'This book convincingly demonstrates the versatility of corpus linguistic methods for the study of legal phraseology, which makes these methods relevant for many different strands of the study of legal communication, among them translation, comparative legal studies and questions of discourse.'

Jan Engberg, Aarhus University, Denmark

'For those of us concerned with legal texts, legal phraseology is a vital but under researched aspect of our daily lives. This timely book is unquestionably invaluable reading, offering an excellent review of carefully researched recent methodological advances. It provides essential, insightful, informative reflections suggesting diverse, innovative avenues of research.'

Catherine Way, University of Granada, Spain

'The nuances of legal language have mystified people inside and outside the legal profession for centuries. This volume provides a major step forward in understanding how and why actors within the legal system write and speak as they do. The book should be of great interest not only to legal and linguistic academics, but also to those who work to craft legal language in legislatures and elsewhere.'

Lawrence M. Solan, Brooklyn Law School, USA

'This volume, edited by two outstanding scholars in the field, gives an impressive overview of cutting-edge approaches to the study of legal phraseology. The combination of quantitative corpus linguistics and qualitative discourse analysis extends our understanding of legal phraseology across a diversity of European legal languages and legal systems. Everybody interested in phraseology, corpus linguistics, and translation studies should read this book.'

Anne Lise Kjær, University of Copenhagen, Denmark

Phraseology in Legal and Institutional Settings

This volume presents a comprehensive and up-to-date overview of major developments in the study of how phraseology is used in a wide range of different legal and institutional contexts. This recent interest has been mainly sparked by the development of corpus linguistics research, which has both demonstrated the centrality of phraseological patterns in language and provided researchers with new and powerful analytical tools. However, there have been relatively few empirical studies of word combinations in the domain of law and in the many different contexts where legal discourse is used. This book seeks to address this gap by presenting some of the latest developments in the study of this linguistic phenomenon from corpus-based and interdisciplinary perspectives. The volume draws on current research in legal phraseology from a variety of perspectives: *translation*, *comparative/contrastive studies*, *terminology*, *lexicography*, *discourse analysis* and *forensic linguistics*. It contains contributions from leading experts in the field, focusing on a wide range of issues amply illustrated through in-depth corpus-informed analyses and case studies. Most contributions to this book are multilingual, featuring different legal systems and legal languages.

The volume will be a valuable resource for linguists interested in phraseology as well as lawyers and legal scholars, translators, lexicographers, terminologists and students who wish to pursue research in the area.

Stanisław Goźdź-Roszkowski is Associate Professor in the Department of Translation Studies, Institute of English Studies, University of Lodz (Poland), where he has been teaching various seminars in discourse analysis and translation studies. His research focuses on functional and corpus-based approaches to the study of legal English in contrast with other languages, as well as their application to translational contexts. His most current research has centred on the expression of evaluation and stance in judicial discourse.

Gianluca Pontrandolfo is currently Adjunct Professor at the University of Trieste (IUSLIT, Department of Legal, Language, Interpreting and Translation Studies), where he lectures on general and specialised translation from Spanish into Italian. His research interests include corpus linguistics, legal phraseology, legal translation training, LSP discourse and genre analysis. He is member of the CERLIS (Research Centre on Languages for Specific Purposes) of the University of Bergamo (Italy).

Law, Language and Communication
Series Editors
Anne Wagner, *Université du Littoral Côte d'Opale*, France
and Vijay Kumar Bhatia, formerly of *City University of Hong Kong*

This series encourages innovative and integrated perspectives within and across the boundaries of law, language and communication, with particular emphasis on issues of communication in specialized socio-legal and professional contexts. It seeks to bring together a range of diverse yet cumulative research traditions in order to identify and encourage interdisciplinary research.

The series welcomes proposals – both edited collections as well as single-authored monographs – emphasizing critical approaches to law, language and communication, identifying and discussing issues, proposing solutions to problems, offering analyses in areas such as legal construction, interpretation, translation and de-codification.

Other titles in the series

Language and Culture in EU Law
Multidisciplinary Perspectives
Edited by Susan Šarčević
ISBN 978-1-4724-2897-4

Towards Recognition of Minority Groups
Legal and Communication Strategies
Edited by Marek Zirk-Sadowski, Bartosz Wojciechowski and Karolina M. Cern
ISBN 978-1-4724-4490-5

The Ashgate Handbook of Legal Translation
Edited by Le Cheng, King Kui Sin and Anne Wagner
ISBN 978-1-4094-6966-7

Legal Lexicography
A Comparative Perspective
Edited by Máirtín Mac Aodha
ISBN 978-1-4094-5441-0

www.routledge.com/Law-Language-and-Communication/book-series/
LAWLANGCOMM

Phraseology in Legal and Institutional Settings

A Corpus-Based Interdisciplinary Perspective

Edited by
Stanisław Goźdź-Roszkowski and Gianluca Pontrandolfo

Routledge
Taylor & Francis Group
LONDON AND NEW YORK

First published 2018 by Routledge

2 Park Square, Milton Park, Abingdon, Oxfordshire OX14 4RN
52 Vanderbilt Avenue, New York, NY 10017

Routledge is an imprint of the Taylor & Francis Group, an informa business

First issued in paperback 2019

British Library Cataloguing-in-Publication Data
A catalogue record for this book is available from the British Library

Library of Congress Cataloging-in-Publication Data
A catalog record for this book has been requested

ISBN: 978-1-138-21436-1 (hbk)
ISBN: 978-0-367-31305-0(hbk)

Typeset in Galliard
by Apex CoVantage, LLC

Contents

Figures

Tables

Contributors

Łucja Biel, University of Warsaw, is Associate Professor and Head of Corpus Research Centre in the Institute of Applied Linguistics. She is a deputy editor of the *Journal of Specialised Translation* and a Secretary General of the European Society for Translation Studies. She was Visiting Lecturer in Legal Translation at City University London (2009–2014). She holds a PhD in Linguistics (University of Gdańsk), Diploma in English and EU Law (University of Cambridge) and a School of American Law Diploma (Chicago-Kent School of Law and University of Gdańsk). Her research interests focus on legal/EU translation, translator training and corpus linguistics. She has published over 40 papers in this area, e.g. in *The Translator*, *Meta*, *The Journal of Specialised Translation*, *Fachsprache*, and a book, *Lost in the Eurofog: The Textual Fit of Translated Law* (Peter Lang, 2014). She has been involved in a number of nationally and internationally funded projects, including *Understanding Justice* (European Commission action grant, Middlesex University), the *Eurolect Observatory* (UNINT, Italy), *Eurofog* and *Polish Eurolect* projects (National Science Centre, Poland).

Ruth Breeze is Senior Lecturer in English at the University of Navarra, Spain, and combines teaching with research as a member of the GradUN Research Group in the Instituto Cultura y Sociedad. Her most recent books are *Corporate Discourse* (Bloomsbury Academic, 2015) and the edited volumes *Interpersonality in Legal Genres* (Peter Lang, 2014) and *Essential Competencies for English-Medium University Teaching* (Springer, 2016). She is currently PI of the project "Imagining the People in the New Politics", funded by the Spanish Ministry of Economy and Competition.

Míriam Buendía Castro is Lecturer in the Department of Modern Philology at the University of Castilla-La Mancha (Spain). She holds a PhD in Translation and Interpreting from the University of Granada, where she was awarded the Outstanding Doctoral Dissertation Award. She has published more than 35 articles, book chapters, and a book in prestigious international journals and publishing houses, such as *Terminology*, or *RESLA*. She has presented her work in international conferences, such as EuraLex, or LREC. She has enjoyed several research stays at the Erasmushogeschool Brussel (Brussels) and at the University of Westminster (London). Her main research interests are terminology, phraseology and corpus linguistics.

Katja Dobrić Basaneže teaches Legal English and Legal German at the Faculty of Law in Rijeka. She is a PhD student of Translation Studies at the Faculty of Arts, University of Ljubljana. Her thesis is entitled *Extended Units of Meaning in the Language of Contracts.* Her academic interests lie in legal phraseology and corpus linguistics. She has participated in several national and international conferences and has authored several research papers on legal translation and legal phraseology. She is a sworn court interpreter for English and German.

Pamela Faber lectures and works in terminology, translation, lexical semantics and cognitive linguistics. She holds degrees from the University of North Carolina at Chapel Hill, the University of Paris IV and the University of Granada, where she has been a full professor in Translation and Interpreting since 2001. She is the director of the LexiCon research group, with whom she has carried out various research projects on terminological knowledge bases, ontologies and cognitive semantics. One of the results of these projects and the practical application of her Frame-based Terminology Theory is EcoLexicon (ecolexicon.ugr.es), a terminological knowledge base on environmental science. She has published close to 100 articles, book chapters and books, and has been invited to present her research in universities in Madrid, Barcelona, Leipzig, Brussels, Zagreb, Mexico D.F., Lodz and Strasbourg, among other places. She serves on the editorial and scientific boards of several journals, such as *Fachsprache*, *Language Design*, *Terminology* and *The International Journal of Lexicography*. She is also a member of the AENOR standardization committee.

Stanisław Goźdź-Roszkowski is Associate Professor in the Department of Translation Studies, Institute of English Studies, University of Lodz (Poland), where he has been teaching various seminars in discourse analysis and translation studies. His research focuses on functional and corpus-based approaches to the study of legal English in contrast with other languages, as well as their application to translational contexts. His most current research has centred on the expression of evaluation and stance in judicial discourse.

Elsa Huertas Barros is Lecturer in Translation Studies in the Department of Modern Languages and Cultures at the University of Westminster. Elsa holds a PhD in Translation from the University of Granada. Elsa's main research interest are translator training, translator competence, assessment practices, collaborative learning and student-centred approaches. Elsa has presented her work at international conferences such as didTRAD and the EST Congress 2016, where she convened a panel on new forms of assessment in translator training. Elsa has published her work in prestigious international journals including *The Journal of Specialised Translation (JoSTrans)*, and has also published book chapters in edited volumes such as *Translation and Meaning*, published by Peter Lang, and *Employability for Languages: A Handbook*.

Joanna Kopaczyk is Research Assistant at the University of Edinburgh and Associate Professor at Adam Mickiewicz University in Poznań. She is a historical linguist with an interest in corpus methods, formulaic language, the history of Scots and historical multilingualism. Her recent books include *The Legal Language of Scottish Burghs: Standardisation and Lexical Bundles (1380–1560)* (Oxford University Press, 2013), *Communities of Practice in the History of English*, co-edited with Andreas H. Jucker (John Benjamins, 2013) and *Binomials in the History of English: Fixed and Flexible*, co-edited with Hans Sauer (Cambridge University Press, 2017), as well as a forthcoming volume on *Patterns in Text: Corpus-Driven Methods and Applications*, co-edited for John Benjamins with Jukka Tyrkkö. She has given talks at conferences in Europe, the USA and Australia, and taught on various aspects of the history of English and Scots at universities in Poland, Germany, Finland and the UK.

Samuel Larner is Lecturer in Linguistics at Manchester Metropolitan University, UK, where he is also Associate Head of the Centre for Applied Pragmatics and Forensic Linguistics. His research interests lie primarily in investigative forensic linguistics, particularly the theory and practice of forensic authorship analysis. His key publications to date have outlined corpus-based approaches to the identification of formulaic sequences and the relationship between formulaic sequences and idiolect.

Davide Mazzi is Research Fellow in English Language and Translation at the University of Modena and Reggio Emilia. His research activity has essentially focused on the following areas: discourse analysis, corpus linguistics and argumentation studies. In particular, his research interests have concentrated on legal, academic, healthcare and news discourse. His recent publications include: *The "Other's" Gaze: The Discursive Construction of Journalists' Professional Identity across Italy and the US* (BrownWalker Press, 2012); "'Our Reading Would Lead To . . .': Corpus Perspectives on Pragmatic Argumentation in US Supreme Court Judgments", *Journal of Argumentation in Context* (2014); "'It Is Natural for You to Be Afraid . . .': On the Discourse of Web-Based Communication with Patients", *Language Learning in Higher Education* (2016); *The Theoretical Background and Practical Implications of Argumentation in Ireland* (Cambridge Scholars Publishing, 2016).

Esther Monzó Nebot is Associate Professor at the Department of Translation and Communication at the University Jaume I. Between 2013 and 2015 she was a full Professor at the Department of Translation Studies of the University of Graz (Austria), were she trained researchers in the field of sociology of translation and interpreting. Her current research focuses on the use of translation and interpreting in the prevention of hate narratives and self-determination in translators' habits. She coordinates the research team TRAP (translation and postmonolingualism) and directs the Master's Degree in Translation and Interpreting Research (*mastertraduccion.uji.es*). Her PhD thesis (2002) focused on the professional practice of sworn translators in Spain from a sociological perspective, combining contributions from the sociology of professions and Bourdieu's economy of practice in an empirical study of certified translators. Her research has focused further on K. Lewin's action-research, computer-assisted translation tools, corpus linguistics and legal translation training. She has taught at different European and Latin American Universities and has also been a practicing translator at the United Nations, the World Trade Organization and the World Intellectual Property Organization (Geneva, Switzerland).

Daniele Orlando is a PhD graduate in Translation Studies at the Department of Legal, Language, Interpreting and Translation Studies (IUSLIT) of the University of Trieste, where he currently holds a position as contract teacher. Based on his participation in the EU project QUALETRA (JUST/2011/JPEN/AG/2975), his PhD research project was a comparative empirical study on the training needs of prospective legal translation trainees, i.e. translation and law graduates. His research interests and publications primarily focus on the definition of legal translation competence, the translation process, translation quality and didactics.

Gianluca Pontrandolfo is currently Adjunct Professor at the University of Trieste (IUSLIT, Department of Legal, Language, Interpreting and Translation Studies), where he lectures on general and specialized translation from Spanish into Italian. His research interests include corpus linguistics, legal phraseology, legal translation training, LSP discourse and genre analysis. He is member of the CERLIS (Research Centre on Languages for Specific Purposes) of the University of Bergamo (Italy).

Raphael Salkie is Professor of Language Studies at the University of Brighton, England. His main research interests are contrastive linguistics, legal language, reported speech and the semantics-pragmatics interface. He compiled the INTERSECT parallel corpus of German, French and English. With Ilse Depraetere he is the co-editor of *Semantics and Pragmatics: Drawing a Line,* due to be published by Springer in 2017.

Magdalena Szczyrbak is Assistant Professor at the Institute of English Studies of the Jagiellonian University in Kraków. Her research interests are mainly in the areas of discourse analysis and corpus-assisted discourse studies applied to legal discourse and, in particular, to the study of stance and evaluation.

Aleksandar Trklja holds a PhD degree in Applied Linguistics from the University of Birmingham. He is a senior lecturer at the Centre for Translation Studies at the University of Vienna. He presently also works as a research fellow at the University of Birmingham on the European Research Council (ERC) projects "Law and Language at the European Court" and "EU Case Law Corpus". His role includes carrying out corpus and discourse analyses of EU jurisprudence and developing a theoretical explanation of relations between law and language in the EU legal order. His research interests lie in the application of corpus linguistics and contrastive linguistic methods to the investigation of lexico-grammatical constructions and discourse organization.

Introduction

Cross-linguistic approaches and applications to phraseology in legal and institutional discourse

Stanisław Goźdź-Roszkowski and Gianluca Pontrandolfo

The collection of articles in this book presents some of the latest developments in the study of the phenomenon of phraseology in legal and institutional discourse. These contributions come from two main sources: selected papers from a workshop devoted to *Corpus Approaches to Legal Phraseology* organised by the editors of this volume during the XX European Symposium on Languages for Special Purposes held in Vienna in July 2015 and some recent invited contributions to the topic made by both renowned linguists and young promising researchers.[1]

This book is an attempt to continue, update and extend different avenues of research signalled in our earlier edited publication of a special issue *Legal Phraseology Today. A Corpus-Based View* in *Fachsprache: The International Journal of Specialised Communication*, in 2015. Much of the ground covered in the next two sections has already been explored in the introduction to that special issue (Goźdź-Roszkowski and Pontrandolfo 2015).

What is (legal) phraseology and how is it analysed?

This apparently simple question will inevitably lead to complex answers given the radical reconceptualisation of phraseology and its meaning that has taken place over the past years and the resulting multitude of linguistic constructs subsumed under the general heading of 'phraseology'. The fundamental change in the way phraseology is now conceptualised is rightly attributed to the British linguist John Sinclair, who made two very important observations:

> (a) more language occurs in 'fixed phrases' than might otherwise be thought and, furthermore, that
> (b) 'fixed phrases' are more varied than might otherwise be thought.
>
> (Sinclair 1991)

Sinclair's ideas provided inspiration for a new approach to phraseology which favours bottom-up methods of identifying lexical co-occurrences. This inductive approach, which is also known as distributional (Evert 2004) and frequency-based (Nesselhauf 2005), has led to the emergence of a wide range of word combinations which do not correspond to predefined linguistic categories. It includes different types of sequences such as frames, collocational frameworks and largely compositional recurrent phrases (e.g. clusters, lexical bundles, n-grams). This perception of phraseology has been systematised in the much cited definition offered by Gries, a computational and cognitive linguist, who defines phraseology as:

> The co-occurrence of a form or a lemma of a lexical item and one more or additional linguistic elements of various kinds which functions as one semantic unit in a clause or sentence and whose frequency of co-occurrence is larger than expected on the basis of chance.
>
> (Gries 2008: 6)

As a result, the boundary of what is perceived as 'phraseological' has been pushed beyond the more traditional approach which focuses on identifying phraseological units on the basis of linguistic criteria (e.g. Burger 1998; Cowie 1994; Mel'cuk 1998).

The contributions to this volume show that that these two major modes of understanding phraseology should be viewed as largely complementary and they are still present in the existing research into phraseology in legal texts. Thus, there are studies that analyse lexico-syntactic combinations in legal language which, based on traditional notions of phraseology, focus on terminological phrases. See, for example, Chapter 4 in this volume, which focuses on phrases centred around the term 'witness' (e.g. 'witness box', 'witness fees', 'witness audit'). There are also studies featured in this volume which are based on the distributional and frequency-based approach with the *lexical bundle* or *n-gram* taking centre stage as the preferred object of analysis (see Chapters 1, 5, 10 and 14). However, analysing phraseology in legal texts should not be seen only in terms of a dichotomy involving these two approaches outlined above. Chapters 8, 12 and 13 demonstrate how legal patterns can weave an intricate web of semantic meanings by relying on a slightly different type of co-occurrence which involves a lexical item (lexical word or grammar word) or a grammar pattern and some semantic unity manifested through a specific discourse function. This different understanding of textual recurrence is particularly well illustrated in Chapter 8, which examines the so-called semantic sequences centred around the head noun *fact* followed by a *that*-clause (a grammar pattern). One of the findings in this study is that *fact that* co-occurs with phraseologies expressing stance, i.e. a writer's 'personal feelings, attitudes, value judgments or assessments' (Biber et al. 1999: 966). In order to capture this type of subtle, context-sensitive meanings, it is necessary to combine statistical, quantitative techniques with methods that pay attention to detail and context (see Partington et al. 2013). Irrespective of different perspectives on what constitutes phraseology, all the studies included in this volume share a corpus perspective.

The growing use and impact of corpus methodology confirms that it is hardly possible to study legal phrasemes manually, as isolated segments of language, thus stressing the need to rely on data-driven research. Contrastive and comparative studies remain relatively scarce, possibly due to the absence of systematic, publicly available corpora for the study of legal language.

This book provides fresh and compelling evidence that corpora and corpus linguistics techniques remain the driving force behind much of the current research into legal phraseology. Yet, it also shows the varying degree to which corpus data and its techniques are used to study word combinations in legal language.

On the one hand, Chapters 1, 5, 9, 11 and 14 adopt a *corpus-driven* methodology where the uninterrupted sequences of words are generated on the basis of frequency alone.

On the other hand, Chapters 6, 7, 8, 10, 12 and 13 rely more on the *corpus-based* approach to multi-word units which involves pre-selecting such expressions and then analysing the corpus data to determine how they are used.

The deductive approach of the former merges with the inductive focus of the latter in the last group of chapters (2, 3 and 4, and partly Chapter 6), which could be defined as *corpus-assisted* (see Partington et al. 2013) in that they have a more qualitative approach to discourse studies; here the corpus is clearly a means to investigate broader linguistic and textual phenomena that need to go beyond the single recurrent strings in order to be appropriately interpreted in legal discourse.

Thus, the contributions in this volume also confirm the importance of combining quantitative approaches to the phenomenon under scrutiny with qualitative focuses.

This 'new wave' of research that we refer to in this section constitutes a broadening and reinterpretation of the term 'phraseology' aided by a varied use of corpus methodologies.

Why study phraseology in legal language?

Phraseology in legal language has been traditionally explored in connection with formulaicity, regarded as one of the most typical and conspicuous features of legal style (Crystal and Davy 1969). Not surprisingly, the earliest studies of phraseology in legal language focused on those lexical items that displayed the highest degree of fixedness and repetition, i.e. binomials (e.g. *signed and delivered*, *act and omission*) and their extended versions: multinomials (e.g. Gustaffson 1984; Mellinkoff 1963: 120; Kopaczyk 2013). The presence of this type of expressions in legal language was rightly perceived as one of the indicators of its formulaicity and standardisation, which can in turn lead us to understand the stylistic preferences in legal drafting. Chapters 9 and 11 address this issue by investigating the roles and functions of binomials in legislative discourse and in contractual instruments respectively. Using uninterrupted sequences of word combinations, i.e. lexical bundles or n-grams, has revived interest in examining patterns of formulaicity in legal discourse in order to gain a better understanding of legal language. This is probably one of the most vibrant strands of phraseology research with a host of possible applications, some of which include standardisation of legal genres (e.g. Kopaczyk 2013), variation within legal discourse (e.g. Goźdź-Roszkowski 2011), and the impact of institutional legal translation on national legal language (e.g. Biel 2014a). In a similar vein, Chapter 14 in this volume is an attempt to see if phraseology, in the form of n-grams, could be applied in forensic settings to determine authorship attribution.

Another area traditionally explored in phraseological research concerns terminology. There is a strand of research which focuses on multi-word terms and collocations where at least one lexeme is a term (e.g. Kjær 2007). What the 'new wave' of research has revealed is that there are word combinations significant for the legal domain but which are not terminological. In addition to that, it is also true that specialised phrasemes tend to cluster around terms, phraseology acting as a link between the term and the text (Pontrandolfo 2015: 148). In this volume, for example, Chapter 1 investigates different multi-word patterns (lexical bundles) and their role in legal translation where some of these significant patterns are non-terminological and fulfil other important functions, such as, for example, text-structuring in legislative instruments. Chapter 4 also demonstrates the close link between legal terminology and phraseology when applied to lexicographic resources.

Phraseology should also be viewed through its close links with discourse. Seen from this perspective, phraseological research involves examining the organisation of language beyond the level of a sentence or a clause and focusing on larger linguistic units, such as conversational exchanges (Stubbs 1983: 1). In Chapter 13 it becomes evident that recurrent patterns play a pivotal role in courtroom discourse, as they explicitly and implicitly show the positioning strategies of legal interactants involved in a trial, including the ways in which they negotiate authority and claim epistemic priority.

Legal phraseology also plays a pivotal role in legal translation, where it has been demonstrated that it is one of the discourse elements which mostly contribute to the naturalness of the translated text (see Chapter 1) and which is one of the most difficult elements translators have to tackle in their job (see Chapters 2 and 3). As a matter of fact, legal translation is not only a question of terminology, but also a problem of phraseological conventions. Beyond lexical and terminological equivalence, translators have to tackle the additional difficulty of acquiring familiarity with the genre structures or routine, if they want to produce a text which is accurate from the discourse and register point of view (Pontrandolfo 2015: 137–138; see also Pontrandolfo 2016: 147–168). Interestingly, the translation of phraseological units can also play a crucial role in understanding how we structure our social experience and crystallise a specific worldview through its use and reproduction in legal documents (see Chapter 6).

Another reason for studying legal phraseology, in its broader meaning, is its strong relationship with legal professional communities. Legal experts and scholars are those who foster the use of phrasemes for a number of reasons, among which is the sense of belonging to a community: often style is a means of ensuring and recognising that membership. If according to these professionals, who are insiders of the law world, formulaicity is a virtue also because it guarantees standardisation, according to outsiders phraseological patternedness of legal texts may result in petrification and lack of spontaneity, therefore a vice (see Biel 2014b: 177).

Last but not least, another strand of research which will be challenging for both the academic and the professional communities in the near future is the link between legal phraseology and plain legal language. Legal phrasemes are often the targets of simplification initiatives worldwide, since they are considered as one of the factors that make texts difficult to read and understand. However, legal texts would be hardly recognisable as such without their phraseological flavour. The debate will remain open in coming years, and corpus-based research will continue to help scholars in the understanding of the quantitative and qualitative scope of this discursive feature.

About the book

The volume is structured into three sections, reflecting essential research areas in which legal phraseology can play a crucial role.

The first part is dedicated to the complex relation between phraseology and legal translation, a binomial that only recently started to gain more attention by legal language scholars (Biel 2014a; Ruusila and Lindroos 2016).

Chapter 1, by Łucja Biel, explores the role played by translation in the patterning of lexical bundles by means of a comparison between Polish-language versions of EU law against English-language versions of EU law and the Polish domestic law. By adopting a frequency-driven approach to legal phraseology, Biel interestingly gets to two important results: a) that Polish EU translated legislation has an increased level of lexical bundles, which apparently confutes the hypothesis that translations are less patterned than original texts; b) that translated texts contain their own lexical bundles rather than priming patterns which are natural and expected in target-language legal texts.

Chapter 2, by Daniele Orlando, presents the results of an empirical study aimed at investigating legal phraseology as a source of translation problems for trainees with different backgrounds (MA-level translation graduates vs. linguistically skilled postgraduate lawyers faced with a translation from English into Italian task). His findings confirm the importance of thematic legal knowledge and familiarity with genre conventions, an added value for lawyers, whose translation process was found to be smoother compared to translation graduates, who encountered a higher number of phraseological problems and performed a higher number of searches compared to lawyers.

Chapter 3, by Elsa Huertas Barros and Míriam Buendía Castro, is closely connected with the previous one, in its methodological approach to the complex relationship between phraseology and legal translation. The paper presents a case study on translation errors made by translation trainees while performing a semi-specialised legal translation from English into Spanish and compares the results of English-native speakers with Spanish-native speakers. The study confirms that legal phraseology is an insidious area, which triggers translation errors for both native and non-native trainees, with the latter category expectedly facing more difficulties in producing idiomatic combinations in their second language. The paper also sheds light on the scarcity of material devoted to the didactics of legal phraseology, a central area to hone phraseological competence which is essential in specialised translation.

Chapter 4, by Míriam Buendía Castro and Pamela Faber, describes the usefulness of some bilingual and multilingual legal resources for translation purposes, with a special focus on legal phraseology information. The paper compares how each resource deals with access to phraseological information and how they describe specialised patterns. On the one hand, the comparative analysis confirms that there is still a lack of high-quality online legal resources, most bilingual or multilingual options being available in paper format, while on the other hand points to some interesting ideas on which elements should be included in a legal translation-oriented resource.

The second section is devoted to the relationship between legal phraseology and contrastive studies, gradually shifting the focus from the translation perspective to the cross-linguistic textual analyses of legal texts. Multilingual translation still plays a role in the studies presented in Chapter 5, 6 and 7 but then leaves the floor to comparative approaches to original legal texts.

Chapter 5, by Aleksandar Trklja, presents an innovative empirical approach for the study of formulaicity and hybridity in legal language, by taking the example of the judgments of the Court of Justice of the European Union. The author addresses the extent to which EU judgments are formulaic and how these formulaic patterns contribute to the discourse organisation of EU texts (in line with Biel's approach to translated phraseology; see Chapter 1). His findings statistically confirm the highly formulaic nature of CJEU judgments compared to national, original judgments, as well as the presence of hybrid expressions, which result from the translation of judgments.

Chapter 6, by Esther Monzó Nebot, proposes an innovative approach to the study of multinomial units in legal language, by adopting a 'philosophical' view. By analysing these types of phrasemes in the International Bill of Human Rights in its English, French and Spanish versions, the author demonstrates that multinomial units can structure our social experience and crystallise our worldview. Thus, the paper investigates if (and how) references to underprivileged groups are made and interestingly gets to the conclusion that although there is no dichotomous view of the international community, which cannot be portrayed as 'good' or 'bad', there is a phraseological tendency which is dominant and can be perceived by looking at the linguistic versions of the texts.

Chapter 7, by Raphael Salkie, is based on two previous contrastive studies on the semantic sequence *the fact that*. It replicates and integrates the study by studying EU legal German. Translation is seen here as a means to engage a contrastive (English-German) investigation of 'the fact that' and its implication not only for legal language and reasoning, but also and most interestingly for phraseology research.

Chapter 8, by Stanisław Goźdź-Roszkowski, adopts a different perspective on phraseology by investigating semantic sequences (functionally motivated series of meaning elements) centred around the phrase *the fact that* and its Polish counterpart in the United States Supreme Court opinions and the judgments given by Poland's Constitutional Tribunal respectively. The goal of the study is to identify characteristic patterns in which the phrase *the fact that* and *fakt, że/iż* are found in judicial discourse and explore the implications of their similarities and differences in terms of epistemology and argumentative strategies. This comparative analysis identifies six major functional categories and corresponding semantic sequences in which this phrase is found in both corpora suggesting that American and Polish judicial writing is underpinned by essentially the same epistemological assumptions.

Chapter 9, by Joanna Kopaczyk, presents a corpus-based analysis of noun binomials in UK and Scottish legislation from a contrastive perspective. The author concentrates on binomials which are shared (and unshared) by both texts, classifies them in semantic fields and then looks at the reasons behind the creation of lexical pairs. The results, which point to a higher percentage of noun binomials in Scottish texts compared to English ones, are also interpreted in the line of the Plain English Campaign directives to legal drafting in both legislative bodies

The third section of the volume focuses exclusively on English legal discourse from various perspectives and with complementary approaches. Legal phraseology is studied intralingually, by looking at recurrent patterns in different genres and contexts.

Chapter 10, by Davide Mazzi, also focuses on lexical bundles and EU legal language (see Chapter 1 and 5), but from a different angle. Forms and functions of lexical bundles are analysed in a monolingual corpus of judgments delivered by the Supreme Court of Ireland dealing with the tension between State law and EU law. Lexical bundles prove to be an essential discourse element with different functions, among others that of bringing insights into the Court's argumentation, which is key to judicial discourse as a practice and system.

Chapter 11, by Katja Dobrić Basaneže, adopts a corpus-driven approach to the study of binomial expressions in English contracts. A detailed classification of binomial realisations in legal language is conducted with a view to confirming the key role played by extended units of meaning in contractual agreements. Results also highlight the importance of binomials for legal professional communities.

Chapter 12, by Ruth Breeze, focuses both on the nature of reporting verbs used to introduce different voices in a corpus of legal academic articles and on the recurrent patterns in which they occur. By taking a wider view of phraseology, it also offers an interesting contrastive perspective on polyphony styles, comparing academic law reports with academic business articles.

Chapter 13, by Magdalena Szczyrbak, is closely connected with the previous chapter as it explores phraseological patterns clustered around verbs in courtroom discourse. Her findings demonstrate the key role of *verba dicendi*'s phraseology in courtroom discourse, as a means to convey evaluative meanings and negotiate the validity of the participants' standpoints. Focus is placed on the patterns with the progressive as a stancetaking discoursive resource.

Chapter 14, by Samuel Larner, adopts quite a different approach from the other chapters included in the volume and mostly focuses on methodological issues related to the potential contribution of phraseology (in particular n-grams) to forensic linguistics and authorship attribution. The author presents a corpus-based method to identify these formulaic sequences and uses short narratives produced by different authors as testbeds for his study. His findings show that, although statistical results demonstrate that formulaic word n-grams were used distinctively between authors, the method was unsuccessful to qualitatively attribute a text whose authorship was unknown to its correct author. Formulaic word n-grams occur too infrequently in short personal narratives to be of practical use as markers of authorship.

Conclusion

In summary, the chapters in this book provide examples of cutting-edge research in phraseological analyses of different languages, all of them with a corpus-based interdisciplinary perspective. The languages included (English, Italian, Polish, Spanish, German, French) cover a range of European legal languages reflecting a diversity of legal systems and legal institutions. The techniques used, combining quantitative statistical methods as well as painstaking qualitative analysis, showcase the variety of approaches to the study of word combinations in legal language. The emergence of specialised tools and large electronic text resources have marked the transition from manual and monolingual studies which focus on a limited number of terminological units in a single genre to large-scale and multilingual explorations into various types of textual recurrence and co-occurrence patterns identified in a wide range of different legal texts.

Note

1 This book is also partially framed within the project entitled "Discurso jurídico y claridad comunicativa. Análisis contrastivo de sentencias españolas y de sentencias en español del Tribunal de Justicia de la Unión Europea" [Legal discourse and clarity. Comparative analysis of Spanish judgments and judgments written in Spanish from the Court of Justice of the European Union] (Referencia FFI2015–70332-P), financed by the Spanish Ministerio de Economía y Competitividad and FEDER funds (Leading Researcher: Estrella Montolío Durán, Universitat de Barcelona).

References

Biber, D., Conrad, S., Finegan, E., Johansson, S., and Leech, G., 1999. *Longman Grammar of Spoken and Written English*. Harlow: Pearson Education Limited.

Biel, Ł., 2014a. *Lost in the Eurofog: The Textual Fit of Translated Law*. Frankfurt am Main: Peter Lang.

Biel, Ł., 2014b. Phraseology in legal translation: A corpus-based analysis of textual mapping in EU Law. In Le Cheng, King Kui Sin, and Anne Wagner (eds.), *Ashgate Handbook of Legal Translation*. London: Ashgate Publishing, 177–192.

Burger, H., 1998. *Phraseologie. Eine Einführung am Beispiel des Deutschen*. Berlin: Erich Schmidt Verlag.

Cowie, A.P., 1994. Phraseology. In R.E. Ashen (ed.), *The Encyclopedia of Language and Linguistics*. Oxford: Pergamon Press, 3168–3171.

Crystal, D. and Davy, D., 1969. The language of legal documents. In D. Crystal and D. Daly (eds.), *Investigating English Style*. Bloomington: Indiana UP, 193–217.

Evert, S., 2004. *The Statistics of Word Cooccurrences: Word Pairs and Collocations*. PhD thesis, Institut für maschinelle Sprachverarbeitung, University of Stuttgart.

Goźdź-Roszkowski, S., 2011. *Patterns of Linguistic Variation in American Legal English: A Corpus-based Study*. Peter Lang: Frankfurt am Main.

Goźdź-Roszkowski, S. and Pontrandolfo, G., 2015. Legal phraseology today: Corpus-based applications across legal languages and genres [Editorial Preface of the Special Issue of *Legal Phraseology Today. A Corpus-based View*]. *Fachsprache*, 3–4: 130–138.

Gries, S. Th., 2008. Phraseology and linguistic theory: A brief survey. In S. Granger and F. Meunier (eds.), *Phraseology: An Interdisciplinary Perspective*. Amsterdam/Philadelphia: John Benjamins, 3–25.

Gustaffson, M., 1984. The syntactic features of binomial expressions in legal English. *Text*, 4(1–3): 123–141.

Kjær, A.-L., 2007. Phrasemes in legal texts. In H. Burger (ed.), *Phraseologie/Phraseology. Ein internationales Handbuchzeitgenössischer Forschung/An International Handbook of Contemporary Research*, Vol. I–II. Berlín: de Gruyter, 506–516.

Kopaczyk, J., 2013. *The Legal Language of Scottish Burghs: Standardization and Lexical Bundles 1380–1560*. Oxford: Oxford University Press.

Mel'cuk, I., 1998. Collocations and lexical functions. In A.P. Cowie (ed.), *Phraseology: Theory, Analysis, and Applications*. Oxford: Clarendon Press, 23–53.

Mellinkoff, D., 1963. *The Language of the Law*. Oregon: Wipf and Stock Publishers.

Nesselhauf, N., 2005. *Collocations in a Learner Corpus*. Amsterdam: John Benjamins.

Partington, A., Duguid, A., and Taylor, C., 2013. *Patterns and Meanings in Discourse: Theory and Practice in Corpus-assisted Discourse Studies (CADS)*. Amsterdam/Philadelphia: John Benjamins.

Pontrandolfo, G., 2015. Investigating judicial phraseology with COSPE. A contrastive corpus-based study. In C. Fantinuoli and F. Zanettin (eds.), *New Directions in Corpus-based Translation Studies, Translation and Multilingual Natural Language Processing* (TMNLP). Berlin: Language Science Press, 137–160.

Pontrandolfo, G., 2016. *Fraseología y lenguaje judicial. Las sentencias penales desde una perspectiva contrastiva*. Roma: Aracne.

Ruusila, A. and Lindroos, E., 2016. Conditio sine qua non: On phraseology in legal language and its translation. *Language and Law/Linguagem e Direito*, 3(1): 120–140.

Sinclair, J., 1991. *Corpus, Concordance, Collocation*. Oxford: Oxford University Press.

Stubbs, M., 1983. *Discourse Analysis: The Sociolinguistic Analysis of Natural Language*. Chicago: Chicago University Press.

Part I

Phraseology, translation and multilingualism

1 Lexical bundles in EU law

The impact of translation process on the patterning of legal language

Łucja Biel

The frequency-driven approach to phraseology: lexical bundles

The growing interest in how language is patterned has been stimulated by corpus linguistics since 1990s. Corpora have shown that language use is highly patterned and that patterns are cognitively motivated (Stubbs 2004: 111). Thanks to its tools and methods, which facilitate studying recurrent patterns of language use, corpus linguistics has shifted attention from a word to a pattern – "phrase-like units, which are the basic unit of meaning" (Stubbs 2004: 118).

Corpus linguistics has not only rekindled interest in patterns and, hence, in phraseology but has also changed our understanding of phraseology.[1] The category of phraseology has been redefined and extended to include new types of word combinations while pushing the hitherto central non-compositional members, such as proverbs, sayings and idioms, to the periphery due to their rare use in language, in particular in specialized genres. The traditional approach has been dethroned by the frequency-based approach, where phrasemes are identified empirically through corpus-driven methods not only on the basis of their co-occurrence but, above all, their recurrence (high frequency) (cf. Granger and Paquot 2008: 28–32). The new centre is occupied by collocations and various types of frequent multi-word units, both continuous and discontinuous ones, such as lexical bundles, phrase frames, skipgrams and phrasal constructions (cf. Nesselhauf 2005: 12; Greaves and Warren 2010: 213). In contrast to the traditional categories which tend to have an ornamental and stylistic function (cf. Grabowski 2015: 82), multi-word units are systematically employed to perform important discourse functions, which will be discussed below.

The most commonly researched multi-word units in the frequency-based corpus-driven approach are lexical bundles, also referred to as clusters, n-grams, chunks or lexical phrases. Lexical bundles are identified solely on the frequency criterion (Biber and Barbieri 2007: 264; Hyland 2008: 6). Even though lexical bundles are very frequent, they are not "perceptually salient" (Biber 2009: 13). They are word sequences that co-occur "irrespective of their idiomaticity" – they are not always meaningful or grammatical units that are structurally complete (Biber et al. 1999: 58–59). Examples of lexical bundles in EU law include: *referred to in Article*, *in accordance with the*, *of regulation EU No.*, *having regard to the*, *for the purposes of*, *the European Parliament and*, *Member States shall ensure that*. Lexical bundles are often transparent in meaning – "semantically transparent" (Cortes 2004: 400; Hyland 2008: 6). They are indicators of genre variation as they have been found to vary across genres (cf. Biber et al. 1999; Hyland 2008: 7).

Lexical bundles may be categorized according to formal criteria (length, structure) or functional criteria. The length-based categorization takes into account a number of constituents in a bundle: if it contains three words, it is referred to as a 3-gram; if four words, a 4-gram; if eight words, an 8-gram. The structural categorization is based on the grammatical structure of lexical bundles, depending on whether they contain noun, verb or prepositional phrases and clause fragments. As for the functional criterion, three main categories of lexical bundles have been identified with reference to the most frequently studied academic discourse: stance bundles, which communicate attitudes, and discourse organizers and referential bundles, which indicate entities and participants (Biber and Barbieri 2007: 265). In general, lexical bundles are "building blocks in discourse" – they provide familiar frames retrieved from memory which are filled in with new information: they are "a kind of pragmatic 'head' for larger phrases and clauses, where they function as discourse frames for the expression of new information" (Biber and Barbieri 2007: 270).

Lexical bundles in legal language

Lexical bundles have been extensively researched in academic genres (see e.g. Biber and Barbieri 2007 for an overview) with few studies into other specialized discourses, including legal language. In general, despite the high formulaicity of legal discourse, legal phraseology has not been a popular topic in legal language studies. This has started to change recently, triggered by the surge of interest in phraseology within corpus linguistics, which found its parallel in the legal domain, as attested, *inter alia*, by this volume. Trends in corpus research into legal phraseology have been classified by Goźdź-Roszkowski and Pontrandolfo into: (1) research into collocations; (2) research into routine formulae, (3) terminographically-oriented studies, (4) cross-linguistic studies of phraseology, including translation, and (5) semantics of legal patterns (2015: 133–134). Research into lexical bundles is subsumed under trend (2).

Lexical bundles do not fit the existing categorizations of legal phraseology. A traditional classification groups legal phrasemes, e.g., into: (1) multi-word terms, (2) collocations with a term and (3) formulaic expressions and standard phrases (Kjær 2007: 509–510). Another classification proposed specifically for the genre of legislation ranges from the global textual level to the local microlevel: text-organizing, grammatical and term-forming patterns as well as term-embedding and lexical collocations (Biel 2014: 36–48). Neither of these classifications embraces lexical bundles, which typically cut across all these categories, both structurally and functionally. Lexical bundles should be viewed as a distinct class of legal patterns in its own right, identified on the basis of frequency-based criteria (and thus incompatible with classifications based on other criteria).

As for lexical bundles in legal language, there are three noteworthy contributions which apply this method: papers by Jablonkai (2010) and Breeze (2013) and a book by Goźdź-Roszkowski (2011). The publications focus on how lexical bundles vary across English-language legal genres in three legal systems: the EU, England and Wales,[2] and the US, respectively.

Starting chronologically, Jablonkai's (2010) study into English-language EU discourse is based on a mixed-genre corpus[3] for ESP purposes and analyzes the corpus of EU genres as a whole against the British National Corpus (BNC) (Sampler, Academic, News, Fiction sections) rather than against a reference corpus of a comparable genre, i.e. a UK legal/administrative corpus. For this reason, Jablonkai's findings cannot be separately related to individual genres, e.g. EU law only, but concern EU administrative discourse in general. The study shows the high formulaicity of EU discourse against the reference corpora attested by the excessively high number of lexical bundles (2010: 258). The EU corpus contains twice as many bundle types and six times as many tokens as the Academic prose section of the BNC; these rates are even higher compared to the fiction, news and general sections of the BNC (2010: 258). As for structural properties of EU bundles, bundles with noun phrases and prepositional phrases dominate the list (80%), but there is also an untypically high number of verb phrase bundles against the reference corpora (2010: 260). As for functional properties of EU bundles, drawing on Cortes (2004) and Hyland (2008), Jablonkai extends Biber's classification to include subject-specific bundles (i.e. context-dependent bundles, topic bundles) and refines the category of referential bundles by quality specification and intertextual bundles (2010: 260–261). Jablonkai finds that the EU corpus contains the largest number of referential bundles which represent quantity, quality, purpose, time and place. The second most prominent group of bundles consists of subject-specific bundles which refer to the European Union; there were few stance and discourse-organizing bundles (2010: 261).

Goźdź-Roszkowski's (2011) in-depth study of lexical bundles across US legal genres (academic journals, briefs, contracts, legislation, opinions, professional articles, textbooks) shows that legislation and contracts are the most formulaic legal genres with the largest range and number of bundles and the highest proportion of words comprised in bundles. As for structural properties, all legal genres frequently use bundles in the form of noun and prepositional phrases. Goźdź-Roszkowski proposes a modified functional classification of bundles into: (1) legal reference (temporal bundles, location bundles, attributive bundles, participative bundles, institutional bundles, terminological bundles, procedure-related bundles), (2) text-oriented bundles (causative/resultative bundles, condition bundles, clarification/topic elaboration bundles, focus bundles, framing signals, structuring bundles, transition bundles) and (3) stance bundles (2011: 113–142). He demonstrates that legislation, contracts and professional articles have the highest number of referential bundles, while academic journals and opinions have the highest proportion of text-oriented and stance bundles (2011).

Breeze (2013) also investigates the variation of lexical bundles across English legal genres (academic articles, legislation, case law and legal documents/contracts) but controls a thematic variable by a corpus design in the area of commercial law. As with Goźdź-Roszkowski's book, her study confirms the highest formulaicity of legislation and documents, both of which use significantly more lexical bundles than case law and academic law articles (2013: 233). Like the other authors, Breeze adjusts Biber's classification to account for topic-specific bundles and proposes a mixed structural and functional classification into four groups: content-related noun phrases and prepositional phrases, non-content noun and prepositional phrases, adjectival phrases, and bundles with a verb phrase (2013: 235). She further divides content bundles into agents (people, institutions), documents (statutes, contracts, sections of documents), dates, actions and abstract concepts (2013: 235). Breeze demonstrates that over 50% of bundles in legislation and documents are content-related noun phrases; compared to case law and academic articles, these two genres also have a high number of verb phrase bundles, which are deontic in nature (2013: 237, 245). Content bundles often indicate agents and institutions, as well as abstract concepts and dates, in particular in legislation (2013: 235). Breeze emphasizes that while content-related noun phrases represent terms, develop a text thematically, and are 'slot fillers', non-content prepositional bundles function as frames – "referential framing to link the ideas in the text together" (2013: 248, 250).

Unlike the above discussed studies, this study is not interested in cross-generic variation but will look into internal variation of a single genre of legislation – translator-mediated multilingual legislation and domestic legislation of a country with a monolingual legal system. To the best of my knowledge, no studies of lexical bundles have been conducted into legal Polish[4] so far.

Translation and phraseology

EU translation – translator-mediated multilingual law

EU legislation, which is applicable in 28 Member States, is produced under a complex array of political, procedural, institutional, legal and cultural constraints. It is drafted in a multilingual environment in 24 official languages. Under the principles of multilingualism and equal authenticity, all language versions have an authoritative status – they are equally valid and are presumed to have the same meaning (cf. Šarčević 1997: 64). They are referred to as 'language versions' rather than translations or target texts. Drafting and translation are concurrent, multistage and multilingual: translation is involved at all stages of the drafting process rather than at the final stage only (cf. Doczekalska 2009: 360). The multilingual procedure implies a constant switching and 'fusion' of languages. These constraints affect the language of EU law – conceptually, lexically, phraseologically, grammatically and stylistically, which creates a hybrid construct – the Eurolect (Biel 2015: 142), perceived as a new legal variant of the official languages (cf. Koskinen 2000: 53).

(Legal) Phraseology in translation

Translations are generally expected to demonstrate the 'phraseological conformity' to target-language phraseology typical of a genre (Gouadec 2007: 23). This expectation extends to legal translation (e.g. Monzó Nebot 2008: 224). Yet the translation process is a complex mental operation involving bilingual processing with frequent switches between the source and target languages; this "interferes with or upsets the spontaneous, or 'ideally monolingual' processing of a native speaker" (Mauranen 2007: 44). As a result, the translation process leaves some traces on the phraseological make-up of the target text.[5] First it may inhibit 'priming' natural recurrent patterns in translation. Patterns may be distorted as a result of pervasive source language interference (cf. Toury 1995: 275). According to Mauranen's untypical collocation hypothesis, translations are assumed to contain collocations which are possible but rare in the target language (TL), have few combinations which are frequent in the nontranslated TL and have more varied, less stable and less frequent patterns (2006: 97). Additionally, there are situations when legal translation may purposefully contain unnatural or untypical phrasemes as a result of conceptual lacunas between the legal systems and the need to convey elements of the source frame which are absent in the target language (cf. Biel 2014: 182).

On the other hand, paradoxically, translations are also hypothesized to show an opposing trend – the increased use of formulaicity and structural flattening, which stems from Toury's law of growing standardization, i.e. translators' tendency to choose "more habitual options offered by a target culture" (1995: 268), and the normalization/conservatism hypothesis – translators' tendency to exaggerate typical features of the TL (Baker 1996: 183). Preliminary findings of my earlier project (Biel 2014: 223–227) show that the genre of multilingual legislation – translated EU law – shows increased patterning; however, it also shows increased variation. Since there are few studies into legal phraseology in translation (Pontrandolfo 2016; Biel 2014, 2015; Ruusila and Lindroos 2016), and even fewer into lexical bundles in translation (Lee 2013; Trklja, this volume), we know very little about how lexical bundles are primed in legal translation.

Corpus design

The main corpus upon which this study is based is the Polish Eurolect corpus. It will be compared against two reference corpora – the corresponding English Eurolect corpus and the Polish Domestic Law corpus (see Table 1.1) – to account for two fundamental relations of translations: the relation to source texts[6] and the relation to nontranslated target-language texts of a comparable genre (cf. Chesterman 2004: 6–7). The corpora used in this study were compiled in 2016 by the author and her research team for the purposes of the Polish Eurolekt Project (2015–2018) (Biel 2016).[7]

The Eurolect corpus was downloaded in the corresponding Polish and English versions from EUR-Lex,[8] the EU database of legislation. Each language-version corpus has the same legal instruments for the period of five years (2011–2015).[9] The corpora comprise two types of complementary legal instruments: regulations and directives. Resolutions, which have general application, are binding in their entirety and are directly applicable in all the Member States, while directives are binding as to the result to be achieved upon each Member State to which they are addressed, but leave the choice of form and methods to national authorities (Article 249 EC Treaty). Because of a different macrostructure of EU and Polish instruments, since the former contain extensive non-normative preambles and technical annexes, only enacting terms (the normative part)[10] were extracted from EU files with the Utilities/Text Converter function of Wordsmith Tools 7.0. This step ensures a much better comparability of the Eurolect corpora to the domestic law corpus and represents an improvement upon the earlier project (Biel 2014: 223–227).

The Polish Domestic Law corpus (PL-DOMESTIC) is a monolingual corpus of non-translated Polish legislation in force as of 31 December 2015, downloaded from the online

Table 1.1 The corpora used in the study

Name of the corpus	*Texts*	*Time depth*	*Tokens (words)*	*Types*
The Polish Eurolect corpus: enacting terms				
PL-EU Regulations	925	2011–2015	1,899,403	39,409
PL-EU Directives	92	2011–2015	768,187	24,288
Total	*1,017*	*2011–2015*	*2,667,590*	*45,249*
The reference corpus 1: the English Eurolect corpus: enacting terms				
EN-PL Regulations	925	2011–2015	2,183,640	13,844
EN-PL Directives	92	2011–2015	884,839	8,843
Total	*1,017*	*2011–2015*	*3,068,479*	*15,462*
The reference corpus 2: the Polish Domestic Law corpus				
PL-DOMESTIC – the standard statutes	135	2011–2015	1,586,725	32,351
PL-DOMESTIC – the core statutes	55	1936–2015	1,868,447	40,085
Total	*190*	*1936–2015*	*3,454,942*	*49,423*

database of Polish legislation *Lex* run by Wolters Kluwer SA. The corpus consists of two components: the standard sub-corpus which covers all statutes (*ustawa*) adopted in the period from 2011 to 2015, excluding amending and repealing acts, and the core sub-corpus with the highest-ranking fundamental statutes of Polish law, which exhaustively regulate branches and thematic fields (the Constitution, codes (*kodeks*) and law-type statutes (*ustawa prawo*)), ranging from 1936 to 2015 and extensively amended, if not rewritten, in the least three decades – first after the fall of Communism, next due to the harmonization with EU law. Even though the time variable is not fully controlled with the core corpus being a diachronic one, this structure ensures a broad representative coverage of the primary legislation passed by the Polish Parliament.

The corpora may be deemed to be comparable due to their corresponding genre and functional qualities. What may pose some comparability issues is a 30% larger size of the Polish reference corpus and a significantly lower number of texts in this corpus.[11] Considering the different sizes of the corpora, frequencies were normalized to 1 million words.

The study was conducted with Wordsmith Tools 7.0.

Method

Lexical bundles are identified on the basis of frequency and dispersion thresholds, both of which are arbitrary to a certain extent. As for the dispersion threshold, the purpose of which is to eliminate idiosyncratic uses of individual authors, the most common threshold is the distribution of a bundle in at least five texts in a corpus (Biber and Barbieri 2007: 267), but there are studies which set the threshold much higher at 10% of texts or more.[12] The more contested issue is the frequency cut-off – the recurrence threshold. It tends to depend on n-gram length, genre, corpus size and research questions. The conservative frequency cut-off is set high at 40 occurrences per million words (pmw) (cf. Biber and Barbieri 2007: 267), but there are studies which use much lower thresholds, e.g. 20, 10 or fewer occurrences pmw, as well as higher thresholds, e.g. 50 occurrences in Breeze's study of legal lexical bundles due to their abundance (2013: 232). Since most work has been done on English so far, it is unclear how the cut-off relates to typologically different languages (cf. Gray and Biber 2015: 144), in particular inflectional languages with many inflectional variants.[13] Owing to the excessive formulaicity of legal discourse and for the sake of comparability with the EU English corpus, this study adopts the conservative cut-off of 40 occurrences pmw,[14] without adjusting it for Polish inflectional variants as in an earlier study (Biel 2014: 223). The dispersion cut-off was set at five texts in a corpus.[15]

Another methodological issue concerns the length of a bundle. As already noted, most studies of bundles involve English and they have examined 4-grams, which is dictated by practical rather than theoretical considerations (e.g. Gries notes "[c]urrently, n = 4 is en vogue" (2010: 329)).[16] If we are interested in cross-linguistic comparisons, which lie at the heart of translation, a question should be asked to what extent a 4-gram reflects the same level of formulaicity across languages; in other words, how we can compare 4-grams across languages. While 4-grams may be optimal for English, they may correspond to shorter sequences in inflectional languages which code grammatical information morphologically (through affixes) and in languages which do not mark (in)definiteness explicitly through articles (as English does, where articles – *the*, *a* – are the most frequent words in the wordlists[17] and are part of numerous bundles), with both features applying to Polish. However, we are at too early a stage to solve the problem of cross-linguistic comparisons of bundles and more field work is required in this area.

The study will first quantitatively analyze the distribution of 3-, 4-, 5-, 6-, 7- and 8-grams in all the corpora and then it will focus in more detail on 4-grams in the translation and nontranslation corpora. When computing bundles, Wordsmith was set to stop at sentence breaks, omit clusters involving numbers and dates, and omit phrase frames.

Distribution of n-grams in the translation corpus and the reference corpora

The quantitative part of the analysis looks into the distribution of n-grams across the corpora in terms of types (number of different bundles, the range of bundles) and in terms of tokens (the aggregate frequency of all bundles, total cases). The distribution of 3–8-grams is shown in Table 1.2 below. The middle column represents the translation corpus of the Polish Eurolect, the column on the left presents n-grams in the English reference corpus with underlying source texts (English Eurolect) and the column on the right shows the second reference corpus with nontranslated domestic legislation (Polish law).

As regards the distribution of n-grams, all the corpora show a similar tendency – namely, they contain the largest number of 3-grams, which are twice as frequent as 4-grams both in English and in Polish. 3-grams constitute 40% of all 3–8-grams in the Eurolect corpora and 54% in the Polish Domestic Law corpus, which may indicate that Polish prefers to rely on smaller units to a larger extent in the uninterfered monolingual production. It should be noted that the results are inflated to a certain extent due to the overlap between bundles as the software splits longer n-grams into smaller ones. This issue will be addressed in the next section.

The total number of types for 3–8-grams, that is a range of lexical bundles in the Polish Eurolect corpus, is high at 1986 occurrences. Compared to the corresponding English Eurolect corpus, the range of Polish lexical bundles is over 50% smaller. Thus, the Polish Eurolect – the translationese – shows a lower degree of formulaicity as regards the range of

Table 1.2 Distribution of lexical bundles in the translation corpus and the reference corpora

	RC: EN Eurolect – enacting terms		*PL Eurolect – enacting terms*		*RC: Polish Domestic Law corpus*	
No. of texts	1,017		1,017		190	
No. of words	3,068,479		2,667,590		3,454,942	
Frequency	RF	**NF**	RF	**NF**	RF	**NF**
3-grams	1,466	n.a.	770	n.a.	502	n.a.
4-grams	813	n.a.	390	n.a.	218	n.a.
5-grams	513	n.a.	274	n.a.	134	n.a.
6-grams	373	n.a.	215	n.a.	56	n.a.
7-grams	305	n.a.	180	n.a.	19	n.a.
8-grams	264	n.a.	157	n.a.	4	n.a.
3–8-grams: total types	*3,734*	n.a.	*1,986*	n.a.	*934*	n.a.
3–8-grams: tokens – total cases	*1,292,820*	***421,323***	*685,990*	***257,007***	*458,760*	***132,784***

RF = raw frequency; NF = normalized frequency per million words (bold type).

n-grams; however, it is impossible to determine to what extent it is attributable to the translation process and/or to morpho-grammatical differences between the two languages. For example, the majority of top ten English 4-grams correspond to shorter word sequences in Polish (three 2-grams, three 3-grams, e.g. *in accordance with the* → *zgodnie z; of the European Union* → *Unii Europejskiej*), although there are also three instances where they correspond to longer 5-grams (*referred to in Article* → *o którym mowa w art.*). Furthermore, the Polish Eurolect shows lower formulaicity as regards the aggregate frequency of all bundles (total cases), which is over 50% higher in the English Eurolect corpus than in the Polish translation corpus.

Interestingly, the Polish Eurolect corpus has nearly two times as many types of bundles and twice as many tokens compared to the domestic law corpus (nontranslations); thus, the translation corpus shows a markedly higher degree of formulaicity than the nontranslations corpus.[18] In respect of the range of bundles, the difference is less pronounced for 3-grams and 4-grams, which are twice as frequent in the Polish Eurolect corpus (1.5 and 1.8 times, respectively), and grows exponentially the longer the gram (two times for 5-grams, four times for 6-grams and ten times for 7-grams). For example, while there are only four sequences with eight words in the Polish domestic law corpus, there are 157 such combinations in the Polish Eurolect and 264 in the English Eurolect. 3-grams and 4-grams seem to be natural 'default' n-grams for Polish since, due to a longer average character length of words, they might be more optimal to handle. Longer n-grams seem to be less 'natural' – they are far less common in nontranslated legal Polish, which appears to be less tolerant of increased formulaicity higher than 5-grams. One of the reasons for the abundance of longer n-grams in the Polish Eurolect corpus may be interference from English combined with tendencies hypothesized to be characteristic of the translation process (explicitation and increased analyticality, failure to lexicalize; see section '(Legal) Phraseology in Translation'), where the formulaicity of English is calqued/transferred in translation. Also, as a guard against jumping to premature conclusions as to the increased formulaicity of translations, it should be noted that the EU corpus has over five times more files than the reference corpus; hence it contains more repetitive closing formulae concerning entry into force, such as: *This Regulation shall be binding in its entirety and directly applicable in all Member States* (RF: 887), *This Regulation shall enter into force on the day following that of its publication in the Official Journal of the European Union* (RF: 461), and *shall enter into force on the* (RF: 1000).

Since the pilot study (Biel 2014: 224) has shown significant differences between the distribution of lexical bundles in regulations and directives (entire instruments), where regulations had nearly 30% more n-grams than directives, the next step of the analysis is to compare the distribution of n-grams in each text type (sub-corpus) in order to evaluate the impact of the variable of text type on the level of formulaicity. Table 1.3 shows the distribution of n-grams in regulations and directives of the Eurolect corpora and in the standard and core sections of the Polish Domestic Law corpus.

The data for each instrument type show that the level of formulaicity is very sensitive to text type, even within the same genre. The enacting terms of directives are more formulaic as regards the range of bundles than regulations in the English Corpus but less formulaic in the Polish corpus even though directives are far less (ten times) numerous in the corpus. On the other hand, regulations have more bundles in terms of tokens (1.2 in English and 1.7 in Polish). Sharp differences are also visible in the reference corpus of Polish domestic law, where the sub-corpus of standard statutes has at least twice as many bundles in terms of types and tokens than the core sub-corpus of codes and law-type statutes. The increased number of n-grams in the sub-corpora compared to the whole corpora may indicate that

Table 1.3 Distribution of lexical bundles in the translation sub-corpora and the reference sub-corpora

	RC: EN Eurolect – enacting terms		*PL Eurolect – enacting terms*		*RC: Polish Domestic Law corpus*	
	Regulations	*Directives*	*Regulations*	*Directives*	*Standard*	*Core*
No. of texts	925	92	925	92	135	55
No. of words (in millions)	2.2	0.9	1.9	0.8	1.6	1.9
3-grams	1,408	1,731	758	866	651	416
4-grams	800	980	413	398	416	152
5-grams	504	593	293	219	218	86
6-grams	371	401	231	143	124	35
7-grams	311	401	196	101	58	18
8-grams	277	247	170	79	34	8
3–8-grams: total types	*3,671*	*4,260*	*2,061*	*1,806*	*1,501*	*715*
3–8-grams: tokens – total cases (normalized pmw)	*470,435*	*401,459*	*307,221*	*201,155*	*195,756*	*100,695*

each sub-corpus seems to be relatively homogenous and have a distinct set of bundles with relatively few shared bundles. Sub-corpus bundles are not able to meet frequency thresholds of the whole corpora.

The link between the level of formulaicity and text type may in some cases override such variables as a language and translatedness of a text. Although in general the above noted tendencies are maintained, certain differences are less pronounced than for the combined corpora. As regards the comparison of the Polish Eurolect to the English Eurolect, the former has a substantially smaller range of bundles than the English Eurolect, as well as a substantially lower number of total tokens.

Comparisons of the Polish Eurolect to Polish Domestic Law are more problematic because there is no direct relationship between the PL-EU texts and PL-Domestic texts, as is the case with the identical instruments of the English and Polish EU corpora. The number of n-grams is highest in regulations and lowest in the core sub-corpus of Polish Domestic Law; however, the difference is less pronounced between directives and the PDL standard sub-corpus. In respect to tokens, they are highest in regulations, similar in directives and the standard component, and lowest in the core component. Overall, it can be argued tentatively that translations – the Eurolect – are more formulaic than non-translated law: they have more tokens (regulations) and types; however, there are areas of ‘convergence’ between translations and nontranslations, where directives have a similar number of tokens as the standard sub-corpus of Polish statutes. It should be noted that the core sub-corpus of Polish statutes has a markedly lower degree of formulaicity, even compared to the other Polish sub-corpus, which shows that formulaicity is strongly linked to text type/sub-genre.

Analysis of 4-grams

Distribution, structure and functions of 4-grams

This section has a narrow focus on 4-grams. First, in order to further verify the increased formulaicity of translations, we will refine the number of 4-grams to eliminate overlapping bundles and bundles at clause boundaries. The refinement will be done only for the main corpora with enacting terms.

There are two types of overlap, referred to by Chen and Baker (2010: 33) as a complete overlap and a complete subsumption. The former occurs when two smaller n-grams come from a longer n-gram (Chen and Baker 2010: 33), e.g. two 4-grams *Member States shall ensure* and *States shall ensure that* are derived from a single 5-gram *Member States shall ensure that*, all of which have a similar distribution in the corpus. The latter, complete subsumption, occurs when "two or more 4-word bundles overlap and the occurrences of one of the bundles subsume those of the other overlapping bundle(s)" (Chen and Baker (2010: 33), e.g. *in the case of* has a raw frequency of 1203 while *the case of a* has a frequency of 268 and is part of the 5-gram *in the case of a* (RF: 268). Although in some studies such sequences are deleted,[19] following Chen and Baker, overlapping 4-grams will be combined into longer sequences to avoid counting them twice. The refinement is shown in Table 1.4.

The highest degree of subsumption has been observed in the translation corpus – 4-grams are often part of (unnaturally) long bundles. After the refinement, translations still have a higher number of bundles than nontranslations; however, overall they have a similar distribution in terms of tokens in both the translation and nontranslation corpora.

Table 1.5 shows top ten 4-grams in the Polish Eurolect corpora and two reference corpora.

Interestingly, the first three most-frequent bundles in the Polish Eurolect and the Polish Domestic Law corpus are identical (although they are twice as frequent in the latter) while the remaining ones differ. The shared bundles are inflectional variants of the referential phrase frame *o który* mowa w* [which is referred to in . . .], which combines with various words on the left *(~Article, Paragraph, the Act, the Annex*, etc.) and on the right (*information, application, case, duty ~*), forming longer but less frequent n-grams.

Table 1.4 Refinement of 4-grams

	RC: EN-EU – enacting terms		*PL Eurolect – enacting terms*		*RC: Polish Domestic Law corpus*	
	RF	*NF*	*RF*	*NF*	*RF*	*NF*
4-grams before refinement: types	813	n.a.	390	n.a.	218	n.a.
Tokens	276,786	**90,203**	137,612	**51,557**	121,915	**35,287**
4-grams after refinement: types	700	n.a.	231	n.a.	137	n.a.
Tokens	217,455	**70,867**	72,734	**21,052**	74,329	**21,514**
% of words in bundles for refined 4-grams	**28%**		**11%**		**8%**	

Table 1.5 Top ten 4-grams after refinement (figures in parentheses provide normalized frequencies per million words/dispersion, i.e. percentage of texts where a given n-gram is found)

RC: EN Eurolect – enacting terms	*PL Eurolect – enacting terms*	*RC: Polish Domestic Law corpus*
referred to in article (1765/39%)	***o których mowa w*** (2243/41%) [which (are) referred to in]	***o których mowa w*** (3703/95%) [which (are) referred to in]
in accordance with article (1401/34%)	***o którym mowa w*** (1031/75%) [which (is) referred to in]	***o którym mowa w*** (3363/94%) [which (is) referred to in]
in accordance with the (1076/29%)	***o której mowa w*** (752/29%) [which (is) referred to in]	***o której mowa w*** (1740/90%) [which (is) referred to in]
referred to in paragraph (1056/34%)	*restrukturyzacji i uporządkowanej likwidacji* (531/0.1%) [(of the) resolution, lit. restructuring and orderly liquidation]	*minister właściwy do spraw* (948/77%) [applicable minister in charge of]
of Regulation EU no. (815/23%)	*w Dzienniku Urzędowym Unii Europejskiej* (404/99%) [in the Official Journal of the European Union]	*w ustawie z dnia* (591/84%) [in the act of day]
referred to in the (641/56%)	*Komisja jest uprawniona do* (274/13%) [The Commission shall be empowered to]	*na terytorium Rzeczypospolitej Polskiej* (545/56%) [in the territory of the Republic of Poland]
the European Parliament and (639/30%)	*we wszystkich państwach członkowskich* (272/89%) [in all the Member States]	*określi w drodze rozporządzenia* (463/72%) [shall specify by way of ordinance]
for the purposes of (586/33%)	*rozporządzenie wiąże w całości i jest bezpośrednio stosowane* (268/91%) [regulation shall be binding in its entirety and shall be directly applicable]	*ministra właściwego do spraw* (353/70%) [(of the) applicable minister – in charge of]
referred to in point (537/21%)	*niniejsze rozporządzenie wchodzi w życie* (267/91%) [this regulation shall enter into force]	*wydanych na podstawie art.* (239/55%) [issued by virtue of article]
of the European Union (527/99%)	*Parlamentu Europejskiego i Rady* (266/24) [(of the) European Parliament and the Council]	*stosuje się odpowiednio przepisy* (221/68%) [provisions are applied accordingly]
9,565	6,308	12,166

This phrase frame plays a fundamental role in legislation: it establishes intratextual and intertextual pointers (Biel 2014: 237–238), contributing to the systemic nature of law. It corresponds to more specific (narrower in meaning) 4-grams in the English Eurolect: *referred to in article*, *referred to in paragraph*, *referred to in the*, *referred to in point*. Owing to structural differences between English and Polish, there is little similarity between the

English and Polish Eurolect bundles since in most cases Polish 4-grams correspond to shorter English grams.

Top bundles in the Polish Domestic Law corpus seem to be more evenly distributed across the texts, i.e. they appear in at last 55% of texts in the corpus. The distribution of top bundles in the Polish Eurolect corpus is more varied, with fourth bundle appearing in only 0.1% of texts (*restrukturyzacji i uporządkowanej likwidacji*, which corresponds to a single term in English – *resolution* (of credit institutions and investment firms)). The dispersion is even lower for the English Eurolect corpus.

The analysis of structural properties of 4-grams confirms Jablonkai's, Goźdź-Roszkowski's and Breeze's findings – the lists are dominated by noun phrases and prepositional phrases with a relatively high percentage of verb phrases. Similarly, as regards the functional properties of 4-grams, there is a majority of referential bundles (participative bundles, institutional bundles, terminological bundles), a small number of text-oriented bundles (purpose, condition, cause-result) and few stance bundles (deontic modality).

Overlap of 4-grams in the translation and nontranslation corpora

The final stage of the analysis is to identify the degree of overlap of 4-grams between the translation and nontranslation corpora. This task will be carried out by comparing the 4-gram lists in the keywords functions (Table 1.6).

Table 1.6 4-grams shared by the translation and nontranslation corpora (the Polish Eurolect corpus against the PL-Domestic corpus)

Shared 4-grams	*Frequency in PL-EU*	*Frequency in PL-Domestic*	*Log_L*	*Log_R*
Parlamentu Europejskiego i Rady [of the European Parliament and the Council]	918	378	392.87	1.65
nie później niż w [not later than in]	129	318	–41.13	–0.93
której mowa w art. [which (is)-FEM referred to in article]	1,703	2,924	–87.79	–0.41
których mowa w ust [which (are) referred to in paragraph]	2,532	4,709	–223.19	–0.52
których mowa w art. [which (are) referred to in]	3,473	6,357	–277.69	–0.50
o których mowa w [about which (are) referred to in]	7,748	12,792	–290.81	–0.35
o której mowa w [about which (is)-FEM referred to in]	2,598	6,012	–653.58	–0.84
której mowa w ust [which (is)-FEM referred to in paragraph]	555	2,548	–924.19	–1.83
którym mowa w art. [which (is)-MASC referred to in article]	1,665	5,281	–1,160.52	–1.29
którym mowa w ust [which (is)-MASC referred to in paragraph]	1,116	4,871	–1,671.08	–1.75
o którym mowa w [about which (is)-MASC referred to in]	3,562	1,1618	–2,675.92	–1.33

The perplexing finding is that there are very few bundles which are shared by the translation and nontranslation corpora – out of 390 4-grams in the Polish Eurolect corpus only 11 bundles are shared (2.8%) and those which are shared are keywords (key bundles) of the nontranslation corpora, except for the first one. The result is slightly higher for a total of 3–8-grams with 5% of shared n-grams between the translation and nontranslation corpora. This suggests that despite the high formulaicity of translations, translations resort to their own bundles prompted by source texts and fail to prime bundles which are typical of the nontranslated texts of a comparable genre. Thus, it seems that translations may create their own 'formulaic profiles' by making uncommon patterns frequent and cognitively salient. In addition to being attributable to complex bilingual processing during the translation process and source text interference, this phenomenon may also be explained by the multilingual and hybrid nature of EU law with its fusion of languages, which may take a toll on the naturalness of patterning in translations. Furthermore, the increased formulaicity of translations confirms Toury's law of growing standardization and Baker's normalization hypothesis while the broader range of n-grams confirms Mauranen's hypothesis that translations use more varied and less stable patterns, thus reconciling the opposing views on the nature of formulaicity in translations.

Conclusions

The study has demonstrated that Polish EU translations seem to have an increased level of formulaicity in respect to types, tokens and percentage of words in bundles, and in particular of bundles which have at least five or more words. Thus, the hypothesis that translations are less patterned and less formulaic than nontranslations has not been confirmed. However, more importantly, it has been shown that translations share very few bundles (3% of 4-grams) with nontranslations – Polish Domestic Law. It implies that translations resort to their own n-grams prompted by source texts rather than prime bundles which are natural and expected in target-language legal texts. This finding might shed new light on the nature of formulaicity of translations, with translations tending to create their own repetitive formulaic sequences and, hence, 'formulaic profiles' affected to a certain degree by source language interference. The findings, in particular those concerning the low overlap of bundles between translations and nontranslations, require further validation and replication in other types of translation, as well as more in-depth studies in the context of EU translation (against various types of reference corpora to reduce the comparability issue). Since another possible explanation of a low percentage of overlapping bundles is an incomplete thematic convergence between EU law and domestic law, due to partially different scopes of regulation, further studies should perhaps attempt to control the thematic variable (text 'aboutness') through corpus design.

Overall, the study has shown that phraseology – understood as recurrent patterns of language use – is central to legal language. The frequency-driven approach to phraseology and the concept of lexical bundles (high frequency multi-word sequences) are well suited to study the nature of patterns in translated texts as they allow us to explore legal translation and legal language from a new angle and give us new tools and theoretical concepts to do it.

Acknowledgement

This work was supported by the National Science Centre (NCN) under Grant 2014/14/E/HS2/00782.

Notes

1 See Gray and Biber (2015) for an overview of current trends and methodological issues in corpus linguistics phraseology.
2 Breeze does not specify it explicitly and only refers to "English legal genres" and "commercial law in English"; however, since the legislation corpus consists of Companies Acts, it may probably be assumed that her texts come from the legal system of England and Wales.
3 The EEUD corpus contains 241 texts which represent 40 EU genres, of which legal texts – including case law – constitute less than 45% of texts (Jablonkai 2010: 256).
4 First studies on Polish lexical bundles concern pharmaceutical Polish (Grabowski 2014).
5 The hypotheses that translations are marked by distinctive features due to the constraint of the translation process are known under the controversial name of translation universals in the Translation Studies literature. See Biel (2014: 96–110) for an overview.
6 Owing to the multilingual and multistage drafting of EU law and the complex relationship between language versions, the English-language version cannot be regarded as a pure source text of the Polish target (although it is often the case, the impact of other languages cannot be entirely eliminated).
7 For more up-to-date information, see also http://eurolekt.ils.uw.edu.pl/.
8 http://eur-lex.europa.eu/browse/directories/legislation.html.
9 All documents were downloaded except for amending, repealing, implementing and delegated acts.
10 Enacting terms constitute ca. 35% of regulations and ca. 50% of directives in the 2011–2015 Eurolect corpus.
11 See also Gray and Biber (2015: 137), who observe that a different corpus size, number of texts and topics may limit the comparability of lexical bundles across corpora.
12 It may, however, be argued whether in the case of legislative texts with collective authorship it is equally necessary to apply the dispersion threshold.
13 For example, as shown in Table 1.1, the Polish corpora have three times as many types as the English corpus due to inflectional variants, which implies a higher variation of n-grams.
14 The same frequency cut-off was applied in Goźdź-Roszkowski's (2011) and Jablonkai's (2010) studies while Breeze (2013) set it higher at 50 pmw.
15 The same dispersion threshold was used in Goźdź-Roszkowski's (2011) study; Jablonkai (2010) applied the threshold of 10% of texts while Breeze (2013) applied none.
16 See Gray and Biber (2015: 136) and Greaves and Warren (2010: 214) for an overview of criticism.
17 *The* is #1 and *a* is #4 in the BNC wordlist, cf. Leech et al. (2001: 120).
18 The difference between translations and nontranslations was not so pronounced in the earlier project (Biel 2014), which, however, compared entire EU instruments, including preambles, to nontranslated Polish documents – regulations had 44% more 3–8-grams and directives 13% more n-grams than Polish law.
19 See also Pęzik (2015) who proposes a more sophisticated approach of counting the Independence-Formulaicity score for n-grams.

References

Baker, M., 1996. Corpus-based translation studies: The challenges that lie ahead. In H.L. Somers (ed.), *Terminology, LSP and Translation: Studies in Language Engineering in Honour of Juan C. Sager*. Amsterdam/Philadelphia: John Benjamins, 175–186.

Biber, D., 2009. Corpus-based and corpus-driven analyses of language variation and use. In B. Heine and H. Narrog (eds.), *The Oxford Handbook of Linguistic Analysis*. [Online] doi:10.1093/oxfordhb/9780199544004.013.0008.

Biber, D. and Barbieri, F., 2007. Lexical bundles in university spoken and written registers. *English for Specific Purpose*, 26(3): 263–286.

Biber, D., Johansson, S., Leech, G., Conrad, S., and Finegan, E., 1999. *Longman Grammar of Spoken and Written English*. Harlow: Longman.

Biel, Ł., 2014. *Lost in the Eurofog: Textual Fit of Translated Law*. Frankfurt am Main: Peter Lang.

Biel, Ł., 2015. Phraseological profiles of legislative genres: Complex prepositions as a special case of legal phrasemes in EU law and national law. *Fachsprache: International Journal of Specialized Communication*, 37(3–4): 139–160.

Biel, Ł., 2016. Mixed corpus design for researching the Eurolect: A genre-based comparable-parallel corpus in the PL EUROLECT project. In E. Gruszczyńska and A. Leńko-Szymańska (eds.), *Polskojęzyczne korpusy równoległe. Polish-Language Parallel Corpora*. Warsaw: The Institute of Applied Linguistics, 197–208. <http://rownolegle.blog.ils.uw.edu.pl/files/2016/03/12_Biel.pdf>

Breeze, R., 2013. Lexical bundles across four legal genres. *International Journal of Corpus Linguistics*, 18(2): 229–253.

Chen, Y.-H. and Baker, P., 2010. Lexical bundles in L1 and L2 academic writing. *Language Learning & Technology*, 4(2): 30–49.

Chesterman, A., 2004. Hypotheses about translation universals. In G. Hansen, K. Malmkjær and D. Gile (eds.), *Claims, Changes and Challenges in Translation Studies. Selected Contributions from the EST Congress, Copenhagen 2001*. Amsterdam: Benjamins, 1–13.

Cortes, V., 2004. Lexical bundles and student disciplinary writing: Examples from history and biology. *English for Specific Purposes*, 23: 397–423.

Doczekalska, A., 2009. Drafting and interpretation of EU law – Paradoxes of legal multilingualism. In G. Grewendorf and M. Rathert (eds.), *Formal Linguistics and Law*. Berlin: de Gruyter, 339–370.

Gouadec, D., 2007. *Translation as a Profession*. Amsterdam: John Benjamins.

Goźdź-Roszkowski, S., 2011. *Patterns of Linguistic Variation in American Legal English: A Corpus-based Study*. Frankfurt am Main: Peter Lang.

Goźdź-Roszkowski, S. and Pontrandolfo, G., 2015. Legal phraseology today: Corpus-based applications across legal languages and genres. *Fachsprache: International Journal of Specialized Communication*, 37(3–4): 130–138.

Grabowski, Ł., 2014. On lexical bundles in Polish patient information leaflets: A corpus-driven study. *Studies in Polish Linguistics*, 9(1): 21–43.

Grabowski, Ł., 2015. *Phraseology in English Pharmaceutical Discourse: A Corpus-driven Study of Register Variation*. Uniwersytet Opolski: Opole.

Granger, S. and Paquot, M., 2008. Disentangling the phraseological web. In S. Granger and F. Meunier (eds.), *Phraseology: An Interdisciplinary Perspective*. Amsterdam: John Benjamins, 27–49.

Gray, B. and Biber, D., 2015. Phraseology. In D. Biber and R. Reppen (eds.), *The Cambridge Handbook of English Corpus Linguistics*. Cambridge: Cambridge University Press, 123–145.

Greaves, Ch. and Warren, M., 2010. What can a corpus tell us about multi-word units? In A. O'Keeffe and M. McCarthy (eds.), *The Routledge Handbook of Corpus Linguistics*. London: Routledge, 212–226.

Gries, S. Th., 2010. Corpus linguistics and theoretical linguistics. A love-hate relationship? Not necessarily . . . *International Journal of Corpus Linguistics*, 15(3): 327–343.

Hyland, K., 2008. As can be seen: Lexical bundles and disciplinary variation. *English for Specific Purposes*, 27: 4–21.

Jablonkai, R., 2010. English *in the context of* European integration: A corpus-driven analysis of lexical bundles in English EU documents. *English for Specific Purposes*, 29(4): 253–267.

Kjær, A.L., 2007. Phrasemes in legal texts. In H. Burger, D. Dobrovol'skij, P. Kühn, and N.R. Norrick (eds.), *Phraseology/Phraseologie: An International Handbook of Contemporary Research/Ein internationales Handbuch der zeitgenössischen Forschung*. Berlin: de Gruyter, 506–516.

Koskinen, K., 2000. Institutional illusions. Translating in the EU Commission. *The Translator*, 6(1): 49–65.

Lee, Ch., 2013. Using lexical bundle analysis as discovery tool for corpus-based translation research. *Perspectives: Studies in Translatology*, 21(3): 378–395.

Leech, G., Rayson, P., and Wilson, A., 2001. *Word Frequencies in Written and Spoken English: Based on the British National Corpus.* London: Longman.

Mauranen, A., 2006. Translation universals. In K. Brown (ed.), *Encyclopedia of Language and Linguistics*, Vol. 13, 2nd ed. Oxford: Elsevier, 93–100.

Mauranen, A., 2007. Universal tendencies in translation. In G.M. Anderman and M. Rogers (eds.), *Incorporating Corpora: The Linguist and the Translator.* Clevedon: Multilingual Matters, 32–48.

Monzó Nebot, E., 2008. Corpus-based activities in legal translator training. *The Interpreter and Translator Trainer*, 2(2): 221–251.

Nesselhauf, N., 2005. *Collocations in a Learner Corpus.* Amsterdam: John Benjamins.

Pęzik, P., 2015. Using n-gram independence to identify discourse-functional lexical units in spoken learner corpus data. *International Journal of Learner Corpus Research*, 1(2): 242–255.

Pontrandolfo, G., 2016. *Fraseología y lenguaje judicial. Las sentencias penales desde una perspectiva contrastiva.* Roma: Aracne.

Ruusila, A. and Lindroos, E., 2016. *Conditio sine qua non:* On phraseology in legal language and its translation. *Language and Law/Linguagem e Direito*, 3(1): 120–140.

Šarčević, S., 1997. *New Approach to Legal Translation.* The Hague: Kluwer Law International.

Stubbs, M., 2004. Language corpora. In A. Davies and C. Elder (eds.), *Handbook of Applied Linguistics.* Oxford: Blackwell, 106–132.

Toury, G., 1995. *Descriptive Translation Studies and Beyond.* Amsterdam: John Benjamins.

2 The problem of legal phraseology

A case of translators vs lawyers

Daniele Orlando

Introduction

Over the past thirty years a growing body of research has focused on the central role of phraseology in language learning (Hoffmann et al. 2015) and teaching (Kennedy 2008: 21), showing a correlation between trainees' L1 and L2 proficiency and adequate phraseological use (e.g. Boers et al. 2006; Eyckmans 2007). Yet, still scarce attention has been paid to phraseology in the LSPs and, more specifically, in the legal field (for an overview on the latter, Pontrandolfo 2016: 69–75). Given the system-bound nature of legal language (e.g. Sandrini 1996), equivalence between legal phrases across different legal languages/systems is not straightforward (e.g. Kjær 1995); hence, the need to reproduce the specific phraseology of legal texts to minimise the risk of impairing communication or losing credibility in the eyes of the (specialised) reader, even when all other aspects of the translated text are perfectly acceptable (cf. Kjær 1990; Garzone 2007). Phraseology has in fact been shown to be a potential cause of translation problems (Osborne 2008; for legal translation, e.g. Šarčević 1997; Garzone 2007); more precisely, Orozco and Sánchez-Gijón (2011: 1–2) observed that legal collocations and phraseology at the micro-textual sentence level might result in difficulties finding a functional equivalent in both the translation process and product. From a didactic perspective, it would therefore seem only appropriate that trainee translators be introduced, and ultimately comply, to the stylistic norms of specialist domains at the collocational and phraseological levels, so as to improve the textual fit of their target texts (cf. Palumbo 2001: 199–200; Biel 2010b). However, the number of specialised mono- and multi-lingual resources to be adopted in both translation practice and training to facilitate the retrieval of phraseology in context, i.e. corpora and concordancers, still appears to be rather low (cf. Vigier Moreno 2016), thus limiting the

> ways of conceiving of the situated user in these environments, of the precise difficulties that multiword expressions present for them there, the new sorts of lexical knowledge that this requires, and novel means of both discovering it and representing it to learners.
>
> (Wible 2008: 180)

Against this background, this chapter addresses the incidence of phraseology in legal translation as a special case in a pedagogical view; particularly, it investigates its problematic nature by focusing on the translation process and product of prospective legal translation trainees with different academic backgrounds and, consequently, different levels of familiarity with the phraseology of legal language.

The empirical study

The research aim

While the special focus of this chapter is on legal phraseology, the analyses presented here are extracted from a larger empirical study conducted at the University of Trieste (Orlando 2016) with the aim of investigating the different (pre-)levels of competence and, ultimately, the different training needs of prospective legal translation trainees with different academic qualifications.

The specific research questions that this chapter seeks to explore are the following:

1. Is legal phraseology a source of translation problems for trainees? If so, can differences be observed as a result of different academic backgrounds?
2. Do these translation problems result in different translation procedures, with particular reference to searches and decision-making?
3. Do these translation problems lead to errors in the translation product?

The research design and methodology adopted to address these questions are presented in the following sections.

The sample

The study analyses thirty translations from English into Italian produced by a sample comprising two different cohorts,[1] including:

- 15 MA-level translation graduates (hereafter, 'Group T' or 'Ts') at the University of Trieste with no specialisation in legal translation, i.e. a limited or lack of knowledge of the legal subject field and no prior experience in legal translation; and
- 15 linguistically skilled postgraduate lawyers ('Group L' or 'Ls') at the Law Faculty of the University of Genova, with no translation background. In other words, their expertise was limited to the legal domain, also in terms of content and formal conventions of the documents produced in this field, as well as mastery of the English language, as testified by fulfilment of a series of minimum requirements (e.g. formal L2 training; official language certifications; research stays in English-speaking countries; publications in English).

The distinctive feature of the empirical study being the participants' prior education is particularly relevant in today's language industry and in the legal context, because while translations to and from the foreign language are mostly produced by professional translators in collaboration with lawyers, occasionally lawyers themselves do their own legal translations (cf. Faber and Hjort-Pedersen 2009: 340; also, Ruusila and Lindroos 2016).

The research design

The thirty participants were asked to translate from English into Italian a 500-word extract from a criminal law document, i.e. a European Arrest Warrant, presenting a variety of translation problems (e.g. comprehension, pragmatic, terminological, and syntactic problems). To ensure ecological validity, the participants were allowed to use any resource they wished.

While most recent studies focused on the different product-related preferences shown by the two groups of participants described above (e.g. Fischer 2008; Faber and Hjort-Pedersen 2009), this study adopted a twofold perspective covering both the translation process and product.

Firstly, procedural data from different collection methods were triangulated, i.e. screen and video recording, and keystroke logging (cf. Enríquez Raído 2011; Göpferich 2009; Martín-Mor 2011; Teixeira 2014; Morado Vázquez 2012) using *Blueberry's BB FlashBack*. The identification of potential occurrences of problems was based on the analysis of the pauses in the translation process; problems were then classified with a specific taxonomy developed for this project, including the main sub-categories of content- and language-related problems. These data have then been correlated with the type of problem-solving procedures and reference materials used, i.e. internal and external support (Alves 1997).

Secondly, all process-related data have been mapped on the quality of the participants' translation products. More specifically, an error analysis (Vollmar 2001; Mossop 2014) and assessment of the translations' *acceptability* (PACTE 2009) have been conducted, to identify which translation processes led to better products and what the main pitfalls and information deficits, i.e. training needs, were for each group of participants.

Methodology

Identification of translation problems

By 'translation problem', we consider "those particular source text items [. . .] problematic for translation [. . .] as manifested in, and inferred from the participants' recorded translation processes and their resulting products" (Enríquez Raído 2011: 151). In a didactic perspective, translation problems are thus to be seen as 'information needs' or 'deficits' (cf. Prahl and Petzolt 1997: 125, 138; Valli 2013: 74–78, respectively), meant both in terms of declarative (i.e. thematic) knowledge of the subject field particular to the source text (ST) and procedural knowledge on how to go about solving said problem.

The identification of problems started with the analysis of pauses, i.e. "observable interruption[s] in the natural flow of translation" (Angelone 2010: 18) which might constitute "potential indicators of mental activity related to the text segments neighbo[u]ring that pause" (Martín 2014: 59).[2] As pointed out by Lörscher (1986: 279), "of course not every pause or hesitation necessarily indicates a translational problem", as ST reception, mental organisation, and target text (TT) formulation – or, in other words, 'cognitive effort' (cf. O'Brien 2006; Lacruz et al. 2012) – may just as well interrupt the process without being caused by a translation problem. Therefore, *problem-related* pauses may be identified based on the occurrence of a series of phenomena. For this purpose, an adapted version of the classification of problem indicators was used, which was originally developed by Krings (1986b: 121; also cf. Englund Dimitrova 2005: 156; Göpferich 2010: 8), who differentiated between: (A) *primary indicators*, e.g. explicit problem identification by the translator, consultations of reference sources, gaps in the translation, of which one occurrence is enough; (B) *secondary indicators*, e.g. alternative translations, repeated changes, underlined units, (non-)lexical phenomena, of which at least two must occur simultaneously for a single segment.

The rhythm and output of the translation may be affected by different types of problems in different ways (Jakobsen 2005: 181); hence, many categorisations of translation problems have been devised through the years (e.g. Nord 1991: 158–160; Hurtado Albir

Table 2.1 Classification of translation problems

Content	**Meaning**	
	Culture-bound differences	
Form	Non-specialised language	
	Sub-language	Terminology
		Phraseology
	Mechanics	
	Style	

2001; PACTE 2011: 327; Krings 1986a; Göpferich 2010). For the purpose of this study, though, a specific taxonomy was developed, paralleling Mossop's (2014) revision parameters as closely as possible, so as to enable for an easier correlation of problems in the translation process and errors in the translation product (see p. 33). The resulting classification of translation problems is summarised in Table 2.1 above.

At the highest level, the categories of *content* and *form* constitute the basic distinction of translation problems (as in Mossop's list below, Table 2.2). In this specific context, the main focus is on the sub-category of *sub-language*, i.e. problems with the LSP (here, legal language) lexical, syntactic, and rhetoric features. In order to gain more specific quantitative and qualitative information on this type of problems, the two further sub-categories of *terminology* and *phraseology* were also analysed separately.

Error analysis

Errors in the translation product can surely be regarded as procedural "problems which the translator was not able to solve" (Palumbo 2008: 47). Despite their (at least partially) inevitably subjective nature, errors are counted, assessed, and classified, mostly in terms of type and severity. Also in this case, many error classifications have been devised (e.g. Pym 1992; Nord 1996; House 1997; Koby et al. 2014); however, Mossop's (2014: 134–149) list of revision parameters was adopted in this study to provide a comparative analysis, both quantitative and qualitative, of the errors found in the translations produced by the two groups of participants. Despite being composite, Mossop's classification (summarised in Table 2.2) is clear and concise, with dynamic distinctions that allow for a wide margin of flexibility. Further, it combines the pedagogical needs of training (especially at the higher MA level, as in this study) and the practical needs of the translation market, by reaffirming the *form/content* dualism.

It should be noted that the category of 'presentation', which pertains to layout, formatting, and other formal aspects, was not part of the translation brief and was not accounted for in the analysis. The three remaining categories are 'transfer', which relates to the accuracy and completeness of the information; 'content', which refers to the logical and factual verity of the translated text; and finally 'language', which includes smoothness (i.e. readability), tailoring to the register and genre conventions of the source text, sub-language, idioms, and mechanics (i.e. grammar, punctuation, and other mechanical aspects of text production). In particular, the analysis presented in this chapter zeroes in on the language

Table 2.2 Mossop's (2014: 134–149) list of revision parameters

	Group	Parameter
Content	A. Transfer	Accuracy
		Completeness
	B. Content	Logic
		Facts
Form	C. Language	Smoothness
		Tailoring
		Sub-language
		Idiom
		Mechanics
	D. Presentation	Layout
		Typography
		Organisation

sub-category of 'sub-language', which addresses the following questions: "Is the style suited to the genre? Has correct terminology been used? Does the phraseology match that used in original target-language texts on the same subject?" (Mossop 2014: 134). For the purposes of this study, again 'terminology' (i.e. domain-specific nouns and noun phrases only) and 'phraseology' (i.e. inter-phrasal combinations of words and, possibly, terms) have been accounted for as two distinct sub-categories.

Finally, the quantitative and qualitative classification of errors was followed by the assessment of their gravity, using Vollmar's (2001) severity scale. It comprises three degrees, which have been combined here with Mossop's parameters in the macro-categories of *form* and *content* errors, as follows:

- *minor errors*, i.e. form errors, which do not affect meaning;
- *major errors*, i.e. form and content errors which result in an ambiguity in the TT; minor errors in a visible or significant part of the text;
- *critical errors*, i.e. form and content errors which result in lack of understanding of the TT; major errors in a visible or significant part of the text.

Results

This section presents the results of the analysis from both a process- and product-oriented perspective. For the former, the occurrences of translation problems will be first observed. In general terms, from a quantitative perspective a strikingly higher number of problems were encountered by Group T, i.e. 55.47, as compared to the average of 24.87 in the case of Group L. Hence, at first sight, it could be assumed that the fewer difficulties faced by Ls might be the result of different levels of competence leading to better translation products. More precisely, a qualitative breakdown of the types of problem per group shows further intergroup differences relevant to this context, with Ts encountering almost twice as many problems in all categories as compared to Ls.

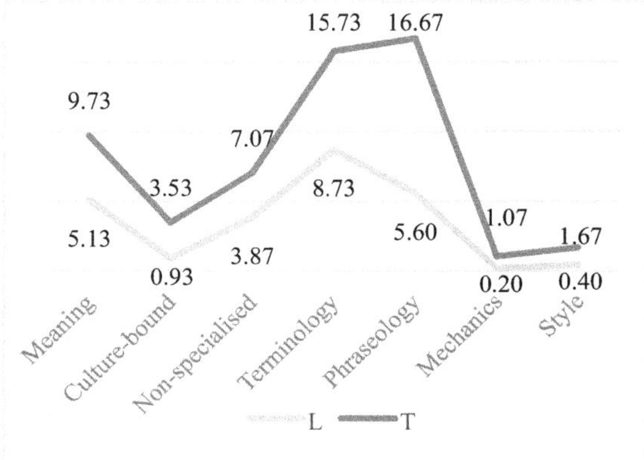

Figure 2.1 Number of problems per type

As can be seen in Figure 2.1, these considerations apply to both content- and form-related problems. From a procedural perspective, both sub-language categories of terminology and phraseology proved especially difficult for Group T (though both categories appeared to be the most problematic for Ls as well), considering their lack of familiarity with the legal content and rhetoric conventions of the document. Particularly, phraseology shows the greatest differences between the two groups, with Ts facing three times as many problems as Ls. These figures suggest that thematic knowledge might, in fact, have proved to be an added value for Ls, whose translation process was found to be smoother with respect to all problem types and legal phraseology in particular.

As mentioned in the previous section, the occurrence of a problem is signalled by, among others, the consultation of a reference source. Quantitatively speaking, as was the case for problems, on average Group T made 3.6 times as many searches as Group L, i.e. 62 and 17, respectively. Such a big difference may find an explanation in the inverse proportionality between the level of domain knowledge and the information needs (cf. Enríquez Raído 2013: 179): the higher the thematic competence, the lower the number[3] and the less specialised the nature of these searches. However, the qualitative analysis of such searches display a more 'interactionist' approach to online searches, i.e. high engagement with and consumption of selected web content, on the part of the participants with a translation-specific background and experience (Group T), who "spent more time on average searching and reading the content retrieved for [their] thematic searches"; by contrast, the less experienced participants generally displayed a "shallow online search style that [. . .] mainly resulted from a desire for fast and easy access to information" (cf. Enríquez Raído 2013: 174). More precisely, the choice of reference sources was rather restricted for Ls, who never developed any translation-specific information mining skills during their studies; as a result, Ls primarily used online bilingual dictionaries (cf. Buendía Castro and Faber, this volume) – more precisely, *WordReference* – for the majority of their searches, including those prompted by comprehension problems (cf. Enríquez Raído 2013: 25) and, more significantly, phraseology, for which they adopted a micro-textual, literal approach focusing on individual lexical items as a cognitive strategy (cf. Barbosa and Neiva 2003: 148). Conversely, the majority of look-ups performed by Group T was not in dictionaries, but rather in concordancers (in particular *Linguee*), i.e. comparable corpora where terms and expressions occur in their original context with reference to the original website; this is the same type of look-up as when googling, which was often adopted by this cohort. With reference to concordancers, the results are partially in line with those reported by Valli in her Ph.D. thesis (2013: 154, 226): nominal strings – but also prepositional phrases – of between 1 and 5 words (2 and 11 in her study) were by far the most frequent type of search; Ts mostly maintained default settings, without applying an actual filter (though EU domains were preferred); finally, almost a third of the searches turned out to be unsuccessful. Still, these retrieval techniques enabled the participants to assess the origin and frequency of use of the lexical units at hand: given the nature of the ST, all Ts who consulted a concordancer, or googled to either retrieve specific information or to find parallel and comparable texts (66.84% of their total searches), assessed the source of the equivalent they found, by only referencing the official websites of the European institutions.

The different levels of problematisation and the resulting use of reference sources ultimately proved crucial in achieving quality in the target text. As a matter of fact, on average Group L made over a third more errors than Group T, with a mean of 31.2 for Group L and 18.33 for Group T, who thus produced translations of an overall better quality. Some (slight) differences can be observed from a qualitative breakdown of the types of errors, summarised in Figure 2.2.

More specifically, the first four categories, i.e. *content*-related errors, prove that Ts managed to overcome the semantic difficulties of the ST better than Ls, despite their lack of familiarity with the subject field, which generally contradicts the initial hypothesis, whereby pragmatic difficulties should have been mostly sustained by Ts rather than Ls, due to their specialisation background. As regards form-related errors, expectedly Group T recorded lower total numbers. Most significantly, though, *sub-language* proved just as problematic for both groups, with an average of almost 3 errors of *terminology* and/or *phraseology* in the major range. On closer inspection, the results for phraseology are rather interesting: though slightly higher in number, in general the errors produced by Ls in this category are less severe than those by Ts, whose renderings mostly failed in terms of function – textual fit, i.e. adherence to the domain – and genre-specific environment – of the phrase selected. It can be thus concluded that in this case Group L appeared to at least partially benefit from their familiarity with the text genre under consideration, thus displaying a partially better mastery of the recurring phraseology of legal documents, unlike Ts who failed in this respect despite their familiarity with the importance of looking for adequate reference sources.

Some examples

In this section, three different examples posing different types of difficulties will be discussed, with a focus on both the translation process and product. More precisely, the first was highly context-dependent; the second could be found in a concordancer; the third was the most easily accessible.

Firstly, a potential source of errors was posed by the phrase ‘contrary to’ referring to an offence (as in, “Affray, *contrary to* section 3 (1) and (7) Public Order Act 1986”). It is a recurring collocation in legal English corresponding in Italian to the expression ‘previsto e punito’ (or its short form, ‘p. e p.’), as well as to a series of other synonymic phrases, which on the linguistic surface appears to adopt the opposite perspective of the English phrase. Though rarely retraceable in its legal meaning and context in the bilingual dictionary, it could have been translated correctly either through adequate searches in comparable, authentic legal texts or, more easily, by relying on prior familiarity with Italian legal

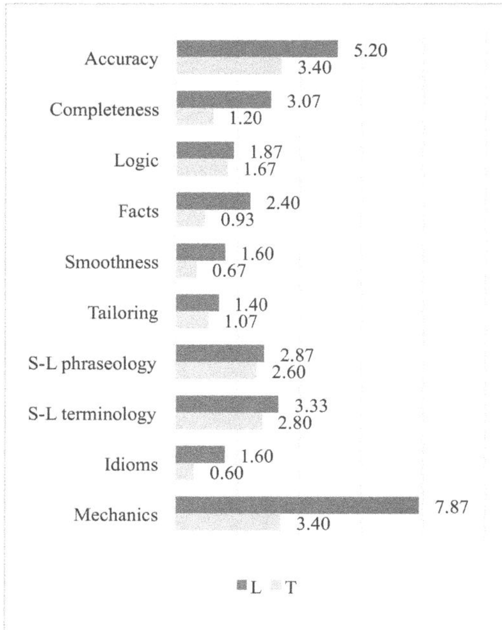

	L	T		L	T		L	T
A	11.08	12.16	**S**	5.56	3.00	**Te**	8.79	10.89
C	10.51	5.50	**Ta**	4.50	3.83	**I**	6.17	3.00
L	12.80	9.03	**P**	5.54	8.62	**M**	6.30	7.18
F	11.81	5.17						

Figure 2.2 Average number and severity of errors per type

phrasemes. As a matter of fact, in this case only 3 Ts found fully acceptable solutions, as compared to 9 Ls, including:

> *L01 punito ai sensi* [di]
> *L03 in violazione* [di]
> *T15 ai sensi* [di]

By contrast, 8 Ts and only 3 Ls rendered the phrase with a literal translation, 'contrario [a]', which is not typical of legal Italian language and only partially acceptable from a semantic viewpoint. In order to understand the different reasonings behind such choices, we now take a look at the translation processes of the participants, as shown in Figure 2.3 below.

It should be noted that this phrase – which appeared twice in the source text – resulted in a problem for 3 Ls and a strikingly higher number of Ts, i.e. 13. However, if we take a look at the decision-making processes, we see Ls relying mostly on *predominantly internal support* (Alves 1997), i.e. they consulted a bilingual dictionary but provided a variant

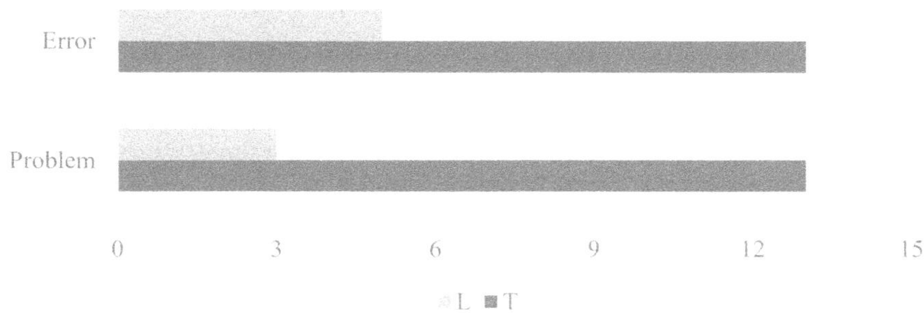

Figure 2.3 'contrary to': translation problems and errors

mostly dependent on their prior knowledge. By contrast, Ts resorted to a greater variety of sources, including concordancers and glossaries, where they did not find the most suitable rendering for the genre under consideration, but rather its literal translation. Ultimately, from a product-oriented perspective this led to a total of 5 errors on the part of Ls and only 2 fully acceptable solutions for Ts; the severity of all these errors, though, is mostly on the major level.

Secondly, a phraseological item which proved to be significantly more problematic for all participants was 'on conviction on indictment' (as in, "A person guilty of affray is liable *on conviction on indictment* to imprisonment for a term not exceeding three years"). From a process-oriented perspective, the prepositional phrase resulted in a translation problem for almost all participants, i.e. 14 Ls and 15 Ts. However, it is quite interesting here to note the very different approaches adopted in solving this problem by the two groups. The former clearly relied on the bilingual dictionary, where they only searched for the translation of each term in the phrase, i.e. mostly 'condanna' or 'sentenza di condanna' for 'conviction', and 'rinvio a giudizio' or 'incriminazione' for 'indictment'. This led to very different solutions, which however resulted in content-related (problems and) errors, given the inability of most members of this group to identify the four-word phrase as a connected entity, as in the examples below:

> *L08 sulla scorta di sentenza o rinvio a giudizio*
> *L13 messa in stato d'accusa e condannata*
> *L14 condannato in via definitiva*

From a cognitive perspective, this was the result of the use of *predominantly external support* (Alves 1997), whereby the translations of the single items of the phrase were arbitrarily connected by Ls based on the context. Conversely, the group of translators resorted to much more suitable reference sources, i.e. a concordancer. All fifteen of them performed a search in the *linguee* online database and found an appropriate solution on their first try, considering that the phrase is typical of legal texts and is a recurring expression in the EU documents which, among others, feed this source. Hence, with the exception of 2 Ts who behaved in a similar manner to the Ls, the decision-making processes of this group clearly tends towards the mere *external support* (Alves 1997), as they trusted the bilingual resource which provided a reliable solution, i.e. 'in caso di condanna con atto formale di accusa'.

Hence, even the severity of the errors made by the two groups appears to be more serious in the case of Ls (i.e. 7 critical errors for Ls and 3 for Ts, 3 major errors for Ls and 2 for Ts). The results of this analysis are summarised in Figure 2.4 below.

The third phraseme under consideration here is 'shall be liable to' (as in, "A person guilty of theft *shall* [. . .] *be liable to* imprisonment for a term not exceeding seven years"), typical of English legal language but not as limited to its realm as the previous example presented above. As a matter of fact, the phrase was the least problematic of the three in the translation processes of the participants; more precisely, only 5 Ls and 9 Ts (see Figure 2.5). Also, it should be noted that in the case of the latter the consultation of external sources mostly occurred on second thought after having already typed a provisional rendering, possibly to find reassurance of the equivalent they already knew. Further, the indicators observed in the translation process of 2 Ls for whom the phrase was a problem show that no consultation of external source was performed, but rather a series of alternatives were considered. The two behaviours mentioned here thus led to decision-making processes relying for the large part on prior knowledge, especially in the case of Ls. From a product-oriented perspective, this resulted in very few errors: more specifically, 1 critical error for Ls and 2 for Ts who translated the phrase as a possibility, thus removing the deontic function of the verb, as in the examples below.

L14 potrà essere sottoposto a
T15 è imputa*bile* [. . .] di
T18 può essere punita con

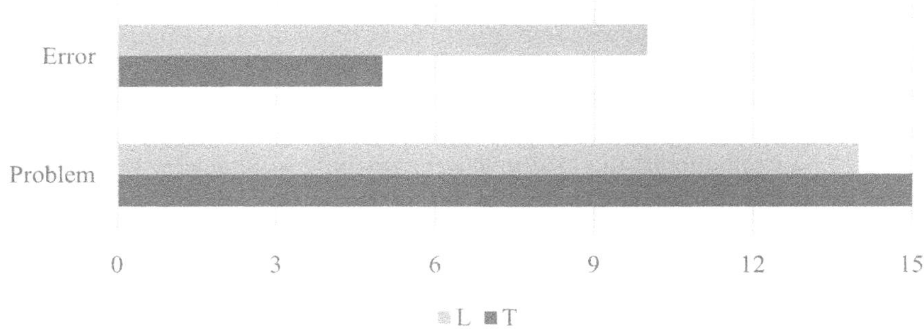

Figure 2.4 'on conviction on indictment': translation problems and errors

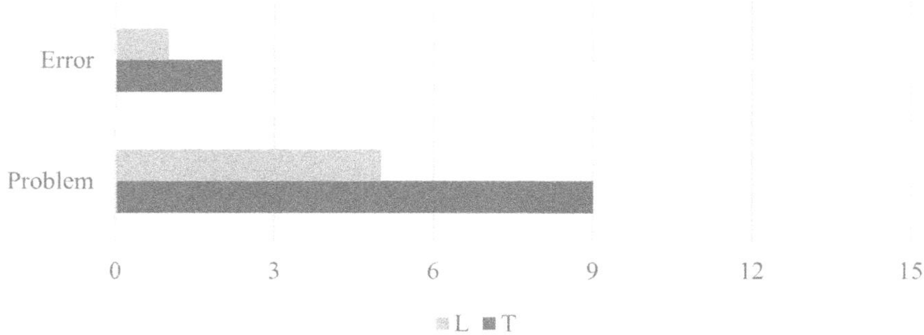

Figure 2.5 'shall be liable to': translation problems and errors

Conclusions

This chapter has attempted to explore the problematic nature of legal phraseology for trainee translators, by analysing and comparing the translation processes and products of two groups of participants, i.e. translation graduates with no specialisation in the legal domain and law graduates with no specialisation in translation. Three phraseological units have also been discussed as examples of different types of difficulties, as reflected in their prompt availability in (non-) specialised bilingual sources and the type of searches conducted by the subjects. In general terms, the different levels of familiarity with legal phraseology appeared to most significantly affect the translation process of the translation graduates, who encountered a higher number of such problems and performed a higher number of searches as compared to the lawyers. However, what emerged from the analysis of the decision-making strategies of the latter and the resulting quality of their texts is that the unexperienced Ls simply tended to "problematise relatively little", translating quickly and effortlessly but ultimately wrongly (cf. novices in Jääskeläinen 1996: 67, who "are blissfully unaware of their ignorance"). Even when searching for specific phrasemes, lawyers displayed an undifferentiated use of the same termino-lexicographic tools and resources, rather than corpus-based ones (cf. Désilets et al. 2009); this led to some critical errors in the case of multiword units for which they only searched the individual components in the bilingual dictionary rather than the phrase as a whole. Conversely, on average Ts still produced a comparable number of phraseological errors mostly affecting the textual fit, rather than the meaning, of the target text. This is the result of a more differentiated use of sources for different types of problems, which however was not sufficient to ensure perfect quality, given their lack of familiarity with the specialised content and rhetorical conventions of the source text. In general, the observation of the processes of the participants appears to confirm both the significance (Vigier Moreno 2016) and current limited availability of contrastive corpus-based and computational approaches to legal phraseology in diverse legal genres (cf. Goźdź-Roszkowski and Pontrandolfo 2015; Ruusila and Lindroos 2016) or, just as lamentably, the participants' lack of awareness of such, however small-sized (Biel 2010a), specialised sources.[4]

Overall, these considerations clearly highlight the need for training to include a special focus on legal phraseology, a seemingly problematic aspect for trainees. On the one hand, the specialised training for translators should aim to increase their awareness of the specific genre conventions of legal texts, thus improving both their translation process and product. On the other hand, lawyers should focus on the study of the LSP beyond the lexical level, considering that their performance appeared to be subpar with reference to all the translation-specific techniques involved, which thus need to be developed and practiced in a thorough manner through proper training.

Notes

1 Given the didactic perspective of this study, a cohort of professional legal translators who are assumed to constitute the *golden standard* in legal translation was not included in the sample.

2 In this analysis, the cut-off length chosen was 1 second, which, despite being low, overcomes any variation of the cognitive rhythms observed within each cohort, the whole sample, and even for each participant in different moments of their translation activity.

3 Based on the participants' responses to a post-task questionnaire, the number of searches observed did not depend on the fact that the translation task was part of an experiment.

4 By way of an example, none of the participants consulted the resources developed in the field of legal translation, e.g. the multi-lingual corpora, translation memories, and termbases developed for the EU project QUALETRA (www.eulita.eu/qualetra).

References

Alves, F., 1997. A formação de tradutores a partir de uma abordagem cognitiva: reflexões de um projeto de ensino. *TradTerm*, 4(2): 19–40.

Angelone, E., 2010. Uncertainty, uncertainty management and metacognitive problem solving in the translation task. In G.M. Shreve and E. Angelone (eds.), *Translation and Cognition*. Amsterdam/Philadelphia: John Benjamins, 17–40.

Barbosa, H.G. and Neiva, A.M.S., 2003. Using think-aloud protocols to investigate the translation process of foreign language learners and experienced translators. In F. Alves (ed.), *Triangulating Translation: Perspectives in Process Oriented Research*. Amsterdam/Philadelphia: John Benjamins, 137–156.

Biel, Ł., 2010a. Corpus-based studies of legal language for translation purposes: Methodological and practical potential. In C. Heine and J. Engberg (eds.), *Reconceptualizing LSP. Online Proceedings of the XVII European LSP Symposium 2009*.

Biel, Ł., 2010b. The textual fit of legal translations: Focus on collocations in translator training. In Ł. Bogucki (ed.), *Teaching Translation and Interpreting: Challenges and Practices*. Newcastle upon Tyne: Cambridge Scholars Publishing, 25–39.

Boers, F., Eyckmans, J., Kappel, J., Stengers, H., and Demecheleer, M., 2006. Formulaic sequences and perceived oral proficiency: Putting a lexical approach to the test. *Language Teaching Research*, 10(3): 245–261.

Désilets, A. et al., 2009. How translators use tools and resources to resolve translation problems: An ethnographic study. In *Proceedings of MT Summit XII, Ottawa, Ontario, Canada, August 26–30, 2009*. <www.mt-archive.info/MTS-2009-Desilets-2.pdf>

Englund Dimitrova, B., 2005. *Expertise and Explicitation in the Translation Process*. Amsterdam/Philadelphia: John Benjamins.

Enríquez Raído, V., 2011. *Investigating the Web Search Behaviors of Translation Students: An Exploratory and Multiple-Case Study*. PhD thesis, Universitat Ramon Llull.

Enríquez Raído, V., 2013. *Translation and Web Searching*. New York/London: Routledge.

Eyckmans, J., 2007. Taking SLA research to interpreter-training: Does knowledge of phrases foster fluency? In F. Boers, J. Darquennes, and R. Temmerman (eds.), *Multilingualism and Applied Comparative Linguistics: Pedagogical Perspectives*. Newcastle: Cambridge Scholars Publishing, 89–104.

Faber, D. and Hjort-Pedersen, M., 2009. Translation preferences in legal translation: Lawyers and professional translators compared. In I.M. Mees, F. Alves, and S. Göpferich (eds.), *Methodology, Technology and Innovation in Translation Process Research: A Tribute to Arnt Lykke Jakobsen*. Copenhagen: Samfundslitteratur, 339–358.

Fischer, M., 2008. *Juridisk oversættelse og en komparativ analyse af to fagekspertgruppers strategier – eller mangel herpå: advokaten i oversætterens univers og translatøren i advokatens univers*. MA thesis, Copenhagen Business School.

Garzone, G., 2007. Osservazioni sulla didattica della traduzione giuridica. In P. Mazzotta and L. Salmon (eds.), *Tradurre le microlingue scientifico-professionali. Riflessioni teoriche e proposte didattiche*. Turin: UTET, 194–238.

Göpferich, S., 2009. Towards a model of translation competence and its acquisition: The longitudinal study TransComp. In S. Göpferich, A.L. Jakobsen, and I.M. Mees (eds.), *Behind the Mind: Methods, Models and Results in Translation Process Research*. Copenhagen: Samfundslitteratur, 11–38.

Göpferich, S., 2010. The translation of instructive texts from a cognitive perspective: Novices and professionals compared. In S. Göpferich, F. Alves, and I.M. Mees (eds.), *New Approaches in Translation Process Research*. Copenhagen: Samfundslitteratur, 5–56.

Goźdź-Roszkowski, S. and Pontrandolfo, G., 2015. Legal phraseology today: Corpus-based applications across legal languages and genres [Editorial Preface of the Special Issue]. *Fachsprache*, 37(3–4): 130–138.

Hoffmann, S., Fischer-Starcke, B., and Sand, A. (eds.), 2015. *Current Issues in Phraseology*. Amsterdam/Philadelphia: John Benjamins.

House, J., 1997. *Translation Quality Assessment: A Model Revisited*. Tübingen: Gunter Narr.

Hurtado Albir, A., 2001. *Traducción y Traductología. Introducción a la Traductología*. Madrid: Cátedra.

Jääskeläinen, R., 1996. Hard work will bear beautiful fruit. A comparison of two think-aloud protocol studies. *Meta: Translators' Journal*, 41(1): 60–74.

Jakobsen, A.L., 2005. Investigating expert translators' processing knowledge. In H.V. Dam, J. Engberg, and H. Gerzymisch-Arbogast (eds.), *Knowledge Systems and Translation*. Berlin: Walter De Gruyter, 173–189.

Kennedy, G., 2008. Phraseology and language pedagogy: Semantic preference associated with English verbs in the British National Corpus. In F. Meunier and S. Granger (eds.), *Phraseology in Foreign Language Learning and Teaching*. Amsterdam: John Benjamins, 21–41.

Kjær, A.L., 1990. Context-conditioned word combinations in legal language. *Terminolgy Science & Research, Journal of the International Institute of Terminology Research*, 1(1–2): 21–32.

Kjær, A.L., 1995. Vergleich von Unvergleichbarem. Zur kontrastiven Analyse unbestimmter Rechtsbegriffe. In H.-P. Kromann and A.L. Kjær (eds.), *Von der Allgegenwart der Lexikologie. Kontrastive Lexikologie als Vorstufe zur zweisprachigen Lexikographie*. Tübingen: Walter de Gruyter, 39–56.

Koby G.S., Fields, P., Hague, D., Lommel, A., and Melby, A., 2014. Defining translation quality. *Tradumàtica*, 12: 413–420.

Krings, H.P., 1986a. Translation problems and translation strategies of advanced German learners of French (L2). In J. House and S. Blum-Kulka (eds.), *Interlingual and Intercultural Communication: Discourse and Cognition in Translation and Second Language Acquisition Studies*. Tübingen: Gunter Narr, 263–275.

Krings, H.P., 1986b. *Was in den Köpfen von Übersetzern vorgeht: Eine empirische Untersuchung zur Struktur des Übersetzungsprozesses an fortgeschrittenen Französischlernern*. Tübingen: Gunter Narr.

Lacruz, I., Shreve, G.M. and Angelone, E., 2012. Average pause ratio as an indicator of cognitive effort in post-editing: A case study. In S. O'Brien, M. Simard and L. Specia (eds.), *Proceedings of the AMTA 2012 Workshop on Post-editing Technology and Practice*. San Diego, CA: Association for Machine Translation in the Americas, 21–30.

Lörscher, W., 1986. Linguistic aspects of translation processes: Towards an analysis of translation performance. In J. House and S. Blum-Kulka (eds.), *Interlingual and Intercultural Communication*. Tübingen: Gunter Narr, 277–292.

Martín, R.M., 2014. A blurred snapshot of advances in translation process research. *MonTI. Monografías de Traducción e Interpretación*. Special Issue 1: 49–84.

Martín-Mor, A., 2011. *La interferència lingüística en entorns de Traducció Assistida per Ordinador. Recerca empíricoexperimental*. Barcelona: Universitat Autònoma de Barcelona.

Morado Vázquez, L., 2012. *An Empirical Study on the Influence of Translation Suggestions' Provenance Metadata*. PhD thesis, Department of Computer Science and Information Systems, University of Limerick.

Mossop, B., 2014. *Revising and Editing for Translators*. Oxon/New York: Routledge.

Nord, C., 1991. *Text Analysis in Translation: Theory, Methodology, and Didactic Application of a Model for Translation-oriented Text Analysis*, 2nd ed. Amsterdam: Rodopi.

Nord, C., 1996. El error en la traducción: categorías y evaluación. In A. Hurtado Albir (ed.), *La enseñanza de la traducción*. Castellón de la Plana: Universidad Jaume I, 91–103.

O'Brien, S., 2006. Pauses as indicators of cognitive effort in post-editing machine translation output. *Across Languages and Cultures*, 7(1): 1–21.

Orlando, D., 2016. *The Trials of Legal Translation Competence: Triangulating Processes and Products of Translators vs. Lawyers*. PhD thesis, Dipartimento di Scienze Giuridiche, del Linguaggio, dell'Interpretazione e della Traduzione, Università degli studi di Trieste.

Orozco, M. and Sánchez-Gijón, P., 2011. New resources for legal translators. *Perspectives: Studies in Translatology*, 19(1): 25–44.

Osborne, J., 2008. Phraseology effects as a trigger for errors in L2 English: The case of more advanced learners. In F. Meunier and S. Granger (eds.), *Phraseology in Foreign Language Learning and Teaching*. Amsterdam: John Benjamins, 67–83.

PACTE, 2009. Results of the validation of the PACTE Translation competence model: Acceptability and decision making. *Across Languages and Cultures*, 10(2): 207–230.

PACTE, 2011. Results of the validation of the PACTE translation competence model: Translation problems and translation competence. In C. Alvstad, A. Hild, and E. Tiselius (eds.), *Methods and Strategies of Process Research: Integrative Approaches in Translation Studies*. Amsterdam/Philadelphia: John Benjamins, 317–343.

Palumbo, G., 2001. The use of phraseology for training and research in the translation of LSP texts. In B. Maia, J. Haller, and M. Ulrych (eds.), *Training the Language Services Providers for the New Millenium, Proceedings of the III Encontros de Tradução de Astra-FLUP*. Porto: Faculdade de Letras, Universidade do Porto, 199–211.

Palumbo, G., 2008. *'Translating Science': An Empirical Investigation of Grammatical Metaphor as a Source of Difficulty for a Group of Translation Trainees in English-Italian Translation*. PhD thesis, Department of Languages and Translation Studies, University of Surrey.

Pontrandolfo, G., 2016. *Fraseología y lenguaje judicial. Las sentencias penales desde una perspectiva contrastiva*. Roma: Aracne.

Prahl, B. and Petzolt, S., 1997. Translation problems and translation strategies involved in human and machine translation. In C. Hauenschild and S. Heizmann (eds.), *Machine Translation and Translation Theory*. Berlin/New York: M. de Gruyter, 123–144.

Pym, A., 1992. Translation error analysis and the interference with language teaching. In C. Dollerup and A. Loddegaard (eds.), *The Teaching of Translation*. Amsterdam/Philadelphia: John Benjamins, 279–288.

Ruusila, A. and Lindroos, E., 2016. Conditio sine qua non: On phraseology in legal language and its translation. *Language and Law/Linguagem e Direito*, 3(1): 120–140.

Sandrini, P., 1996. *Terminologiearbeit im Recht*, IITF Serie. Vienna: TermNet.

Šarčević, S., 1997. *New Approach to Legal Translation*. The Hague/Boston: Kluwer Law International.

Teixeira, C., 2014. Data collection methods for researching the interaction between translators and translation tools: An ecological approach. In A. Ferreira and J.W. Schwieter (eds.), *The Development of Translation Competence: Theories and Methodologies From Psycholinguistics and Cognitive Science*. Newcastle upon Tyne: Cambridge Scholars Publishing, 267–284.

Valli, P., 2013. *Concordancing Software in Practice: An Investigation of Searches and Translation Problems Across EU Official Languages*. PhD thesis, Dipartimento di Scienze Giuridiche, del Linguaggio, dell'Interpretazione e della Traduzione, Università degli studi di Trieste.

Vigier Moreno, F.J., 2016. Teaching the use of ad hoc corpora in the translation of legal texts into the second language. *Language and Law/Linguagem e Direito*, 3(1): 100–119.

Vollmar, G., 2001. Damit die Qualität nicht in der Übersetzungsflut untergeht: Ein Modell für eine pragmatische Qualitätssicherung bei Übersetzungsprojekten. *Lebende Sprachen*, 46(1): 2–6.

Wible, D., 2008. Multiword expressions and the digital turn. In F. Meunier and S. Granger (eds.), *Phraseology in Foreign Language Learning and Teaching*. Amsterdam: John Benjamins, 163–181.

3 Analysing phraseological units in legal translation

Evaluation of translation errors for the English-Spanish language pair

Elsa Huertas Barros and Míriam Buendía Castro

Introduction

It seems that about 80% of the words in discourse are chosen according to the co-selection principle rather than for purely syntactic or grammatical reasons (Sinclair 2000: 197). Thus, the analysis of how words co-select with other words is a necessary focus of study for any translator wishing to create a text that is as natural and linguistically correct as possible.

The interest in the didactics of phraseology has increased substantially in the last few decades. Most studies concerning the teaching and learning process of phraseology have been accomplished from the perspective of foreign or second language acquisition (Higueras García 2006; Meunier and Granger 2008; Penadés Martínez 1999; Qi 2016; Ruiz Gurillo 2002; *inter alia*). However, research on the didactics of phraseology in translation training is still scarce, particularly in specialised translation, such as legal translation. The specificities of a translator as a linguistic and cultural mediator require a specific teaching methodology. In this sense, it is necessary for trainee translators to acquire what has been referred to as *phraseological competence* (Howarth 1998), i.e. a kind of "learner's ability to produce conventional collocations and formulaic sequences" (Turner 2014: 222).

This phraseological competence becomes evident in legal translation since legal documents often use grammatical structures typical of the field, such as redundancy, foreign words and Latinisms, syntactic discontinuity, impersonal and passive constructions, nominalisation, complex sentences, and formulaic expressions (Alcaraz Varó and Huges 2014; Borja 2000: 23–30, 2015: 123–150). Of these elements, formulaic language, i.e. phraseological units (PU), seems to be at the core of legal documents (Tiersma 1999: 100–104). This chapter describes a comparative case study on how students deal with PU in a piece of legal translation coursework.

The chapter is organised as follows. The next section provides an overview of our approach to phraseology and PU, followed by the classification of translation errors used in our case study. Then, we set out our practical case study, including a module overview, a description of the students' profile and other key questions such as the text type, the brief, and the assessment criteria used at the University of Westminster (UoW). Next, we analyse and discuss the most recurrent translation errors made by students when dealing with certain PU in a semi-specialised legal text. The subsequent section summarises the main results of our study, with a focus on the most common translation errors made by English native speakers (ENS) and Spanish native speakers (SNS). Finally, we highlight the main conclusions drawn from our study and to some approaches to developing and honing the phraseological competence required in semi-specialised legal translation courses.

Our approach to phraseology and phraseological units

Phraseology is the study of phrases, where phrases are "any multi-word expression up to sentence level" (Pawley 2001: 122). As with other linguistic phenomena, there is still no consensus regarding the term used to designate phrases:[1] *multi-word unit* appears to be the preferred term within the natural language processing community, whereas *phraseological unit* seems to be the preferred term in the field of phraseology (Corpas Pastor 2013). Briefly speaking, a *phraseological unit* is a stable combination of at least two words which, depending on the approach, can have either a phrase or a whole sentence as an upper limit (Corpas Pastor 2003: 134). We follow a broad conception of phraseology (Roberts 1994/95; Hausmann 1989; Corpas Pastor 2003, *inter alia*), which regards PU as all combinations of words with a certain degree of stability. This includes not only idioms, but also collocations and compounds.

As such, in our approach, a *collocation* can be defined as the combination of two or more words which frequently appear in combination with each other and where each lexical unit retains its meaning. The collocate (the verb or the adjective) is constrained by the meaning of the base (normally the noun), but at the same time the collocate constrains the kind of nouns that can combine with it.[2] As such, for example, in the collocation 'do checks' (see source text in the Annex), both 'do' and 'check' keep their respective meanings. In this sense, 'check' (an examination of something to make certain that it is correct or the way it should be) can appear with verbs that indicate performing a task (e.g. 'do'), and, at the same time, the predicate 'do' (to perform, take part in, or achieve something[3]) requires, among others, nouns or noun phrases designating examination (e.g. 'check'). In line with semantically-based approaches, what distinguishes a combination such as 'do checks' from 'criticise the checks' are the definitions of both elements. As shown, the definition of 'check' makes no reference to verbs such as 'criticise'. Therefore, the combination 'criticise the checks' is a free combination, whereas 'do checks' is a collocation.

In contrast to collocations, compounds are often defined as "one word (in the sense of lexeme) that is made up of two other words (in the sense of a lexeme)" (Bauer 1988: 65). That means that they designate a single concept. Since nominal compounds in English are either noun + noun or adjective + noun combinations, and collocations can have a similar structure, it is often difficult to differentiate them from compounds. In this regard, Meyer and Mackintosh (1996: 3) coin the term *phraseme* to refer to both collocations and compounds.[4]

Our case study analyses both compounds and collocations. More specifically, the PU under analysis were the following: 'local adoption agency', '(local) Health and Social Care Trust', 'voluntary agency', 'health and criminal record', 'home study report', 'adoption panel', 'agency's decision maker', 'senior manager', and 'do some checks'.

Translation errors and translation evaluation

The concept of translation error has been addressed by many scholars over the past few decades. As noted by Hansen (2010: 385), "the perception of what constitutes a translation 'error' varies according to translation theories and norms". Hurtado Albir (2001/2004: 289) defines a translation error as an inadequate equivalence for the translation task that has been commissioned (our translation). From a functionalist perspective, for example, the notion of translation error is closely intertwined with the purpose of the translation process or product. From this perspective, Nord defines the term error as "a failure to carry out the

Table 3.1 Summary of revision parameters proposed by Mossop (2001/2014: 134–149)

1) TRANSFER	*2) CONTENT*	*3) LANGUAGE*	*4) PRESENTATION*
a) Accuracy	a) Logic	a) Smoothness	a) Layout
b) Completeness	b) Facts	b) Tailoring	b) Typography
–	–	c) Sub-language	c) Organization
–	–	d) Idiom	–
–	–	e) Mechanics	–

instructions implied in the translation brief and as an inadequate solution to a translation problem" (1997/2012: 75).[5]

There are also several classifications of translation errors associated with both the source and the target text (e.g. Gouadec 1981; Delisle 1993; Nord 1996, 1997/2012; Hansen 2006; Hurtado Albir 2001/2004, 2015a, 2015b), and some scholars also make a distinction between the nature of translation errors (e.g. Pym 1992; Kussmaul 1995) and distinguish between binary and non-binary errors, and scholars such as Nord (1996: n.p.) and Williams (2009: 6) classify errors according to their level of seriousness (i.e. major or minor error).[6]

The notion of translation error is closely linked to the notion of translation quality and translation evaluation. The identification and classification of errors in our case study draws on the assessment criteria and rubric used at the UoW (see page 45). This classification of errors bears a strong resemblance to the revision parameters (i.e. the type of errors) proposed by Mossop (2001/2014: 134–149), which we summarise in Table 3.1. Given that our case study focuses on the analysis of specific PU and not the entire translation as such, the presentation parameter has not been factored in the analysis and classification of errors discussed in subsequent sections.

A comparative case study at the University of Westminster: Spanish translation 2 (English-Spanish)

The following section presents a practical case study undertaken with second-year undergraduate students taking the BA Translation course at the UoW. The object of our study is to analyse the translation strategies used by translation students when they deal with certain PU in a piece of legal translation coursework. We will first provide a contextualisation of the module in question and the students' profile, followed by a text type description and an overview of the assessment parameters used at the UoW. Then, we will analyse the main results and conclusions drawn from our case study.

Contextualisation: overview of the BA Translation course at the UoW

The BA Translation is a three- or four-year professionally oriented training course that provides students with the necessary skills, knowledge and competences to embark on a career as professional translators or linguists. The course offers French and Spanish as main languages and consists of 120 credits per year, spread across three levels: Level 4 (first-year students); Level 5 (second-year students); and Level 6 (third-year students or fourth-year students if they spend a year abroad).

Module overview and students' profile

Our case study will focus on the Level 5 module 'Spanish Translation 2', a 30 UK credit module (i.e. equivalent to 15 ECTS) in which students translate from English into Spanish and vice versa, and work with real-world texts within the following subject areas: Business, Health, Law and Technical. The module combines both language-specific translation seminars and theory lectures. In terms of assessment methods, students are required to complete four practical pieces of coursework (one for each subject area), one theoretical essay and one exam (i.e. a translation). Formative tasks are also used to prepare students for summative assessment.

Our case study will focus on the piece of coursework devoted to the subject area of Law, which consisted of a source text of 350 words (see Annex). The data was collected for the English into Spanish language pair during the academic year 2014–2015. There were 14 students enrolled on this module, including six native speakers of Spanish and eight native speakers of English. All the students in the sample received the same training at university since they attended the same core modules in their first year of study, including the Level 4 module 'Spanish Translation 1'. Prior to the study, we completed a research ethics application to obtain full approval from both the participants of the study and the Research Ethics Committee.

While we are aware of the relatively small size of the sample and, therefore, we cannot generalise our results to larger populations, this is a standard class size for translation modules in the UK. Our sample could serve as a first step to identify and analyse some common translation errors and translation patterns and strategies used by translation students when dealing with PU in a legal translation context and to point to some guidelines for teaching phraseology in a legal translation course.

Text type

The source text (see Annex) is of a legal nature since its focus is the "creation, implementation, (and) dissemination (. . .) of Law" (Borja 2007: 151, our translation). Following Reiss's (1977/1989: 108–109) text types and text varieties and Borja's (2007/2015: 161) classification of legal texts, the source text can be considered informative, given that it is concerned with plain communication of facts. In other words, the source text provides information about the adoption process and how to facilitate the placement of children to families in Northern Ireland. The source text is also of a normative nature (Borja 2007/2015) given that it concerns regulations of the Adoption Law and how the potential adopters should comply with the relevant adoption procedures (e.g. "the first thing you should do is . . ."). Some language structures also induce behavioural responses to persuade potential adopters to act in a specific way (e.g., "you must . . ."), which means the source text can also be considered operative (Reiss 1977/1989: 108–109). On the whole, the source text could be considered a hybrid of general information text and legal text, since it contains language structures that could be placed between both the general language and the special language continuum (Snell-Hornby 1988/1995: 32).

Translation brief

In a translation training context, providing a brief is essential so that students can draw relevant source text and target text profiles and produce a translation that is suitable for

Table 3.2 Translation brief

Please translate the following text, which is an edited extract taken from the official government website for Northern Ireland (www.nidirect.gov.uk/). You are requested to translate it into Spanish for publication in a multilingual section in the same website that provides information about the adoption process and how to facilitate the placement of children to families in Northern Ireland.

its purpose. As suggested by Nord (1997/2012: 60), the translation brief provided to the participants of our case study contained the following information: 1) the (intended) text function(s), 2) the target text addressee(s), 3) the (prospective) time and place of text reception, 4) the medium over which the text would be transmitted, and 5) the motive for the production or reception of the text. Table 3.2 displays the translation brief provided to students for this particular task.

Assessment criteria

The classification of errors used in our case study is based on the assessment criteria and the rubric used in the module 'Spanish Translation 2', which includes the following main categories:

- Accuracy in rendering source-text message, i.e. the extent to which the translation coveys the source-text message in a complete and accurate manner.
- Target text language quality, in other words, the use of the target language, including grammar, spelling, lexis, and punctuation.
- Translation according to the brief, i.e. the extent to which the translation complies with the requirements of the specific brief and is written in a register and style that is appropriate to both client and audience expectations.

In a broad sense, these categories resemble Mossop's types of errors/revision parameters (2001/2014: 134–149), except for the fact that the transfer and content categories which appear as different parameters in Mossop's proposal are considered under the overarching category of "Accuracy in rendering the source-text message" in the rubric used at the UoW. Given that Mossop's classification (see page 43) provides a more detailed breakdown of the aforementioned categories, our analysis and discussion will draw upon his proposal.

Analysis and discussion of the case study

The following section analyses the translation patterns and strategies used by translation students, including both ENS and SNS, when dealing with certain PU in a piece of legal translation coursework (see source text in Annex). For each PU, a table is displayed which includes the translation solutions provided by both ENS (column on the right) and SNS (column on the left). Acceptable translations are included in normal typeface, and those which contain errors are shown in italics and boldface along with an asterisk (*) indicating where the mistake is. The number of students who opted for each translation option is also specified between parentheses after each rendering.

As previously mentioned, the PU under analysis were the following: 'local adoption agency', '(local) Health and Social Care Trust', 'voluntary agency', 'health and criminal record', 'home study report', 'adoption panel', 'agency's decision maker', 'senior manager', and 'do some checks'.[7] The reasons for choosing these particular PU were, on the one hand, the fact that they pertain to the subdomain of adoption, and, on the other hand, because they were the units which posed more problems for students. It was not necessary to extract them automatically with a term extractor or corpus analysis tool due to the short length of the source text.

(1) local adoption agency

Table 3.3 offers the various translations proposed by both SNS and ENS for the PU 'local adoption agency'. As shown, only one of the SNS provided an accurate translation ('*agencia de adopción de su zona*') compared to 5 ENS with good solutions such as '*agencia de adopción local*', '*agencia de adopción de su localidad*', '*agencia de adopción de su área*'. In percentage terms, 16.7% of SNS offered a correct translation compared to 62.5% of ENS. Sometimes (2 SNS and 3 ENS) the problem lies in the use of word combinations that are not idiomatic or do not fully comply with the rhetorical preferences of Spanish (i.e. LANGUAGE > IDIOM). As pointed out by Mossop, this example shows that some students "(. . .) are prone to producing, under the influence of the source text, unidiomatic combinations" (Mossop 2001/2014: 146). The term '*local*' should modify the entire collocation '*agencia de adopción*' and not just the term '*agencia*' ('*agencia local* de adopción*'). In other cases, the solution offered is excessively long and the style is not suited to the genre (e.g., '*oficina local de un organismo competente en materia de adopción*') (LANGUAGE > SMOOTHNESS and LANGUAGE > IDIOM). As recommended by Mossop (*ibid.*: 143), "In some genres, (. . .) action should be taken to reduce them". Other renderings provide inaccurate information to the reader if we take into consideration the translation brief (e.g. 1 SNS provided the rendering '*servicios específicos de adopción, SEA*', which are services available only in Spain but not in Northern Ireland) (TRANSFER > ACCURACY; LANGUAGE > TAILORING). As noted by Mossop (*ibid.*: 136), there are limits when replacing or using a functional equivalent of a cultural feature in a translation. Reiterative translations are also found within SNS (i.e. '*agencia local de adopción más cercana*', where *más cercana* [Spanish term for 'local'] is reiterative), and clarifications such as '*agencia de adopción local (local adoption agency)*' are unnecessary since the audience would know that the translation refers to 'adoption agency' due to the similarity between both terms. In these two cases, students would be expected to render the message with "No additions, No Subtractions" (*ibid.*: 137) (TRANSFER > ACCURACY and TRANSFER > COMPLETENESS).

Table 3.3 Translations given by SNS and ENS for 'local adoption agency'

Spanish native speakers (SNS)	*English native speakers (ENS)*
agencia de adopción de su zona (1SNS)	agencia de adopción local (2ENS)
servicios específicos de adopción (SEA)* (1SNS)	agencia de adopción en su localidad (2ENS)
agencia local* de adopción (2SNS)	agencia de adopción en su área (1ENS)
agencia de adopción local más cercana* (1SNS)	***agencia local* de adopción*** (2ENS)
agencia de adopción local (local adoption agency)* (1SNS)	***oficina local de un organismo competente en materia de adopción**** (1ENS)

In conclusion, except for three transfer problems in which the students overlook the translation brief or do not convey the complete message, the rest of the translation errors are associated with linguistic features since students struggle to express in the target language a linguistic element that they seem to understand. These errors are related to the use of unidiomatic and unsmooth expressions in Spanish.

(2) (local) Health and Social Care Trust

On this occasion, 50% of SNS provided an acceptable translation compared to 37.5% of ENS. Some good options included renderings such as '*Health and Social Care Trust (más cercana)*', '*Health and Social Care Trust local*', '*Health and Social Care Trust de la localidad*', or a short explanation ('*Health and Social Care Trust (centro de servicios sociales y sanitarios)*)'.

As shown in Table 3.4, most translation issues are linked to problems of meaning transfer (i.e., TRANSFER > ACCURACY and TRANSFER > COMPLETENESS; see table 3.1), since some students opted for replacing the cultural element Health and Social Care Trust with a potential functional equivalent in Spanish. As mentioned in the previous example, considering the target text is addressed to Spanish speakers who are hoping to adopt in Northern Ireland, the option of replacing the Trust with an equivalent cultural feature in Spanish should be discarded. This translation error disregards the importance of TAILORING the message to the audience (i.e. LANGUAGE > TAILORING). As pointed out by Mossop (*ibid.*: 143), "the translation has to be suited to its readers and to the use they will make of it". One SNS and one ENS also encountered problems to ensure idiomatic word combinations (i.e. LANGUAGE > IDIOM) and placed the term '*local*' at the beginning of the combination (i.e., '*Local* Health and Social Care Trust*', which is not a correct combination in Spanish). An important TRANSFER error was made by 1 SNS who, in an attempt to provide an explanation for the Trust, introduced a major inaccuracy in the target text by stating that the Trust operates in the entire United Kingdom. One ENS also encountered problems of language and style (i.e. LANGUAGE > SMOOTHNESS and LANGUAGE > TAILORING), since the explanation provided for the Trust was not concise enough and the degree of formality was not correct ('*un*

Table 3.4 Translations given by SNS and ENS for '(local) Health and Social Care Trust'

Spanish native speakers (SNS)	*English native speakers (ENS)*
Health and Social Care Trust (más cercana) (1SNS)	Health and Social Care Trust de la localidad (1ENS)
Health and Social Care Trust (local) (1SNS)	Health and Social Care Trust, organismo público del norte de Irlanda que presta servicios de adopción a escala local (1ENS)
Health and Social Care Trust de tu zona (1SNS)	Health and Social Care Trust (centro de servicios sociales y sanitarios) (1ENS)
Entidad pública de Servicios Sociales* (1SNS)	***Local* Health and Social Care Trust*** (1ENS)
Local* Health and Social Care Trust (1SNS)	***Ministerio de Salud Pública y Asistencia Social local**** (1ENS)
Health and Social Care Trust (Organismo del Reino Unido* más cercano) (1SNS)	***Centro de salud y asistencia social**** (1ENS)
	Health and Social Care Trust (Fundación* de la Salud y de Servicios Sociales) (1ENS)
	Health and Social Care Trust local (un fideocomiso dedicado a proveerle al público de Irlanda del Norte con servicios sociales a escala local y regional*) (1ENS)

fideocomiso dedicado a proveerle al público de Irlanda del Norte con servicios sociales a escala local y regional').

(3) voluntary agency

As shown in Table 3.5, for the combination 'voluntary agency', all students but 1 SNS used terms that are not associated with the adoption context at all (e.g. '*agencia voluntaria*', '*organismo de carácter voluntario*', '*organismo voluntariado de ayuda*'). Students should have paid more attention to the brief, particularly the final reader and the context in which the translation would be used (i.e., LANGUAGE > TAILORING). In addition to this, while the term 'adoptive' is not included in the combination in the source text, it is indeed implicit, and it can be argued that "this information in the translation will be very important to the readers" (Mossop 2001/2014: 138). Therefore, it is necessary to make this term explicit in the target-language text, otherwise the translation into Spanish loses an important aspect of its content (i.e., TRANSFER > ACCURACY and TRANSFER > COMPLETENESS).

(4) health and criminal record

On this occasion (see Table 3.6), 2 SNS (33.3%) and 3 ENS (37.5%) offered a good translation ('*estado de salud y antecedentes penales*', '*expediente médico y antecedentes penales*', '*chequeo médico y un certificado de antecedentes penales*'). The rendering provided by 1 SNS ('*exámenes médicos* y comprobación de sus antecedentes penales*') and 1 ENS ('*pruebas de*

Table 3.5 Translations given by SNS and ENS for 'voluntary agency'

Spanish native speakers (SNS)	*English native speakers (ENS)*
agencia de adopción voluntaria (1SNS)	***agencia voluntaria**** (5ENS)
agencia voluntaria* (2SNS)	***organismo de carácter voluntario**** (2ENS)
a voluntary agency* (1SNS)	***organización de voluntariado**** (1ENS)
organismo voluntariado de ayuda* (1SNS)	
agencia de voluntariado adoptivo* (1SNS)	

Table 3.6 Translations given by SNS and ENS for 'health and criminal record'

Spanish native speakers (SNS)	*English native speakers (ENS)*
expediente médico y antecedentes penales (1SNS)	su estado de salud y antecedentes penales (2ENS)
estado de salud y certificado de antecedentes penales (1SNS)	chequeo médico y un certificado de antecedentes penales (1ENS)
exámenes médicos* y comprobación de sus antecedentes penales (1SNS)	***pruebas de salud* o antecedentes penales*** (1ENS)
historial clínico e historial criminal* (1SNS)	***su salud y su historial criminal**** (1ENS)
historial médico y expediente delictivo* (1SNS)	***estado de salud y antecedentes criminales**** (1ENS)
su salud y antecedente penal* (1SNS)	***su estado de salud y cualquier antecedente penal**** (2ENS)

salud o antecedentes penales*') resulted in a TRANSFER problem and, more specifically, an ACCURACY issue. The term 'record' in English refers to "information about someone or something that is stored by the police or by a doctor".[8] This definition does not correspond to the definition of '*exámenes*' or '*pruebas*' in Spanish, both of which refer to a particular test. In addition, 1 SNS ('*historial clínico e historial criminal**') and 2 ENS ('*su salud y su historial criminal**'; '*estado de salud y antecedentes criminales**'), seem to have understood the source language PU, but they did not offer a natural combination in Spanish, resulting thus in a LANGUAGE error that can be more concretely assigned to the IDIOM subcategory. Finally, some SUB-LANGUAGE/SMOOTHNESS errors were also detected. Two SNS and 2 ENS provided translations such as ('*su salud y antecedente penal**', '*su estado de salud y cualquier antecedente penal**', '*historial médico y expediente delictivo**'. As shown, 'criminal record' was lexicalised in singular by 2 ENS and 1 SNS, following thus the same grammar pattern as in the source text, which does not work in Spanish. These students therefore made a LANGUAGE > SUB-LANGUAGE error, given that Spanish lexicalises the general concept of 'criminal record' in a plural form (i.e. '*antecedentes penales*'). The rendering '*expediente delictivo*' can also be assigned to this category of error (LANGUAGE > SUB-LANGUAGE) since it is not the combination normally used in this context.

(5) home study report

For the PU 'home study report' (see Table 3.7), only 1 SNS (16.7%) compared to 3 ENS (37.5%) solved the translation problem satisfactorily. This term refers to a report that the caseworker writes about the family interested in adopting. Drawing from interviews with members of the family and third parties, this report contains basic information such as family background, financial statements, education and employment, relationships and social life, daily routines, parenting experiences, etc.[9] In Spanish, equivalents such as '*informe de valoración de idoneidad*', '*informe de idoneidad*', or even '*informe de valoración*' could be considered suitable renderings. However, some of the translations options proposed resulted in problems associated with TRANSFER < ACCURACY. In other words, 2 SNS and 2 ENS offered options such as '*informe del estudio del hogar de adopción**', or '*informe de la visita domiciliaria**', which do not fully reflect the definition of 'home study report' provided above. While a suitable equivalent for this PU cannot easily be retrieved in monolingual or bilingual lexicographic or terminographic resources, this error could have been avoided by undertaking extensive research about the topic and consulting parallel texts in both English and Spanish. Other options provided (2 ENS

Table 3.7 Translations given by SNS and ENS for 'home study report'

Spanish native speakers (SNS)	*English native speakers (ENS)*
informe de valoración (1SNS)	informe de valoración de idoneidad (2ENS)
informe del estudio del hogar de adopción* (1SNS)	informe de idoneidad (1ENS)
informe de la visita domiciliaria* (1SNS)	***informe de estudio en el hogar**** (1ENS)
estudio* de idoneidad (1SNS)	***informe de estudio del hogar de adopción**** (1ENS)
certificado* de idoneidad (1SNS)	***certificado* de idoneidad*** (1ENS)
informe del examen de idoneidad (1SNS)	***informe del examen* de idoneidad*** (1ENS)
	estudio* de idoneidad (1ENS)

Table 3.8 Translations given by SNS and ENS for 'adoption panel'

Spanish native speakers (SNS)	*English native speakers (ENS)*
comité de adopción (3SNS)	comité de adopción (4ENS)
comisión de adopciones (1SNS)	***panel de adopción**** (2ENS)
panel de adopción* (1SNS)	***jurado de adopción**** (2ENS)
adoption panel (servicio social del Reino Unido)* (1SNS)	

and 2 SNS), such as '*estudio* de idoneidad*', or '*certificado* de idoneidad*' are not correct as the Spanish terms '*estudio*' and '*certificado*' do not convey exactly the same meaning as '*informe*' (report). This would be a LANGUAGE > SUB-LANGUAGE issue which would also affect the meaning TRANSFER < ACCURACY.

(6) adoption panel

Six students (2 SNS and 4 ENS), i.e. 33.3% of SNS and 50% of ENS, provided an inaccurate translation for this collocation by translating the English noun 'panel' as '*panel*' in Spanish, resulting in a calque of the source language (i.e. LANGUAGE > IDIOM). As shown in Table 3.8, ENS seem to be more prone to producing unidiomatic combinations in this case, probably due to "the engrossing effect of source text patterning" (Baker 2011: 58):

> It is easy to assume that as long as a collocation can be found in the target language which conveys the same or a similar meaning to that of the source collocation, the translator will not be confused by differences in the surface patterning between the two.

The transference pitfall above has been caused by the influence that the collocational patterning of the source text has on the target language, which resulted in an interference problem for some students. In other words, terms such as '*comité*' and '*comisión*' should have been used in Spanish to avoid a calque of the source language (i.e. '*panel*').

The amplification offered by 1 SNS is incorrect, given that the adoption panel would be based in Northern Ireland as specified in the translation brief (TRANSFER < ACCURACY). An amplification of this sort, i.e. '*adoption panel (servicio social de Irlanda del Norte)*' would not be necessary in any case, since the term 'adoption panel' is fairly transparent and even has a counterpart in the target language. In other words, the pertinence of a translation technique depends on the genre and the purpose of the translation (Hurtado Albir 2015a: 173), and, considering the brief provided to students, this technique would be redundant and unnecessary in this case.

(7) agency's decision maker

On this occasion (see Table 3.9), 3 SNS (50%) and 6 ENS (75%) provided an acceptable translation solution (e.g. '*persona responsable de tomar decisiones en la agencia*', '*responsable de la toma de decisiones de la agencia*', etc.). However, renderings such as '*alto cargo de la agencia**' or '*autoridades**', do not convey the meaning of the source language PU in an accurate manner (TRANSFER < ACCURACY), and '*tomador de decisiones de la agencia**' or '*fabricante de la decision de la agencia**' make little sense as they are not idiomatic

Table 3.9 Translations given by SNS and ENS for 'agency's decision maker'

Spanish native speakers (SNS)	*English native speakers (ENS)*
persona responsable de tomar decisiones en la agencia (2SNS)	responsable de tomar la decisión final en la agencia (1ENS)
responsable en materia de adopción (1SNS)	responsable de tomar decisiones de la agencia de adopción (3ENS)
alto cargo de la agencia, el cual estará encargado de tomar la última decisión* (1SNS)	responsable de la toma de decisiones del organismo competente (1ENS)
autoridades* (1SNS)	responsable de la toma de decisiones de la agencia (1ENS)
responsable de tomar las decisiones en la agencia de adopción (agency's decision maker*) (1SNS)	***tomador de decisiones de la agencia**** (1ENS)
	fabricante de la decisión de la agencia* (1ENS)

Table 3.10 Translations given by SNS and ENS for 'senior manager'

Spanish native speakers (SNS)	*English native speakers (ENS)*
alto cargo de la agencia (1SNS)	***(omitted)**** (3ENS)
directivo* (2SNS)	***directivo de la agencia de adopción**** (1ENS)
alto cargo directivo* (2SNS)	***personal de alta dirección**** (1ENS)
persona que ocupa el alto cargo directivo* (1SNS)	***directivo superior**** (2ENS)
	director* de la agencia de adopción (1ENS)

combinations in Spanish (LANGUAGE > IDIOM). Finally, 1 SNS provided a good translation equivalent in Spanish, but then opted to leave the source PU as well. This is not necessary and is redundant bearing in mind that this particular sentence offers an explanation of who this particular person is. Taking into account the use that the readers will make of the text, it is not necessary to make this explicit, as it will rather "cause confusion or slow the process of reading" (Mossop 2001/2014: 144). This could be considered as a LANGUAGE error, within the TAILORING category, but also a TRANSFER < COMPLETENESS issue.

(8) senior manager

On this occasion (see Table 3.10), only 1 SNS provided a suitable solution for the combination 'senior manager' (i.e., '*alto cargo de la agencia*'). As observed in previous examples, the vast majority of pitfalls in this particular example are associated with problems of language and style (LANGUAGE > SUB-LANGUAGE), due to the use of terminology or style which are not suited to the genre. In other words, "each genre (text type) and each field of writing draws on a different selection of the lexical, syntactic and rhetorical resources of that language" (Mossop 2001/2014: 144) and combinations such as '*directivo*', '*director*' or '*personal de alta dirección*' are characteristic of the business and finance fields. This error has been made by 5 ENS and 5 SNS. Three ENS have even omitted this PU in their translations, as they felt it was redundant given that the same sentence previously refers to this individual (i.e. the agency's decision maker). However, as noted by Mossop (*ibid.*: 137), "Unless

Table 3.11 Translations given by SNS and ENS for 'do some checks'

Spanish native speakers (SNS)	*English native speakers (ENS)*
proceder a hacer algunas comprobaciones (1SNS)	llevar a cabo algunas comprobaciones (2ENS)
realizar algunas comprobaciones (1SNS)	hacer una serie de comprobaciones (1ENS)
realizar algunas verificaciones (1SNS)	realizar algunas verificaciones (1ENS)
llevar a cabo algunas verificaciones (1SNS)	***hacer algunas pruebas**** (1ENS)
realizar diversos reconocimientos* (1SNS)	***proceder algunas verificaciones**** (1ENS)
la agencia le realizará una serie de pruebas* (1SNS)	***hacer unas* comprobaciones*** (1ENS)
	informarse sobre su persona* (1ENS)

specifically asked to write a summary or gist, or provide an adaptation, translators are usually expected to render all the message (. . .) that is in the source text." Mossop's point is particularly relevant in this case, since the source text author seems to have added the term '*senior manager*' to ensure readers are aware of the role of the agency's decision maker (i.e. TRANSFER > COMPLETENESS). In a broad sense, in the PU 'senior manager', language errors go hand in hand with an incomplete transfer of the message.

(9) do some checks

As shown in Table 3.11, 2 SNS and 4 ENS offered an inaccurate translation for the verb collocation 'do some checks', this being motivated by either the wrong choice of the noun (e.g. '*pruebas*', '*reconocimientos*' instead of '*comprobaciones*' or '*verificaciones*') (TRANSFER > ACCURACY) or an incorrect use of grammar (e.g. '*hacer unas* comprobaciones*' instead of '*hacer algunas* comprobaciones*' and '*proceder* algunas verificaciones*' instead of '*proceder a realizar*') (LANGUAGE > MECHANICS). The use of prepositions is indeed a recurrent problem in the English-Spanish language pair (Beeby Lonsdale 1996: 242), and the example '*proceder* algunas*' shows that some ENS have been heavily influenced by the source language structure. While not an error as such, it is interesting to highlight that ENS adopted a less formal register in the sense that 3 out of 8 used the verb '*hacer*' instead of '*realizar*'. Finally, the combination '*informarse sobre su persona*' does not convey the meaning of the source text PU and, consequently, has been categorised as another error of TRANSFER > ACCURACY.

Discussion of results

From the data analysis presented in the previous section, interesting conclusions can be drawn. As shall be seen, most errors are associated with the category of TRANSFER, followed by errors pertaining to the category of LANGUAGE errors (see Mossop's classification in section 3). It is important to emphasise here that CONTENT errors were not spotted since no factual or mathematical errors were detected. Given that the focus of our study was on specific PU and not on the text as a whole, the sequence of ideas was not analysed either. This means that logic errors, which also belong to the category of CONTENT, have not been considered in our study. In line with this, as previously mentioned, PRESENTATION errors were not relevant for the purposes of our study either and, thus, were not taken into consideration.

Table 3.12 includes a summary of the results of our analysis. The column on the right refers to ENS and the column on the left to SNS. Each column is further subdivided into *percentage of errors* and *categorisation of errors*. The column *percentage of errors* includes the percentage of ENS or SNS who did not provide an acceptable translation for the given PU, and the number of students this percentage represents. In other words, as shown in Table 3.12, for the PU 'local adoption agency', we can see that 83.3% of the total number of SNS (which amounts to 5 students out of 6 SNS), and 37.5% of the total number of ENS (i.e. 3 students out of the 8 ENS) did not offer a good translation solution.

Subsequently, the column *categorisation of errors* classifies each error according to Mossop's proposal (see table 3.1). Within the TRANSFER category, ACCURACY and COMPLETENESS errors were observed, and within the LANGUAGE one, SMOOTHNESS, TAILORING, SUB-LANGUAGE, IDIOM, and MECHANICS errors were detected. At this point it is important to clarify that sometimes the number of students specified in *percentage of errors* does not coincide with the number of errors highlighted in the *categorisation of errors*. The reason is that some mistakes can fall within the scope of more than one subcategory. For example, as specified in Table 3.12, 5 SNS out of 6 did not offer an acceptable solution for 'local adoption agency'. However, the *categorisation of errors* column refers to six errors. This is because the incorrect translation provided by 1 of the 5 SNS for the PU 'local adoption agency' was categorised under two separate error types (i.e. TRANSFER>ACCURACY and LANGUAGE>TAILORING) and this counts as two errors.

Table 3.12 Results of the evaluation analysis

	SNS (6 students)			*ENS (8 students)*		
	Percentage of errors	*Categorisation of errors*		*Percentage of errors*	*Categorisation of errors*	
'local adoption agency'	83.3% (5 students)	2 (33.3%)	LANGUAGE > IDIOM	37.5% (3 students)	3 (37.5%)	LANGUAGE > IDIOM
		2 (33.3%)	TRANSFER > ACCURACY		1 (12.5%)	LANGUAGE > SMOOTHNESS
		1 (16.7%)	LANGUAGE > TAILORING		–	–
		1 (16.7%)	TRANSFER > COMPLETENESS		–	–
'(local) Health and Social Care Trust'	50% (3 students)	2 (33.3%)	TRANSFER > ACCURACY	62.5% (5 students)	1 (12.5%)	LANGUAGE > IDIOM
		1 (16.7%)	TRANSFER > COMPLETENESS		1 (12.5%)	LANGUAGE > TAILORING
		1 (16.7%)	LANGUAGE > IDIOM		1 (12.5%)	LANGUAGE > SMOOTHNESS
		–	–		3 (37.5%)	TRANSFER > ACCURACY
		–	–		1 (12.5%)	TRANSFER > COMPLETENESS
'voluntary agency'	83.3% (5 students)	2 (33.3%)	TRANSFER > COMPLETENESS	100% (8 students)	7 (87.5%)	TRANSFER > COMPLETENESS
		3 (50%)	TRANSFER > ACCURACY		1 (12.5%)	TRANSFER > ACCURACY

(Continued)

Table 3.12 (Continued)

	SNS (6 students)			*ENS (8 students)*		
	Percentage of errors	*Categorisation of errors*		*Percentage of errors*	*Categorisation of errors*	
'health and criminal record'	66.7% (4 students)	1 (16.7%)	TRANSFER > ACCURACY	62.5% (5 students)	1 (12.5%)	TRANSFER > ACCURACY
		1 (16.7%)	LANGUAGE > IDIOM		2 (25%)	LANGUAGE > IDIOM
		2 (33.3%)	LANGUAGE > SUB-LANGUAGE		2 (25%)	LANGUAGE > SMOOTHNESS
'home study report'	83.3% (5 students)	4 (66.7%)	TRANSFER > ACCURACY	62.5% (5 students)	4 (50%)	TRANSFER > ACCURACY
		2 (33.3%)	LANGUAGE > SUB-LANGUAGE		2 (25%)	LANGUAGE > SUB-LANGUAGE
'adoption panel'	33.3% (2 students)	1 (16.7%)	LANGUAGE > IDIOM	50% (4 students)	2 (25%)	LANGUAGE > IDIOM
		1 (16.7%)	TRANSFER > ACCURACY		1 (12.5%)	LANGUAGE > SUB-LANGUAGE
'agency's decision maker'	50% (3 students)	2 (33.3%)	TRANSFER > ACCURACY	25% (2 students)	2 (25%)	LANGUAGE > IDIOM
		1 (16.7%)	LANGUAGE > TAILORING		–	–
		1 (16.7%)	TRANSFER > COMPLETENESS		–	–
'senior manager'	83.3% (5 students)	5 (83.3%)	LANGUAGE > SUB-LANGUAGE	100% (8 students)	3 (37.5%)	TRANSFER > COMPLETENESS
		–	–		5 (62.5%)	LANGUAGE > SUB-LANGUAGE
'do some checks'	33.3% (2 students)	2 (33.3%)	TRANSFER > ACCURACY	50% (4 students)	2 (25%)	TRANSFER > ACCURACY
		–	–		2 (25%)	LANGUAGE > MECHANICS

From our analysis, it can be inferred that SNS made a total of 38 mistakes, of which 22 (57.9%) were associated with TRANSFER errors, and 16 (42.1%) with LANGUAGE issues. More concretely, of those 22 TRANSFER errors, 17 (44.7%) were related to the level of ACCURACY and only 5 (13.2%) were linked to COMPLETENESS. As for the LANGUAGE parameter, no errors regarding SMOOTHNESS and MECHANICS were spotted. Of the 16 errors associated with LANGUAGE, 9 (23.7%) corresponded to SUB-LANGUAGE, 2 (5.2%) to TAILORING, and 5 (13.1%) to IDIOM.

ENS made 47 mistakes, of which 22 (46.8%) corresponded to TRANSFER errors (11, i.e. 23.4%, were issues related to ACCURACY; and 11, i.e. 23.4%, to COMPLETENESS), and 25 (53.2%) were errors associated with LANGUAGE (4, i.e. 8.5%, related to SMOOTHNESS; 8, i.e. 17%, to SUB-LANGUAGE; 1, i.e. 2.1%, to TAILORING; 10, i.e. 21.3%, to IDIOM; and 2, i.e. 4.3%, to MECHANICS). See Figure 3.1 for a breakdown of errors.

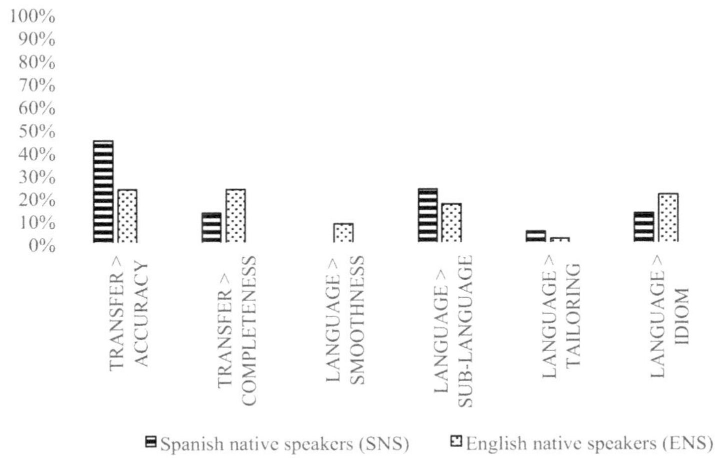

Figure 3.1 Breakdown of errors associated with SNS and ENS

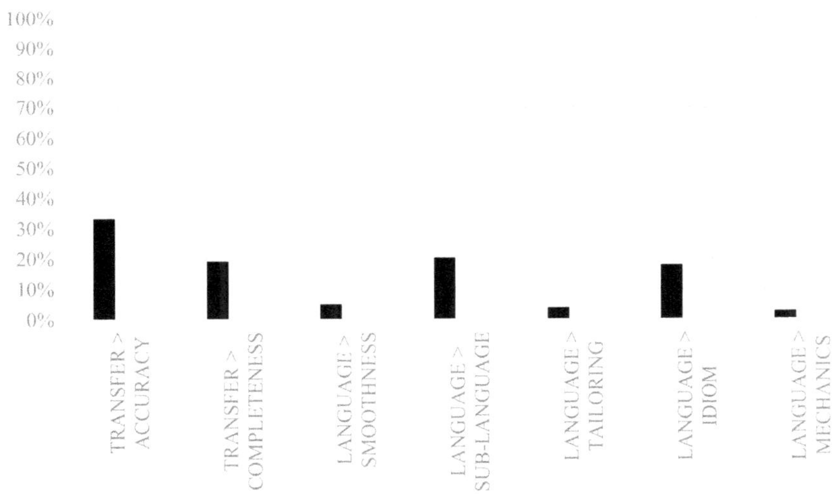

Figure 3.2 Breakdown of errors including the entire sample (n = 14 students)

The total number of errors made by both ENS and SNS was 85, of which 44 (51.8%) resulted in TRANSFER issues, and 41 (48.2%) in problems related to the LANGUAGE category. More concretely, 28 errors (33%) fall within the subcategory of ACCURACY, and 16 errors (18.8%) within the subcategory of COMPLETENESS. As LANGUAGE errors are concerned, 4 (4.7%) are associated with SMOOTHNESS, 17 (20%) with SUB-LANGUAGE, 3 (3.5%) with TAILORING, 15 (17.6%) with IDIOM, and 2 (2.4%) with MECHANICS. See Figure 3.2 for a breakdown of errors of the entire sample.

Conclusions

Following the analysis and discussion of our case study, this section suggests some approaches that could minimise the most recurrent translation errors made by students when dealing with PU in a semi-specialised legal text. Our case study and similar research recently undertaken in the field of legal translation (Pontrandolfo 2016) identify both TRANSFER and LANGUAGE as the main areas in which trainee translators need further training. Within these two overarching categories, issues related to ACCURACY of the message, SUB-LANGUAGE, and (UN)IDIOM(ATIC) combinations seem to be the most problematic areas for the students in our sample.

As shown in the data analysis and discussion of results, SNS are more prone to make TRANSFER > ACCURACY and LANGUAGE > SUB-LANGUAGE errors, whereas ENS seem to incur TRANSFER > ACCURACY, TRANSFER > COMPLETENESS, and LANGUAGE > IDIOM errors. From these findings, we can infer that SNS do not seem to always understand both the explicit and implicit message conveyed by the source text, perhaps because it is written in their second language, whereas ENS seem to experience more difficulties in producing idiomatic combinations in their second language. Interestingly, our results also show that while ENS tend to understand the source text well, they do not always convey the COMPLETE message in Spanish and sometimes leave out important elements. A remarkable number of SNS also experiences problems with LANGUAGE > SUB-LANGUAGE, which may show a lack of effective preliminary research on the topic and relevant parallel texts and resources.

Given the relatively small size of our sample, we cannot generalise our findings to other translation students and we can only make some tentative conclusions. However, if considered together with similar studies in legal translation modules (e.g. Pontrandolfo 2016), our comparative case study can serve as a first step to identifying general trends of translation errors made by similar samples. For future research, we intend to build upon our current work and conduct similar case studies involving not just a larger sample but also other fields of specialisation, e.g. economics.

Despite the increasing number of studies in comparative phraseology in the last few decades, our study evidences the need for further research on the didactics of phraseology in translation training, particularly in specialised translation. Some of the existing approaches that can mitigate the type of translation errors and specific needs identified in our case study include: task-based approaches (e.g. Hurtado Albir 1999/2003, 2015a, 2015b; González Davies 2004; Borja 2007/2015 in particular; Huc-Hepher and Huertas Barros 2016), critical discourse analysis (Way 2012), and approaches based on decision making and problem solving (Prieto Ramos 2014; Way 2014). These approaches can develop and hone the *phraseological competence* (Howarth 1998) required in semi-specialised legal translation courses, by making students aware of the conventional collocations and formulaic sequences that characterise this field.

Acknowledgements

This research was carried out within the framework of project FF2014–52740-P, *Cognitive and Neurological Bases for Terminology-Enhanced Translation* (CONTENT) funded by the Spanish Ministry of Economy and Competitiveness.

Notes

1 Wray (2000) provides a complete description of the many terms used to refer to phraseological units (i.e., phrase, phraseme, phraseological term, multi-word unit, multi-word lexical unit, formulae, word combination, phrasal lexeme, formulaic language, etc.).

2 In contrast to meaning-based approaches which believe the base to be autonomous and the collocate to be dependent, in our approach both elements depend on each other.
3 The definition of 'do' and 'check' has been extracted from *Cambridge Dictionary online:* <www.dictionary.cambridge.org> [12/12/2016].
4 We distinguish between compounds and collocations and refer to both as phraseological units.
5 As highlighted by Martínez Melis and Hurtado Albir (2001: 280–281), it is important to establish the difference between the notion of translation problem and translation error. The former is defined by Nord as "an objective (or inter-subjective) transfer task which every translator (irrespective of their level of competence and technical working conditions) has to solve during a particular translation process" (1988/2005: 166–167).
6 For a comprehensive overview on Translation Quality Assessment (TQA) models based on error typology see e.g. Waddington (1999, 2001, 2006) and Williams (2004).
7 Many PU suffer a process of terminologisation in legal language and acquire a specific meaning within this specific domain.
8 This definition has been extracted from the *Cambridge Dictionary Online*: http://dictionary.cambridge.org/dictionary/english/record
9 Information extracted from the website AdoptUSKids: http://adoptuskids.org/adoption-and-foster-care/how-to-adopt-and-foster/getting-approved/home-study

References

Alcaraz Varó, E. and Huges, B., 2014. *Legal Translation Explained.* Abingdon/New York: Routledge.

Baker, M., 2011. *In Other Words: A Coursebook on Translation.* London/New York: Routledge.

Bauer, L., 1988. When is a sequence of two nouns a compound in English? *English Language and Linguistics*, 2(1): 65–86.

Beeby Lonsdale, A., 1996. *Teaching Translation From Spanish to English: Worlds Beyond Words.* Ottawa: University of Ottawa Press.

Borja, A., 2000. *El texto jurídico inglés y su traducción al español.* Barcelona: Ariel.

Borja, A., 2007/2015. Estrategias, *materiales y recursos para la traducción jurídica (inglés-español).* Castelló de la Plana: Publicacions de la Universitat Jaume I; Madrid: Edelsa.

Buendía Castro, M., 2013. *Phraseology in Specialized Language and Its Representation in Environmental Knowledge Resources.* PhD thesis, Universidad de Granada, Granada, Spain.

Buendía Castro, M., Montero Martínez, S., and Faber, P., 2014. Verb collocations and phraseology in EcoLexicon. *Yearbook of Phraseology*, 5(1): 57–94.

Corpas Pastor, G., 2003. *Diez años de investigación en fraseología: análisis sintáctico-semánticos, contrastivos y traductológicos.* Madrid: Iberoamericana.

Corpas Pastor, G., 2013. All that glitters is not gold when translating phraseological units (abstract). In J. Monti, R. Mitkov, and G. Corpas Pastor (eds.), *Proceedings of the Workshop on Multi-word Units in Machine Translation and Translation Technologies*, 9–10. <www.mt-archive.info/10/MTS-2013-W4-TOC.htm> [Accessed: 15/12/2016].

Delisle, J., 1993. *La traduction raisonnée.* Ottawa: Presses de l'Université d'Ottawa.

González Davies, M., 2004. *Multiple Voices in the Translation Classroom: Activities, Tasks and Projects.* Amsterdam/Philadelphia: John Benjamins.

Gouadec, D., 1981. Paramètres de l'évaluation des traductions. *Meta*, 26(2): 99–116.

Hansen, G., 2006. *Erfolgreich Übersetzen. Entdecken und Beheben von Störquellen.* Tübingen: Narr, Francke, Attempto.

Hansen, G., 2010. Translation errors. In Y. Gambier and L. van Doorslaer (eds.), *Handbook of Translation Studies: Volume 1.* Amsterdam: John Benjamins, 385–388.

Hausmann, F.J., 1989. Le dictionnaire de collocations. In F.J. Hausmann, O. Reichmann, H.E. Wiegand, and L. Zgusta (eds.), *Wörterbücher/Dictionaries/Dictionnaires – Ein internationals Handbuch zur Lexikographie/An International Enyclopedia of Lexicography/Enyclopédie internationale de lexicographie.* Berlin/New York: Walter de Gruyter, 1010–1019.

Higueras García, M., 2006. *Las colocaciones y su enseñanza en la clase de ELE*. Madrid: Arco/Libros.

Howarth, P., 1998. Phraseoloy and second language proficiency. *Applied Linguistics*, 19(1): 24–44.

Huc-Hepher, S. and Huertas Barros, E., 2016. Up-skilling through e-collaboration. In E. Corradini, K. Borthwick, and A. Gallagher-Brett (eds.), *Employability for Languages: A Handbook*. Dublin, Ireland/Voillans, France: Research-publishing.net, 139–148.

Hurtado Albir, A., 1999/2003. *Enseñar a traducir. Metodología en la formación de traductores e intérpretes*. Madrid: Edelsa.

Hurtado Albir, A., 2001/2004. *Introducción a la Traductología*. Madrid: Cátedra.

Hurtado Albir, A., 2015a. *Aprender a traducir del francés al español: competencias y tareas para la iniciación a la traducción*. Castelló de la Plana: Publicacions de la Universitat Jaume I; Madrid: Edelsa.

Hurtado Albir, A., 2015b. The acquisition of translation competence. Competences, tasks, and assessment in translator training. *Meta: Journal des Traducteurs/Meta: Translators' Journal*, 60(2): 256–280.

Kussmaul, P., 1995. *Training the Translator*. Amsterdam: John Benjamins.

Martínez Melis, N. and Hurtado Albir, A., 2001. Assessment in translation studies: Research needs. *Meta*, 46(2): 272–287.

Meunier, F. and Granger, S., 2008. *Phraseology in Foreign Language Learning and Teaching*. Amsterdam/Philadelphia: John Benjamins.

Meyer, I. and Mackintosh, K., 1996. Refining the terminographer's concept-analysis methods: How can phraseology help? *Terminology*, 3(1): 1–26.

Mossop, B., 2001/2014. *Revising and Editing for Translators*. Manchester: St. Jerome Publishing.

Nord, C., 1988/2005. *Text Analysis in Translation: Theory, Methodology, and Didactic Application* of *a Model for Translation-oriented Text Analysis*. Amsterdam: Rodopi.

Nord, C., 1996. El error en la traducción: categorías y evaluación. In A. Hurtado Albir (ed.), *La enseñanza de la traducción*. Castelló: Universitat Jaume I, 91–108.

Nord, C., 1997/2012. *Translating as a Purposeful Activity: Functionalist Approaches Explained*. Manchester: St. Jerome.

Pawley, A., 2001. Phraseology. Linguisitcs and the dictionary. *International Journal of Lexicography*, 14(2): 122–134.

Penadés Martínez, I., 1999. *La enseñanza de las unidades fraseológicas*. Madrid: Arco/Libros.

Pontrandolfo, G., 2016. La evaluación en el aula de traducción jurídica. Una experiencia de análisis de errores en la combinación español-italiano. *Revista Española de Lingüística Aplicada/Spanish Journal of Applied Linguistics*, 29(1): 296–331.

Prieto Ramos, F., 2014. Parameters for problem-solving in legal translation: Implications for legal lexicography and institutional terminology management. In L. Cheng, K. Kui Sin, and A. Wagner (eds.), *The Ashgate Handbook of Legal Translation*. Farnham: Ashgate, 121–134.

Pym, A., 1992. Translation error analysis and the interface with language teaching. In C. Dollerup and A. Loddegaard (eds.), *Teaching Translation and Interpreting: Training, Talent and Experience. Papers presented at the First Language International Conference, Elsinore, Denmark, 31 May–2 June, 1991*. Amsterdam: John Benjamins, 279–288.

Qi, X., 2016. Formulaic sequences and the implications for second language learning. *English Language Teaching*, 9(8): 39–45.

Reiss, K., 1977/1989. Text-types, translation types and translation assessment. Translation by Andrew Chesterman: 105–115. Original: Texttypen, Übersetzungstypen und die Beurteilung von Übersetzungen. *Lebende Sprachen*, 22(3): 97–100.

Roberts, R., 1994/1995. Identifying the phraseology of LSPs. *ALFA*, 7(8): 61–73.

Ruiz Gurillo, L., 2002. *Ejercicios de fraseología*. Madrid: Arco/Libros.

Sinclair, J., 2000. Lexical grammar. *Darbai Ir Dienos*, 24: 191–204. <http://donelaitis.vdu.lt/publikacijos/sinclair.pdf> [Accessed 08/12/2015].
Snell-Hornby, M., 1988/1995. *Translation. Studies: An Integrated Approach*. Amsterdam/Philadelphia: John Benjamins.
Tiersma, P., 1999. *Legal Language*. Chicago: University of Chicago Press.
Turner, S., 2014. *The Development of Metaphoric Competence in French and Japanese Learners of English*. PhD thesis, University of Birmingham.
Waddington, C., 1999. *Estudio comparativo de diferentes métodos de evaluación de traducción general*. Madrid: Publicaciones de la Universidad Pontificia Comillas.
Waddington, C., 2001. Should student translations be assessed holistically or through error analysis? *Hermes*, 26: 15–37.
Waddington, C., 2006. Measuring the effect of errors on translation quality. *Lebende Sprachen. Zeitschrift für interlinguale und interkulturelle Kommunikation*, 51(2): 67–71.
Way, C., 2012. A discourse analysis approach to legal translator training: More than words. *International Journal of Law, Language and Discourse*, 2(4): 39–61.
Way, C., 2014. Structuring a legal translation course: A framework for decision-making in legal translator training. In L. Cheng, K. Kui Sin, and A. Wagner (eds.), *The Ashgate Handbook of Legal Translation*. Farnham: Ashgate, 135–152.
Williams, M., 2004. *Translation Quality Assessment: An Argumentation-centred Approach*. Ottawa: University of Ottawa Press.
Williams, M., 2009. Translation quality assessment. *Mutatis Mutandis*, 2(1): 3–23.
Wray, A., 2000. Formulaic sequences in second language teaching: Principle and practice. *Applied Linguistics*, 21(4): 463–489.

Annex

The adoption process and where to get support

If you are thinking about adopting a child, the first thing you should do is contact your local adoption agency. This can be your local Health and Social Care Trust or a voluntary agency. Your adoption agency will ask you to a meeting where you can learn more about what is involved and the types of children who need to be adopted.

Application and preparation

If you wish to go ahead, the agency will do some checks - including your health and any criminal record you may have. A health condition or criminal record may not necessarily exclude you from the process. Adoption agencies are mainly interested in your suitability to care for a child and meet their needs into adulthood.

If the checks are satisfactory, you will be invited to attend a preparation course where you will learn more about caring for an adopted child.

Assessment

If the agency accepts your application, an assessment process will begin. The social worker will make some visits to your home and will:

- ask you questions about your own family background, your childhood, your present circumstances and your attitude to parenting
- speak with other members of your family
- interview two personal referees named by you

The assessment is demanding, it can feel intrusive and will take several months. Everything is explored in depth with you.

Adoption is for life and the agency must be sure you are right for the role. Just as importantly, you must be certain you can make a success of it.

Once you have seen and agreed the content of the home study report, it will be considered by an adoption panel and then by the agency's decision maker, who is a senior manager in the adoption agency.

What is an adoption panel?

An adoption panel is a group of people who have to consider whether:

- adoption would be in the best interests of a child
- the person who wants to adopt should be approved
- particular people are suitable for a particular child or children

The panel's recommendation is passed to the agency's decision maker for a final decision to be made.

Source: nidirect Government Services

http://www.nidirect.gov.uk/index/information-and-services/parents/adoption-fostering-and-children-in-care/adoption/the-adoption-process-and-where-to-get-support.htm

Figure 3.3 Source text

4 Online resources for phraseology-related problems in legal translation

Míriam Buendía Castro and Pamela Faber

Introduction

Legal language is known for having very specific syntactic, semantic, and pragmatic features (Tiersma 1999: 15–133). Legal documents often use grammatical structures typical of the field, such as redundancy, foreign words and Latinisms, syntactic discontinuity, impersonal and passive constructions, nominalization, complex sentences, and formulaic expressions (Williams 2004: 112–115). Of these elements, formulaic language seems to be at the core of legal documents (Tiersma 1999: 100–104), and can be defined as follows (Wray 2000: 465):

> A sequence, continuous or discontinuous, of words or other meaning elements, which is, or appears to be, prefabricated: that is, stored and retrieved whole from memory at the time of use, rather than being subject to generation or analysis by the language grammar.

Other frequent names for a *formulaic sequence* include "multiword unit, multiword lexeme, multiword lexical unit, fixed expression, *phrase figée*, set expression, set phrase, and phraseological unit" (Corpas Pastor 1996: 17). It seems that *multi-word unit* is the preferred term within the Natural Language Processing community, and *phraseological unit* is the preferred term in phraseology (Corpas Pastor 2013).[1] In line with Corpas Pastor, we use the umbrella term *phraseological unit* to refer to formulaic sequences.

Gustaffson (1984) performed one of the earliest quantitative analyses of phraseological units in legal language, which reflected the prevalence of repetitive and fixed expressions in legal discourse. In line with Gustaffson, Goźdź-Roszkowski and Pontrandolfo (2015: 131) highlight the potential of repetition, fixedness, and frequency to identify phraseological units in legal language.

In specialized translation, it is crucial for translators to have access to the most recent information and documents, in both the target-language and source-language cultures. However, it is particularly important in the field of law, especially when legal systems are not closely related (Buendía Castro and Faber 2015: 164) since "legal translation tends to involve more culture-specific than universal components" (Biel 2008: 22). Nevertheless, when searching for phraseological equivalents in target-language legal documents, legal translators still depend on monolingual, bilingual, and multilingual dictionaries (Buendía Castro and Faber 2015: 164).

De Groot and Van Laer (2011, 2005) classified hundreds of legal dictionaries containing the languages of the European Member States into the following categories:

(i) *word lists*, i.e. bilingual or multilingual lists of terms with poor translations and with no explanations regarding meaning; (ii) *explanatory dictionaries*, which include usage contexts; (iii) *comparative dictionaries*, which also refer to legal systems or legal sources or legal areas or comparative law and differentiate between legal systems that share the same language. According to de Groot and Van Laer (2005), most legal dictionaries fall within the scope of *word lists*, which means that no information regarding phraseology is provided.

Paper dictionaries seem to be the one of the main sources of documentation for legal translation. This limits access to information since searches are only possible from the base term (i.e. the noun). In addition, there is the risk of not including the most recent concepts or new senses because of the length of the publishing process (Biel 2008: 29). Consequently, there is currently an increasing tendency to use online resources since, if designed properly, they can provide easier access to phraseological information in a wide range of professional and linguistic contexts. Besides offering more search options, specialized electronic resources can be continuously updated, whereas paper dictionaries are often out of date from the first day of publication. In line with this, more and more publishing houses offer electronic versions of specialized dictionaries. However, the problem is that most of them are not open-access resources, which means that the purchase or subscription prices are usually very high.

This study describes and compares a set of the most widely used bilingual/multilingual legal digital resources that contain phraseological information in their entries, with a view to evaluating the advantages and disadvantages of these resources from the perspective of legal translation.

Online resources containing legal phraseological information

This section provides a brief description of the most representative bilingual or multilingual legal resources that include phraseological information. The headword 'witness' is used as an example to describe and compare the set of legal resources. The focus of our analysis is on how each resource deals with the access to phraseological information and the description of phraseological units. The resources analyzed are the following: (i) *InterActive Terminology for Europe* (IATE); (ii) *TERMIUM* Plus®; (iii) JURITERM; (iv) Evroterm; (v) JuriDiCo; and (vi) MuLex.

InterActive Terminology for Europe *(IATE)*

IATE (*InterActive Terminology for Europe*) is the EU's multilingual terminology database which has been available online since 2007.[2] It contains all the information included in former EU databases such as EURODICAUTOM (Commission), TIS (Council), and EUTERPE (Parliament), *inter alia*.[3] IATE contains more than 8 million terms, including 130,000 phrases in all 24 official EU languages. It is growing at a pace of 300 new terms every day, and it receives about 3,600 visits per hour with 70 million queries per year.[4] IATE covers a wide range of domains including politics, law, economics, science, etc. It is operated by a management group with representatives from various institutions including the European Parliament, the European Commission, the Council of the European Union, the European Court of Justice, the European Court of Auditors, the European Economic and Social Committee, the Committee of the Regions, the Translation Centre for the Bodies of the European Union, and the European Central Bank.[5]

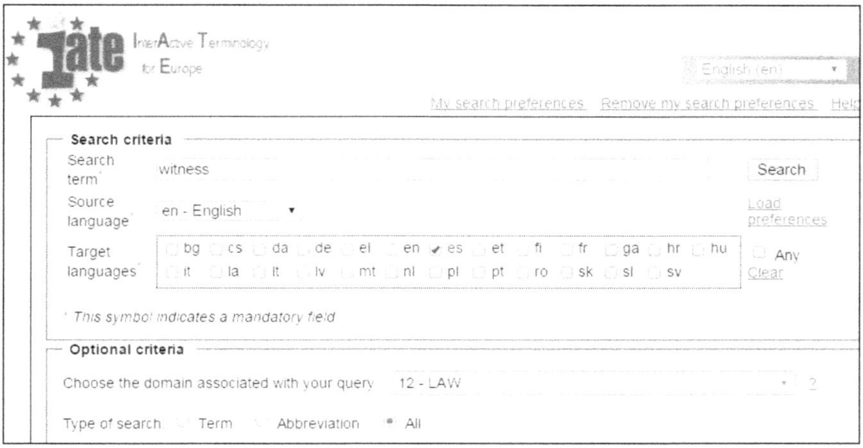

Figure 4.1 Search interface of IATE

Figure 4.1 displays the search interface in IATE. Users enter the keyword in the search box, and choose the source language and target language. They can also restrict the search query to a given domain.

When typing 'witness' in the search engine, the system displays a list with all combinations starting with 'witness'. These include 'witness', 'witnesseth', 'witnessing', 'witness box', 'witness fees', 'witness audit', 'witness chair', 'witness point', 'witness stand', 'witness summons', 'witness to will', 'witness in court', 'witness testimony', 'witness to a deed', 'witness inspection', 'witness protection', 'witness whereof/in', 'witness as expenses', 'witness against'. The user can also specify several words in the search box at once, and IATE will retrieve entries that contain all the words. In addition, IATE offers the possibility of including a word combination in double quotation marks, which means that the system retrieves the exact word combination in that order. This is especially interesting for phraseological units. Wildcards can also be used to replace any number or character.

For 'witness' restricted to the domain of law, IATE offers a total of 54 hits, which include all hits where 'witness' is part of the phraseological unit. In 'witness for the defence', 'in witness whereof', 'cooperative witness', 'statement by witness', 'eye witness', 'to summon witnesses', etc., 'witness' is a noun. In 'witness protection' and 'witness testimony', 'witness', though a noun, functions as an adjective since it modifies another noun; and in 'to witness', 'witness' is a verb.

Figure 4.2 displays an extract of the results with the matching term highlighted in the hit list. Apart from providing information regarding the domain in which the search term is included (e.g. 'object to a witness' is found within the domain of *EU institution, Operation of the Institutions, Judicial proceedings [COM]*), for every entry, IATE provides access to the term reference (+@), context, note section, and definition. Users can also retrieve this information by placing the mouse over each symbol. In addition, IATE also includes a reliability code. Four stars mean that the information given is very reliable, whereas one star signifies that its reliability cannot be verified.

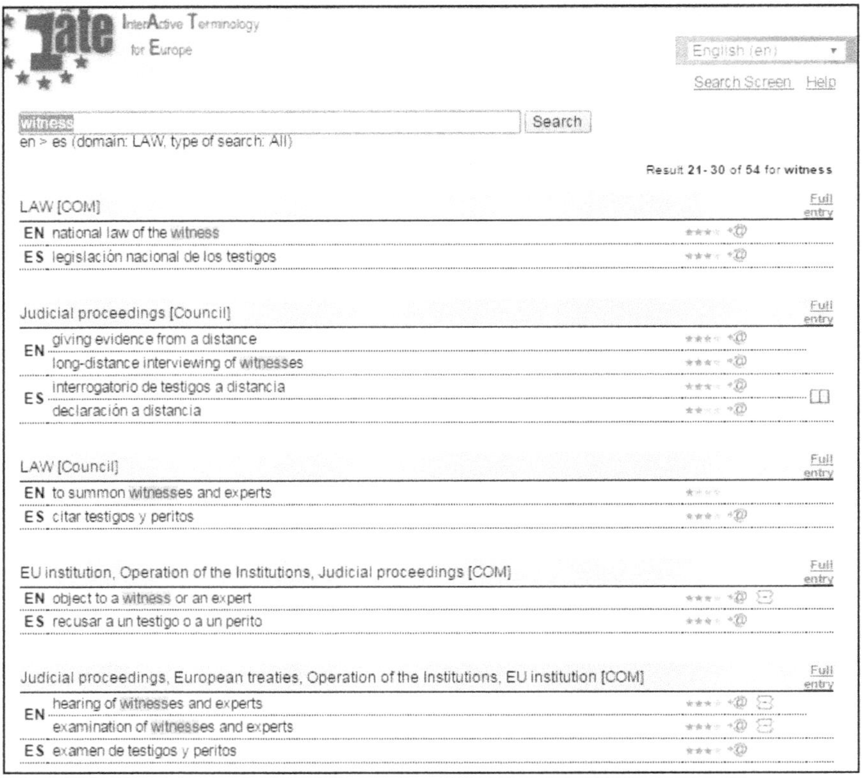

Figure 4.2 Extract of the results for 'witness' in IATE

Users can also access all of the details of the term entry (see Figure 4.3) by clicking on 'full entry'. For example, when this is done for 'object to a witness or an expert', another window is displayed, which contains the term reference as well as a reliability code for both the source term and its target-language equivalent. The source term also contains an explanatory context, which acts as a definition, and the reference from which it was taken.

Apart from the number of phraseological units that IATE contains, the main advantages of this resource are that it includes specialized verbs and also provides usage contexts for most phraseological units, the reference of the context, and a reliability code. In addition, searches are permitted both from the noun and the verb. In other words, if 'object' is typed in the search box, IATE will offer, among others combinations, 'object to a witness or an expert'.

However, the information could be further enhanced. When more than one phraseological unit is given for a certain term entry in one language, IATE does not indicate the degree of equivalence. For example, the database gives the impression that 'hearing of witnesses and experts' is synonymous with 'examination of witnesses and experts' since no indication is given of the extent to which they differ. The Spanish equivalent seems to be '*examen de testigos y peritos*', but once again, it is very difficult to know whether this is a good equivalent for the first phraseological unit, the second, or both.

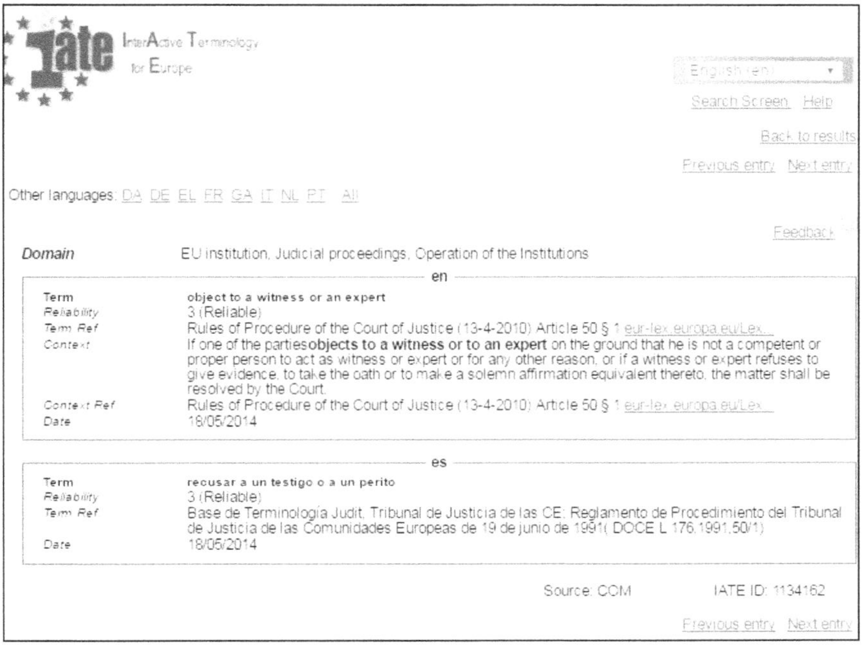

Figure 4.3 Full entry of 'object to a witness or an expert' in IATE

TERMIUM *Plus*®

TERMIUM Plus®[6] is a terminological and linguistic database created by the Government of Canada. It is the result of over 35 years of research and development in Terminology. It is one of the largest terminology and linguistic databases in the world. It contains millions of terms in English, French, Spanish, and Portuguese. Queries can be formulated in any of the four languages. It is a work in progress, which includes record creation, deletion of obsolete data, and expansion of existing records.

According to the information on its previous website, *TERMIUM* Plus® covers "almost every field of human endeavour [. . .] from a simple tool or a complex machine, to a disease or plant, association or committee". *TERMIUM* Plus® is a resource created to facilitate standardization. As such, it gives access to 16 electronic resources and also provides writing assistance.

Figure 4.4 displays the search interface of *TERMIUM* Plus®. The search term (which may be composed of several words) appears in the search box. In the 'where' section, a drop-down menu displays where users can specify the scope of the search. The options provided are the following:

- *All terms.* The application searches the entries where the term appears exactly as entered in all languages contained in *TERMIUM* Plus®.
- *All records.* The application searches all sections of the record and in all four languages. In other words, the system searches for the term in all entry fields (head terms, spelling variants, synonyms, abbreviations, and key terms) and in the rest of sections (definitions, contexts, observations, and phraseologisms).

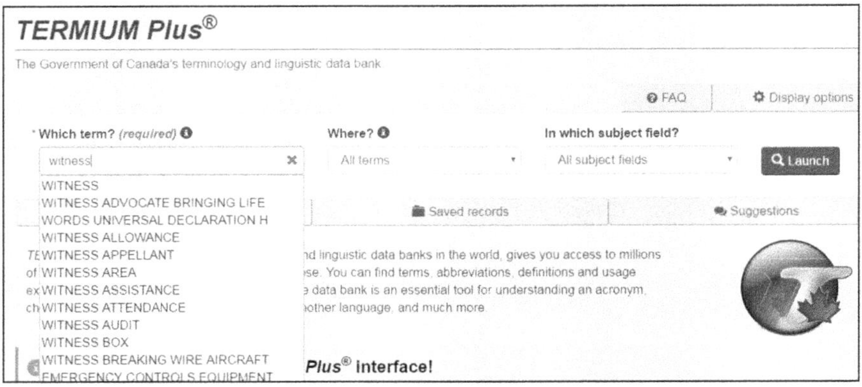

Figure 4.4 Search interface of *TERMIUM* Plus®

Apart from these two options, for each language (e.g. for English) additional search options are offered:

- *English terms (exact term)*. This search is similar to the *all terms* search option, but only retrieves English terms.
- *Words in English terms*. This option is interesting for users looking for all records in which two or more words appear in the entry, though not in a certain order.
- *Words in English definitions and contexts*. This option allows users to search for words in *textual supports*[7] (definitions, contexts, observations, and phraseologisms) in the selected language. This is useful for phraseology-related searches.
- *English records*. The system searches in all record sections: entries (head terms, spelling variants, synonyms, abbreviations, and key terms) and in textual support (definitions, contexts, observations, and phraseologisms) in English.

Finally, users can restrict the search to a certain domain. For example, one of the domains is *law and justice*. Within this domain, the users can select, among others, *administrative law*, *commercial law*, *copyright*, *patent and trademark law*, *international law*, etc. However, general domains such as *law and justice* cannot be chosen, only a specific subdomain. This can be a problem for users who are not specialists in the field, and who cannot judge whether a specific combination belongs to *commercial* or *administrative law*, for instance.

By default, the *TERMIUM* Plus® search engine searches in *all terms* and in *all fields* in all languages. The number of results is limited to the 100 most recent records.[8]

Figure 4.5 shows the *TERMIUM* results for 'witness' in a search in *all records* and *all fields*, in all languages. Nonetheless, if the search is for *all terms*, there are only six hits since the system only retrieves exact matches. This option is thus not useful for phraseology. The options *all records* and *words in English terms* give users the same information. As such, we opted for *all records* to be able to identify as much phraseological information as possible. The search was not limited to a specific domain since, as previously mentioned, general domains cannot be chosen (i.e. *law and justice*). Since the results totalled 100 hits, because of space constraints only two extracts of a record are shown as an example.

As shown in Figures 4.5 and 4.6, the subject field is specified in each entry. It is followed by the term or phraseological unit in which the search word appears (e.g. 'present a witness', 'material witness', 'key witness'). If the term is a noun or noun phrase, a definition is provided, headed by DEF. For example, for the noun phrase 'material witness' (Figure 4.6), the following definition is given: "A witness who can testify about matters having some logical connection with the consequential facts, esp. if few others, if any, know about those matters". Since the example displayed in Figure 4.5 is a verbal collocate, no definition is given.

In Figure 4.5, there is also a usage context, headed by CONT (context). The two examples displayed show that most of the time, within each term entry, *TERMIUM* opts for

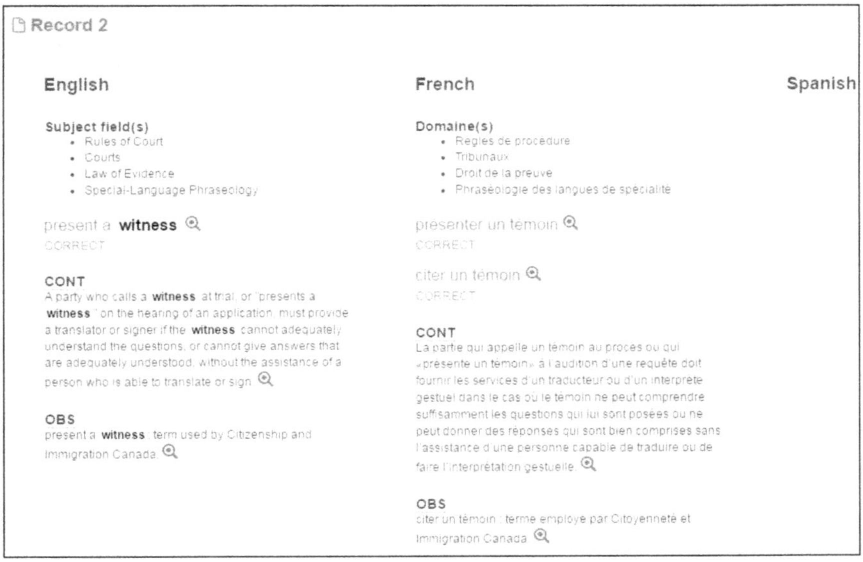

Figure 4.5 Extract of the results for 'witness' in *TERMIUM* Plus®. Example of a verbal collocate.

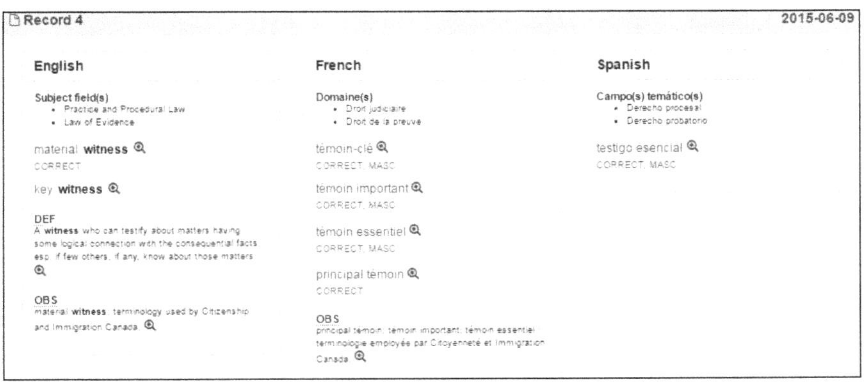

Figure 4.6 Extract of the results for 'witness' in *TERMIUM* Plus®. Example of a noun phrase.

either a definition or a context. In this regard, Reimerink et al. (2010) distinguish between *meaningful context* and *defining context*. Definitions in *TERMIUM* consist of a *defining context*, namely, a context that includes all or most of the elements necessary to understand a concept, whereas the contexts in *TERMIUM* are formed by a *meaningful context*, namely, a context that includes at least one knowledge element.

After the contextual information, there is an *observation section* (OBS), i.e. a section that provides more information related to the term entry. Lastly, collocational information or information regarding phraseologisms (PHR) is given. Collocations are classified in terms of part of speech (noun, adjective, or verb). For the example of 'witness', combinatorial information is offered. Although the phraseological units appear as term entries, none of these records includes a specific section for phraseological information.

Needless to say, *TERMIUM* Plus® is a huge database which is a veritable goldmine of information. It is an extremely valuable repository when looking for phraseological units in both general language and specialized language, and more specifically within the domain of law. In addition, like IATE, though unlike most specialized resources in other domains, it includes verbal collocates (e.g. 'present a witness', 'appear as a witness', 'summon as a witness', 'subpoena as a witness'), which are of paramount importance especially for text encoding purposes. In addition, it also allows searches by noun or by verb. It also includes a definition or usage context for most combinations, which is very useful for translators.

However, *TERMIUM* Plus® has certain limitations in regard to phraseology. Although it claims to have a special section within each term entry that includes phraseological information, collocates only appear in a limited number of term records, and when they are listed, they are incomplete (Buendía Castro 2013: 197). As shown, this section did not appear in the search for 'witness' combinations in *TERMIUM*. In addition, the information is provided mostly for English and French. The information in Spanish and Portuguese is extremely limited. Of the 100 records displayed for 'witness', all of them were explained in English and French, whereas only seven were explained in Spanish, and two in Portuguese.

JURITERM

JURITERM[9] is a bilingual (English-French) online resource for Common Law terminology. It was created by the *Centre de Traduction et de Terminologie Juridiques (CTTJ)* of the Université de Moncton, and was funded by the Ministry of Justice of Canada. It contains about 18,200 entries in every domain of private common law, including the full standardization in French of common law as well as hundreds of definitions in French from *La common law de A à Z* (Vanderlinden et al. 2010). JURITERM is for all users interested in legal language (i.e. translators, writers, teachers, or students).

Figure 4.7 shows the JURITERM search interface. As shown, the application is in French. After entering the term in the search box, users choose English (*terme anglais*) or French (*terme français*) as the search language in the *champ cible* [target field] section. Finally, the results are obtained by pressing Enter or clicking on *lancer la recherche* [launch the search]. Users can also launch advanced searches by linking two words with a plus sign (+) in the search box. This is useful to retrieve phraseological units since the search engine will retrieve all term entries containing both words.

In Figure 4.7, the screen shows the results of a search for all term entries containing the word 'witness' and lists them in the section *fiches traitées* (upper left-hand side).

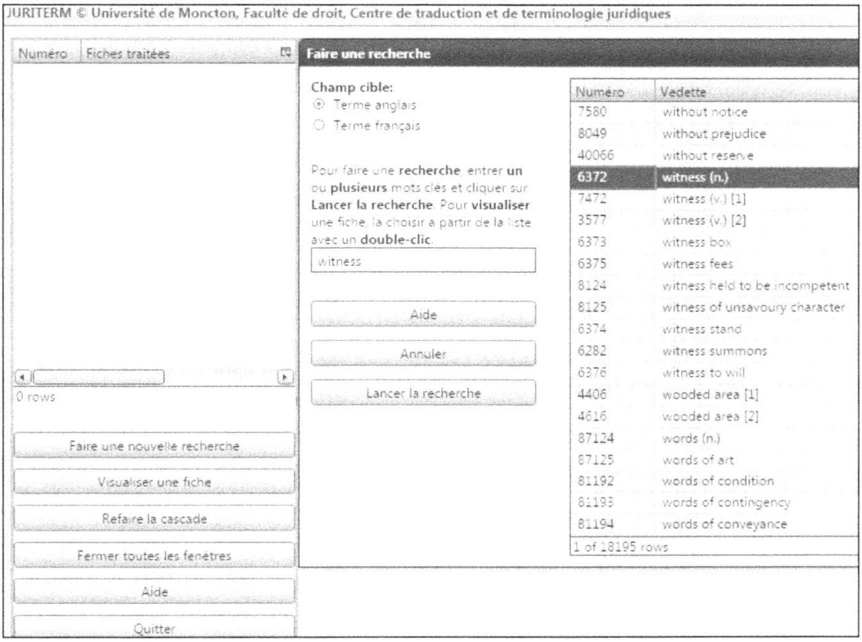

Figure 4.7 JURITERM search interface

As shown in Figure 4.8, the system retrieves a total of 79 hits (e.g. 'adverse witness', 'attendance of a witness', 'attesting witness', 'authenticating witness', 'competent witness', 'corroborative witness', 'credible witness', key witness', 'lay witness', 'material witness', 'non-compellable witness', 'non-expert witness', 'opposing witness', etc.). Thirteen of these hits correspond to verbal phraseological units (i.e. 'appear (v.) as a witness', 'call (v.) a witness', 'call (v.) as a witness', 'cross-examine (v.) a witness', 'discredit (v.) a witness', 'excuse (v.) a witness', 'hear (v.) a witness', 'impeach (v.) a witness', 'impeach (v.) the credibility of a witness', 'impeach (v.) the credit of a witness', 'impugn (v.) the credibility of a witness', 'lead (v.) the witness', 'witness (v.)').

Figure 4.9 shows two extracts of two entries in JURITERM, a noun phraseological unit ('material witness') and a verbal phraseological unit ('impugn (v.) the credibility of a witness').

As shown in Figure 4.9, each term entry describes the phraseological unit highlighted. Also provided are the sources from which it was taken (i.e. *Black's Law Dictionary* and the *Vocabulaire Bilingue de la Common* Law), and the synonyms, antonyms, generic, specific, analogous terms, and variant forms, if any, specified by hyperlinks. This enables users to easily navigate from one term entry to another in search of more information. For instance, according to Figure 4.9, 'material witness' has a synonym ('key witness'), whereas 'impeach (v.) a witness' has three synonyms ('impeach (v.) a witness', 'impeach (v.) the credibility of a witness', and 'impeach (v.) the credit of a witness'). In addition, the French equivalents appear along with their standardization status and information regarding the sources, and notes on meaning and usage.

Numéro	Fiches traitées
5742	**adverse witness**
7607	appear (v.) as a witness
6479	attendance of a witness
3076	attesting witness
5755	authenticating witness
7692	blank summons to witness
6510	call (v.) a witness
5772	call (v.) as a witness
6512	capacity (n.) [4] (of witness)
5957	character witness
5791	commission for examination of witnesses
5792	commission to examine witnesses
5795	compellable witness
5796	competence (n.) [2] (of witness)

1 of 79 rows

Figure 4.8 Phraseological units retrieved for 'witness' in JURITERM

INFORMATIONS SUR LA VEDETTE

VEDETTE: material witness
SOURCE 1: Black's Law Dictionary, 6e éd., St. Paul (Minn.), West Publishing Co., 1990, p. 977.
SYNONYMES: key witness (7903)

INFORMATIONS SUR LES SOLUTIONS

ÉQUIVALENT 1: témoin-clé (m.)
PONDÉRATION: Recommandé par le CTTJ

CONSTATS
CONSTAT 1: témoin-clé
SOURCE 1: Centre de traduction et de terminologie juridiques (CTTJ), Vocabulaire de la common law, tome 3 : Procédure civile et Preuve, Moncton, Université de Moncton, Faculté de droit, 1983, p. 126.

RÉDACTION: CBL
DATE DE RÉDACTION: 27/09/1989
DATE DE MISE À JOUR: 28/07/1997
NUMÉRO: 7022

INFORMATIONS SUR LA VEDETTE

VEDETTE: impugn (v.) the credibility of a witness
SOURCE 1: PAJLO, Vocabulaire bilingue de la Common Law : Droit de la preuve, Coll. La Clef, Ottawa, Ass. Bar. can., 1984, p. 110.
SYNONYMES: impeach (v.) a witness (6086),
impeach (v.) the credibility of a witness (6087),
impeach (v.) the credit of a witness (6088)

INFORMATIONS SUR LES SOLUTIONS

ÉQUIVALENT 1: attaquer la crédibilité d'un témoin
PONDÉRATION: Normalisé par PAJLO
ÉQUIVALENT 2: reprocher un témoin
PONDÉRATION: Normalisé par PAJLO

CONSTATS
CONSTAT 1: attaquer la crédibilité d'un témoin
SOURCE 1: PAJLO, Vocabulaire bilingue de la Common Law : Droit de la preuve, Coll. La Clef, Ottawa, Ass. Bar. can., 1984, p. 110.
CONSTAT 2: reprocher un témoin
SOURCE 2: PAJLO, Vocabulaire bilingue de la Common Law : Droit de la preuve, Coll. La Clef, Ottawa, Ass. Bar. can., 1984, p. 110.

Figure 4.9 Term entry examples in JURITERM

Of the resources in this paper, JURITERM provides the most phraseological information. It is also the most reliable, since unlike IATE and *TERMIUM*, it only focuses on the domain of law. Furthermore, the sources of both the source language terms and their correspondences are truly representative of the domain and are always provided. Searches can also be launched both from the noun or the verb, which is absolutely essential when looking for phraseological information. This database is extremely valuable for translators working with English and French combinations. Nevertheless, users may find it difficult to ascertain how a particular legal phraseological unit can be used in texts since no usage contexts are included.

Evroterm

Evroterm[10] is a multilingual terminological database that was created from the Slovene version of the legal documents of the European Union. It was compiled by terminologists in the Translation Unit of the Government Office for European Affairs of the Republic of Slovenia. The compilation process began in 1997, and since 2000, Evroterm has been freely available on the web. It currently contains about 130,000 entries.

In line with specialized resources in other subdomains, such as EcoLexicon,[11] a database on environmental science (Faber and Buendía Castro 2014), Evroterm makes the distinction between concept and term. In other words, one concept (in the form of a database entry) can be activated by various terms in the same language and in different languages. For this reason, the database contains terms that are apparently the same but which refer to different concepts. For this reason, they are included in different entries (e.g. 'witness' as a noun and 'witness' as a verb are listed separately). Most entries are bilingual (English-Slovene), but there are also multilingual entries (mostly German and French, but also Croatian, Czech, Danish, Dutch, English, Finnish, Hungarian, Italian, Latin, Polish, Portuguese, Slovak, Spanish, and Swedish). Some terms from other terminological databases are also available (e.g. IATE).

Figure 4.10 shows the Evroterm search interface and the results obtained when searching for 'witness'. As shown, the search interface is very simple. It only contains a search window where users can type the search term in any of the languages in the database. In a search for 'witness', the application gives 19 results (e.g. 'witness against the suspect', 'witness disk', 'witness file share', 'witness for the defence', 'witness for the prosecution', 'witnessed assessments', etc.).

It is important to emphasize that by default, the system searches by *terms beginning with the search query*. By clicking on each phraseological unit, users access the complete description of the term entry. Figure 4.11 shows the term entry of 'witness for the defence' as an example of the information included. As can be observed, an Evroterm entry first includes the creation date, modification date, the subject domain in Slovene and English, and the term entry number. The phraseological unit is then given along with its synonyms in the source language (i.e. 'defence witness', 'witness for the defence', 'witness in behalf of the suspect'). The definition of the main term ('defence witness') is also provided along with the definition source. In addition, it also includes a *see also* section in most of the phraseological units, which refers users to other dictionaries, glossaries, and terminological databases with more information pertaining to the term. Finally, translations are provided.

In Figure 4.11, a translation into Slovene and French are given. For these correspondences, Evroterm includes a reliability index, ranging from 1 (unreliable) to 5 (very reliable). It also includes the reference of the translation (*TermRef*), the institution that recommended the translation (*TermSource*), and cross references to other resources.

Users can also launch an advanced search (Figure 4.12), which allows them to choose the source language and the target language or languages. The search query can also be restricted to a certain domain (e.g. *law*).

Figure 4.10 Search interface and results for 'witness' in Evroterm

Figure 4.11 Entry of 'defence witness' in Evroterm

Figure 4.12 Advanced search in Evroterm

#	Term (EN)	Translation	Language	Subject
1	appear as witness	nastopiti kot priča	SL	law JU

Figure 4.13 Results for 'witness' in the advanced search *terms containing search query*

In theory, the advanced search option allows users to customize searches and obtain, for example, *terms containing search query*. This should help retrieve more phraseological units that contain 'witness'. However, as shown in Figure 4.13, this search only produced one phrase ('appear as witness'). Despite the fact that the target languages were all languages in Evroterm, the only result was the correspondence in Slovene. By clicking on the term entry, users see a new window with all the term entry information.

The rest of the search options in Evroterm (*terms matching search query*, *terms ending with search query*, *fuzzy search*, *terms containing search query in additional data fields*) do not work properly since the only result given is the term entry for 'witness'.

Evidently, Evroterm is a work in progress. Therefore, the information regarding phraseological units is still very limited, except for the combination English-Slovene. There are no usage contexts or specification of the degree of equivalence between source and target-language correspondences. Nonetheless, Evroterm is an interesting resource because in the same way as other resources described in this paper (and unlike most specialized knowledge resources), it includes verb phraseological units. Moreover, searches can also be launched from the noun or from the verb. In addition, for some phraseological entries, the definition, the definition reference, and a reliability code for translations are provided.

JuriDiCo

JuriDiCo[12] is a freely available online multilingual lexical knowledge resource (English-Portuguese-French) for legal terminology. It is based on Frame Semantics (Fillmore 1977,

1982, 1985; Fillmore and Atkins 1992) and the FrameNet project (Ruppenhofer et al. 2010). The methodology used to compile it is the same as that used in DiCoInfo (*Dictionnaire fondamental de l'informatique et de l'Internet*)[13] and DicoEnviro (*Dictionnaire fondamental de l'environnement*),[14] created by the *Observatoire de linguistique Sens-Texte* at the University of Montreal (L'Homme 2008, 2016; *inter alia*).

More specifically, JuriDiCo describes specialized verbs in texts of Supreme Court judgments in Canada and Portugal. It provides users with both linguistic information (i.e. syntactic structure patterns, actantial (argument) structure, collocations), and extralinguistic information (i.e. the *frames* or conceptual scenarios to which the term refers (Pimentel 2015: 428)).

Generally speaking, *frames* are regarded as a cognitive structuring device, based on experience, which provide the background knowledge for the words in a language. Accordingly, in order to understand word meaning, it is first necessary to know the conceptual structures underlying their usage (Faber and López Rodríguez 2012: 23). Target users of JuriDiCo are anyone interested in legal terminology, especially translators and technical writers.

The novelty of JuriDiCo is that it focuses on verb description. As is well known, terminology has always been centred on the description of nouns and noun phrases and has played down the description of verbs (Buendía Castro 2012; L'Homme 1998; Lorente and Bevilacqua 2000; *inter alia*). Nevertheless, verbs are considered to be the most important lexical and syntactic category of language since they provide the relational and semantic framework for sentences (Fellbaum 1990: 278). Pimentel (2015: 428) writes:

> [V]erbs should be included in multilingual terminological resources, in general, and in resources covering the specialized field of law, in particular, because they pose decoding, encoding and translation challenges.

The JuriDiCo search engine can be alphabetically queried by either a term index (*list of terms*) or a frame index (*list of frames*). The list of terms is in English, French, and Portuguese. However, frames are only described in English since semantic frames are thought to be language independent to a certain degree (Baker 2009). The search engine (Figure 4.14) allows users to perform searches based on the following: (i) *language* (Portuguese, English, or French, or the three languages together); (ii) *mode*, by term, frame, or both frames and terms; (iii) *precision*, which permits searches by *exact matching*, *starting with*, or *containing* the word entered in the search box.

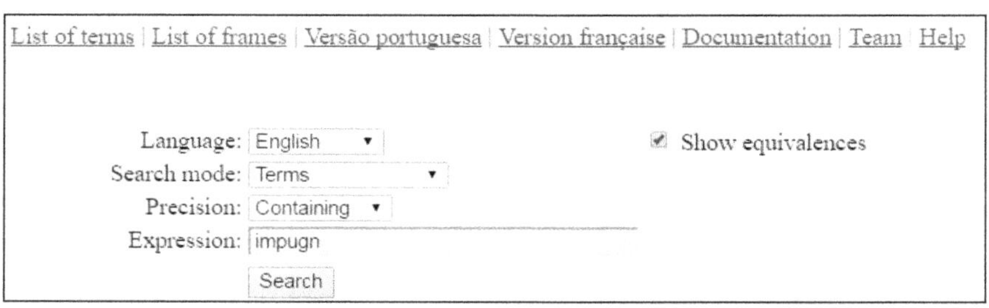

Figure 4.14 JuriDiCo search interface

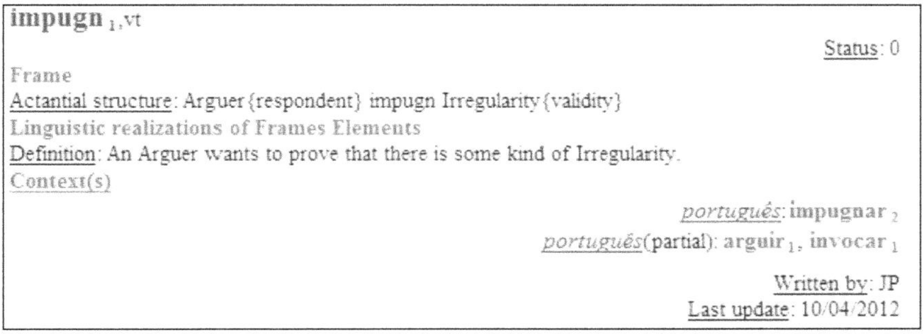
impugn $_{1}$,vt

Status: 0

Frame

Actantial structure: Arguer{respondent} impugn Irregularity{validity}

Linguistic realizations of Frames Elements

Definition: An Arguer wants to prove that there is some kind of Irregularity.

Context(s)

português: **impugnar** $_{2}$

português(partial): **arguir** $_{1}$, **invocar** $_{1}$

Written by: JP

Last update: 10/04/2012

Figure 4.15 The term entry 'impugn$_1$' in JuriDiCo

Since JuriDiCo focuses on verbs, the search for 'witness', used for the other resources, cannot be launched. Therefore, the verb 'impugn' is given as an example to explain the information in JuriDiCo since it is one of the most complete entries. Figure 4.15 shows the search results for 'impugn'.

As can be observed in Figure 4.15, entries in JuriDiCo have the following data fields:

- *Headword.* The sense number of the specialized verb is given.[15]
- *Grammatical information.* Verbs can be transitive (*vt*) or intransitive (*vi*).
- *Degree of completion of the entry.* For example, 0 means the entry is completed; 1 means that the sections are in an advanced stage of editing; and 2 means that the entry is still being developed.
- *Frame.* By clicking on *frame*, a new window is displayed with frame information (see Figure 4.16).
- *Actantial structure.* This field specifies the typical actants[16] or arguments activated by a verb and their semantic role. For example, 'impugn1' has two arguments: ARGUER and IRREGULARITY.
- *Linguistic realizations of frame elements.* The terms that can instantiate each argument are shown. They are the potential collocates of the verb. For example, terms with the role of ARGUER are 'appellant' and 'respondent', and terms with the role of IRREGULARITY are 'accuracy', 'communication', 'conduct', 'credibility', 'finding', 'integrity', 'interview', 'lawfulness', 'order', 'principle', 'proceeding', 'reason', 'reliability', 'statement', and 'validity').[17]
- *Definition.* This information is only provided for terms whose state is 0. For example, the definitional context of 'impugn' is *an arguer wants to prove that there is some kind of irregularity.*
- *Context(s).* This data field shows short extracts of corpus texts.
- *Correspondences.* All of the full equivalents of the term in other languages are given. When no full equivalent is available, a partial equivalent is provided. For example, in Portuguese, 'impugn$_1$' has one full equivalent '*impugnar$_2$*', and two partial equivalents, '*arguir$_1$*', '*invocar$_1$*'.
- *Administrative information.* This field shows the most recent update of the entry and the person responsible for its compilation.

Frame Definition:	
This frame is related to the Argumentation frame. Whereas in the Argumentation frame the Arguer presents a statement, a reason or fact for or against the matter under discussion, in this frame the Arguer questions the validity of a statement or of a fact. This frame has three core FEs, i.e. Arguer, Irregularity and Evidence. Not all terms that evoke this frame profile the FE Evidence.	
Core Elements:	
Arguer : It can refer to the accuser or to the defendant (criminal suit), to the petitioner or to the respondent (civil suit). The terms that instantiate the role of the Arguer are most often: Crown, appellant, accused, plaintiff, and respondent. However, the Arguer can also be instantiated by terms denoting a different specialized nature such as court and judge. Whereas the Protagonist is anyone who plays a given role, i.e. the role of the accused or of the accuser (criminal suit), the role of the petitioner or of the respondent (civil suit) and even the role of the judge, the Arguer is a Protagonist who plays the specific role of providing argumentation support. The Arguer has the right and duty to present arguments so as to keep the role of Protagonist in different moments of the lawsuit. Therefore, the Arguer is a type of Protagonist and the Protagonist becomes the Arguer at certain moments of the lawsuit.	
Evidence : The Black Law's Dictionary – Free online edition defines Evidence as "the means by which any alleged matter of fact, the truth of which is submitted to investigation, is established or disproved".	
Irregularity : The Black Law's Dictionary – Free online edition defines Irregularity as a "violation or nonobservance of established rules and practices [...] defect in practical proceedings, or the mode of conducting an action or defense [...] The doing or not doing that, in the conduct of a suit at law, which, conformably with the practice of the court, ought or ought not to be done". Irregularity is a core FE in frames in which verbs usually combine with terms denoting negative events.	
Non-Core Elements:	
Basis, Case, Condition, Manner, Mode, Place, Purpose, Reason, Text	
English Terms:	**Portuguese Terms:**
allege 1 impugn 1 rebut 1	arguir 1 impugnar 2 invocar 1

Figure 4.16 Contesting frame in JuriDiCo

Figure 4.16 displays the frame activated by 'impugn$_1$', which is the *Contesting* frame. As shown, each frame template is composed of three parts: (i) a frame definition; (ii) the frame participants, who are divided into core (obligatory) participants and non-core (optional) participants; (iii) the verbs that activate the frame in the languages contained in JuriDiCo. This example only has verbs in English and Portuguese.

Over all, JuriDiCo provides valuable information regarding verbs within the legal domain. Since it is one of the few resources that focuses on verbs, it can provide relevant information for users interested in legal phraseology and legal knowledge. Nevertheless, it only contains a limited number of entries, and the information in many entries is not complete.

In addition, even though the search template of JuriDiCo is designed for both encoding and decoding purposes, this is really not the case. Despite the fact that users can search by term or by frame (by entering previous knowledge of the concept), searches can only be launched with the verb and not with the noun or noun phrase that can collocate with a specific verb. For example, when 'appellant' and 'respondent' are entered in the search window, both of which collocate with 'impugn', the system states that *no information has been found*. The frame search option is not user-friendly since it is necessary to have previously memorized the name of the frames. Otherwise no information is offered. Finally, JuriDiCo should include an explanation of its theoretical premises since most users are not familiar with concepts such as *actant*.

MuLex

The *Multilingual Legal Terminological Knowledge Base*, MuLex[18] (Peruzzo 2013, 2014), is a translation-oriented terminological knowledge base (English-Italian) developed at the

University of Trieste, which contains terminology related to the legal subdomain of crime victims. It integrates three different legal systems: the European Union system, the British system, and the Italian system. It offers conceptual and linguistic information pertaining to crime victims. The resource is mainly for translators, but it can also be useful for anyone interested in legal terminology.

The design of MuLex entailed a preliminary conceptual structuring of the legal area of crime victims, based on the premises of Frame Semantics (Fillmore 1977, 1982, 1985; Fillmore and Atkins 1992). These are the principles applied, for instance, in Frame-based Terminology (Faber 2009, 2011, 2012) and in EcoLexicon for the specialized subdomain of the environment. This type of preliminary conceptual structure permitted the specification of a frame or event template (Faber 2012), typical of this legal subdomain. This template was then subdivided into *concept fields*, which provide the initial structure for the classification of concepts (Peruzzo 2014: 157):

> In line with the prototypical conceptual structures reproducing events or processes proposed by Frame-Based Terminology, [. . .] event templates are considered useful from a terminological perspective for two reasons. On the one hand, they can be exploited to reconstruct and represent a prototypical model of an event or process which allows for a TKB to be both managed and monitored effectively and integrated and updated consistently by terminologists, whereas on the other, they can be accessed and consulted by the end users of the TKB.

Therefore, concept fields were created for a more efficient management of the database and to categorize and identify concepts as objects or entities. MuLex differentiates between three concept fields or subframes: (i) persons involved in criminal justice/*soggetti della giustizia penale*; (ii) harm and damage suffered by crime victims/*pregiudizi subiti dalle vittime di reato*; (iii) rights of crime victims/*diritti delle vittime di reato*.

Figure 4.17 displays the search interface of MuLex. As can be observed, after entering the term in the search window, users can directly query the list of English or Italian terms. In addition, it is possible to search by *concept field*. Clicking on a concept field gives users access to all its member concepts, which provides more contextual knowledge.

Figure 4.18 shows the results of a search for ‘witness’. As previously mentioned, each entry in MuLex offers both conceptual and linguistic information. The conceptual information provided is the following:

- *Subject, subfield, and concept field* (upper left-hand side). Since MuLex focuses on the legal area of crime victims, all terminographic entries share the same *subject* (*criminal law*), and the same subfield (*victims of crime*). As shown, ‘witness’ is found in the concept field of *persons involved in criminal justice*. This section would be even more useful if MuLex was expanded to cover other areas of law.
- *Definition and the source of the definition*. WITNESS is defined as “anyone called to testify by either side in a trial who is sworn in and who offers evidence deemed relevant to the case; also, one who has observed an event, such as a crime”).
- *Graphic visualization boxes*. These display the conceptual relations linking the search concept to other concepts in MuLex. The four conceptual relations are superordinate, subordinate, coordinate, and general. For instance, WITNESS is linked to the general concept of VICTIM in the EU system, as well as in the UK legal system.[19]

Figure 4.17 MuLex search interface

The linguistic information included for each entry in MuLex is the following:

- *Language* (i.e. English, Italian);
- *Part of speech*, which can be either noun or noun group;
- *Gender* for Italian terms (*m* for masculine and *f* for feminine);
- *Regional label*, i.e. EU, Italy, UK, CoE (Council of Europe), UN;
- *Style label* (official, potentially official, obsolete);
- *Phraseology*, which shows noun, adjective, and verbal phraseological units regarding the term entry (e.g. 'to hear a witness', 'to provide protection for witnesses', 'witnesses attend in court', etc.);
- *Contexts of use*, which include only one context when a term is found in texts in only one legal system, and include two different contexts when two legal systems are involved (Peruzzo 2013: 237);
- *Equivalent terms in Italian* (i.e. testimone, persona che puó riferire circostanze utili al fini delle indagini).

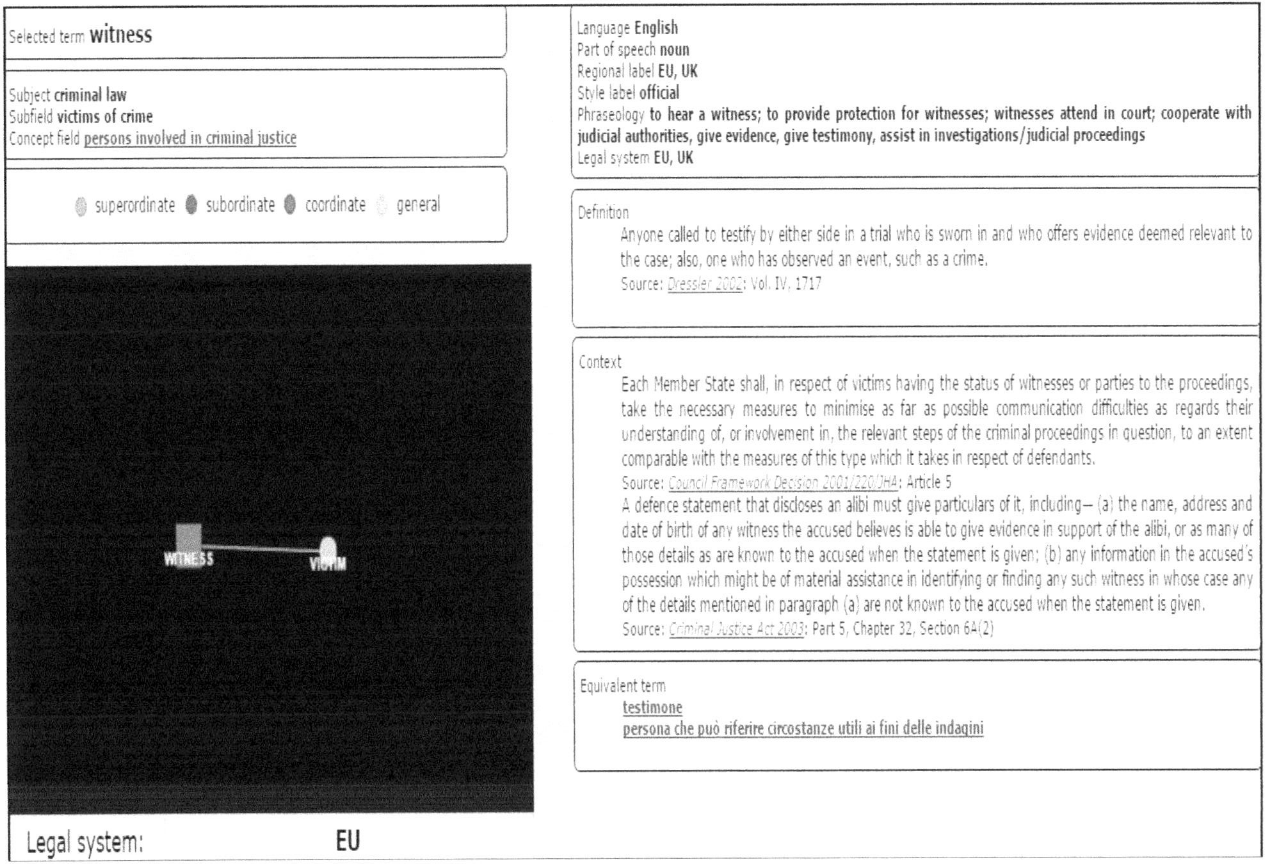

Figure 4.18 Extract of the entry of 'witness' in MuLex

MuLex is a potentially valuable resource for legal translators dealing with the subdomain of crime victims. It allows users to access conceptual and linguistic information for each term entry, and includes phraseological information. MuLex also provides an indirect correspondence between collocations in English and Italian. In other words, after accessing the term and its collocations in one language, users must click on the target-language equivalent and view its collocations. If direct correspondence could be established between collocations in the two languages, this would be useful for translators since otherwise it is difficult to infer the degree of equivalence.

Comparative analysis of online legal resources

In this section, we provide a comparative analysis of all the resources described in Section 2 in regard to the following features: (i) macrostructure of the dictionary; (ii) information included for source terms; and (iii) information given for translation correspondences.

As shown in Table 4.1, IATE, *TERMIUM*, and JURITERM include a large number of phraseological entries. All the resources analyzed include verb phraseological units. This is positive since such information is not generally found in lexicographic and terminographic resources. Moreover, all of them, except for JuriDiCo and MuLex, allow users to access phraseological information by the verb as well as by the noun, which enhances searches and information retrieval. As previously mentioned, all resources except MuLex provide direct translation equivalences.

Regarding the microstructure of source terms, JURITERM and Evroterm are the only termbases that do not include usage contexts. As observed by Faber and León-Araúz (2016), contextual information is vitally important because user understanding of an entity or group of entities depends on having access to the necessary information to activate the right frame or knowledge structure in which the word or term should be processed. In turn, the effective production of a specialized utterance also depends on the user having access to the combinatorial potential of the terms involved. When a terminological resource includes multilingual correspondences, contextual information becomes even more crucial because of the lack of isomorphism between languages and cultures

Apart from contextual information, IATE, *TERMIUM*, MuLex, and Evroterm also include a definition for some of the term entries. In addition, IATE and Evroterm offer a reliability code for each phraseological unit, whereas IATE and *TERMIUM* also contain a usage note for some entries. Finally, IATE, JURITERM, Evroterm, and MuLex provide the reference for each phraseological unit. It should be noted that JuriDiCo is the only resource whose metalanguage may sometimes be difficult to understand.

As for the translations of phraseological units, although the information provided for translations is supposed to be the same as for the source terms in each resource, this is not the case in practice. All resources offer one or various translations for a specific source phraseological unit, but they do not specify the degree to which the various translation options differ. It is true that JuriDiCo claims to specify the degree of equivalence of the various translation correspondences provided for the same source terminological unit. However, this is not always the case since most entries are incomplete. Moreover, extra theoretical knowledge is required to decipher the metalanguage. Table 4.1 summarizes the information contained by each resource:

Table 4.1 Comparative analysis of online legal resources

Resource	*Macrostructure of the resource*	*Information given for the source term entry*	*Information given for the translated terms*
IATE	• Large number of entries • Inclusion of verbal collocates • Retrieval by means of verbs or nouns	• Definition (for some entries) • Usage context • Reliability code • Reference from which the phraseological unit was taken • Usage notes (for some entries)	• Definition (for some entries) • Usage context • Reliability code • Reference from which the phraseological unit was taken • Usage notes (for some entries) • Synonyms. No degree of equivalence
TERMIUM	• Large number of entries (primarily for French and English) • Inclusion of verbal collocates • Retrieval by means of verbs or nouns	• Definition (for some entries) • Usage context • Usage notes	• Definition (for some entries) • Usage context • Usage notes • Synonyms. No degree of equivalence
JURITERM	• Large number of entries • Inclusion of verbal collocates • Retrieval by means of verbs or nouns	• Representative references from which the phraseological unit was taken • Lack of usage contexts	• Representative references from which the phraseological unit was taken • Synonyms. No degree of equivalence • Lack of usage contexts
Evroterm	• Limited number of entries • Inclusion of verbal collocates • Retrieval by means of verbs or nouns	• Definition (for some entries) • Reliability code (for some entries) • Reference from which the phraseological unit was taken (for some entries) • Lack of usage contexts	• Reliability code (for some entries) • Reference from which the phraseological unit was taken (for some entries) • Synonyms. No degree of equivalence • Lack of usage contexts
JuriDiCo	• Limited number of entries • Inclusion of verbal collocates • Only searches via the verb • Difficult theoretical metalanguage	• Frame • Actantial structure • Linguistic realizations of frame elements • Definition • Usage contexts (it requires theoretical knowledge)	(most terms) • Frame • Definition • Synonyms
MuLex	• Limited number of entries • Inclusion of verbal collocates • Only searches via the noun • No direct correspondences	• Definition • Usage context • Reference from which the term entry was taken • Collocations	(in another window) • Definition • Usage context • Reference from which the term entry was taken • Collocations • Synonyms. No degree of equivalence

Conclusions

Bilingual and multilingual legal resources play an essential role in the legal translation process. The problem is that most of these repositories are not well designed and, therefore, they cannot meet translators' needs. De Groot and Van Laer (2008) provide evidence of the poor quality of legal resources. They analyzed more than 200 bilingual paper legal dictionaries containing languages of Member States of the European Union, and concluded that only 12 dictionaries were of good quality. They underlined that most of these dictionaries were simply a list of legal terms in the source language and a list of translations in the target language without any further information regarding the legal context.

Because of the specificities of legal language, "legal dictionaries must be frequently reassessed and updated" (De Groot and Van Laer 2008). This is the reason why the internet seems to be the ideal platform for legal resources since it allows easier updates and no space constraints. In this regard, this paper describes a set of the most representative bilingual and multilingual legal online resources that contain phraseological information. The task of finding high-quality resources was far from easy since the web offers a large number of monolingual legal dictionaries, but still suffers from a lack of high-quality online legal resources. In other words, most bilingual or multilingual options are still only available in paper format.

The comparative analysis shows that a useful resource for legal translators who must deal with phraseology-related problems would include the following information:

- Noun and verb collocations since verbs are an essential category of language and verb collocations are very frequent in legal documents.
- Various ways of accessing phraseological information via the noun as well as the verb so as to enhance the retrieval of phraseological units.
- A definition and usage contexts to enhance knowledge acquisition and an understanding of the phraseological unit.
- Reference to the translation as evidence of its reliability.
- Direct correspondences between phraseological units in the various languages as well as an evaluation of the degree of equivalence in the same language or different languages.
- User-friendly interface without complicated metalanguage.

It goes without saying that legal paper dictionaries should not be set aside. Evidently, legal translators will continue to depend on a combination of digital resources and paper dictionaries to perform legal translation assignments.

Acknowledgements

This research was carried out within the framework of project FF2014–52740-P, *Cognitive and Neurological Bases for Terminology-Enhanced Translation* (CONTENT) funded by the Spanish Ministry of Economy and Competitiveness.

Notes

1 www.mt-archive.info/10/MTS-2013-W4-Corpas-Pastor.pdf
2 http://iate.europa.eu
3 http://iate.europa.eu/brochure/IATEbrochure_EN.pdf

4 According to https://tke2014.coreon.com/slides/2014_06_19_104_1150_Maslias_et_al.pdf
5 http://termcoord.eu/iate/about-iate
6 www.btb.termiumplus.gc.ca
7 We use the term *textual support* in line with *TERMIUM* Plus® terminology. www.btb.termiumplus.gc.ca/tpv2alpha/alpha-eng.html?lang=eng&srchtxt=&i=1&index=alt&codom2nd_wet=1&page=aide-help-eng#resultrecs
8 For more information regarding searches in *TERMIUM* Plus®, please visit: www.btb.termiumplus.gc.ca/tpv2alpha/alpha-eng.html?lang=eng&srchtxt=&i=1&index=alt&codom2nd_wet=1&page=aide-help-eng#resultrecs
9 www.juriterm.ca
10 www.evroterm.gov.si
11 ecolexicon.ugr.es
12 http://olst.ling.umontreal.ca/cgi-bin/juridico/search.cgi
13 http://olst.ling.umontreal.ca/cgi-bin/dicoinfo/search.cgi
14 http://olst.ling.umontreal.ca/cgi-bin/dicoenviro/search_enviro.cgi
15 The number is always included, even when the term has only one sense since it might be used in other sections in which the term entry appears.
16 *Semantic actants* are the arguments or participants associated with the predicate (see Mel'čuk 2004).
17 A screenshot is not provided since at the time of the query, the interface did not display properly.
18 http://mulex.altervista.org
19 The graphical symbol for the UK legal system has not been included for space constraints.

References

Baker, C.F., 2009. La sémantique des cadres et le projet FrameNet: une approche différente de la notion de 'valence'. *Languages*, 4: 32–49.

Biel, Ł., 2008. Legal terminology in translation practice: Dictionaries, Googling or discussion forums? *SKASE Journal of Translation and Interpretation*, 3(1): 22–38. <www.skase.sk/Volumes/JTI03/pdf_doc/BielLucja.pdf> [Accessed: 15/07/2016].

Buendía Castro, M., 2012. Verb dynamics. *Terminology*, 18(2): 149–166.

Buendía Castro, M., 2013. *Phraseology in Specialized Language and Its Representation in Environmental Knowledge Resources*. PhD thesis, University of Granada, Granada, Spain.

Buendía Castro, M. and Faber, P., 2015. Phraseological units in English-Spanish legal dictionaries: A comparative study. *Fachsprache: International Journal of Specialized Communication*, 37(3–4): 161–175.

Corpas Pastor, G., 1996. *Manual De Fraseología Española*. Madrid: Editorial Gredos.

Corpas Pastor, G., 2013. All that glitters is not gold when translating phraseological units (abstract). In J. Monti, R. Mitkov, and G. Corpas Pastor (eds.), *Proceedings of the Workshop on Multi-Word Units in Machine Translation and Translation Technologies*, 9–10. <www.mt-archive.info/10/MTS-2013-W4-TOC.htm> [Accessed: 15/07/2016].

De Groot, G.-R. and Van Laer, C.J.P., 2005. *Bilingual and Multilingual Legal Dictionaries in the European Union: A Critical Bibliography*. Maastricht. <http://arno.unimaas.nl/show.cgi?did=6364> [Accessed: 15/07/2016].

De Groot, G.-R. and Van Laer, C.J.P., 2008. *The Quality of Legal Dictionaries: An Assessment*. Working Paper. Maastricht Faculty of Law. <http://ssrn.com/abstract=1287603> [Accessed: 15/07/2016].

De Groot, G.-R. and Van Laer, C.J.P., 2011. Bilingual and multilingual legal dictionaries in the European Union: An updated bibliography. *Legal Reference Services Quarterly*, 30(3):149–209.

Faber, P. (ed.), 2012. *A Cognitive Linguistics View of Terminology and Specialized Language*. Berlin/Boston: Mouton de Gruyter.

Faber, P. and Buendía Castro, M., 2014. EcoLexicon. In A. Abel, C. Vettori and N. Ralli (eds.), *Proceedings of the 16th EURALEX International Congress*. Bolzano: EURALEX, 601–607.

Faber, P. and León-Araúz, P., 2016. Specialized knowledge representation and the parameterization of context. *Frontiers in Psychology*, 7(196). doi:10.3389/fpsyg.2016.00196

Faber, P. and López Rodríguez, C.I., 2012. Terminology and specialized language. In P. Faber (ed.), *A Cognitive Linguistics View of Terminology and Specialized Language*. Berlin/Boston: Mouton de Gruyter, 9–32.

Faber, P., 2009. The cognitive shift in terminology and specialized translation. *MonTI. Monografías de Traducción e Interpretación*, 1(1): 107–134.

Faber, P., 2011. The dynamics of specialized knowledge representation: Simulational reconstruction or the perception-action interface. *Terminology*, 17(1): 9–29.

Fellbaum, C., 1990. English verbs as a semantic net. *International Journal of Lexicography*, 3(4): 279–301.

Fillmore, C.J., 1977. Scenes and frame semantics. In A. Zampolli (ed.), *Linguistic Structures Processing*. Amsterdam: North Holland, 55–83.

Fillmore, C.J., 1982. Frame semantics. In The Linguistic Society of Korea (ed.), *Linguistics in the Morning Calm*. Seoul: Hanshin, 111–137.

Fillmore, C.J., 1985. Frames and the semantics of understanding. *Quaderni Di Semantica*, 6: 222–254.

Fillmore, C.J. and Atkins, B.T., 1992. Toward a frame-based lexicon: The semantics of RISK and its neighbors. In A. Lehrer and E.F. Kittay (eds.), *Frames, Fields and Contrasts: New Essays in Semantic and Lexical Organization*. Hillsdale: Erlbaum, 75–102.

Goźdź-Roszkowski, S. and Pontrandolfo, G., 2015. Legal phraseology today: Corpus-based applications across legal languages and genres [Editorial Preface of the Special Issue]. *Fachsprache*, XXXVII(3–4): 130–138.

Gustaffson, M., 1984. The syntactic features of binomial expressions in legal English. *Text. Interdisciplinary Journal for the Study of Discourse*, 4(1–3): 123–141.

L'Homme, M.C., 1998. Le Statut Du Verbe En Langue De Spécialité Et Sa Description Lexicographique. *Cahiers De Lexicographie*, 73(2): 61–84. <www.ling.umontreal.ca/lhomme/docs/cahiers-lexico-98.PDF> [Accessed: 22/02/2011].

L'Homme, M.C., 2008. Le DiCoInfo. Méthodologie pour une nouvelle génération de dictionnaires spécialisés. *Traduire*, 217: 78–103.

L'Homme, M.C., 2016. Terminologie de l'environnement et Sémantique des cadres. In *Congrès Mondial de Linguistique Française* (CMLF 2016). <http://olst.ling.umontreal.ca/pdf/LHomme_CMLF2016.pdf> [Accessed: 22/07/2016].

Lorente, M. and Bevilacqua, C., 2000. Los verbos en las aplicaciones terminográficas. In M. Correia (ed.) *Actas del VII Simposio Iberoamericano de Terminología RITerm 2000*. Lisboa: ILTEC.

Mel'čuk, I., 2004. Actants in semantics and syntax. I. *Linguistics*, 42(1): 1–66.

Peruzzo, K., 2013. *Terminological Equivalence and Variation in the EU Multi-level Jurisdiction: A Case Study on Victims of Crime*. Doctoral thesis in Interpreting and Translation Studies, IUSLIT, University of Trieste. <www.openstarts.units.it/dspace/ handle/10077/8592> [Accessed: 22/02/2016].

Peruzzo, K., 2014. Term extraction and management based on event templates: An empirical study on an EU corpus. *Terminology*, 20(2): 151–170.

Pimentel, J., 2015. Using frame semantics to build a bilingual lexical resource on legal terminology. In H.J. Kockaert and F. Steurs (eds.), *Handbook of Terminology*, Vol. 1. Amsterdam/Philadelphia: John Benjamins, 427–450.

Reimerink, A., García de Quesada, M., and Montero Martínez, S., 2010. Contextual information in terminological knowledge bases: A multimodal approach. *Journal of Pragmatics*, 42(7): 1928–1950.

Ruppenhofer, J., Ellsworth, M., Petruck, M., Johnson, C., and Scheffczyk, J., 2010. FrameNet II: Extended theory and practice. *ICSI Technical Report*. <http://framenet2.icsi.berkeley.edu/docs/r1.5/book.pdf> [Accessed: 22/02/2016].

Tiersma, P., 1999. *Legal Language*. Chicago: University of Chicago Press.

Vanderlinden, J., Snow, G. and Poirier, D., 2010. *La common law de A à Z*. Éditions Yvon Blais: Montréal.

Williams, C., 2004. Legal English and plain language: An introduction. *ESP Across Cultures*, 1: 111–124.

Wray, A., 2000. Formulaic sequences in second language teaching: Principle and practice. *Applied Linguistics*, 21(4): 463–489.

Part II

Phraseology and contrastive studies

5 A corpus investigation of formulaicity and hybridity in legal language

A case of EU case law texts

Aleksandar Trklja

Introduction

The aims of the present chapter are twofold. First, it contributes to the field of legal linguistics by providing evidence for the use of formulaic and hybrid expressions in legal language. The study will in particular focus on judgments of the Court of Justice of the European Union (CJEU). Second, it proposes new empirical methods for the study of discourse organization on the one hand and of semantic and grammatical profiles of lexical items on the other.

Traditionally, legal linguistic studies focus on the recurrent use of legal terms that have specific ideational meanings (e.g. Tiersma 1999) or on the impact that the rigid nature of formulaic expressions might have on law. However, there are no theoretical or methodological reasons why the study of repetition in legal language should be restricted to legal terminology understood in a narrow sense. In fact, legal terminology is part of formulaicity as a more general phenomenon. Apart from the fact that it is often very difficult to distinguish between legal and non-legal meanings of lexical items (e.g. Goźdź-Roszkowski 2011), formulaicity includes the types of expressions that have non-ideational meaning. Montolío (2001) and Goźdź-Roszkowski (2011), for example, illustrate how recurrent expressions contribute to the textuality of legal texts. McAuliffe (2009) also shows that drafters of the judgments at the CJEU are constrained by the formulaic style of these documents. This paper demonstrates that the investigation of types of formulaic expressions that signal discourse organization is key for an understanding of how information and argumentation develop in legal texts.

Another well-known feature of legal language is the use of idiosyncratic expressions. The expressions typically discussed in the literature (e.g. Charrow et al. 1982; Tiersma 1999) include legal archaisms (e.g. *further affiant sayeth not*, *be it known*) or formal and ritualistic words and phrases (e.g. *Wherefore the Plaintiff prays for relief as follows*). However, more recent studies (Kermas 2010; McAuliffe 2011; Biel 2014) indicate that such expressions in legal texts can also be created through translation. This is especially the case in the context of EU institutions where communication takes place to a large extent through translation. The language of EU institutions is described as being 'strange' because it departs from 'normal' use observed in non-translated texts (Born 1995; Muhr and Kettemann 2002; Tirkkonen-Condit 2001). This phenomenon is referred to as *hybrid language* (Schäffner and Adab 2001; McAuliffe 2011). However, linguistic aspects of hybrid languages have not been investigated in a systematic manner. The present paper demonstrates that this gap can be filled by using an approach based on a quantitative comparative analysis of local grammars. Hybrid expressions are considered as lexical items which are produced through translation into a target language, and the semantics of which depart from the semantics observed in 'standard' use.

The next section sets out the notions of formulaicity and hybridity. The subsequent two sections describe the role of the CJEU, as well as the data, methodology and theory used. Methods of analysis and results are then presented in the penultimate section in three individual studies.

Formulaicity and hybridity

In one of the earliest linguistic investigations of formulaic language, Pawley and Syder (1983) suggest that language users' mental lexicon consists of holistically stored linguistic sequences. They refer to these sequences as 'lexicalized or institutionalized sentence stems'. These units are of clause length or longer and according to the authors such expressions facilitate language processing. A similar view was expressed by Sinclair (1991) in his formulation of 'idiom principle':

> The principle of idiom is that a language user has available to him or her a large number of semi-preconstructed phrases that constitute single choices, even though they might appear to be analysable into segments.
>
> (Sinclair 1991: 110)

Subsequent empirical research both in corpus linguistics (e.g. Biber 2009) and psycholinguistics (e.g. Schmitt 2004; Wray 2005; Conklin and Schmitt 2012) provided further evidence for these claims.

Biber and Conrad (1999) proposed a corpus-driven method of investigation of formulaic language. The method, which was further elaborated in subsequent studies (e.g. Biber et al. 2004; Biber 2009) focuses on the distribution of frequently recurring fixed sequences of words called *lexical bundles*. Lexical bundles can be of various lengths but are typically 3- to 6-word long sequences. These sequences are incomplete structural units both in semantic and grammatical terms and can be classified into different classes according to their functions. These functions include epistemic meaning, the expression of attitudes, indication of references and signalling textual or discourse organization. To date the most comprehensive investigation of the lexical bundles that have textual function is Nesi and Basturkmen (2006). Goźdź-Roszkowski (2011) identifies typical lexical bundles in US legal texts and demonstrates how their distribution reveals variation of legal genres in American legal English.

The present study adopts the general principle of the analysis of lexical bundles. However, that principle is further developed here by introducing two new methodological features. First, previous studies say almost nothing about the degree of formulaicity of texts. They are concerned with the distribution of lexical bundles across registers and ignore individual texts. This paper addresses that issue using a new approach, set out in the section 'The Theory of Information Distribution in Text'. Secondly, as mentioned above, lexical bundles are structurally incomplete units. In contrast, the present paper focuses on units which are not only functionally and structurally complete but which are also associated with a specific textual position. These units are part of information structure in language and they signal discourse organization of texts.

The paper examines the following research questions in relation to formulaicity:

1. To what extent are CJEU judgments formulaic?
2. How do formulaic units contribute to the discourse organization of CJEU judgments?

The notion of hybridity that has its origin in the 19th century discourse of race (Young 2000) was first introduced to social science as an analytical tool by Bakhtin (1981) in *The Dialogic Imagination*. Since then, the term has been used in various disciplines such as social anthropology (Hannerz 1987), cultural studies (Bhabha 1994) or translation studies (Schäffner and Adab 2001). What is common to different definitions offered so far is that hybridity is seen as a force that creates new cultural forms, undermines the established ways of thinking and increases variety.

Schäffner and Adab argue that hybridity is the defining feature of translated texts because these texts do "not conform to established norms and conventions" (Schäffner and Adab 2001: 169). The 'strangeness' of translated texts relies on the fact that they contain linguistic features that do not occur in non-translated texts. It is because of these features that the language of translated text deviates from the use of language in non-translated texts (Bond 2001). Neubert (2001) warns that although translated texts might contain hybrid texts it would be wrong to consider them in their totality as hybrid. The present paper adopts the latter position.

In the context of legal studies, McAuliffe (2011, 2013) argues that legal judgments produced by the CJEU are hybrids because a) they are produced in a multilingual context and b) they are produced through translation. In an in-depth description of the work and procedures employed by the Court the author demonstrates how various types of legal texts are first produced in French and then translated into other languages. French serves as the working language of the CJEU but the majority of those involved in the text production process are non-native French speakers. In addition, these drafters work under time pressure and are expected to ensure coherence of EU law. All these factors contribute to the stylistic peculiarity of CJEU judgments.

The above research serves as a starting point to address the third research question:

3 Can we find linguistic evidence of hybridity of CJEU judgments?

CJEU judgments

The Court of Justice of the European Union is the highest court in the EU legal order. The main role of the CJEU as stated in Article 220 Treaty of Rome is to "ensure that in the interpretation and application of the Treaty the law is observed". The Court delivers binding judgments regarding questions of interpretation of EU law in up to 24 language versions (the 24 official languages of the EU) and those judgments constitute an EU case law.[1] Although the Court produces judgments in all EU official languages, for practical reasons that institution works in one language – French. Thus, all judgments are first drafted in French and then translated into the other EU official languages. However, only one version of a judgment is considered 'official', the version in the language of the case, which is rarely French.[2] In other words the official version of a judgment is more often than not a translation. A judgment is a collegiate text, the final version of which is agreed on by the relevant judges in secret deliberations in chambers. This final version, which is in French, is translated into the other official EU languages by lawyer-linguists who are professional lawyers by vocation but who are usually not trained translators. It is not uncommon that a lawyer linguist at one point moves to the position of référendaires who are legal assistants in judges' cabinets (McAuliffe 2011). CJEU judgments are thus multi-authored texts, created through translation. From the fact that the authentic version of a CJEU judgment is usually a translation it can be concluded the Court perceives translation as a neutral medium of communication that does not have any important impact on the form and content of EU case law.

The corpus of CJEU judgments

CJEU judgments have been collected in the present study and stored into several corpora and sub-corpora[3] to answer the three research questions introduced in the 'Introduction'.

The degree of formulaicity in CJEU judgments is investigated in a comparative study using two sets of sub-corpora. The first set consists of the English, French, German and Italian language version of CJEU judgments. Because an analysis of all available judgments in all official languages would be prohibitively time consuming for the purposes of the present paper, the relevant sample is restricted to 1140 CJEU judgments and to four languages. These judgments were produced in the period between 1955 and 2011 and the corpus comprises between 8 and 9 million tokens depending on individual languages. These judgments make up the EU *acquis communautaire* case law and are as such considered to be the most important judgments in EU law. The second set contains judgments produced by constitutional or supreme courts of EU member states in which English, French, German and Italian are official languages. This second corpus covers the same time period as the corpus of CJEU judgments and contains approximately the same number of words. Since the first three languages are used in two member states this second set includes judgments from seven national courts.[4] National constitutional or supreme courts were chosen since they are the closest types of national courts for comparative purposes to the CJEU.

Owing to limits of time and requirements regarding the length of the present paper, the second and the third questions are addressed only by focusing on the English-language versions of CJEU judgments. Analysis of the use of lexical items signalling discourse organization of judgments is based on CJEU judgments only. The occurrence of hybrid expressions is studied in a comparative analysis between CJEU judgments, UK Supreme Court (UKSC) judgments and texts from the British National Corpus (BNC).[5]

In addition to courts' decisions, the texts of judgments contain other sections consisting of summaries of facts and/or law, keywords or party names. Since the present analysis focuses on the language of decisions such sections have been removed from corpora by means of a Python script created for the purposes of the present paper. Other tools used in the studies and the procedure of analysis are described in the section with the case studies.

Theoretical and methodological issues

The theory of information distribution in text

Although sentences unfold in a linear fashion in a text, discourse has a structure (Hobbs 1985). Texts consist of discourse units which are semantically organized in terms of various types of relations. Discourse units have different discourse values or communication functions which are "determined largely with respect to the interaction between sentence meaning and context" (Crombie 1985: 2). This means that information development in discourse can be understood by looking at the ways in which sentences are related to each other.

The basic functional units in information structure are Theme and Rheme (Halliday 1985), which give a clause the character of a message. These two units are associated with specific positions in a clause. Theme refers to all the elements in a clause that start from a clause boundary and end with a finite verb and Rheme covers the rest of the clause. Theme serves as "the point of departure for the message . . . that with which the clause is concerned" (Halliday 1985: 38). The content of the message is developed in Rheme, which is typically associated with new information. The elements that occur in the Theme position, therefore, signal how the message will develop and the content of this message is located in Rheme. According to Halliday, there are three kinds of Themes: ideational or topical, interpersonal and textual. Ideational Themes indicate the propositional content of a clause or message, interpersonal Themes signal the writer-reader relationship and textual Themes are about how the distribution of information is signalled.

Building on this theory of information structure, Fries (1981) proposes a 'method of development' that goes beyond the analysis of clause relations and that demonstrates how information flows at the level of text. Lexical items that occur in the Theme position serves as cohesive ties and the method demonstrates how ideas develop in texts. Fries' method, in other words, imply that thematic items signal information structure not only of a clause and sentence but also of a discourse. For example, 'In those circumstances' typically indicates that the information in a given clause serves as a conclusion that follows from a unit of information provided in the previous stretch of discourse. This is illustrated in the following extract. Sentences are enumerated for the ease of referencing.

> 1) The Italian Government further claims that, without a guaranteed market outlet, the cultivation of durum wheat would disappear from the regions of the Mezzogiorno where it is practised. . . . 2) The statistics supplied to the Court show a steady increase in the market share held by pasta products made exclusively from durum wheat in other Member States in which they already face competition from pasta made from common wheat or from a mixture of common wheat and durum wheat. 3) **In those circumstances**, it is clear that the fears expressed by the Italian Government as to the disappearance of durum-wheat growing are unfounded.

The first sentence introduces a claim for which contradictory evidence was provided in the second sentence. The textual Theme 'In those circumstances' from the third sentence finally refers to the content of the previous sentence and signals that if this is true then it can be concluded that the original claim is wrong and should be rejected.

The studies conducted to date (e.g. Halliday 1985; Fries 1995; Martin 1995) have been concerned with the flow of information investigated in terms of ideational meaning or ideational motifs. It means that the contribution of interpersonal and textual Themes has been ignored. Since the objective of the present paper is to investigate how the flow or organization of information in text is signalled, the most relevant kinds of Theme are those that denote textual meaning. In addition, unlike previous studies which are concerned with short texts, the results presented in the study below derive from a quantitative analysis.

Halliday (1985) proposes a system of logico-semantic relations that accounts for relations between clauses.[6] This system provides a sound basis for the study of the functions of textual Themes. Due to word limits this system can only briefly be described here and for a more detailed explanation an interested reader is referred to Halliday (1985) or Martin (1992). Halliday distinguishes between three kinds of logico-semantic relations: Elaboration, Extension and Enhancement.

Elaboration items serve to signal that one clause "elaborates on the meaning of another by further specifying or describing it" (Halliday 1985: 203). These items indicate that the subsequent clause does not contain new information but instead provides further characterization of a previous clause. There are three types of Elaboration items:

- Exposition indicates restatement (e.g. *in other words*);
- Exemplification indicates providing examples (e.g. *for example*);
- Clarification indicates further clarification of a message (e.g. *in other words*).

Extension items signal that a clause adds new information to a previously introduced message.

Distinctions can be made between:

- Addition indicates adding new content to an existing message (e.g. *in addition*);
- Alternation indicates variation in the content of a message (e.g. *in the alternative*);
- Variation indicates replacement of the content of a previous message (e.g. *on the contrary*).

Enhancement items signal qualifying the content of a message by reference to time, place, manner, cause or condition:

- Temporal relations indicate successive or simultaneous order (e.g. *at the same time*);
- Spatial relations indicate at what point something happened (e.g. *in the present case*);
- Manner relations indicate by what means something happened (e.g. *in this way*);
- Causal-conditional relations indicate for what purpose something happened (e.g. *for this reason*).

Information structure and logico-semantic relations are defined in terms of the position of lexical items in a clause. Since the automatic identification of textual Themes in CJEU judgments at clause level is not possible and a manual analysis is not practically possible for the purposes of the present paper, the present study is restricted to the sentence level.

Following Fries' (1981: 135) findings that "the information contained within the Themes of all the sentences of a paragraph creates the method of development of that paragraph", it is assumed that the study of textual Themes in sentences can indicate the organization of discourse at paragraph level. In addition, Moore (2016: 10) argues that "the fundamental function of INFORMATION STRUCTURE is to divide the flow of discourse into manageable units . . . that punctuation functions to divide written discourse into manageable units". Relying on this, it is assumed that commas demarcate the items that have textual meaning in text. The units of analysis selected to deal with the second research question are all multi-word, sentence-initial expressions that end with a comma.

The local grammar approach

The local grammar approach was developed by Gross (1987, 1993, 1997) and its purpose was to account for how rules locally constrain co-occurrence of words. The approach relies on Harris' distributional theory of language (e.g. Harris 1954, 1988) and the theory of finite-state local automata (e.g. Roche and Schabes 1997).

First it is assumed that "the occurrence of each word in an utterance depends on the occurrence there of an element – any element – of some stated subset of words" (Harris 2002: 216). This claim is similar to the notion of s(semantic)-selection introduced by

Chomsky (1965), which specifies restrictions between lexical items that co-occur in the same textual context. With any lexical item there will be a limited number of co-occurring items that will constitute a sub-set within a general grammar category. For example, *beautiful* and *poor* are both adjectives that can be preceded by adverbs. However, it does not mean that these two adjectives select any type of adverbs. Thus, according to the BNC, *beautiful* collocates with *stunningly*, *breathtakingly*, *strikingly* but not with *desperately* or *pretty*, which are found with *poor*.

The co-selection of lexical items[7] is of a finite-state nature because "short range constraints between words in sentences are crudely accounted for by Markovian [or finite-state] models" (Gross 1997: 330). In other words, local co-selection relations between lexical items, unlike relations in general syntax, include restricted options because they involve constraints of combination of words. Finite-state automata are powerful devices that can account for constraints operating on a local syntactic level (Roche and Schabes 1997). These constraints allow or preclude particular classes of combinations (Harris 1991). One simple example of a finite-state automaton is illustrated in Figure 5.1, which presents the finite-state nature of the co-occurrence of *beautiful* and *poor* and their collocates. As can be seen, each finite-state automaton has one initial state and one finite state denoted by the leftmost arrow and the rightmost square respectively. These states simply mean that a linguistic unit has a beginning and end. The central rectangles represents an inventory of options available for the construction of a lexical item. As in this example, the options include sets or paradigms that might contain one or more elements.

The diagram represents only a segment of the local grammars of *beautiful* and *poor*. In reality the number of elements would be much higher and the relations between them much more complex.

The structure of strings generated through a local grammar can be represented by means of phrase structure rules introdu/ced by Chomsky (1957). This type of string rewriting system has an initial string and a string derived by means of a rule. Although this algorithmic device has been mainly used to show relations between lexical items and general parts-of-speech categories it will be demonstrated below that it can be adopted to describe relations at the local grammar level.

Staying with the same example, the adverbs observed above with *beautiful* do not occur with equal likelihood (*strikingly* is found in a stronger collocation in this context than

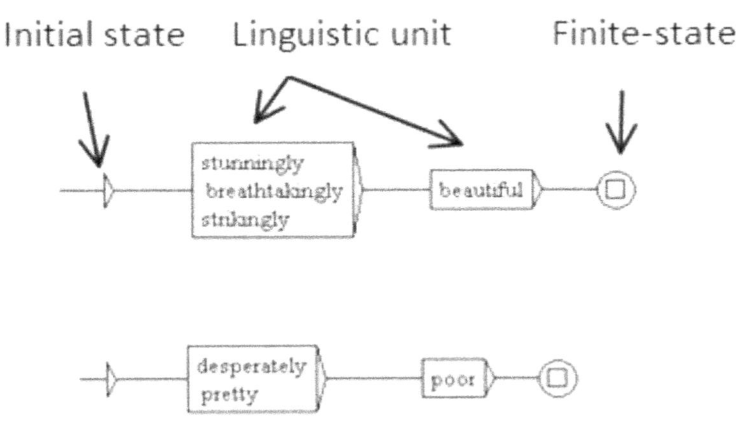

Figure 5.1 An example of a finite-state automaton

stunningly, which is found in a stronger collocation than *breathtakingly*). This is because linguistic systems are probabilistic (Halliday 1991: 42) and with every lexical item there will be inequalities or grading from most to least likely collocates (Harris 1991). Through the investigation of these inequalities we can identify typicality of co-occurrence of lexical items.

It is the probabilistic nature of co-occurrence of lexical items that can help to distinguish between hybrid and non-hybrid expressions. In other words, the question of whether a lexical item 'departs' or not from a usual usage will depend on whether the likelihood of co-occurrence of collocates corresponds or not to that which is found in a corpus that represents a standard language use. The finite-state automata make it possible to capture the types of lexical items that characterize the use of hybrid items in a systematic manner.

Linguistic analysis of formulaicity and hybridity in CJEU judgments

Study I: degree of formulaicity

This study addresses the first research question introduced above. In order to deal with this question, it is first necessary to establish a method of measuring the degree of formulaicity of CJEU judgments and to find a model of investigating this extent at the textual level. To deal with the first requirement the study compares the degree of formulaicity in CJEU and in national judgments. The judgments produced by supreme or constitutional courts of EU member states will serve as yardsticks that reflect a 'standard' level of formulaicity in the register of legal judgments. The extent of formulaicity in CJEU judgments will therefore be measured with respect to these standard values. The second requirement is captured by calculating the percentage of repeated expressions in individual judgments.

The units of analysis used in the study are all repetitive lexical bundles that are at least five words long. The only two criteria for deciding the length of lexical bundles are the size of corpora and the frequency of lexical items (Biber 2006). The preliminary investigation shows that 5-word lexical bundles are sufficient to mirror adequately the occurrence of formulaic expressions in the relevant corpora. Owing to the practice of citation and to the principle of precedent in common law systems in particular (e.g. Brenner 1992), judgments might occasionally contain longer textual chunks. For this reason, those expressions which are longer than 5-word lexical bundles are also included in the present analysis.

Preliminary analysis indicates that there are two factors that can influence results: a) the number of texts compared and b) the length of texts. In addition, corpora with fewer texts tend to have a lesser degree of repetition and corpora with a larger number of texts have more variations in the length of texts. For example, 50 repeated words found in a text that has 300 words comprises 17% and in a text that has 3000 words less than 1%. To overcome these problems a range of samples that consist of 100 texts (from CJEU and reference corpora) was created. In both corpora the number of texts from different years varies and there are more texts from more recent periods. In the CJEU corpus 32% of the texts analyzed are from the 1990s, 23% from the 1980s, 22% from the period between 2000 and 2010, 4% from 1960, about 1% from the period between 2010 and 2012 and less than 1% from the 1950s. For this reason texts are selected at the proportional rate for each decade. Whenever possible the same proportion and decades were reflected in the reference corpora. There are also significant differences in the style of reporting judgments between different countries; therefore an attempt was made to select texts of similar size and to exclude those that are either very short or very long.

Because investigations of this kind are extremely time- and resource-consuming the findings presented below are based on analysis of five samples of 100 judgments. For the same reason, it was not possible to carry out an analysis covering all 24 official languages. Instead, the study is restricted to four languages: English, German, French and Italian. The first three languages are used in two EU member states and it means that the study covers four languages and seven national courts.

At the next stage, a calculation was carried out to show in terms of percentage values expressions that occur in other texts. The analysis was divided into two steps. First, all 5-word or longer multi-word expressions that occur in samples and in the rest of the corpus are identified. This analysis was carried out in both sets of corpora. A Python script was created to compare each text from the five samples to all other texts from the corpus in order to identify repetitive multi-word expressions that occur in study texts. After that the average values for these texts were calculated and results between CJEU and national judgments were compared.

The average values of degree of formulaicity for all relevant judgments are displayed in Figure 5.2. Bars with striped lines denote the results of CJEU judgments and dotted bars of national judgments.

It can be observed that, with the exception of judgments of the French Constitutional Court, in all instances CJEU judgments tend to contain more formulaic expressions than national judgments. The first conclusion to be drawn is that there is more similarity it terms of formulaicity between national judgments than between them and CJEU judgments. The high formulaicity degree of CJEU judgments and this difference highlight the unique linguistic style of these judgments. Differences that can be observed across languages are due to structural differences between languages which have an impact on the size and number of n-gram constructions. These differences, therefore, do not demonstrate that, for example, English judgments are more formulaic than German judgments. German is a synthetic and English is an analytic language, which means that the same unit of meaning can be realized in the former as one word and in the latter in two or more words.[8]

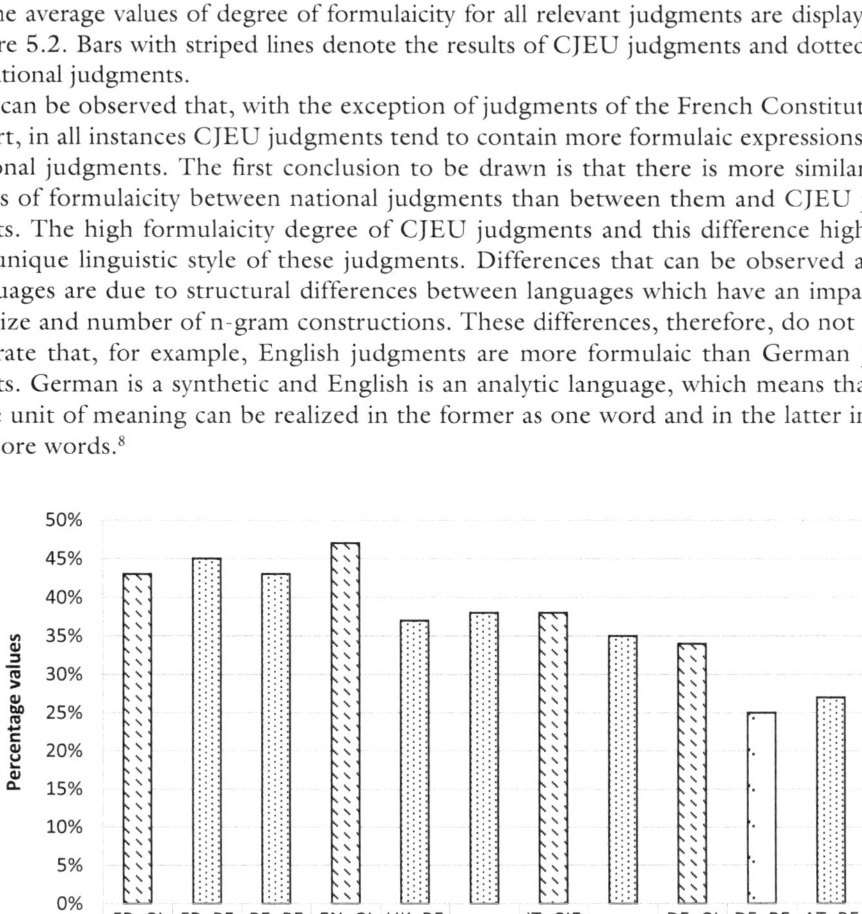

	FR_CJEU	FR_REF	BE_REF	EN_CJEU	UK_REF	IE_REF	IT_CJEU	IT_REF	DE_CJEU	DE_REF	AT_REF
Series1	43%	45%	43%	47%	37%	38%	38%	35%	34%	25%	27%

Figure 5.2 Degrees of formulaicity in CJEU and national judgments

A test of significance was conducted to determine whether the differences between formulaicity values in CJEU and national judgments are statistically significant. A one-way Anova test was performed for German, English and French because these data sets contain three variables and an independent t-test for Italian because there are only two variables here. The results indicate that the difference between CJEU and national judgments is statistically significant ($F = 12.8$, $p = 0.000$) only for English versions of judgments. Statistically significant differences cannot be observed in French ($F = 1.5$, $p = 0.218$), German ($F = 1.8$, $p = 0.156$) and Italian (t-score (298) = -1.3, $p = 0.200$).

The results demonstrate that the method employed can successfully provide the values of the degree of formulaicity at the textual level. These values indicate that formulaicity is one of the features of CJEU judgments because the degree of formulaicity tends to be beyond the standard level observed in national judgments. The statistical tests indicate that formulaicity is especially strongly associated with the English version of CJEU judgments. Finally, the fact that judgments of the French Constitutional Court have a high degree of formulaicity is indicated. French is the working language of the CJEU and French administrative law served as a model for EU case law in its formative years. From this one can assume that legal French has influenced the linguistic shape of CJEU judgments. This hypothesis deserves further investigation.

Study II: discourse organization and formulaicity

As mentioned above, the units of analysis selected to address the second research question are all multi-word, sentence-initial expressions that are at least two words long and that end with a comma. In the first stage of analysis, 1760 linguistic units that met the above criteria were extracted in the English version of CJEU judgments by means of Corpus Query Processor (CQP) tools. These units are between two and six words long. Their frequency and quantity are displayed in Figure 5.3. Since the figures for the two variables differ in scale the results are summarized in terms of their log values.

Biber (1995) reports that correlation between the length and frequency of lexical bundles can be observed in his data. In contrast, in the present data the most numerous items

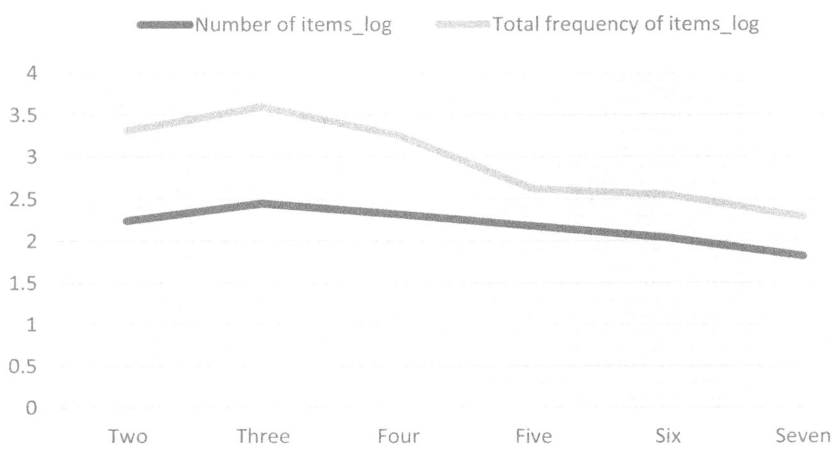

Figure 5.3 The frequency and number of Themes in CJEU judgments

are not the shortest linguistic units. This might suggest that structurally and functionally complete formulaic expressions have preferences regarding length. Figure 5.3 also shows that the number of items corresponds to their frequency, which means that once their length is established the frequency of lexical items can be predicted.

In the next stage of analysis, the identified linguistic units were classified into three types of textual Themes following Halliday's system. First, it is assumed that the least frequent items do not contribute to the formulaicity of judgments. This assumption is justified by the results which show that items occurring five times, or more frequently, make up 67% of the frequency of all items identified. These more frequent items, therefore, reflect the typical use of thematic items and they were thus selected for further investigation. Out of 248 Themes 49% have a textual function, 26% interpersonal and 25% ideational function. In terms of frequency of occurrence, 80% are textual Themes and the other two types 10% each. These results indicate that the beginning of sentences in CJEU judgments typically serve to signal organization of discourse. It can also be concluded that the same items tend to be more often re-used when it denotes the meaning of textual rather than interpersonal or ideational Themes.

At the next stage all textual Themes identified (108 items) are classified into categories in terms of the system of logico-semantic relations. Since the focus of the study is on the method of development of texts, all ideational and interactional Themes are excluded from further consideration. Figure 5.4 displays the distribution of textual Themes in relation to all categories and sub-categories from the system of logico-semantic relations.

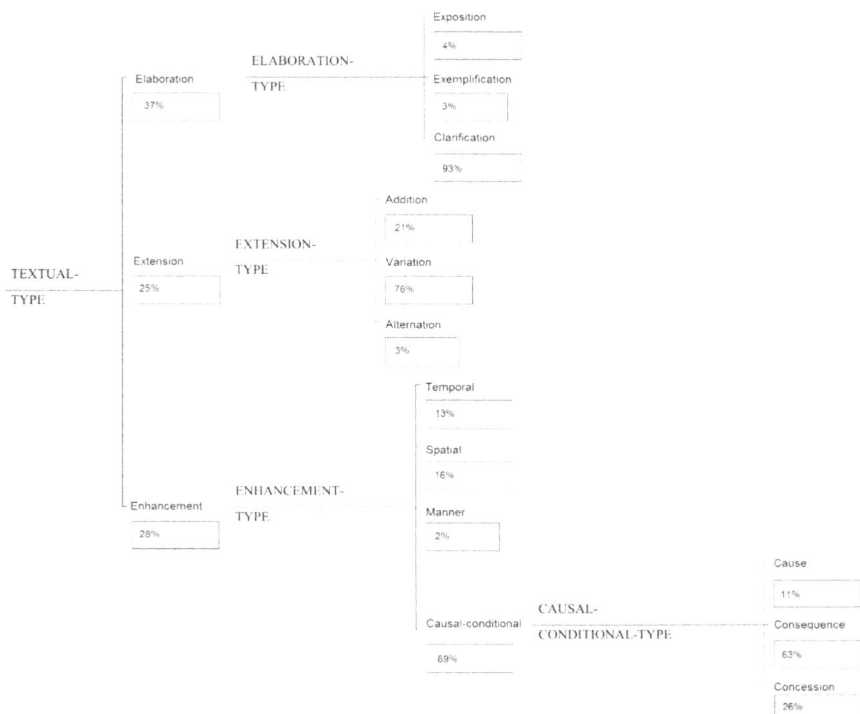

Figure 5.4 Frequency of textual Themes in terms of logico-semantic relations

There are, at first sight, no important differences between the three kinds of relations (Enhancement, 38%; Elaboration, 37%; and Extension, 25%) but greater variations can be observed with respect to more delicate options. Thus, textual Themes that denote Causal-conditional relations occur with higher likelihood than other types of Enhancement. It follows that it is very typical for the Court to reason its decision by first developing certain points and then clarifying its position towards issues expressed by means of these points. This type of relation is most frequently realized by means of the lexical items such as *In those circumstances*, *On those grounds*, *In that case*, *For that reason*, *In such circumstances*, *As a result*, *It follows that*, *On that basis*, *That being the case*. Similarly, Clarification is the most typical kind of Elaboration and Variation is the most typical kind of Extension found in CJEU judgments. This means that textual Themes in CJEU judgments often signal that a subsequent piece of discourse will contain an additional explanation or correction or contrasting view. The most frequently used Clarification items are *In particular*, *On the one hand*, *In effect*, *In this connection*, *In any case*, *What is more*, *In reality*, *In essence*, and the most frequently occurring Verification items are *On the contrary*, *On the one hand*, *By contrast*, *In contrast*.

Grammatically, 92% of all textual Themes are prepositional phrases. The items from the same categories usually consist of identical grammatical and lexical elements. For example, the majority of Clarification items have the structure <in + DET + connection|regard|respect> such as in *In that regard*, *In that respect* or *In this connection*. Vertical bars here indicate alternative options and DET denote determiners. To give another example, Causal-conditional items have the following structure: <In|Under + those|these|those|the + circumstances|situation>. These results indicate the formulaic nature of textual Themes by showing that individual types of textual Themes are made up of restricted sets of lexical items.

Figure 5.4 displays the distribution of textual Themes in terms of their frequency. Figure 5.5, on the other hand, shows the number of items found within individual categories and sub-categories. The items belonging to the category Enhancement appear to be most numerous. However, this has to do with the nature of taxonomy rather than with linguistic devices used in CJEU judgments, because the Enhancement category contains more sub-categories than the other two categories. One striking feature in the data is that two types of the most frequently used types of textual Themes (Clarification and Variation) have lower figures in this second graph. Thus, the Clarification items that in terms of frequency make up 93% of all Elaboration items occur with the value 75% in terms of the number of items per categories. The respective values for the Variation items are 76% and 44%. At first sight, this does not seem to be the case with the items from the category Consequence but this is only true as long as we compare the three most delicate sub-categories of Enhancement items. However, if we compare figures globally we can see that the value for this category is 34% in terms of frequency and 23% in terms of the number of items. All these differences demonstrate that the most frequently used types of textual Themes tend to be re-used more often than the less frequent types. It follows that drafters of CJEU judgments tend to re-select from a small set of available resources. This has a direct impact on how the flow of information and reasoning is organized in CJEU judgments.

The results of the present analysis show that textual Themes serve as formulaic expressions that signal discourse organization of CJEU judgments. The flow of information in these judgments is typically based on the devices signalling that the subsequent discourse provides more information, contrasting views or that the content of the subsequent discourse is conditioned by what was said before. In terms of argumentation theory it can

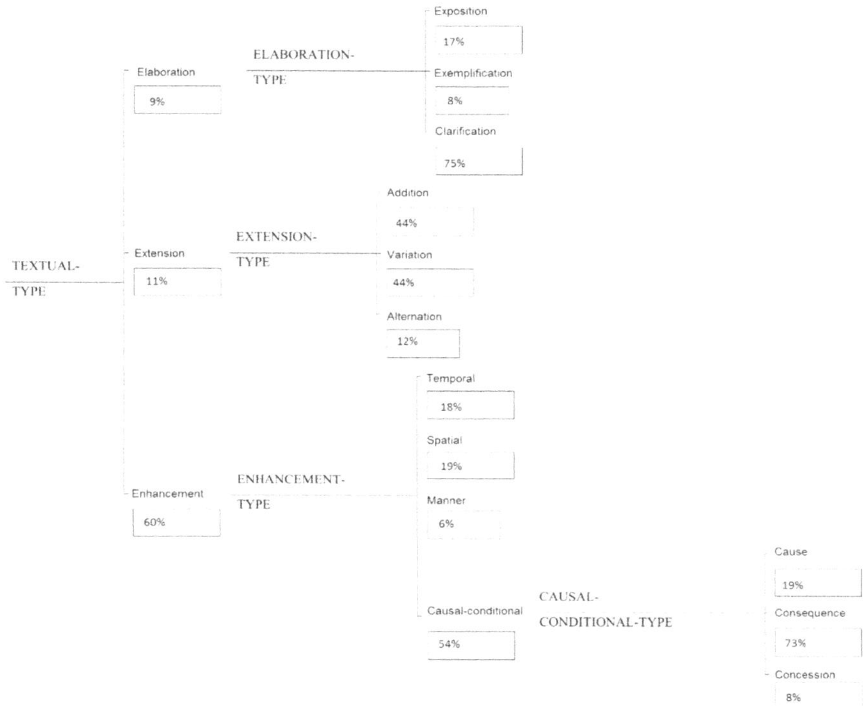

Figure 5.5 Numbers of textual Themes in terms of logico-semantic relations

be said that the Court puts emphasize on providing clear arguments and creating logically valid inferences.

Study III: hybrid expressions

To identify potential candidates to be considered as hybrid expressions, two keyword analyses were carried out using WordSmith tools (Scott 2012). As explained above, the reference corpora used in the study are the BNC and a corpus of judgments of UK Supreme Court (UKSC). The purpose of conducting two instead of one analysis is to identify expressions with high keyness values with respect to general English and the UK legal English. These values indicate that items depart from the standard use as reflected in the BNC and the UKSC.

First, the keyword lists obtained in the two analyses were compared and only those items that occurred with high keyness value in both analyses were selected for further analysis. Since the purpose of the present study is to explore the occurrence of hybrid expressions created through translation, only those linguistic items with suffixes historically borrowed from French were taken into account. The assumption here is that the influence of French as a source language will be more visible for those English lexical items which are historically related to French. Some of the suffixes imported from French in the Middle English period which are still in use are *–bility*, *–ble*, *–nym*, *–ary*, *–ment* (Dalton-Puffer 1996;

Zergollem-Miletic 1997). These lexical items are mainly nouns and the final stage of analysis involved the creation of a keyword list of all nouns that occur in CJEU judgments. The candidates identified in the data in this way include *interoperability* (198), *compatibility* (56), *competition* (5), *concentration* (17), *consumption* (38), *cooperation* (24), *distribution* (36), *inadmissibility* (88), *notification* (46), *objections* (26), *production* (19), *treatment* (92). The numbers in parenthesis indicate words' ranks in the keyword list of nouns that contain 8300 nouns that occur at least five times in the corpus of CJEU judgments.

To explore whether these items depart from established use it is necessary to fully understand their distribution. Such analysis is demonstrated here by exploring the use of the lexical item *compatibility*. First its most typical collocates are identified across three corpora and the results are compared. Then the local grammar approach is used to conduct a fine-grained analysis of its grammatical and semantic profile.

The lexical item *compatibility* is 22 times more likely to occur in CJEU judgments than in the BNC and 11 times more likely in CJEU judgments than in the UKSC. It follows that it generally prefers occurring in the legal register. It occurs in a verb and noun phrase: a) as an argument in the frame V + *compatibility*, and ii) as a complement in the frame N + of + *compatibility*.

With regard to the frequency of occurrence of verbs and nouns from these two grammatical frames, the items that occur only once can be ignored because they do not reflect typical collocates. The lexical item *compatibility* occurs with a larger number of verbs in CJEU judgments (37) than in the BNC (23) or UKSC (29). Also, there are four nouns that colligate with *compatibility* in CJEU judgments, one in the UKSC and none in the BNC. The BNC is 17 and the UKSC 5 times bigger than the corpus of CJEU judgments and one would therefore expect inverse results.

A closer investigation of the types of words that occur with *compatibility* shows that it is most typically associated with expressions that denote assessment. There are eight verbs with this meaning in the first structure and four nouns in the second structure. As can be observed from Table 5.1, all these items occur with the highest likelihood in CJEU judgments. The figures show raw frequency values and the occurrence of lexical items per million words. For example, <assess> is 84 and <examine> 53 times more likely in CJEU

Table 5.1 Collocates of *compatibility*

Lexical items	*Freq_CJEU*	*Per mil_CJEU*	*Freq_UK*	*Per mil_UK*	*Freq_BNC*	*Per mil_BNC*
assess	49	7.332098	3	0.087351	2	0.017811
examine	41	6.135021	4	0.116467		
consider	10	1.496347	10	0.291169		
review	4	0.598539	2	0.058234		
prejudge	2	0.299269				
enquire	2	0.299269				
appraise	2	0.299269				
verify	2	0.299269				
assessment	16	2.394154				
examination	15	2.24452				
analysis	4	0.598539	2	0.058234		

judgments than in UK judgments. The first item is 412 times more common in the CJEU corpus than in the BNC. Using the understanding of hybridity formulated above it can be concluded that *compatibility* occurs in hybrid expressions in CJEU judgments.

However, the collocation analysis is insufficient because it does not provide a comprehensive description of the distribution of this item. It is only through such a description that we can understand the 'strangeness' of a hybrid expression. At the next stage of analysis, the rules that govern the relationship between *compatibility* and its collocates are established.

Such a description is presented below first in the form of rewriting rules (Chomsky 1957) and then a finite-state diagram. [1] and [2] below show first the structure of the verbal and determiner phrase in which *compatibility* occurs. After that, the members of the parts-of-speech categories are specified. The local grammar sets identified here are ASSESS and COMPATIBILITY in [1] and ASSESSMENT and COMPATIBILITY in [2]. They contain the collocates listed in Table 5.1.

1 VP → V + DP
V → ASSESS
DP → D + NP
D → the
NP → COMPATIBILITY
ASSESS → assess, examine, consider, review, prejudge, enquire, appraise, verify
COMPATIBILITY → compatibility

2 DP → D + NP
D → the, a, possessives
NP → NP + PP
NP → ASSESSMENT
PP → P + DP
P → of
DP → D + NP
D → the
NP → COMPATIBILITY
ASSESSMENT → assessment, examination, analysis, review
COMPATIBILITY → compatibility

A further investigation shows that both structures further colligate with the prepositional phrase PP + DP. In [3] first the general phrasal structures and then the local grammar categories are described. The nouns that occur in this prepositional phrase can be classified according to their denotation into three classes: legal acts (coded as LEGAL ACT), international companies (coded as COMPANY) and financial support (coded as AID).

3 PP → P + DP
P → of
DP → D + NP
D → the, a, that, zero plural
NP → LEGAL ACT, COMPANY, AID
LEGAL ACT → legislation, right, rule, decision, decree
COMPANY → concentration, merger
AID → aid, measure, transaction

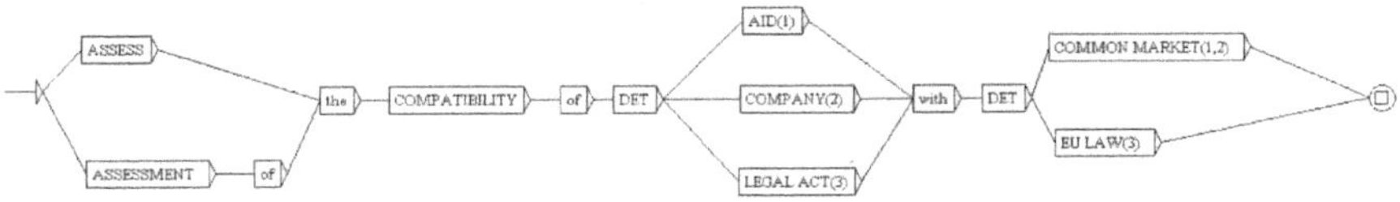

Figure 5.6 A local grammar diagram of *compatibility*

The data in the present study allow further specification of the semantic and grammatical profile of *compatibility* [4]. The existing structure colligates with another prepositional phrase. The preposition observed here is *with*, the determiner is either *the* or zero plural and the types of nouns observed are conditioned by the items established at the previous stage. The items from the categories AID and COMPANY collocates only with *common market* (coded as COMMON MARKET), whereas the items from the category LEGAL ACT collocates with expressions that refer to EU law (coded as EU LAW).

4 PP → P + DP
P → with
DP → D + NP
D → the, zero plural
N → COMMON MARKET | EU LEGAL DOCUMENT
COMMON MARKET → common market
EU LAW → Treaty, Second Directive, EU or Community Law

With this, the final stage of the analysis of the local grammar associated with *compatibility* is reached. [5] shows the complete structure in terms of parts of speech categories. LU here refers neutrally to the whole construction as a linguistic unit. The entire local grammar is displayed in the form of a finite-state graph in Figure 5.6. Numbers indicate which types agree with each other. For example, AID(1) and COMPANY(2) agree with COMMON MARKET(1) but not with LEGAL ACT(3). Vertical bars again indicate alternatives.

$$LU \rightarrow \begin{matrix} VP + \\ \\ NP + \end{matrix} \left[PP + PP \right]$$

This analysis demonstrates that CJEU judgments contain hybrid expressions which result from the translation of judgments from French into English. As illustrated through the analysis of *compatibility* such hybrid expressions have a unique grammatical and semantic profile and as such are less typically occurring in the standard UK English varieties. A repeated use of the same lexical items with *compatibility* indicates also the formulaic nature of this hybrid expression.

The results of this analysis also demonstrate that a combination of a keyword analysis with the investigation of words that have origin in a specific language can help identify potential candidates for hybrid expressions. Whether a candidate is a hybrid expression or not is then established through a comparative analysis collocation analysis. Finally, a local grammar analysis provides a detailed description of the types of structures, patterns and items associated with a given hybrid expression.

Conclusion

The following conclusions about the nature of CJEU judgments follow from the above studies:

- The high degree of formulaicity is one of the defining features of CJEU judgments;
- The argumentation of CJEU judgments relies on a limited number of textual devices;
- CJEU judgments contain hybrid expressions which are created through translation.

Furthermore, the studies prove the validity of the models proposed in the present paper. The first study demonstrates how the degree of formulaicity can be studied at the textual level. The second study illustrates that an investigation of sentence-initial textual Themes can show how these expressions signal the development of information in texts. Finally, the local grammar approach provides a fine-grained description of grammatical and semantic structures of hybrid expressions.

In a previous study (Trklja and McAuliffe, forthcoming) it was demonstrated that paragraph initial multi-word units signal the discourse organization of the entire texts of CJEU judgments. The main pattern observed in that study was that the argumentation is based on the Consideration-Conclusion pattern. Semantically, this pattern corresponds to the consequential type of Causal-conditional types of logico-semantic relations. The lexical items that signal this type of relations also occur with high frequency in the position of textual Themes. It follows that the same kind of devices are used as discourse organizers both at the macro level of entire texts of judgments and at the paragraph level. These relations serve as the primary principle of argumentation in CJEU judgments. Following Koestler (1964) it can be argued that these devices indicate routinization of thinking at the CJEU. Routinization is understood as the process of selection of "the sub-codes of grammar and syntax . . . [which are] are almost wholly automatized" (Koestler 1964: 12).

One might wonder how the evidences of routinized thinking may be reconciled with the findings that demonstrate the use of hybrid expressions. Hybrid expressions are associated with the creation of new cultural forms, undermining the established ways of thinking, and variety. This question can be answered only briefly here. First, although it is true that translation creates semantic diversity in CJEU judgments due to re-selection of established translation candidates it also serves as a force that ensures that this diversity does not devolve into chaos and disintegration. Second, once new concepts have been created they become established and through repetitive and routinized reasoning they play an important role in embedding the rule of law. Through its case law, the early CJEU developed and extended its own jurisdiction and transformed the European Union from a traditional international organization into a new type of legal order (Harmsen and McAuliffe 2014). As the EU legal order became more established, the level of lexical variation in CJEU judgments seems to have dropped.

Acknowledgements

The research for this paper was carried out as part of the European Research Council (ERC) funded project 'Law and Language at the European Court of Justice'. For more details of this project please see www.llecj.karenmcauliffe.com. I wish to thank anonymous reviewers, the editorial team of the book and Karen McAuliffe for constructive and helpful comments on the earlier version of the paper. The usual disclaimers apply.

Notes

1 At the time of going to press there are 24 official EU languages. These are, in English alphabetical order: Bulgarian, Croatian, Czech, Danish, Dutch, English, Estonian, Finnish, French, German, Greek, Hungarian, Irish, Italian, Latvian, Lithuanian, Maltese, Polish, Portuguese, Romanian, Slovakian, Slovenian, Spanish, Swedish.

2 Each case has a 'language of procedure' and only the judgments produced in the language of procedure are considered 'authentic', in spite of the fact that they are usually translations. For more information on the language regime at the CJEU see McAuliffe (2011, 2013).

3 These corpora have been compiled within the European Research Council (ERC) project 'Law and Language at the European Court of Justice'.

4 These courts are: *Verfassungsgerichtshof Österreich* (the Constitutional Court of Austria), *Bundesverfassungsgericht* (German Federal Constitutional Court), *UK Supreme Court*, the *Supreme Court of Ireland*, *Corte costituzionale della Repubblica Italiana* (the Constitutional Court of the Italian Republic), *Conseil constitutionnel* (French Constitutional Council) and *Grondwettelijk Hof* or *Cour constitutionelle* (the Constitutional Court of Belgium).

5 A fuller and more cohesive study relating to these questions is being carried out in the ERC-funded 'Law and Language at the European Court of Justice' project. For further information see www.llecj.karenmcauliffe.com.

6 Although called *logico-semantic relations* these are purely semantic relations because they do not include logically valid inference relations between propositions. However, for the sake of clarity the established term is used here.

7 Chomsky (1957) argues that finite-state grammars present a model which is too simple to describe the syntax of natural languages. They have a too limited expressive power to capture complex combinatorial options available in the syntax of general language.

8 To get more comparable results of formulaicity across languages it would be necessary to identify appropriate lengths of lexical bundles for each language. Although of interest, this is beyond the scope of the present paper.

References

Bakhtin, M.M., 1981. *The Dialogic Imagination: Four Essays* (C. Emerson, Trans., M. Holquist, Ed.). Austin, TX: University of Texas Press.

Bhabha, H.K., 1994. *The Location of Culture*. New York: Routledge.

Biber, D., 1995. *Dimensions of Register Variation: A Cross-Linguistic Comparison*. Cambridge: Cambridge University Press.

Biber, D., 2006. *University Language: A Corpus-Based Study of Spoken and Written Registers*. Amsterdam: John Benjamins Publishing.

Biber, D., 2009. A corpus-driven approach to formulaic language in English: Multi-word patterns in speech and writing. *International Journal of Corpus Linguistics*, 14(3): 275–311.

Biber, D. and Conrad, S., 1999. Lexical bundles in conversation and academic prose. *Language and Computers*, 26: 181–190.

Biber, D., Conrad, S., and Cortes, V., 2004. If you look at . . . : Lexical bundles in university teaching and textbooks. *Applied Linguistics*, 25(3): 371–405.

Biel, Ł., 2014. *Lost in the Eurofog: The Textual Fit of Translated Law*. Frankfurt am Mein: Peter Lang.

Bond, N., 2001. Interpreting the objectively 'strange' and the strangely 'objective'. *Across Languages and Cultures*, 2(2): 251–259.

Born, J.S.W., 1995. *Eurotexte: Textarbeit in einer Institution der EG*. Tübingen: Gunter Narr.

Brenner, S., 1992. *Precedent Inflation*. New Brunswick, NJ: Transaction Publishers.

Charrow, V.R., Crandall, J.A., and Charrow, R.P., 1982. Characteristics and functions of legal language. In R. Kittredge and J. Lehrberger (eds.), *Sublanguage: Studies of Language in Restricted Semantic Domains*. Berlin: Walter de Gruyter, 175–190.

Chomsky, N., 1957. *Syntactic Structures*. New York: Mouton.

Chomsky, N., 1965. *Aspects of the Theory of Syntax*. Cambridge: MIT Press.
Conklin, K. and Schmitt, N., 2012. The processing of formulaic language. *Annual Review of Applied Linguistics*, 32: 45–61.
Crombie, W., 1985. *Process and Relation in Discourse and Language Learning*. Oxford: Oxford University Press.
Dalton-Puffer, C., 1996. *The French Influence on Middle English Morphology: A Corpus-based Study on Derivation*. Berlin: Walter de Gruyter.
Fries, P.H., 1981. On the status of theme in English: Arguments from discourse. *Forum Linguisticum*, 6(1): 1–38.
Fries, P.H., 1995. A personal view of theme. In M. Ghadessy (ed.), *Thematic Development in English Texts*, 1–19. London: Pinter, 1–20.
Goźdź-Roszkowski, S., 2011. *Patterns of Linguistic Variation in American Legal English: A Corpus-based Study*. Frankfurt am Mein: Peter Lang.
Gross, M., 1987. The use of finite automata in the lexical representation of natural language. In M. Gross and D. Perrin (eds.), *Lecture Notes in Computer Science 377, Electronic Dictionaries and Automata in Computational Linguistics*. Berlin: Springer-Verlag, pp. 34–50.
Gross, M., 1993. Lexicon based algorithms for the automatic analysis of natural language. In F. Beckmann and G. Heyer (eds.), *Theorie und Praxis des Lexikons*. Berlin: Walter de Gruyter, pp. 218–239.
Gross, M., 1997. The construction of local grammars. In E. Roche and Y. Schabes (eds.), *Finite-State Language Processing*. Cambridge, MA: The MIT Press, 329–354.
Halliday, M.A.K., 1985. *An Introduction to Functional Gramm*ar. London: Edward Arnold.
Halliday, M.A.K., 1991. Towards probabilistic interpretations. In E. Ventola (ed.), *Functional and Systemic Linguistics: Approaches and Uses*. Berlin and New York: Mouton de Gruyter, 39–61.
Hannerz, U., 1987. The world in creolisation. *Africa*, 57(4): 546–559.
Harmsen, R. and McAuliffe, K., 2014. The European courts. In J.M. Magone (ed.), *The Handbook of European Politics*. London: Routledge.
Harris, Z.S., 1954. Distributional structure. *Word*, 10(2/3): 146–162.
Harris, Z.S., 1988. *Language and Information*. New York: Columbia University Press.
Harris, Z.S., 1991. *A Theory of Language and Information: A Mathematical Approach*. Oxford and New York: Clarendon Press.
Harris, Z.S., 2002. The structure of science information. *Journal of Biomedical Informatics*, 35(4): 215–221.
Hobbs, J.R., 1985. On the coherence and structure of discourse. *Technical Report*: 85–37, Center for the Study of Language and Information (CSLI), Stanford, CA.
Kermas, S., 2010. English legal discourse and the French continuum. In D. Giannoni and C. Frade (eds.), *Researching Language and the Law*. Berna: Peter Lang, 49–69.
Koestler, A., 1964. *The Act of Creation*. London: Hutchinson.
Martin, J.R., 1992. *English Text: System and Structure*. Amsterdam: Benjamins.
Martin, J.R., 1995. More than what the message is about: English theme. In M. Ghadessy (ed.), *Thematic Development in English Texts*. London: Pinter, 223–259.
McAuliffe, K., 2009. Translation at the Court of Justice of the European Communities. In F. Oslen and D. Stein (eds.), *Translation Issues in Language and Law*. New York: Palgrave Macmillan.
McAuliffe, K., 2011. Hybrid texts and uniform law? The multilingual case law of the Court of Justice of the European Union. *International Journal for the Semiotics of Law*, 24: 97–115.
McAuliffe, K., 2013. The limitations of a multilingual legal system. *International Journal for the Semiotics of Law*, 26(4): 861–882.
Montolío, E., 2001. *Conectores de la Lengua Escrita*. Barcelona: Ariel Practicum.
Moore, N., 2016. What's the point? The role of punctuation in realising information structure. *Written English Functional Linguistics*, 3/6: 1–23.

Muhr, R. and Kettemann, B. (eds.), 2002. *Eurospeak: der Einfluss des Englischen auf europäische Sprachen zur Jahrtausendwende*. Frankfurt am Mein: Peter Lang.

Nesi, H. and Basturkmen, H., 2006. Lexical bundles and discourse signalling in academic lectures. *International Journal of Corpus Linguistics*, 11(3): 283–304.

Neubert, A., 2001. Some implications of regarding translations as hybrid texts. *Across Languages and Cultures*, 2(2): 181–193.

Pawley, A. and Syder, F.H., 1983. Two puzzles for linguistic theory: Nativelike selection and nativelike fluency. In J.C. Richards and R.W. Schmidt (eds.), *Language and Communication*. London: Longman, 191–225.

Roche, E. and Schabes, Y., 1997. *Finite-State Language Processing*. Cambridge, MA: MIT Press.

Schäffner, C. and Adab, B., 2001. The idea of the hybrid texts and translation: Contact as conflict. *Across Languages and Cultures*, 2: 167–180.

Schmitt, N. (ed.), 2004. *Formulaic Sequences: Acquisition, Processing, and Use*. Amsterdam: John Benjamins Publishing.

Scott, M., 2012. WordSmith Tools, version 6. Stroud: Lexical Analysis Software.

Sinclair, J.M., 1991. *Corpus, Concordance, Collocation*. Oxford: OUP.

Tiersma, P., 1999. *Legal Language*. Chicago, IL: University of Chicago Press.

Tirkkonen-Condit, S., 2001. EU project proposals as hybrid texts: Observations from a Finnish research project. *Across Languages and Cultures*, 2(2): 261–265.

Trklja, A. and McAuliffe, K., forthcoming. Metadiscursive signalling devices in legal language: A corpus-based model for studying discourse organisation. *Journal of Applied Linguistics*.

Wray, A., 2005. *Formulaic Language and the Lexicon*. Cambridge: Cambridge University Press.

Young, L., 2000. Hybridity's discontents: Rereading Science and 'race'. In A. Brah and A. Coombes (eds.), *Hybridity and Its Discontents: Politics, Science and Culture*. London: Routledge, 154–170.

Zergollem-Miletic, L., 1997. Morphological adaptation of the suffixes of English nouns borrowed in French. *Studia Romanica et Anglica Zagrabiensia*, 42: 411–416.

6 The out-grouping society

Phrasemes othering underprivileged groups in the International Bill of Human Rights (English-French-Spanish)

Esther Monzó Nebot

This chapter will focus on how binomials and multinomials structure our social experience and crystallize a specific world view through their use and reproduction in legal documents. Through the study of these types of phrasemes in the International Bill of Human Rights (IBHR), this contribution will explore what divisions are operated by the international community to organize our shared social experience (Foucault 1991a). The study builds on Sinclair's stress on the relation between meaning and choice (1998: 2), his focus on the mutual influence of form and meaning (1998: 12), and the distinction between phrasemes' phraseological and terminological tendencies. By scrutinizing how fixed the divisions by which the international community organizes the world behave, I will explore whether the prevailing social divisions crystalized in binomials and multinomials are dichotomous by studying whether references to underprivileged groups have been lexicalized and are together understood as the specific set of humans which requires protection or whether these groups are considered individually in discourse.

To develop the hypothesis that divisions represented in binomials and multinomials can shed light on how society structures the world, this contribution will first explore the cognitive and social foundations of groupings. To justify the choice of the IBHR as the focus of the study, the chapter will then proceed to discuss theoretical approaches and empirical studies on how international human rights legislation exerts cognitive colonialism by dictating domestic sociopolitical structures. It will be further suggested that cognitive biases crystallizing in international documents can endanger the goal of uniting the 'human family' (UNGA 1948). The analysis of these biases in the IBHR will be used to determine how international societies are developing and resisting the international discursive order with the support of translation. To do so, the discursive choices of the English, French, and Spanish versions of the documents composing the IBHR will be discussed.

Grouping, in and out

As our ancestors were evolving from ape-like societies to modern human societies (Barkow et al. 1992), inter-group contacts and conflicts were a matter of life and death (Alexander 1987; Shaw and Wong 1989; Ghiglieri 1999). Resources within a territory were limited and invasions were threats to survival. The fact that groups were small and isolated increased their possibilities in such an environment, but precluded internal division of labor and the appearance of any motivation for external exchanges (Edgerton 1992; Stiner et al. 1998). The ability to quickly identify group members and react against outsiders made social and biological sense (Turner et al. 1987), so in- and out-grouping individuals on the spot became powerful survival mechanisms. With larger and more complex societies, trade made its appearance and those mechanisms lost their relevance (not necessarily their ascendancy) when the need to cooperate with other groups became the real vantage point (Cosmides and Tooby 1992).

Societies have become ethnically diverse and are expected to increase their diversity (Cornelius and Rosenblum 2005). Identities are now not only based on ethnical grounds, and the features ensuring membership to a group are subject to change (Van den Berghe 1981). Yet, however defined, identities remain a central issue in human life (Tajfel 1982). In- and out-grouping are still very powerful mechanisms and even if conflicts resulting from out-grouping others may under present social and historical circumstances do more harm than good to societies (Eibl-Eibesfeldt 1998; Goetze 1998; Salter 2008), we construct out-groups that we can judge as inferior and stereotype (Matsumoto 2009: 355). Whereas out-grouping triggers hostility, in-grouping is the source of care. Self-categorization with a group makes us process in-group members individually (Sporer 2001), and it is individualizing and in-depth contact that precludes stereotyping and other mechanisms associated with discrimination, bias, and hate (Beck 2002; Broockman and Kalla 2016). As social structures increase their complexity, population grows, globalization reinforces divisions of labor, and trade exchanges intensify, reciprocal altruism (Trivers 1971) seems a fitter strategy (Correll and Park 2005; Dovidio et al. 2005), promoted by the international legal order (see UNGA 1948).

As an elaborated method to address conflicts in attaining common social goals and to provide remedies, the law plays a crucial role in ensuring we all know what societies expect from us and what we can expect from them. When embarking on the ambitious enterprise of sharing complex social spaces regardless of our manifold differences, historical and social evolution are strong determinants of our values and policies (see Koopmans and Michalowski 2016: 25). Even if the rules of the game are clearly worded and commonly accepted, controversies over desirable values and degrees of equalities are often present in all sorts of discourses involving all kinds of individuals. The question is whether in drafting the laws humans were able to defy primal behavioral patterns. Are all human beings equally human before the law? As conveniently put by Barthes (1953: 20), language is never innocent and, even inadvertently, our use of language reveals the boundaries we draw between our own conceptions of *wedom* (in-group) and *theydom* (out-group). Also through language, we can access, expose, discuss, and review our struggles to become productive members of diverse social organizations.

Human rights

Some disciplines travel well. Some scholars work on the assumption that their objects of study behave in the same way anywhere on the planet. Law, however, represents a special case as it is essentially local and closely tied to – even embedded in – language in various ways. Every culture has developed throughout its own history its own set of rules on how to better solve its own issues and conflicts, and its own rationality on which issues deserve problematizing and how to address them (Smith 1968; Connolly 2010). Even the concept of 'right' is far from present in every human culture whereas to some it is "the maker of citizenship, our relation to others" (Williams 1991: 164).

Of course, human rights are first and foremost 'rights' and therefore constructs. Their particularity, however, is that an international system has evolved to such an extent that no State can now legitimately deal with human rights issues as they do with domestic matters (Joseph 2010: 35). One of the claims of the law on human rights is indeed universality

(UNGA 1948; Turner 2006: 3). The ambition is that any individual, irrespective of their circumstances,[1] can enjoy the protection of their human rights. This claim does not obscure the fact that rights are social constructs based on particular values, purportedly those put forward by liberal democratic states (see UNGA 1993), which brings the issue of cultural incommensurability to the fore. Building on cultural relativism, incommensurabilists claim that the way we frame the world is not only defined by culture but disables us from fully understanding another culture's *Anschauung*. As a consequence, whoever has been raised and exposed to the ideas of one legal culture becomes cognitively biased in approaching any other (see, for instance, Geertz 1983: 170–175). Arguments (Singh 2003; Legrand 2005) and counter-arguments (Connolly 2010; Baaij 2014) have been proposed building on different dogmas, and they have also been taken by governments themselves to advance some regime's interests (Le 2012). Indeed, an international governance system implies a displacement of the power to define what is the competence of the State and what is not, to restructure the categories and essential dualisms (good/bad, reasonable/unreasonable, licit/illicit) by which societies are organized. Within structures, resistance against the established divisions and categories develops and, if successful, replaces them continuously in a cycle of creative destruction.

The issue of incommensurability is relevant – especially to Translation Studies (TS) – in a world that sees itself as globalized, but it remains empirically unsolved. A hurdle to that enterprise is that the foundations of the law on human rights are largely hidden (Mooney 2014) and that the dynamics of multilateralism, with a focus on generalized principles of conduct (Ruggie 1992: 571), have traditionally allocated testimonial presence to minorities. These issues loom large in human rights legal and political studies, trigger discontent, and threaten adherence to and compliance with international agreements. From the linguascape of international organizations (see, for instance, UNGA 1946) to the location and workload of their headquarters, minority cultures have been less present and represented in multilateral negotiations, even when a degree of ethnolinguistic democracy was available through translation and interpreting.

The cultural imbalance can be equated with a social imbalance. Indeed "feminism and cultural relativism have been among the most vigorous and the most visible critiques of human rights discourse" (Brems 1997: 136). Globally disprivileged cultures and socially disprivileged identities share an imposed delegation of voice and agency. They are categorized in groups that frame their possibilities within development plans contrived by those who are indeed well represented in the international community and hold the power to distribute individuals in groups. Categories 'other' these individuals, in-group some and out-group others, and specific identities are minored in a process where representation simplifies instead of exposing individualized complexities. Labels help the international legal system profess aims of protection. In so doing, however, are they defining underprivileged groups altogether as the out-group in the collective imaginary and sentencing them to the lower positions in society? How meaningful can recognition be when framed in the mainstream constructions of the in-grouped? Reconciling the need for recognition and protection under the law and the benefits of individualization to prevent discrimination is indeed a difficult enterprise. How does human rights legislation solve the issue?

Other studies dealing with the language of human rights have dealt with how 'human rights' are understood in society in general (Stenner 2011) and the media in particular (Mooney 2012), how human rights discourse is used in (anti-)European nation-building efforts (Kjær and Palsbro 2008), how technical language can prevent vulnerable and minoritized groups from benefitting from the rights that the instruments and institutions purport to protect (Ochoa 2003), how language shapes rationalities and policies (Cohn 1987), how it is used to build common enemies and strengthen identities (Stychin 2004), to silence other identities (Brems 1997), or to advance justice and counter terrorism (Teitel 2002). Underlying some of these studies, a recurrent idea suggests that rationalities and divisions, especially dichotomist divisions, voiced in human rights discourse exert a spooky disciplinary action by normalizing identities according to streamlined (and simplified) bureaucratic models (Baca 2009).

We will approach such a question by focusing on the binomials and multinomials designating and organizing human groups in the International Bill of Human Rights (IBHR). The IBHR consists of the Universal Declaration of Human Rights (UNDHR) (UNGA 1948), the International Covenant on Economic, Social and Cultural Rights (ICESCR) (UNGA 1966b), and the International Covenant on Civil and Political Rights (ICCPR) (UNGA 1966a) and its two Optional Protocols (UNGA 1966c, 1989). The Bill was adopted in the aftermath of WWII, in a traumatized world that had been witness to the blatant violation of basic rights by the government of a prosperous country. The defeated regime was based on the unlimited powers of a State against individuals. The signatories of the UN Charter (United Nations 1945) were determined to establish a direct relationship with individuals, irrespective of their nationality, that could offer human beings protection against any particular government. The question arises: are the divisions of human beings portrayed in the IBHR conducive to the advancement of human rights?

Dichotomous and categorical thinking in othering and ordering

Dichotomous thinking is the tendency to think in 'black and white'. In this 'all-or-nothing' thinking, nuances are reduced to binary oppositions, leading to extreme evaluations. Empirical studies have linked this style of thought with cognitive disorders that impede or even deter optimal adaptation (Beck 1999; Oshio 2009; 2012). Dichotomous thinking is deemed to be a cognitive bias that prevents the holder from capturing the complexities of the world, and distorts perceptions by diminishing differences within categories and exaggerating discrepancies between different groups (Krueger and Clement 1994; Rothbart and Davis-Stitt 1997).

Categorical thinking is the tendency to assign subjects and objects to categories, in a way that those subjects and objects are simultaneously perceived with whatever attributes the perceiver assigns to the category. For over 40 years, the bias was deemed inevitable, as human minds need the help of categories, and the related prejudice, to understand and be operative in the world (Allport 1954: 20). However, more recent studies have gathered data attesting to the centrality of attitudes of perceivers towards the members of the target group (Lepore and Brown 1997; Wittenbrink et al. 1997), and to the relevance of motivation (Bargh 1994; Spencer et al. 1998), as categorical thinking has been proved to be activated when judging a member of the 'othered' group increases the perceivers' self-worth.

Both cognitive biases lead to stereotyping and reality distortion, and both have been seen to ameliorate when increasing the exposure of the individual to the object of such evaluations (Allport 1954; Brendel et al. 2016). To produce durable changes in perception, however, exposure should be activated on a regular basis (Macrae and Bodenhausen 2000). By developing the perception of nuances along continuums such as race, sex, or age, simplistic views of identities can be prevented.

Othering builds on those two biases to out-group a culture by dividing and distinguishing. Othering is "essentially about constructing dualisms" (Maccallum 2002: 88; see also

Bruce and Yearley 2006). In times of social distress, it signals difference and associates the target with danger (Finney and Simpson 2009: 167). Translation Studies has extensively explored how cultures other one another and how translation can bring the other home (Carbonell i Cortés 2000). Whether translators' sensitivity and efforts to provide nuances and build a continuum have the expected impact on the public has yet to be answered (Tymoczko 2012: 94). Linguistic, textual, and cultural hybridities that mimic other cultures in home-relevant shapes have been suggested as a strategy to reconstruct otherness, challenge established categories, and build non-dichotomous representations.

And yet political discourses stress oppositions between a group to which voters can relate and the 'others', which can be portrayed as a threat to security, cultural values, or 'home' identities, or as the origin of unpopular measures. Nation-building efforts are particularly keen on those practices (Stychin 2004; Chin 2009), but also migration policies (Ghorashi 2010) seem to work on the assumption that one is either the national 'normal' or the foreign 'other'. Also, governance builds partially on those biases in structuring the range of possibilities others live by. In order to govern, divisions need to be posited and operated (Foucault 1991b: 74). Particular views on identities are enshrined in the normative logic and ontology that shape practices and naturalize the positions of the so-formed groups as either dominant or needing protection (see Foucault 1982), present in the rationale or referred to in the text. How could we reveal those views in order to approach them critically? How could phraseology play its part in advancing a critical perspective on society and the establishment?

Phrasemes, binomials, and multinomials

When approaching multiword units as phrasemes, two distinctions have been objects of controversy: the limits between compounds and phraseological units and the differences between phrasemes and multiword terms (see Granger and Paquot 2008). The issues arising from the conceptualization of multiword units as compounds or phrasemes focus on their morphology (lexical units written as either one word, a hyphenated word, or two consecutive words with no punctuation or grammatical words acting as link) (Bauer 1988; Sager 1997). Granger and Paquot suggest including multiword compounds as referential phrasemes, together with binomials and trinomials (Granger and Paquot 2008: 42), which solves the question by adopting an eclectic position. What is relevant to this study is that a compound usually designates a single concept (Meyer and Mackintosh 1994: 3), whereas phrasemes may maintain the meaning of their integral parts.

The second distinction, between 'terms' and 'phrasemes', has produced a number of commentaries (Meyer and Mackintosh 1994; Cabré et al. 1996; Oster 2004, 2005). A widely accepted criterion is based on Sinclair's (1991) differentiation of open and restricted co-selection rules among words. The 'open-choice principle' (Sinclair 1991: 109) or 'terminological tendency' states that language is the result of a great number of complex choices, restricted only by grammaticalness and local restraints. This tendency would account for unrandomness in word choices when there are experiential and social relations between the notions covered by the words and the participants they address in communicative situations. Another principle, the 'idiom principle' or 'phraseological tendency', is needed to explain those choices which "have little or nothing to do with the world outside" (Sinclair 1991: 110). Sinclair argues that words related in such a way have unclear meanings and the debate must therefore focus on uses, since the compounding words are often even delexicalized and users have no real option to choose other alternatives. Mel'čuk (1995:

168) also stresses the fixed (set, frozen) nature of these combinations, which the author calls 'phrasemes'.

Whether the list of words used to identify human groups in the IBHR are sequences of words whose combination is determined by linguistic convention or by individualized reference to concepts or participants will be the focus of this study. Some of those groupings are binomials (Malkiel 1959: 113; Bhatia 1993: 197–198), whose use has been abundantly documented and explored in the study of legal language (Koskenniemi 1968; Gustafsson 1984); others are multinomials (an extension of the same concept), which have attracted less attention in studies of legal phraseology. Together they are defined as "a sequence of two or more words or phrases belonging to the same grammatical category having some semantic relationship and joined by some syntactic device such as 'and' or 'or'" (Bhatia 1993: 197). The issue posed by 'some semantic relationship' is controversial, as a great part of the available research has focused on synonymic expressions. In these cases, studies argue that binomials are used for rhetorical emphasis and precision, constitute an important ingredient of legal language (Charrow et al. 1982: 179–180; Hiltunen 1990: 55; Bhatia 1993: 108; Tiersma 1999: 31–32, 61–65), and may have their origin in the translation of Latin sources of law where vernacular words were used as glosses for the unfamiliar Latin terminology (Mellinkoff 1963: 345–349; Jumpertz-Schwab 2000: 84–107; Mattila 2012).

In this research, binomials and multinomials are studied as the divisions which the international community operates to organize our shared social experience (Foucault 1991a). By designating specific individuals or groups and silencing others, categories are conveyed that may or may not be faithful to the complex identities of the members of the human family, but that will consequently be used to organize human beings in their political spaces and, when relevant, to distribute resources. To participate in the system and become politically relevant, that categorical language must be learned and acted on. And yet, by accommodating our discourse to the established divisions, by taking those multinomials as a reference in our shared experiences and discourses, we limit what we can say and, in the long run, think. That discipline, in Foucault's terms (1975), or 'spooky action at a distance', in Einstein's (Einstein et al. 1935), has political and physical consequences in the empirical world and its inhabitants.

Sinclair's (1998: 2) stress on the relation between meaning and choice implies that patterns of co-selection are most relevant when determining meaning. If the particularized analysis of binomials and multinomials can provide insights into the divisions by which the international community organizes the world, the phraseological or terminological behavior of the different items within those phrases can help us see whether the prevailing divisions are dichotomous. By determining the (in)variability of these phrases we can observe whether there is a phraseological tendency, and whether references to underprivileged groups have been lexicalized and are together understood as the specific set of human groups which requires protection. If the expressions behave as lexicalized phrases, internal distinctions would bear little relevance to the construction of meaning (since co-selection is based on text-construction rules), even though their compound nature may recall their origins in a number of groups (see Sager 1990: 73). On the other hand, if the patterns of co-selection ruling the behavior of those phrases are open, that is, if meaning is the key in the co-occurrence of the elements in the phrase, the focus would be on their relative specificity vis-à-vis other vulnerable groups, as the particular integrating items would behave as distinct terminological units (co-selection based on meaning).

Binomials and multinomials in the International Bill of Human Rights

To approach the question of how bureaucratic divisions designing vulnerable groups are, the IBHR will be used to explore the international consensus on how individual identities were identified and organized in the international society at its conception, what divisions were recognized and accepted to distinguish types of human beings before the law, and what kind of *Anschauung* can be identified between categories and, if applicable, dichotomies. Words and sequences of words referring to human groups will be first identified in the English, Spanish, and French versions of the instruments (a corpus of 44,981 words). This will shed light on the categories used for international governance at a time in history when protection of and care for human beings had peaked. To observe how othering the discourse in these documents acts, that is, to what degree distinctions are based on antagonizing dualisms, the textual functioning of binomials and multinomials will be studied to determine whether they posit a dichotomous view of humanity. Further, a synchronic study of the documents issued by the Security Council in 2015[2] will reveal how fixed or 'frozen' the phrases used are. This will allow us to determine whether these phrases present a terminological tendency, focusing on the specific nature of each group, or a phraseological one, blurring the lines between groups and focusing on their otherness.

A first analysis of the IBHR was conducted using TAMSAnalyser (Weinstein 2002–2012) for Macintosh OS X to manually code all references to human beings and human groups in the English, French, and Spanish versions of the five instruments included in the IBHR. The coding, which will be used only partially in the present study, was based on a primary distinction between human beings and human groups, but no other subcode was predefined. The resulting codification was structured as follows:

- Human > being > Neutral
- Human > being > Male
- Human > being > Female
- Human > being > TwoGenders
- Human > being > Underaged > neutral
- Human > being > NonPolitician
- Human > being > OfficeProfession > neutral
- Human > being > OfficeProfession > male
- Human > being > Vulnerable
- Human > group > Family
- Human > group > Social
- Human > group > State
- Human > group > Demographic
- Human > group > OfficeProfession
- Human > group > Everyone
- Human > group > Vulnerable

It should be noted that female human beings first appeared in the 1966 instruments, although they are included in the phrase 'all men and women' in the 1948 document. This binomial was coded as detailing two genders and reflects the traditional Western categories to classify human beings. In opposition to the binomial 'peoples and nations', the expression 'men and women' is used as a lexicalized phrase, as it is premodified as a unit in 'all men and women'. On the contrary, in the phrase 'all peoples and all nations', which appears three times in the IBHR, both terms are treated separately as two distinct notions. Even though the use of 'and' does not allow us to understand the binomial as a compound, the fact that 'men', 'he', 'himself', or 'his' are used in the same document to refer to human beings as a whole seems to give 'women' an accessory function, with the purpose of closer determining one same concept (Sager 1990: 73).

This phraseological behavior is not matched in the French version, which premodifies both terms of the equation separately ('à l'homme et à la femme', 'des hommes et des femmes'), thereby conferring women a particularity which is absent in the English version. In the Spanish version, the binomial does not behave consistently, as it is used both as a phrase ('a hombres y mujeres') and as two distinct terms ('del hombre y de la mujer', or 'al hombre y a la mujer').[3] No instances of 'women and men' occur, nor are 'she', 'her', or 'herself' used to refer to the whole group of human beings, which testifies to a consistent division that, in this case, is dichotomous.

The categories ordering society are clear in the IBHR as far as gender is concerned, but they may have been overcome in institutional usage, especially considering the advancements society has accomplished in the area of LGBT rights. To find out whether the tendency found in the IBHR is reflected in the language and world view of the present international community, the 2015 proceedings of the Security Council of the United Nations were analyzed using AntConc (Anthony 2014). Two searches – 'men and women' and 'men and * women'[4] – were conducted. Results showed one case (out of 26 occurrences) where 'women' behaved individually in the binomial ("That means encouraging the broadest selection of credible candidates – men and particularly women – and setting a clear timeline for appointment"). Contrary to the use in the treaties, proceedings in 2015 used the binomial in the reversed order ('women and men') on 12 additional occasions (see Table 6.1). By reversing the order, the phraseological tendency is questioned and so is the vision of women being second to men in ordering our society.

When taking all public documents published by the UN between 1990 and 2014 (Ziemski et al. 2016), the phrase 'men and women' appears 36,152 times and 'women and men' is used 27,913 times, which seems to suggest that the terminological tendency seen in the French version of the IBHR is now present in the English version of UN documents.

The French version of the proceedings shows only three instances of 'femmes et hommes' but it is worth noticing that in one of those the article is used only once, in front of the feminine noun modifying both ('les femmes et hommes' in document SPV7530). This would be contrary to French linguistic usage, which seems to signal a strong interference of divisions as expressed in English. The inversion with a phraseological behavior happens also once in the Spanish version (see sentence *g* in Table 6.1). The masculine + feminine version is used 37 times and among these it is striking to find some examples where other languages choose the reverse order. Those discrepancies between linguistic versions can be found in *f–j* in French and *h–j* in Spanish:

It is also worth noticing how the French version individualizes the different terms in the multinomials by repeating the corresponding articles even when that article keeps the same form in different genders, such as 'des hommes et des femmes', when 'des hommes et femmes' would be rare but possible (see *a*, *b*, *d*, *f*, *g*, *j*, and *l*). In two cases (*a* and *c*), the French version even prefers a distributive structure ('les femmes comme les hommes'), which suggests the tendency to individualize both groups as distinct is not determined by linguistic usage only. In this instance, the Spanish version follows suit. In the Spanish version of sentence *e*, 'children', which is gendered in Spanish ('niño' for the masculine and

Table 6.1 All occurrences of 'women and men' in the English proceedings of the Security Council (2015) aligned to French and Spanish versions

EN	*FR*	*ES*	*Doc.*
a. Both women and men alike	Les femmes comme les hommes	Tanto la mujer como el hombre	SPV7361
b. for women and men	entre les femmes et les hommes	las mujeres y los hombres	SPV7361
c. participation of both women and men	La participation des femmes comme celle des hommes	la participación tanto de mujeres como de hombres	SPV7374
d. that children, women and men	des enfants, des femmes et des hommes	los niños, las mujeres y los hombres	SPV7374
e. All persons, women and men, girls and boys,	Tous les êtres humains, femmes, hommes, filles ou garçons sont,	Todas las personas, mujeres y hombres, niñas y niñas,	SPV7374
f. equality between women and men	des droits des hommes et des femmes	la igualdad entre las mujeres y los hombres	SPV7389
g. brave women and men	des hommes et des femmes courageux	a las mujeres y hombres valientes	SPV7389
h. women and men	des hommes et des femmes	de los hombres y las mujeres	SPV7403
i. tens of millions of Afghan women and men	des dizaines de millions d'hommes et de femmes	decenas de millones de hombres y mujeres afganos	SPV7467
j. to the women and men	par les hommes et les femmes	por los hombres y las mujeres	SPV7467
k. Palestinian children, women and men	des enfants, des femmes et des hommes palestiniens	de niños, mujeres y hombres palestinos	SPV7490
l. civilians – children, women and men, day and night	civils innocents, des enfants, des femmes et des hommes	civiles inocentes, niños, mujeres y hombres,	SPV7490

'niña' for the feminine) is rendered as a double feminine ('niñas y niñas'). This can only be explained as a mistake, maybe as a consequence of the translators' reflecting on the order of the gendered words. In the remaining cases, only the masculine word for 'children' is used. The French version uses either a non-gendered word or two words representing these two genders.

In any event, the binomials 'men and women' and 'women and men' leave intersexual individuals out of the equation. These have at times been grouped with other individuals defined by their gender, and not sex, under the lexicalized acronym LGBTI, which does not appear in the 2015 proceedings corpus nor in the 1990–2014 UN corpus. Such grouping causes confusion, especially when texts do not address intersex-specific issues.

Other phrases silence different identities:

1 'without any limitation due to race, nationality or religion'

(UNDHR)

2 'ethnic, religious or linguistic minorities'

(ICCPR)

3 'all nations, racial or religious groups'

(UNDHR)

4 'all racial, ethnic or religious groups'

(ICESCR)

The wording shows a discursive order where everyone has a language and ethnic origin and also a religion. One can have one religion or another, but no religion is not an option. The variable position of the concepts in these cases does not show phraseological patterns of how nationalities, race, and religions are positioned as defining features of identities.

The same categories are maintained in the French and Spanish versions. However, the French version adds articles in front of each of the groups on only one occasion, thereby stressing the individuality of the different elements ('sans aucune restriction quant à la race, la nationalité ou la religion', UNDHR). Also the French version alters the grouping in another instance ('toutes les nations et tous les groupes raciaux ou religieux', UNDHR). The Spanish version of the UNDHR also stresses the distinction between a nation and a racial or religious group in this latter case ('todas las naciones y todos los grupos étnicos o religiosos'), which may be due to the Spanish being a translation of the French and not the English text.

In 2015 ethnic groupings are further specified as 'tribes' (12 occurrences) or 'clans' (10), which responds to the more specific nature of the documents (treaties are expected to cover a high number of possible cases) and a greater familiarity with the issues considered by the Security Council in 2015. The French and Spanish versions depict this same specification of social groupings.

As far as 'nationality' is concerned, of the 15 times it is used in the 2015 documents, 8 multinomials are found (see Table 6.2). It is remarkable how often in these multinomials (*a–f*) the category 'religion' ('beliefs', 'faith') is linked to nationality, which abounds in the idea that normal identities (authority and truths, in a Foucauldian sense) within States are defined multidimensionally and that State limits are identified with cultural boundaries, which is clearly detrimental to migration movements. This is noticeable also in phrase *d*, where 'nationality' and 'faith' share the same premodifier ('no'), whereas it was reiterated for the remaining elements in the phrase. Phraseologically, there is an exact match in *a* and *b* in the English version, but free co-selection otherwise.

When compared with the English version, the tendency of the French version to modify each group independently (partially in *b*, and more clearly in *c–h*) individualizes the groups. This is less patent in the Spanish versions (*d–g*), which still provide more instances of individualization (*see d*) than the English texts.

Other phrases identifying vulnerable groups in need of special protection in the IBHR include a wider range of lexical units:

5 'without distinction of any kind, such as race, colour, sex, language, religion, political or other opinion, national or social origin, property, birth or other status'

(occurring in the UNDHR and the ICCPR)

Table 6.2 Occurrences of 'nationality' in the English, French, and Spanish versions of the Security Council public proceedings (2015)

EN	*FR*	*ES*	*Doc.*
a. any religion, nationality, civilization or ethnic group	à une religion, nationalité ou civilisation ni à un groupe ethnique	a ninguna religión, nacionalidad, civilización o grupo étnico	SPV7362
b. any religion, nationality, civilization or ethnic group	à aucune religion, nationalité, civilisation, ni à aucun groupe ethnique	a ninguna religión, nacionalidad, civilización, ni a ningún grupo étnico	SPV7389
c. regardless of religion, ethnicity or nationality	sur la religion, l'appartenance ethnique ou la nationalité	cualquiera sea su religión, origen étnico o nacionalidad	SPV7360
d. knows no colour, no ethnicity, no nationality or faith, and it knows no borders	ne connaît ni couleur, ni origine ethnique, ni nationalité, ni croyance, ni frontière	no sabe de color ni de origen étnico, de nacionalidad ni de religión, y no conoce fronteras	SPV7466
e. their religion, nationality and beliefs	à cause de leur religion, de leur nationalité, de leurs croyances	por su religión, su nacionalidad y sus creencias	SPV7389
f. whatever their religious belief and nationality	en raison de leur croyance religieuse et de leur nationalité	sin otro motivo que su creencia religiosa y su nacionalidad	SPV387
g. Regardless of where you come from and of your nationality, race or political ideology	notre lieu de naissance ou notre nationalité, notre race ou notre idéologie politique	Con independencia de la procedencia, la nacionalidad, la raza o la ideología política	SPV361
h. regardless of their ethnicity, nationality or race	indépendamment de leur origine ethnique, de leur nationalité ou de leur couleur de peau	independientemente de su origen étnico, nacionalidad o raza	SPV7466

6 'without discrimination of any kind as to race, colour, sex, language, religion, political or other opinion, national or social origin, property, birth or other status'

(ICESCR)

7 'discrimination on any ground such as race, colour, sex, language, religion, political or other opinion, national or social origin, property, birth or other status'

(ICCPR)

8 'without any discrimination as to race, colour, sex, language, religion, national or social origin, property or birth'

(ICCPR)

9 'do not involve discrimination solely on the ground of race, colour, sex, language, religion or social origin'

(ICCPR)

Four of these five multinomials use exactly the same words and order to refer to these identities. Reduced versions of the phrase use the same order as in the longer list even though they include fewer groups. This is clearly due to semantic reasons: no consideration is given to specific opinions in cases 8 and 9, and property or birth are not taken into account nor protected in sentence 9. However, the invariability in order shows a phraseological tendency which we can contrast with other UN documents. Translations of the IBHR follow this phraseological tendency with only one exception in the Spanish version of the instruments, which uses 'condición' in one instance and 'condición social' in two cases.

Such extended multinomials are not to be found in the Security Council proceedings, which may be due to the greater specificity of the issues discussed in its sessions and meetings.

A final phrase testifies to the importance of birth for group definition in the international community. Indeed parentage defines one's race beyond any physical or social traits in American society and this conception of the category is colonizing Western society and beyond (Bourdieu and Wacquant 1998).

10 'without any discrimination for reasons of parentage or other condition'

(ICESCR)

The issue of birth (or parentage) does not appear in the 2015 proceedings of the Security Council. 'Origin', however, is a frequent word, which suggests that the category is still very much in use in the way the international community structures our world.

The perception of otherness as a concern for the international community

The issue this paper wanted to tackle is how our human tendency to in- and out-group individuals based on certain traits is solved in international legislation to achieve the goal "to practice tolerance and live together in peace with one another as good neighbours" (United Nations 1945: 190). Being such a pervasive behavioral issue, wired in our brains but also our social structure, the way we organize our identities and allot them spaces of political action and resistance is a critical issue in the path to those goals. The study aimed at offering an overview of the issue from different perspectives as well as critical insight through studying the use of phrasemes.

The question of whether the language used by the international community is an instrument for in-group affiliation as "members of the human family" (UNGA 1948) or a testimony of the alienating out-group biases used in othering human beings and groups was approached by studying references to underprivileged groups present in the IBHR. More specifically, the phraseological behavior of binomials and multinomials was examined first in the IBHR and then the public proceedings of the Security Council published in 2015. The aim was twofold: to test whether usage was consistent in a larger corpus and to check whether social structuring has evolved in the era of international cooperation.

Results do not offer a dichotomous view of the international community, as the texts show complex behaviors. Categories are indeed present and made pervasive, and they are used to impose local views through international action. Racial, ideological, and gender categories are largely based on specific Western societies (Bourdieu and Wacquant 1998: 112–113; Stychin 2004: 954), and their use as a bureaucratic instrument for governance allows for acceptance and reproduction or resistance, whereby individuals are demoted to marginal spaces of political representation. This allodoxia and the resulting colonization of our minds has been a successful process and, even though categorical structure is subject to change, these changes appear to be minimal in the data studied in this paper.

Regarding dichotomous thinking, the second bias on which othering is grounded, results are not conclusive but a phraseological tendency is indeed dominant. There are clear differences across linguistic versions, among which the French versions of the international documents seem to be the most terminology-oriented and socially engaged, by harnessing the potential of language for individualizing groups, even though originally the very concept of 'human rights' is termed as 'men's rights' in French ('droit des hommes'). In other versions, especially the English texts, chances to facilitate the in-depth and individualized representation that can avoid discrimination are missed. Non-optional co-selection patterns within phrasemes obscure the characteristics of the members of vulnerable groups, making them out-grouped and othered. The terminological principle, which seems to prevail in the French texts, focuses on the individual components and gives them separate identities. Against the current political background, such tendencies can provide constructs and relations which the empirical world can appropriate.

How can we overcome the divisions imposed upon us by the international order? How can we free ourselves from the dichotomies we are entrapped in? Opening up discussion on the linguistic aspects and political consequences of the terminological ethnocentrism embedded in our categorical and dichotomous thinking can help us promote more inclusive social constructs. The relationship between form and meaning is intimate; both evolve and influence each other: "variation in one normally leads to variation in the other" (Sinclair 1998: 12).

Notes

1 Exceptions would include the right to free movement for individuals convicted of serious crimes.
2 This corpus comprises 2,645,018 words in English, 2,847,630 in French, and 2,851,219 in Spanish.
3 Actual appearances of women in the IBHR are also worth noticing, as they made it to the IBHR as 'pregnant women' and 'mothers' (three occurrences) and in one case as 'women' requiring special protection. In general statements of rights they are semantically included (or blurred) in 'parents or legal guardians'.
4 In AntConc '*' substitutes for zero or more characters, '#' for one word, and '@' for zero or one word. Since the relevant options included two words, '*' was preferred.

References

Alexander, R.D., 1987. *The Biology of Moral Systems.* New York: Aldine de Gruyter.
Allport, G., 1954. *The Nature of Prejudice.* Reading: Addison Wesley.
Anthony, L., 2014. *AntConc.* 3.4.3. Tokyo: Waseda University. <www.laurenceanthony.net/>
Baaij, C.J.W., 2014. Confronting the conjecture of cultural incommensurability in comparative law. *King's Law Journal*, 25(2): 287–300.
Baca, G., 2009. Neoliberalism and stories of racial redemption. *Dialectical Anthropology*, 32(3): 219–241.

Bargh, J.A., 1994. The four horsemen of automaticity: Awareness, intention, efficiency, and control in social cognition. In R.S. Wyer and T.K. Srull (eds.), *Handbook of Social Cognition*. Hillsdale: Erlbaum, 1–40.

Barthes, R., 1953. *Le degré zéro de l'écriture*. Paris: Éditions du Seuil.

Bauer, L., 1988. When is a sequence of two nouns a compund in English? *English Language and Linguistics*, 2(1): 65–86.

Beck, A.T., 1999. *Prisoners of Hate: The Cognitive Basis of Anger, Hostility, and Violence*. New York: Perennial.

Beck, A.T., 2002. Prisoners of hate. *Behaviour Research and Therapy*, 40: 209–216.

Bhatia, V.K., 1993. *Analysing Genre: Language Use in Professional Settings*. Essex: Longman.

Bourdieu, P. and Wacquant, L., 1998. Sur les ruses de la raison impérialiste. *Actes de la recherche en sciences sociales*, 121–122: 109–118.

Brems, E., 1997. Enemies or Allies? Feminism and cultural relativism as dissident voices in human rights discourse. *Human Rights Quarterly*, 19: 136–164.

Brendel, N., Aksit, F., Aksit, S., and Schrüfer, G., 2016. Multicultural group work on field excursions to promote student teachers' intercultural competence. *Journal of Geography in Higher Education*, 40(2): 284–301.

Broockman, D. and Kalla, J., 2016. Durably reducing transphobia: A field experiment on door-to-door canvassing. *Science*, 352(6282): 220–224.

Bruce, S. and Yearley, S., 2006. *Sage Dictionary of Sociology*. London: Sage.

Cabré, M.T., Estopà, R., and Lorente, M., 1996. Terminología y fraseología. In *Actas del V Simposio Iberoamericano de Terminología: Terminología, Ciencia y Tecnología*. Mexico. <www.ufrgs.br/riterm/esp/simposios_anteriores_1996.html>

Carbonell i Cortés, O., 2000. Exoticism in translation: Writing, representation, and the postcolonial context. In I. Santaolalla (ed.), *'New' Exoticisms: Changing Patterns in the Construction of Otherness*. Amsterdam: Rodopi, 51–63.

Charrow, V.R., Crandall, J.A., and Charrow, R.P., 1982. Characteristics and functions of legal language. In R. Kittredge and J. Lehrberger (eds.), *Sublanguage: Studies of Language in Restricted Semantic Domains*. Berlin: Walter de Gruyter, 175–190.

Chin, R. 2009. Guest worker migration and the unexpected return of race. In R. Chin, H. Fehrenbach, G. Eley, and A. Grossmann (eds.), *After the Nazi Racial State: Differences and Democracy in Germany and Europe*. Ann Arbor: University of Michigan, 80–101.

Cohn, C., 1987. Sex and death in the rational world of defense intellectuals. *Signs*, 12: 687–718.

Connolly, A.J., 2010. *Cultural Difference on Trial: The Nature and Limits of Judicial Understanding*. Farnham: Ashgate.

Cornelius, W.A. and Rosenblum, M.R., 2005. Immigration and politics. *Annual Review of Political Science*, 8(1): 99–119.

Correll, J. and Park, B., 2005. A model of the ingroup as a social resource. *Personality and Social Psychology Review*, 9: 341–359.

Cosmides, L. and Tooby, J., 1992. Cognitive adaptations for social exchange. In J.H. Barkow, L. Cosmides, and J. Tooby (eds.), *The Adapted Mind*. New York: Oxford University Press, 163–228.

Dovidio, J.F., Glick, P., and Rudman, L.A. (eds.), 2005. *On the Nature of Prejudice: Fifty Years After Allport*. Malden: Blackwell Publishing.

Edgerton, R.B., 1992. *Sick Societies: Challenging the Myth of Primitive Harmony*. New York: Free Press.

Eibl-Eibesfeldt, I., 1998. Us and the others: The familial roots of ethnonationalism. In I. Eibl-Eibesfeldt and F. Salter (eds.), *Indoctrinability, Ideology, and Warfare*. New York: Berghahn Books, 21–53.

Einstein, A., Podolsky, B., and Rosen, N., 1935. Can quantum mechanical description of physical reality be considered complete? *Physical Review*, 47: 777–780.

Finney, N., and Simpson, L., 2009. *'Sleepwalking to Segregation'? Challenging Myths About Race and Migration*. Bristol: The Policy Press.

Foucault, M., 1975. *Surveiller et punir: naissance de la prison*. Paris: Gallimard.

Foucault, M., 1982. Le sujet et le pouvoir. In D. Defert, F. Ewald, and J. Lagrange (eds.), *Dits et écrits II, 1976–88*. Paris: Gallimard, 222–243.

Foucault, M., 1991a. Governmentality. In G. Burchell, C. Gordon, and P. Miller (eds.), *The Foucault Effect: Studies in Governmentality With Two Lectures By and an Interview With Michel Foucault*. Chicago: The University of Chicago Press, 87–104.

Foucault, M., 1991b. Questions of method. In G. Burchell, C. Gordon, and P. Miller (eds.), *The Foucault Effect: Studies in Governmentality With Two Lectures By and an Interview With Michel Foucault*. Chicago: The University of Chicago Press, 73–86.

Geertz, C., 1983. *Local Knowledge: Further Essays in Interpretative Anthropology*. London: Basic Books.

Ghiglieri, M.P., 1999. *The Dark Side of Man: Tracing the Origins of Male Violence*. Reading, MA: Perseus Books.

Ghorashi, H., 2010. From absolute invisibility to extreme visibility: Emancipation trajectory of migrant women in the Netherlands. *Feminist Review*, 94: 75–92.

Goetze, D., 1998. Evolution, mobility, and ethnic group formation. *Politics and the Life Sciences*, 17(1): 59–71.

Granger, S., and Paquot, M., 2008. Disentangling the phraseological web. In S. Granger and F. Meunier (eds.), *Phraseology: An Interdisciplinary Perspective*. Amsterdam/Philadelphia: John Benjamins, 27–50.

Gustafsson, M., 1984. The syntactic features of binomial expressions in legal English. *Text*, 4: 123–142.

Hiltunen, R., 1990. *Chapters on Legal English*. Helsini: Suomalaisen Tiedeakatemia.

Joseph, S., 2010. The United Nations and human rights. In S. Joseph and A. McBeth (eds.), *Research Handbook on International Human Rights Law*. Cheltenham: Edward Elgar Publishing, 1–35.

Jumpertz-Schwab, C., 2000. *The Development of the Scots Lexicon and Syntax in the 16th Century Under the Influence of Translations From Latin*. Frankfurt am Main: Peter Lang.

Kjær, A.L. and Palsbro, L., 2008. National identity and law in the context of European integration: The case of Denmark. *Discourse & Society*, 19(5): 599–627.

Koopmans, R. and Michalowski, I., 2016. Why do states extend rights to immigrants? Institutional settings and historical legacies across 44 countries worldwide. *Comparative Political Studies*, 50(1): 1–34.

Koskenniemi, I., 1968. *Repetitive Word-Pairs in Old and Early Middle English Prose*. Turku: Turun Yliopisto.

Krueger, J. and Clement, R.W., 1994. The truly false consensus effect: An ineradicable and egocentric bias in social perception. *Journal of Personality and Social Psycholog*, 67(4): 596–610.

Le, U.P., 2012. A culture of human rights in East Asia: Deconstructing 'Asian values' claims. *UC Davis Journal of International Law and Policy*, 18: 469–504.

Legrand, P., 2005. Issues in the translatability of law. In S. Bermann and M. Wood (eds.), *Nation, Language, and the Ethics of Translation*. Princeton: Princeton University Press, 30–50.

Lepore, L. and Brown, R., 1997. Category and stereotype activation: Is prejudice inevitable? *Journal of Personality and Social Psycholog*, 72: 275–287.

Maccallum, E.J., 2002. Othering and psychiatric nursing. *Journal of Psychiatric and Mental Health Nursing*, 9: 87–94.

Macrae, C.N. and Bodenhausen, G.V., 2000. Social cognition: Thinking categorically about others. *Annual Review of Psychology*, 51: 93–120.

Malkiel, Y., 1959. Studies in irreversible binomials. *Lingua*, 8: 113–160.

Matsumoto, D., 2009. *The Cambridge Dictionary of Psychology*. Cambridge: Cambridge University Press.

Mattila, H., 2012. Legal vocabulary. In L.M. Solan and P.M. Tiersma (eds.), *The Oxford Handbook of Language and Law*. New York: Oxford University Press.
Mel'čuk, I., 1995. Phrasemes in language and phraseology in linguistics. In M. Everaert, E.-J. van der Linden, A. Schenk, and R. Schreuder (eds.), *Idioms: Structural and Psychological Perspectives*. Hillsdale, NJ: Lawrence Erlbaum Associates.
Mellinkoff, D., 1963. *The Language of the Law*. Boston: Little Brown & Co.
Meyer, I., and Mackintosh, K., 1994. Phraseme analysis and concept analysis: Exploring a symbiotic relationship in the specialized lexicon. In W. Martin, W. Meijs, M. Moerland, E. ten Pas, P. van Sterkenburg, and P. Vossen (eds.), *Euralex 1994 Proceedings*. Amsterdam: Euralex, 339–348.
Mooney, A., 2012. Human rights: Law, language and the bare human being. *Language & Communication*, 32(3): 169–181.
Mooney, A., 2014. *Human Rights and the Body: Hidden in Plain Sight*. Farnham: Ashgate.
Ochoa, C., 2003. Advancing the language of human rights in a global economic order: An analysis of a discourse. *Boston College Third World Law Journal*, 23(1): 57–88.
Oshio, A., 2009. Development and validation of the dichotomous thinking inventory. *Social Behavior and Personality: An International Journal*, 37: 729–742.
Oshio, A., 2012. An all-or-nothing thinking turns into darkness: Relations between dichotomous thinking and personality disorders. *Japanese Psychological Research*, 54(4): 424–429.
Oster, U., 2004. From relational schemas to subject-specific semantic relations: A two-step classification of compound terms. *Annual Review of Cognitive Linguistics*, 2: 235–259.
Oster, U., 2005. *Las relaciones semánticas de términos polilexemáticos. Estudio contrastivo alemán-español*. Frankfurt am Main: Peter Lang.
Rothbart, M. and Davis-Stitt, C., 1997. Effects of arbitrarily placed category boundaries on similarity judgments. *Journal of Experimental Social Psychology*, 33: 122–145.
Ruggie, J.G., 1992. Multilateralism: The anatomy of an institution. *International Organization*, 46: 561–598.
Sager, J.C., 1990. *Practical Course in Terminology Processing*. Amsterdam/Philadelphia: John Benjamins.
Sager, J.C., 1997. Term formation. In S.E. Wright (ed.), *Handbook of Terminology Management*. Amsterdam/Philadelphia: John Benjamins, 25–41.
Salter, F., 2008. Evolutionary analyses of ethnic solidarity: An overview. *People and Place*, 16(2): 1–11.
Shaw, R.P., and Wong, Y., 1989. *Genetic Seeds of Warfare: Evolution, Nationalism, and Patriotism*. Boston: Unwin Hyman.
Sinclair, J.M., 1991. *Corpus, Concordance, Collocation*. Oxford: Oxford University Press.
Sinclair, J.M., 1998. The lexical item. In E. Weigand (ed.), *Contrastive Lexical Semantics*. Amsterdam/Philadelphia: John Benjamins, 1–24.
Singh, M.P., 2003. Human rights in the Indian tradition – Alternatives in the understanding and realization of the human rights regime. *Zeitschrift für ausländisches öffentliches Recht und Völkerrecht*, 63: 551–584.
Smith, J.C., 1968. The unique nature of the concepts of Western law. *The Canadian Bar Review*, 46(2): 191–225.
Spencer, S.J., Fein, S., Wolfe, C.T., Fong, C., and Dunn, M.A., 1998. Automatic activation of stereotypes: The role of self-image threat. *Personality and Social Psychology Bulletin*, 24: 1139–1152.
Sporer, S.L., 2001. Recognizing faces of other ethnic groups: An integration of theories. *Psychology, Public Policy, and Law*, 7(1): 36–97.
Stenner, P., 2011. Subjective dimensions of human rights: What do ordinary people understand by 'human rights'. *The International Journal of Human Rights*, 15(8): 1215–1233.
Stiner, M.C., Munro, N.D., Surovell, T.A., Tchernov, E., and Bar-Yosef, O., 1998. Paleolithic population growth pulses evidenced by small animal exploitation. *Science* September 25.

Stychin, C.F., 2004. Same-sex sexualities and the globalization of human rights discourse. *McGill Law Journal*, 49: 951–968.

Tajfel, H. (ed.), 1982. *Social Identity and Intergroup Relations.* Cambridge: Cambridge University Press.

Teitel, R., 2002. The future of human rights discourse. *St. Louis University Law Journal*, 46: 449–463.

Tiersma, P.M., 1999. *Legal Language.* Chicago: The University of Chicago Press.

Trivers, R.L., 1971. The evolution of reciprocal altruism. *Quarterly Review of Biology*, 46: 35–57.

Turner, B.S., 2006. *Vulnerability and Human Rights.* University Park, PA: The Pennsylvana State University Press.

Turner, J., Hogg, M.A., Oakes, P.J., Reicher, S.D., and Wetherell, M.S., 1987. *Rediscovering the Social Group: A Self-Categorization Theory.* Oxford: Blackwell.

Tymoczko, M., 2012. The neuroscience of translation. *Target*, 24: 83–102.

UNGA (United Nations General Assembly), 1946. *Rules of Procedure Concerning Languages.* London: United Nations. <www.un.org/documents/ga/res/1/ares1.htm>

UNGA, 1948. Universal Declaration of Human Rights. In *Resolution 217A (III).* Paris: United Nations. <www.un.org/en/universal-declaration-human-rights/>

UNGA, 1966a. International Covenant on Civil and Political Rights. In *Resolution 2200A (XXI) of 16 December 1966.* New York: United Nations. <https://treaties.un.org/Pages/ViewDetails.aspx?src=IND&mtdsg_no=IV-4&chapter=4&clang=_en>

UNGA, 1966b. *International Covenant on Economic, Social and Cultural Rights.* New York: United Nations. <https://treaties.un.org/Pages/ViewDetails.aspx?src=IND&mtdsg_no=IV-3&chapter=4&clang=_en>

UNGA, 1966c. *Optional Protocol to the International Covenant on Civil and Political Rights.* New York. <https://treaties.un.org/Pages/ViewDetails.aspx?src=IND&mtdsg_no=IV-5&chapter=4&clang=_en>

UNGA, 1989. *Second Optional Protocol to the International Covenant on Civil and Political Rights.* New York. <https://treaties.un.org/Pages/ViewDetails.aspx?src=IND&mtdsg_no=IV-12&chapter=4&clang=_en>

UNGA, 1993. *Report of the Regional Meeting for Asia of the World Conference on Human Rights.* Bangkok: Association of Southeast Asian Nations.

United Nations, 1945. United Nations: Charter of the United Nations. *The American Journal of International Law*, 39(3): 190–229.

Van den Berghe, P., 1981. *The Ethnic Phenomenon.* New York: Elsevier.

Weinstein, M., 2002–2012. *TAMSAnalyser.* 4.48b5: SourceForge.net. <http://tamsys.sourceforge.net>

Williams, P.J., 1991. *The Alchemy of Race and Rights.* Cambridge, MA: Harvard University Press.

Wittenbrink, B., Judd, C.M., and Park, B., 1997. Evidence for racial prejudice at the implicit level and its relationship with questionnaire measures. *Journal of Personality and Social Psycholog*, 72: 262–274.

Ziemski, M., Junczys-Dowmunt, M., and Pouliquen, B., 2016. The United Nations parallel corpus. In *Language Resources and Evaluation (LREC'16).* Portorož, Slovenia.

7 Legal phraseology in contrast

The fact that and its German counterparts

Raphael Salkie

Introduction

Expressions with *the fact that* are common in spoken and written English, with nearly 13,000 occurrences in the British National Corpus. This chapter analyses such expressions when they are used in legal language, with the help of their translation equivalents in German.

To set the scene, here is an example from the *Acquis Communautaire* archive (see 'Corpus and Methodology' for more about this corpus):

(1) In setting the fines, the Commission also took into account the duration of the infringement, the large size and overall resources of some of the undertakings and ***the fact that*** some of the undertakings were addressees of previous Commission decisions establishing infringements of the same type.

In (1) we have a construction consisting of *the fact that* followed by the noun complement clause *some of the undertakings were addressees of previous Commission decisions establishing infringements of the same type.*[1] The entire construction functions as the object (in fact, the third of three conjoined objects) of the multi-word verb *take into account* in the matrix clause. One can get a sense of the extraordinary range and versatility of the phraseological unit *the fact that* from Hunston (2011): five pages in that study list 43 sub-types with different verbs and prepositions in the *New Scientist* corpus (*due to the fact that, stems from the fact that, lose sight of the fact that*, etc.). Hunston also presents six more examples where the expression is clause-initial (e.g. *The fact that P. suturalis has two different forms of shell . . . needs a different kind of explanation*) (2011: 112–116). Illuminating though her discussion is, it serves to indicate only some of the wide variety of uses of *the fact that* (Hunston does not mention examples like (1) where the construction is in object position), and to show the pressing need for more extensive analysis.

Despite the frequency of expressions with *the fact that*, they have hitherto been the subject of rather sparse and fragmentary research, probably for two main reasons. One is the relatively limited literature on noun complement clauses in general (but see Francis (1993), Ballier (2007) and Kanté (2010) for some enlightening analysis and reviews of the literature). The second reason is that the field of phraseology did not become firmly established until recent times. Theoretical models which take phrases seriously, such as Pattern Grammar and Construction Grammar, are still quite new; and large corpora, along with the software to recognise and quantify the occurrence of words and phrases, have only been widely available in the last two decades. Lexicographers have, of course, long been very aware of multi-word expressions (MWEs), but detailed discussion of the practical and theoretical issues of identifying and classifying them has been rare: see Atkins and Rundell (2008: 166ff.) for a rare exception.

Two recent studies discuss the use of constructions with *the fact that* in legal English and their counterparts in other languages, namely Goźdź-Roszkowski and Pontrandolfo (2014) for Italian, and Zeleňáková (2014) for French. These scholars have raised interesting issues about *the fact that* as an MWE, about phraseology in general, about languages in contrast, and about legal language and legal reasoning.

This chapter is a modest attempt to build on the foundations laid by these two studies. The next section reviews some of the work on *the fact that* in English and in contrastive studies, and the following section introduces the corpus and methodology, and extends the data to legal German. Subsequent sections consider the implications of the corpus data for the analysis of expressions with *the fact that*, for English and German in contrast, for legal language and legal reasoning, for plain legal language, and for phraseology.

Previous studies of *the fact that*

Monolingual research

To the best of my knowledge, the first substantial examination of *the fact that* was Mair (1988), a pioneering corpus-based study which lists only two previous research articles in its short bibliography: Christophersen (1979), which only mentions *the fact that* briefly in passing, and Kiparsky and Kiparsky (1971), a paper which is not relevant to our concerns here. Mair's main intentions were firstly to defend *the fact that* from prescriptive grammarians who discourage its use, and secondly to argue that '*the fact that* is not a mere variant of the conjunction *that* but a genuinely suppletive form which substitutes for *that* in contexts where the latter is ruled out' (1988: 70). He adds another dimension to the observed variety of the construction by noting that the word *fact* can be pre- or post-modified by an adjectival, as in:

(2) But what finally knocks the theory on the head is ***the fact***, not to be denied however wrong or puzzling it may seem, ***that*** long-haired men are interested in women – and women are interested in long-haired men.

(Mair 1988: 68)

Compare:

(3) I note not only that the numbers of people in residential and nursing care have increased substantially, as we all know, but also ***the surprising fact that*** there has been only a modest fall in the numbers of people in local authority care.

(British National Corpus, BNC)

Subsequently Granath (2001) searched the Frown and FLOB corpora (see Smith 2014 for details) and found around 200 instances of *the fact that*, which she subclassified on the basis of their function in the matrix clause (as we did above when we noted that in (1) the construction functions as object). She raises the question of why the verb *regret* (along with 27 other verbs in her corpus) usually took a bare *that*-clause complement, and was only rarely followed by *the fact that*; whereas with *dislike* and 40 others, it was the other way round – but concedes that currently this is an area of language 'that cannot be wholly explained in terms of one system or another' (2001: 240). She goes on to note that the word *the* is not always present in this construction, that the word *that* is sometimes omitted too, and that *the facts that* also occurs, though infrequently. She observes finally that instances can be found where the situation referred to in the complement clause is not regarded by the speaker as a fact:

(4) Quite frankly, it is not a tax break for the rich. . . . It would be first dollar coverage, it would be a high deductible, it would be very, very affordable for those people and unfortunately I just cannot buy ***the fact that*** it is a tax break for the rich.
(CNN Domestic News, 25 Apr 1996) (Granath 2001: 242)

Similar examples where the factuality of the complement clause situation is at least in doubt are:

(5) 1803 G. Moore Diary 15 Jan. in *Mem. Life Sir J. Mackintosh* (1835) I. iv. 175, I would not agree to ***the fact that*** ennui prevailed more in England than in France.
(*Oxford English Dictionary*)

(6) I think you hinted at ***the fact that*** they perhaps are not quite so good at maybe the harder sciences.
(BNC)

(7) All the evidence points to ***the fact that*** he will overrule Roe and he has said nothing to allay our concerns.
(COCA)

The observations in these two works are useful, but they do not answer the question of whether *the fact that* has a basic function in English. A plausible answer is offered by Schmid (2007), who argues that the central function of *the fact that* and similar constructions is to 'reify' the information expressed in the sentential complement into a nominal concept. Schmid acknowledges that similar proposals were made by Francis (1986) and Conte (1996), but his statement is admirably clear:

> The crucial cognitive function of the abstract nouns I am concerned with here is to 'encapsulate' the complex pieces of information expressed in the sentential complements as nominal concepts.
> (Schmid 2007: 516)

We shall draw heavily on this proposal below, but first we must look at contrastive studies.

Bilingual research

Zeleňáková (2014: 257ff.) looked at *the fact is that* and French *le fait est que* in legal texts as 'emergent discourse markers', following Aijmer (2004). Space prevents us from developing this topic, except to make this anecdotal observation: the expression *the fact of the matter is that* seems to have been used extensively by Conservative members of the UK cabinet for decades to add credibility and weight to their assertions and to suggest that their opponents are not dealing with facts. Here is one example:

(8) The Prime Minister: ***The fact of the matter is that*** it is not, as I have explained to the right hon. Gentleman on many occasions, happening only in this country. If the right hon. Gentleman is so concerned about unemployment and recession, why does he not acknowledge the impact that his minimum wage would have upon unemployment?

(BNC)

A more significant bilingual study is Goźdź-Roszkowski and Pontrandolfo (2014), where the notions of *evaluation* and *epistemic stance* were used to pinpoint the functions of this construction and Italian *il fatto che* in legal texts. The authors note that evaluation construed narrowly ('the good or bad dichotomy' is the sense specified in another paper, Pontrandolfo and Goźdź-Roszkowski (2014: 72), citing Hunston (2004)), only applies to some uses of *the fact that*, and not to others. Only 5% of their English examples, and 10% of their Italian examples, involved 'affective reaction to a fact' (Goźdź-Roszkowski and Pontrandolfo 2014: 23). However, they also make the interesting proposal that this explicit evaluation is not the only kind: they also found traces of covert evaluation in their data. Consider this example:

(9) The artificial (and consequently unfair) nature of the resulting sentence *is aggravated by **the fact that*** prosecutors must charge all relevant facts about the way the crime was committed.

(Goźdź-Roszkowski and Pontrandolfo 2014: 21)

They list this example under 'Fact is the cause of a problem or its solution', but *aggravated* often carries negative connotations (less so in legal discourse, but the writer could have used the neutral *increased* or *amplified* instead). The nearby words *artificial* and *unfair* are also evaluative. We shall see similar findings in our data from English and German below.

Corpus and methodology

Like Zeleňáková, but unlike Goźdź-Roszkowski and Pontrandolfo, we used a parallel (translation) corpus of English and German texts: the *Acquis Communautaire* corpus of EU law. The corpus contains over a billion words in 22 languages (Steinberger et al. 2014). We extracted 100 random examples of *the fact that* from the corpus, and matched them with their German counterparts. This sample is too small for meaningful quantitative analysis: only in relation to examples (39–44) below is there a numerical reference to the infrequency of overtly evaluative verbs taking *fact* as their object.

An advantage of using a parallel corpus is that each English example can be compared directly with its German counterpart. In a comparable corpus this is not possible. Goźdź-Roszkowski and Pontrandolfo used a corpus of US Supreme Court judgements and a corpus of judgements delivered by the Italian Supreme Court. So to compare the two languages directly, they had to hunt through their corpus for similar examples: so they contrast their English example, reproduced as (9) above, with this one:

(10) . . . una evidente contradizzione dovuta al fatto che la Corte ha ritenuto . . .
. . . *a clear contradiction due to the fact that the Court believed* . . .

The advantage of a comparable corpus is that we can be confident that the examples are authentic and natural. With a parallel corpus, there is always the risk that the translated language is unnatural 'translationese'. This danger is 'aggravated' by 'the fact that' the *Acquis Communautaire* corpus does not systematically indicate which is the source text and which the translated text. These are genuine problems, but the reader is free to examine the data in the many examples presented below, and to draw her own conclusions about their quality – and, of course, about the value of conclusions based on these examples.

A further problem with the *Acquis Communautaire* corpus is that it includes a wide variety of documents, some of them only marginally 'legal' and some of them not involving judgements. Bonde describes the corpus as follows:

> [It] covers all treaties, EU legislation, international agreements, standards, court verdicts, fundamental rights provisions and horizontal principles in the treaties such as equality and non-discrimination. In short: EU-law.
>
> (Bonde 2016)

It will be clear that this covers a wide range of text genres. Examples (33–34) below, for example, may form part of a legal text, but out of context they look like engineering language. In constructing the sample of 100 examples, I tried to exclude any that were clearly remote from the type of judgements that Goźdź-Roszkowski and Pontrandolfo examined, so that their data could be compared, at least to some extent, with mine.

In presenting the data below, I have given the English first, followed immediately by the corresponding German text. I have not systematically provided glosses of the German examples: they are published by the EU as translation equivalents, so even readers with limited or no German should be able to understand them to some extent by looking for proper names or cognate words. Where German examples are discussed in detail, I have tried to provide word for word glosses. Note that German has two dictionary equivalents for *fact*: *Tatsache* and *Umstand*. Studying the differences between them is beyond the scope of the paper, but see Endnote 4 for a brief comparison.

Constructions with *the fact that* in contrast with German

Consider again example (1), reproduced here as (11), this time with its German counterpart:

(11) In setting the fines, the Commission also took into account the duration of the infringement, the large size and overall resources of some of the undertakings and ***the fact that*** some of the undertakings were addressees of previous Commission decisions establishing infringements of the same type.

(12) Bei der Festsetzung der Geldbußen berücksichtigte die Kommission auch die Dauer der Zuwiderhandlung, die erhebliche Größe und die Gesamtressourcen einiger der Unternehmen sowie ***die Tatsache, dass*** die Kommission an einige der Unternehmen bereits frühere Entscheidungen aufgrund von Zuwiderhandlungen der gleichen Art gerichtet hatte.

Here the English multi-word verbal construction *take into account* and its German single-word counterpart *berücksichtigen* govern a series of object noun phrases: the construction introduced by *the fact that/die Tatsache dass* is the last of these object noun phrases. I would argue, following Schmid (2007), that the fundamental reason for using *the fact that/die Tatsache dass* here is to enable the writer to reify the information in the sentential complement by nominalising it so that it patterns along with the other noun phrases.[2] It is true that Mair's (1988) line of argument applies here: it would be clumsy, if not impossible, to leave out *the fact/die Tatsache* in these examples. However, this syntactic fact about the two languages does not apply to every instance of *the fact that/die Tatsache dass*, as we shall see. Notice also that the notions of evaluation and epistemic stance do not appear to shed light on these examples. Some of the things that you can do to noun phrases headed by *duration*, *size*, and *resources* can also be done to the construction introduced by *the fact that*: you can note them, deplore them, or analyse them, for instance. Once a piece of information has been nominalised, it is fair game for any appropriate verb, not only evaluative ones like *deplore*.

Among the small number of nouns which can take sentential complements (*claim*, *theory*, *assumption*, etc.), *fact* is notable for its frequency and its semantic near-emptiness, two characteristics which are no doubt connected. Instances of *the fact that* range from those like (13) where the word *fact* is virtually devoid of meaning and is omissible, to those such as (15) where the writer apparently wants to make it clear that the situation in the complement is indeed a fact:

(13) LDCOM further stresses ***the fact that*** the State cannot go back on its declarations without harming its own financial credibility.
(14) LDCOM hebt ferner hervor, ***dass*** der Staat seine Erklärungen nicht zurücknehmen könne, ohne seine eigene Kreditwürdigkeit zu beeinträchtigen.
(15) This is reinforced by ***the fact that*** the overall performance of the Community producers is negative.
(16) Dies wird durch ***die Tatsache*** untermauert, ***dass*** die Geschäftsergebnisse aller Gemeinschaftshersteller zusammengenommen negativ sind.

Here again, syntactic constraints mean that *the fact* could have been left out in (13), so that it mirrored its German counterpart in (14), whereas this is not possible in (15) (though in (66) the writer could have said 'Dies wird dadurch untermauert, dass . . .' – cf. examples (34), (50), (68), and (70) below). The crucial difference, however, seems to be that in (13) the writer wants to assert a fact, whereas in (15) the information in the sentential complement is assumed to be true and is used to support the conclusion referred to by *this*. There are many ways to assume or presuppose the factual status of a proposition, one of them being to nominalise it without using *Tatsache*, as in (18):

(17) According to the case law of the Court of Justice, where private investors are prepared to intervene only after the authorities have decided to grant aid, ***the fact that those investors are then prepared*** to intervene at the same time is no longer relevant.
(18) Nach der Rechtsprechung des Gerichtshofs sei ***die Bereitschaft privater Investoren***, gleichzeitig mit dem Staat aktiv zu werden, nicht mehr relevant, wenn sie diese Bereitschaft erst nach der Entscheidung der Regierung zur Gewährung einer Beihilfe entwickeln würden . . .

Here the English version could have paralleled the German by reading 'the preparedness/readiness/willingness of those investors to intervene'.

In all the examples given so far, the reified proposition in the sentential complement of *the fact that* is used as part of a chain of reasoning. In (11), the proposition is used to justify the size of the fines; in (13) it is used to support an argument about the credibility of the (French) state; in (15), it supports a claim in the previous sentence (not included in the example) that the overall picture is 'injurious'; and in (17), the proposition is said to be not relevant. Most of the examples in our sample have a similar function with a chain of reasoning. Here are some typical ones (we do not comment on the German equivalents here – see the next section):

The complement clause supports a conclusion:

(19) The low cooperation by unrelated importers and ***the fact that*** after the imposition of measures on the PRC, importers do not seem to have experienced particular difficulties further underscores this conclusion.

(20) Die geringe Mitarbeit seitens der unabhängigen Einführer und ***die Tatsache, dass*** die Einführer nach der Einführung der Maßnahmen gegenüber der VR China nicht mit besonderen Schwierigkeiten konfrontiert waren, bekräftigen diese Schlussfolgerung noch.

The complement clause does not alter an assessment:

(21) ***The fact that*** the investment concerned headquarters rather than production capacity did not alter this assessment.

(22) ***Die Tatsache, dass*** die Investition anstelle der Schaffung von Produktions-kapazitäten die Errichtung eines Firmensitzes betraf, änderte nichts an dieser Einschätzung.

A third party is said to ignore the proposition in the complement clause:

(23) by proposing to . . . , the Commission is in practice penalising the eligible regions and overlooking ***the fact that*** in 2001 the new legislative framework had not come into force . . .

(24) mit dem Vorschlag . . . benachteiligt die Kommission in Wirklichkeit die Empfängerregionen und missachtet ***die Tatsache, dass*** der neue Rechtsrahmen 2001 noch nicht in Kraft war . . .

The complement clause is the basis of a decision:

(25) However, based ***on*** the environmental logic of the scheme and ***the fact that*** the relevant state aid rules expressly refer to property tax as one way to counterbalance new environmental taxes, the Commission has decided . . .

(26) Ausgehend von dem der Regelung zugrunde liegenden Umweltschutz-gedanken und ***von der Tatsache, dass*** die Grundsteuer in den einschlägigen Beihilfevorschriften ausdrücklich als ein Ausgleichsinstrument für neue Umweltabgaben genannt wird, hat die Kommission daher beschlossen . . .

(27) In its decision, . . . the Commission took account of ***the fact that*** the heavy debt burden, the loss of markets and the excessive workforce were all inherited from a period when the Lithuanian economy was still in transition.

(28) In ihrer Entscheidung, . . . trug die Kommission ***dem Umstand*** Rechnung, ***dass*** die enorme Schuldenbelastung, das Wegbrechen von Märkten und die zu hohe

Mitarbeiterzahl Altlasten aus einer Zeit waren, als sich die litauische Volkswirtschaft noch im Übergang befand.

The complement clause was recognised as part of the approach relied upon:

(29) In terms of impact, the report relied, for most regions, on a macro-modelling approach to assess the impact of the SFs on economic and social cohesion. It recognised ***the fact that***: 'The emerging results inevitably flow to some extent from assumptions made within the modelling process.'
(30) Zur Bewertung der Auswirkungen der Strukturfonds auf den wirtschaftlichen und sozialen Zusammenhalt stützte sich der Bericht bei den meisten Regionen auf ein makroökonomisches Modell. Es wird eingeräumt, ***dass*** die erzielten Ergebnisse unweigerlich zu einem gewissen Grad aus während des Modellgestaltungsprozesses getroffenen Annahmen abgeleitet wurden.
(31) Moody's decision at that time ***was based on the fact*** that the agency did not expect France Télécom and Orange to be in a position to generate sufficient cash flow to reduce the group's consolidated debt.
(32) Der Entscheidung der Ratingagentur ***lagen*** Zweifel an der Fähigkeit von FT und Orange ***zugrunde***, einen ausreichenden Cashflow zu erzielen, um die Schuldenlast des Konzerns zu verringern.

The complement clause is important and needs to be highlighted:

(33) It is necessary to draw attention to ***the fact that*** the value of *s* is specific to the situation calculated and can, therefore, be influenced by the action of the body tilt system.
(34) Es ist ***darauf*** hinzuweisen, ***dass*** *s* den spezifischen Wert nur in dem betrachteten Berechnungsfall aufweist und folglich durch die erzwungene Wagenkastenneigung beeinflusst werden kann.

The complement clause is a good example of the content of another proposition:

(35) Moreover, the widespread existence of slitting companies and steel service centres in the Community ***illustrates the fact that*** the GOES do not always leave the factories of the producers in dimensions specifically required by the end-user.
(36) Zudem ***lässt sich*** aus der großen Zahl von Unternehmen mit Spaltbandanlagen (Slitting-Anlagen) und von Stahlservicezentren in der Gemeinschaft durchaus ***schließen, dass*** die GOES auch in nicht kundenspezifischen Abmessungen ab Werk geliefert werden.

The complement clause explains something:

(37) The increase between 2003 and the IP ***can be explained by the fact that*** the Community industry decreased its sales prices (see below) in order regain market share.
(38) Der Anstieg zwischen 2003 und dem UZ ***war nur möglich, weil*** der Wirtschaftszweig der Gemeinschaft seine Verkaufspreise senkte (siehe unten), um so seinen Marktanteil halten zu können.

We have not included examples here of the type *in view of the fact that/despite the fact that*, which need separate discussion – see next section. In none of these examples is evaluation by the writer (in the narrow sense) a factor. In (36), the German version in its use of the word *schließen* 'conclude' makes the chain of reasoning, implicit in the English (35), explicit. Only in three out of our hundred examples is the proposition in the sentential complement explicitly evaluated, positively in (39–42), negatively in (43–44):

(39) [The committee] welcomes ***the fact that*** NCTS, by simplifying the administrative tasks of customs workers, can help free up human resources . . .

(40) [Der Ausschuss] begrüßt ***die Tatsache, dass*** das NEVV, da es die Verwaltungsaufgaben der Zollbediensteten vereinfacht, dazu beitragen kann, Humanressourcen freizustellen . . .

(41) [The committee] welcomes ***the fact that***, in practice, the Court contributes not only to correcting mistakes, but also to developing and improving management in the EU.

(42) [Der Ausschuss] würdigt ***die Tatsache, dass*** der Rechnungshof mit seiner Arbeit nicht nur dazu beiträgt, Mängel zu berichtigen, sondern auch das Management der Europäischen Union weiterzuentwickeln und zu verbessern.

(43) [The committee] deplores ***the fact that*** the Commission has not made efforts to establish an appropriate mechanism to measure such impacts.

(44) [Der Ausschuss] bedauert ***die Tatsache, dass*** die Kommission es versäumt hat, einen entsprechenden Mechanismus zur Beurteilung dieser Auswirkungen zu entwickeln.

This low number of explicitly evaluative examples seems to match the findings of Goźdź-Roszkowski and Pontrandolfo (2014: 23, Figures 1–3), where, as we noted above, their category 'affective reaction to a fact' has a small number of examples, and the largest number are classified as 'fact is the basis for a practical outcome or reasoning'.

Connecting propositions in chains of reasoning

We also find *the fact that* as part of a larger connective structure involving a preceding preposition or phrasal preposition – the 'recurring prepositions' of Hunston (2011: 13). Usually this structure makes explicit the connection between two or more propositions. Here are some typical examples, starting with those that involve a positive connection between the two propositions:

(45) ***In view of the fact that*** the quantities traded would be substantial and that the agreement was made between the two largest undertakings active in trading rough diamonds, competition would be substantially weakened as a result of the trade agreement.

(46) ***Angesichts der Tatsache, dass*** der Handel beträchtliche Mengen betrifft und die Vereinbarung von den beiden größten, auf dem Gebiet des Rohdiamanthandels agierenden Unternehmen abgeschlossen würde, wäre eine spürbare Beeinträchtigung des Wettbewerbs auf dem Markt . . . zu erwarten.

(47) . . . the principle's applicability in the present case is incontestable ***in view of the fact that*** the State is acting as a shareholder . . .

(48) . . . die Anwendbarkeit dieses Grundsatzes im vorliegenden Fall sei unstreitig ***angesichts der Tatsache, dass*** der Staat hier als Aktionär . . . agiert habe.

(49) The main build up occurred during 2003 and the IP and was ***due to the fact that*** one of the sampled producers had to satisfy a very big delivery immediately after the end of the IP.

(50) Der Anstieg war im Jahr 2003 und im UZ am ausgeprägtesten und ***darauf*** zurückzuführen, ***dass*** die Stichprobenhersteller unmittelbar nach Ende des UZ einen sehr großen Auftrag erfüllen mussten.

(51) ***In view of the fact that***, in the present case, the investor is the State, the study of domestic law also included administrative law.

(52) ***Da*** im vorliegenden Fall der Staat der Investor ist, wurde auch das Verwaltungsrecht in diese Untersuchung des innerstaatlichen Rechts einbezogen.

(53) The necessary amendment or repeal may arise ***due to the fact that*** the products upon which measures have been imposed by Regulation (EC) No 151/2003 fall within the scope of the products subject to the proceeding . . .

(54) Eine solche Änderung oder Aufhebung könnte eventuell erforderlich sein, ***weil*** die Waren, für die die mit der vorgenannten Verordnung eingeführten Maßnahmen gelten, unter die Warendefinition des Verfahrens . . . fallen.

(55) However, ***owing to the fact that*** in most Member States there is no or insufficient export-credit insurance cover offered by private insurers to micro and small companies, the Commission decided . . .

(56) ***Weil*** jedoch in den meisten Mitgliedstaaten Klein – und Kleinstunternehmen von Seiten privater Versicherer keine oder nur eine unzureichende Ausfuhrkreditversicherungsdeckung angeboten wird, beschloss die Kommission, . . .

In the next group, the two propositions are in contrast:

(57) ***Despite the fact that*** the sampled producers recovered to a certain extent from past dumping of imports originating in the PRC, it was also found that the sampled producers still suffered material injury within the meaning of Article 3 of the basic Regulation.

(58) ***Obwohl*** sich die Stichprobenhersteller bis zu einem gewissen Grad von dem früheren Dumping der Einfuhren mit Ursprung in der VR China erholt haben, erlitten sie den Untersuchungsergebnissen zufolge dennoch eine bedeutende Schädigung im Sinne des Artikels 3 der Grundverordnung.

(59) . . . the distinction between data on telecommunications and Internet data, ***despite the fact that*** the distinction becomes technologically less important.

(60) . . . der Unterscheidung zwischen Telefon – und Internetdaten, ***obgleich*** diese Unterscheidung technisch betrachtet an Bedeutung verliert.

(61) ECTA is of the opinion that the following measures constitute state aid: (i) the ministerial declarations of July and October 2002 informing the market that the State would not leave France Télécom in financial difficulties; . . . and (v) the apparent transfer of France Télécom's employees within ERAP ***despite the fact that*** they continue to work for France Télécom.

(62) Nach Auffassung von ECTA stellen die folgenden Maßnahmen staatliche Beihilfen dar: (i) die ministeriellen Erklärungen zwischen Juli und Oktober 2002, mit denen der Markt darüber informiert worden sei, dass der Staat FT in finanziellen Schwierigkeiten nicht allein lassen würde; . . . und (v) die augenscheinliche Übernahme von – ***gleichwohl*** weiterhin für FT tätigen – FT-Mitarbeitern durch ERAP.

In (46) and (48), the German version closely parallels the English one. Such examples were outnumbered in our sample, however, by the types illustrated in (49–62), where a single word in German corresponds to the more complex English structure. Arguably the factual status of the proposition in the clausal complement is more important in (45–48); in the remaining examples, a single word in English, paralleling the German, would have been possible.

In (62), the clause introduced by *despite the fact that* corresponds to *gleichwohl weiterhin für FT tätigen* ("although further active for FT") – an adjectival phrase without a verb, and thus a further simplification of the structure. Anticipating our discussion of plain legal language below, it is worth pointing out that the less elaborate structure in (62) is not necessarily easier to understand than the more complex (61). Sometimes elaborate syntax aids comprehension.

English and German legal language in contrast

We have already noted in relation to examples (17–18) that nominalisation can fulfil the same function as a construction with *the fact that*. Here is a similar example:

(63) Hence, ***owing to the fact that*** the Company's fundamentals ***were healthy***, France Télécom's situation cannot be compared to that of companies such as Vivendi Universal or Crédit Lyonnais.
(64) ***Angesichts der gesunden Grundlagen*** von FT lasse sich die Situation des Konzerns nicht mit der anderer Unternehmen wie Vivendi Universal oder Crédit Lyonnais vergleichen. (The German starts with "In view of the healthy foundations of FT".)

In other cases, we found German using nominalisation as part of a radical difference from the English structure. Examples (31–32) above are one such pair. Here is another:

(65) The authorities maintain that the loan proposal was never signed by France Télécom ***owing to*** the excessive cost of the financial terms proposed to it ***and the fact that*** the Commission was raising doubts.
(66) Nach Auskunft der Regierung hat FT den vorgesehenen Vorschuss niemals in Anspruch genommen, zum einen ***aufgrund*** der hohen Kosten, die mit den angebotenen Finanzierungsbedingungen verbunden gewesen seien, zum anderen ***aufgrund der Bedenken***, die die Kommission geäußert hätte. (The German text here ends with "owing to the doubts that the Commission had voiced".)

We have seen several examples where an elaborate construction with *the fact that* corresponds to a single word in German, among them *in view of the fact that* > *da* "since" in (51–52), *owing to the fact that* > *weil* "because" in (55–56), and *despite the fact that* > *obgleich* "although" in (59–60).

Examples where a construction with *the fact that* had as its German counterpart a construction with *da* – "there" were common in our sample.[3] Examples (33–34) and (49–50) illustrate this contrast: *It is necessary to draw attention to the fact that* in (33) corresponds to (34) *Es ist darauf hinzuweisen, dass* "It is thereupon to be insisted that". Here are some more:

(67) Although the Council has decided that the Member States should benefit from Community financial support to eradicate the disease, this does not alter ***the fact***

that the specific financing decisions adopted by the Commission after receiving a request for reimbursement . . . point out that this is contingent on the planned action being taken immediately . . .

(68) Zwar hat der Rat beschlossen, dass die Mitgliedstaaten eine Finanzhilfe der Gemeinschaft zur Tilgung der Seuche erhalten müssen, jedoch ändert dies nichts ***daran, dass*** in den von der Kommission nach Erhalt eines Erstattungsantrags verabschiedeten spezifischen Entscheidungen über eine Finanzhilfe darauf hingewiesen wird . . . dass dieser Anspruch an die unmittelbare Anwendung der geplanten Maßnahmen gebunden ist . . .

(69) Despite the difficulties in obtaining data ***due to the fact that*** different types of building work were interconnected, the evaluators attempted . . .

(70) Trotz der Schwierigkeiten bei der Sammlung von Daten, die ***darauf*** zurückzuführen waren, ***dass*** unterschiedliche Arten von Bauarbeiten miteinander verbunden waren, versuchten die Prüfer, . . .

In (70), the German version uses *die darauf zurückzuführen waren, dass* "which were thereto to be traced back, that", where the English has [understood: *which were*] *due to the fact that.*

Finally we reproduce here some of the instances where the German structure diverges sharply from the English one. In a few cases we found the German word *Tatsache* or *Umstand* used:[4]

(71) As regards applications for a reduction in fines, ***the statistics provided should be seen in the light of the fact that*** in a single investigation normally more than one undertaking applies for a reduction in fines.

(72) Im Hinblick auf Anträge auf eine Ermäßigung von Geldbußen ***sollte bei der Betrachtung der vorgelegten Statistik die Tatsache berücksichtigt werden, dass*** im Normalfall bei einer einzigen Ermittlung mehr als ein Unternehmen eine Geldbußenermäßigung beantragt. (The words in bold translate as "in the consideration of the provided statistics, the fact should be considered that".)

(73) ***Where the incurrence of the debt is due to the fact that*** the goods covered by the ATA carnet have not been re-exported or have not been assigned a customs-approved treatment or use within the periods laid down by the ATA Convention . . .

(74) ***Hat die Entstehung der Abgabenschuld ihren Grund in dem Umstand, daß*** Waren, für die ein Carnet ATA ausgestellt worden ist, nicht wiederausgeführt oder nicht innerhalb der gemäß dem ATA-Übereinkommen festgelegten Frist ordnungsgemäß erledigt worden sind . . . (The words in bold translate as "If the incurrence of the debt has its origin in the fact that".)

In other cases the structures diverged even more radically:

(75) . . . the consultant is wrong to carry out his analyses in the light of a single factor (the ministerial interview on 12 July 2002) to the exclusion of all others (***despite the fact that there are no grounds for asserting*** that market operators considered the ministerial interview to be an important factor for investors).

(76) Der Berater kann seine Analysen also nicht auf einen einzigen Faktor (das Ministerinterview vom 12. Juli 2002) stützen und sämtliche anderen Faktoren ignorieren (***wobei nichts für die Behauptung spricht, dass*** das Minister-interview nach

Einschätzung der Marktteilnehmer für die Investoren von Bedeutung gewesen wäre). (The words in bold translate as "in which connection nothing speaks for the claim, that.")

(77) ***The discussion*** also ***highlighted the fact that*** active competition law enforcement is likely to be required to avoid incumbent firms' behaviour limiting competition from the substitute services.

(78) ***In der Diskussion wurde deutlich, dass*** eine aktive Durchsetzung des Wettbewerbsrechts erforderlich sein dürfte, um zu vermeiden, dass etablierte Firmen durch ihr Verhalten den von alternativ angebotenen Dienstleistungen ausgehenden Wettbewerb beschränken. (The words in bold translate as "In the discussion [it] became clear, that".)

(79) ***The fact that*** the Directive on the retention of data generated or processed in connection with the provision of publicly available electronic communications services or of public communications networks and amending Directive 2002/58/EC ***was adopted*** on 21 February 2006, only five months after the presentation of the Commission proposal, following the agreement reached at first reading between Parliament and the Council, was an inter-institutional success symbolising the Union's political will.

(80) Die Richtlinie über die Vorratsspeicherung von Daten, die bei der Bereitstellung öffentlicher elektronischer Kommunikationsdienste verarbeitet werden, und zur Änderung der Richtlinie 2002/58/EG, die am 21. Februar 2006 nur fünf Monate nach Vorlage des Vorschlags der Kommission nach der Einigung zwischen Parlament und Rat in erster Lesung ***verabschiedet*** wurde, war ein interinstitutioneller Erfolg, der den politischen Willen der EU deutlich macht. (The structure of the German sentence is: "The Directive . . . , which was adopted at first reading . . . was an inter-institutional success".)

(81) In a 1989 report on Member States' policies for controlling FMD, the Commission noted that some Member States that did not practise preventive vaccination of livestock could impose restrictions on trade in animals with Community partners that did vaccinate. The restrictions ***were justified by the fact that*** even though vaccinated animals appear clinically normal they may be carrying the virus.

(82) In einem Bericht über die Politiken der Mitgliedstaaten zur Bekämpfung der MKS stellte die Kommission im Jahr 1989 jedoch fest, dass einige Mitgliedstaaten, die keine prophylaktischen Impfungen ihres Viehbestands durchführten, ***berechtigt waren***, gegenüber den Mitgliedstaaten der Gemeinschaft, die prophylaktische Impfungen praktizierten, Beschränkungen beim Handelsverkehr mit Tieren anzuwenden ***mit der Begründung***, äußerlich gesunde, geimpfte Tiere könnten Virusträger sein. (The words in bold translate as "were justified . . . on the grounds [that]".)

There are no apparent general patterns at work in this group of examples, but they do indicate one of the advantages of working with a translation corpus: a rich and sometimes surprising array of equivalents often comes to light. General patterns might well appear in a larger sample, of course.

Plain legal language

In some instances, using a construction with *the fact that* is a simple and efficient way to get the message across. This is certainly the case in (11), where a series of NPs appear in object position and the proposition in the complement clause is conveniently added to the series; and a similar point can be made about the pair of NPs in subject position in (19). We have also noted instances like (15), where the writer apparently uses the word *fact* to mark the factual status of the proposition in the complement clause.

In other cases, the single-word counterparts of the construction involving *the fact that* provide cross-linguistic support for the argument that the construction can be unnecessarily cumbersome: examples (49–62) illustrate this clearly, and it would be perfectly possible to simplify (45–48) in similar ways, in both languages. The admirable guidelines from the EU translation unit, known in English as *How to Write Clearly* (European Commission 2012a), advise writers to avoid the expression *in view of the fact that*, and to use *as* instead. The German counterpart *Klar und deutlich schreiben* (European Commission 2012b) likewise rejects *in Anbetracht des Umstands, dass* (not attested in our corpus) in favour of *weil*. (The French *Rédiger clairement* (European Commission 2012c) advises *comme* rather than *en raison du fait que*, and the Italian *Scrivere chiaro* (European Commission 2012d) rejects *in considerazione del fatto che* in favour of *poiché*. I am not competent to check all the available language versions, but the Dutch and Spanish guidelines give similar advice, although the longer phrase in these two languages (*i betragtning af at/habida cuenta de que*) does not contain an equivalent of the word *fact*.)

We thus have some limited evidence that a contrastive, corpus-based approach can supplement efforts to simplify legal language.

Implications for phraseology

In studying constructions like *the fact that*, it is a familiar principle that we need to distinguish between the phrase on its own, and the phrase as part of a larger expression such as *in view of the fact that*. The contrastive data presented here also indicate that we often need to look at the wider context to analyse the function of *the fact that* – not just the immediate context, but also at least the sentence as a whole, as the divergent equivalents in (75–82) indicate clearly. It would also be interesting to compare related expressions with *the fact* across languages, as these two pairs of examples indicate:

(83) As to the compatibility of the support measures within the meaning of the Guidelines, Bouygues Telecom argues that. . . . Basically, ***the fact is that*** the Ambition 2005 plan does not satisfy the minimum requirements of the Guidelines.

(84) Zur Frage der Vereinbarkeit dieser Maßnahmen mit den Leitlinien ***macht BT geltend, dass*** . . . der Plan Ambition 2005 erfülle die in den Leitlinien aufgestellten Mindestanforderungen nicht. (The words in bold translate as “BT argues, that.”)

(85) The very first contact can win or lose a client, so ***it’s an incredible fact that*** 30% of all artists don’t say their name when answering the phone.

(86) Schon der erste Kontakt kann einen Kunden gewinnen oder verlieren, daher ***ist es erstaunlich, dass*** sich 30% aller Künstler nicht mit ihrem Namen melden. (The words in bold translate as “it is astonishing that.”)

The role of *the fact that* constructions in what we have called ‘chains of reasoning’ has come out clearly in the data here, and this is one advantage of focusing on legal language, where chains of reasoning are frequent and usually explicit. However, by limiting the data here to legal genres, it remains an open question whether our results apply to other genres or to the two languages as a whole. Surely the frequent occurrence of constructions with *da–* in our data (cf. examples (67–70) above) is a reflection of their frequent occurrence in other German genres. It is likely that one can find a similar range of uses of *the fact that* in academic writing and other genres where explicit reasoning is frequent, but demonstrating that will need further research.

Conclusions

Noun complement constructions introduced by *the fact that*, and their equivalents in other languages, seem to yield helpful insights into legal reasoning. We have taken the view that such constructions enable propositions to be nominalised, and thus reified and used in chains of argumentation. Legal texts, with their often complex patterns of reasoning, are particularly good illustrations of this analysis.

Using a parallel corpus has shown that other constructions can be employed in a similar way. Viewing two languages in direct contrast can shed light on each of them, and can bring to light modes of expression which are less obvious in monolingual work. By taking an expression in one language, and looking at its counterpart in the other, we can ask whether the formulation in the second language would have been available in the first one. Sometime it is not available: the German constructions using *daran dass* and *darauf . . . dass* in (68) and (70) have no direct English equivalents. In other cases, an equivalent formulation could have been used in the first language: in (64), the German construction *Angesichts der gesunden Grundlagen von FT* raises the intriguing question of why the perfectly acceptable English equivalent *In view of FT's healthy foundations* was not used. Similarly, instances where the counterpart is simpler than the original can also illustrate some ways in which legal language can be simplified in the first language.

Much work remains to be done on *the fact that* and related constructions, notably in relation to Construction Grammar (cf. Bergs and Diewald 2008) and to phraseological theory. This paper has tried to open up some paths for such future research.

Notes

1 Only a small group of nouns (*idea*, *suggestion*, *claim*, etc.) can take complement clauses, and *fact* is by far the most common of these. Huddleston and Pullum (2002: 965) give a fuller list. Like most nouns, *fact* can also be followed by a relative clause, so we can contrast:

(a) The fact that he arrived on time surprised us. [*fact that* + noun complement clause]
(b) The fact that he mentioned surprised us. [*fact that* + relative clause]

The most common distinguishing feature is that relative clauses like *he mentioned* would be grammatically incomplete if they were main clauses, whereas *he arrived on time* would be complete. Also, in (b) the word *that* could be replaced by the relative pronoun *which*; this is not possible in (a). In this paper we are only concerned with *the fact that* + noun complement clause, as in (a). Another name for noun complement clauses is *appositive clauses*: this is the term used by Quirk et al. (1985: 1321). Some reasons to avoid the latter term are given by Huddleston and Pullum (2002: 1016ff.).

2 Cf. also Huddleston and Pullum (2002: 965): '*the fact (that)* . . . serves as a device for nominalising clauses by incorporating them into an NP that can occupy any ordinary NP position'.

3 German has two homonyms: *da* can be a subordinating conjunction ("since"), as in (52), and it can be a locative adverb ("there"). As a separate word there are no corpus examples of the latter in this paper, but the famous words of the poet and activist Heinrich Heine were: *Hauptsache ist: Ich bin da!* ("The main thing is: I am there!"). Just as in (formal) English, the word *there* combines with prepositions (*thereby*, *thereupon*, etc.), we find in all varieties of German very frequent combinations such as *darauf* in (34) and *daran* in (68).

4 It is possible that *Umstand* is a more natural word than *Tatsache* in our data, suggesting that some of the examples with *Tatsache* are translations from the English. Perhaps (72) with *Tatsache* reads like translationese whereas (74) using *Umstand* could be original German. Further research would be necessary to verify this suggestion.

References

Aijmer, K., 2004. *The fact is* – An emergent discourse marker? In G. Bergh, J. Herriman, and M. Mobärg (eds.), *An International Master of Syntax and Semantics. Papers presented to Aimo Seppänen on the Occasion of His 75th Birthday*. Gothenburg studies in English, Vol. 88. Gothenburg: University of Gothenburg, 1–9.

Atkins, B. and Rundell, M., 2008. *The Oxford Guide to Practical Lexicography*. Oxford: Oxford University Press.

Ballier, N., 2007. La complétive du nom dans le discours des linguistes. In D. Banks (ed.), *La coordination et la subordination dans le texte de spécialité*. Paris, L'Harmattan, 55–76.

Bergs, A. and Diewald, G. (eds.), 2008. *Contexts and Constructions*. Amsterdam: Benjamins.

Bonde, J.-P., 2016. *Acquis communautaire*. <http://en.euabc.com/word/12>

Christophersen, P., 1979. Prepositions before noun clauses in present-day English. In M. Chesnutt, C. Faerch, T. Thrane, and G.D. Caie (eds.), *Essays Presented to Knud Schibsbye on His 75th Birthday*. Copenhagen: Akademisk Forlag, 229–234.

Conte, M.-E., 1996. Anaphoric encapsulation. In W. de Mulder and L. Tasmowski (eds.), *Coherence and Anaphora* (*Belgian Journal of Linguistics* 10), 1–10 [Reprinted in Conte, M.-E., 1999. *Condizioni di coerenza. Ricerche di linguistica testuale*. Alessandria: Edizioni dell'Orso, 107–114].

European Commission, 2012a. *How to Write Clearly*. <http://bookshop.europa.eu/is-bin/INTERSHOP.enfinity/WFS/EU-Bookshop-Site/en_GB/-/EUR/ViewPublication-Start?PublicationKey=HC3212148>

European Commission, 2012b. *Klar und deutlich schreiben*. <http://bookshop.europa.eu/is-bin/INTERSHOP.enfinity/WFS/EU-Bookshop-Site/en_GB/-/EUR/ViewPublication-Start?PublicationKey=HC3212148>

European Commission, 2012c. *Rédiger clairement*. <http://bookshop.europa.eu/is-bin/INTERSHOP.enfinity/WFS/EU-Bookshop-Site/en_GB/-/EUR/ViewPublication-Start?PublicationKey=HC3212148>

European Commission, 2012d. *Scrivere chiaro*. <http://bookshop.europa.eu/is-bin/INTERSHOP.enfinity/WFS/EU-Bookshop-Site/en_GB/-/EUR/ViewPublication-Start?PublicationKey=HC3212148>

Francis, G., 1986. *Anaphoric Noun*. Unpublished MS, University of Birmingham.

Francis, G., 1993. A corpus-driven approach to grammar – Principles, methods and examples. In M. Baker, G. Francis, and E. Tognini-Bonelli (eds.), *Text and Technology: In Honour of John Sinclair*. Amsterdam: Benjamins, 137–156.

Goźdź-Roszkowski, S. and Pontrandolfo, G., 2014. Facing the facts: Evaluative patterns in English and Italian judicial language. In V.K. Bhatia, G. Garzone, R. Salvie, G. Tessuto, and C. Williams (eds.), *Language and Law in Professional Discourse: Issues and Perspectives*. Newcastle: Cambridge Scholars, 10–28.

Granath, S., 2001. Is that a fact? A corpus study of the syntax and semantics of *the fact that*. In P. Rayson, A. Wilson, T. McEnery, A. Hardie, and S. Khoja (eds.), *UCREL Technical Papers Special Issue: Proceedings of the Corpus Linguistics 2001 Conference*, 234–244. <https://pdfs.semanticscholar.org/a01e/3a0c851b14b18de79d795b0f0e24ad9c3ac8.pdf>

Huddleston, R. and Pullum, G.K., 2002. *The Cambridge Grammar of the English Language*. Cambridge: Cambridge University Press.

Hunston, S., 2004. Counting the uncountable. Problems of identifying evaluation in a text and in a corpus. In A. Partington, J. Morley, and L. Haarman (eds.), *Corpora and Discourse*. Bern: Peter Lang, 157–188.

Hunston, S., 2011. *Corpus Approaches to Evaluation: Phraseology and Evaluative Language*. London: Routledge.

Kanté, I., 2010. Mood and modality in finite noun complement clauses: A French-English contrastive study. *International Journal of Corpus Linguistics*, 15(2): 267–290.

Kiparsky, P. and Kiparsky, C., 1971. Fact. In M. Bierwisch and K.E. Heidolph (eds.), *Progress in Linguistics: A Collection of Papers*. The Hague: Mouton, 143–173.

Mair, C., 1988. In defense of *the fact that*: A corpus-based study of current British usage. *Journal of English Linguistics*, 21(1): 59–71.

Pontrandolfo, G. and Goźdź-Roszkowski, S., 2014. Exploring the local grammar of evaluation: The case of adjectival patterns in American and Italian judicial discourse. *Research in Language*, 12(1): 71–92.

Quirk, R., Greenbaum, S., Leech, G., and Swartvik, J., 1985. *A Comprehensive Grammar of the English Language*. London: Longman.

Schmid, H.-J., 2007. Non-compositionality and emergent meaning of lexico-grammatical chunks: A corpus study of noun phrases with sentential complements as constructions. *Zeitschrift für Anglistik und Amerikanistik*, 55(3): 313–340.

Smith, N., 2014. *Categories in LOB/FLOB/Brown/Frown*. <www.lancaster.ac.uk/fss/courses/ling/corpus/blue/l02_1.htm>

Steinberger, R., Ebrahim, M., Poulis, A., Carrasco-Benitez, M., Schlüter, P., Przybyszewski, M. and Gilbro, S., 2014. An overview of the European Union's highly multilingual parallel corpora. *Language Resources and Evaluation*, 48(4): 679–707. <https://ec.europa.eu/jrc/sites/jrcsh/files/2014_08_LRE-Journal_JRC-Linguistic-Resources_Manuscript.pdf>

Zeleňáková, M., 2014. *English and French Terminology Within the Field of EU Law: Noun That-Complement Clauses and the Expression of Stance*. PhD dissertation, University of Košice and Université Paris Diderot.

8 Facts in law

A comparative study of *fact that* and its phraseologies in American and Polish judicial discourse

Stanisław Goźdź-Roszkowski

Introduction

Few disciplines are more concerned with facts than Law. Facts play a crucial role in determining the content of the law. This is particularly true of empirical, descriptive facts, which provide knowledge about human conduct in various circumstances (Greenberg 2004). In judicial writing, and especially in judicial opinions, marking a proposition as factual or non-factual means engaging in law-determining as well as in epistemic and evaluative practices. When judges state that a legal proposition (understood as a legal standard or requirement) is a true statement of the law in a particular legal system, they effectively determine the content of the law. When a judge, writing a dissenting opinion, labels an argument as an *assumption* or *notion*, they evaluate it by assigning a non-factual status to the proposition.

However, indicating a factual status can be problematic. As Hunston (2011: 108) notes in her study of facts in science writing, the use of the word *fact* "potentially leads to contentious discussions about the nature of facts and reality". If, for example, a proposition is labelled as *hypothesis* in a research paper then it becomes one. But this alignment is not always so straightforward with factual propositions, especially in legal discourse. A proposition can have the status of *fact* without being explicitly assessed as such. On the other hand, a proposition could be marked as *fact* not so much for its factual status but to express other functions. Quantitative data relating to the word *fact* in the Academic sections of the British National Corpus show that Law is among disciplines (along with Politics and Education) with the highest occurrence of *fact*.[1] The central question addressed in this chapter concerns the use of *fact* in the domain of law represented by judicial opinions. Previous research on status-indicating nouns (nouns which aver alignment between a proposition and the world) (Goźdź-Roszkowski and Pontrandolfo 2013; Goźdź-Roszkowski forth 2017) and particularly one study which focuses on the use of *the fact that* in American and Italian judicial discourse (Goźdź-Roszkowski and Pontrandolfo 2014) demonstrates that their use may be mapped onto several different discourse functions with evaluation or stance being particularly prominent. The findings also suggest that the way *fact* and other status nouns are used is genre-specific and should be accounted for in terms of the nature of judicial argumentation irrespective of a particular language and legal system.

This chapter aims to explore this hypothesis further by adopting a comparative and cross-lingual perspective. In doing so, I investigate how the phrase *the fact that* and its Polish counterpart *fakt, że* are used in US Supreme Court opinions and Poland's Constitutional Tribunal, respectively. It is argued that the use of *fact* is highly patterned and judicial writing shows a clear preference for certain phraseological patterns (referred to here as semantic sequences) which reflect the epistemic practices inherent in the nature of judicial argumentation. In what follows I elaborate on *status* and *stance*, two concepts most relevant to the present analysis. The analytical framework adopted in Goźdź-Roszkowski and Pontrandolfo (2014) is revisited and refined to establish its suitability between the English and Polish data. The next section brings the presentation of bilingual data and the discussion of findings, followed by a summary and conclusions.

Status and stance

Most, if not all writing involves specifying the type of relationship that exists between propositions and the world. Writers, irrespective of academic discipline or professional field, are inevitably faced with the task of reifying propositions by assigning them an epistemic status. An assignment of status, understood as a type of alignment between a text or proposition and the world, involves labelling a proposition as *discovery*, *hypothesis*, *claim* or *fact*. The practice of indicating status is informed by the broader phenomenon known as stance, which refers to the expression of a writer's "personal feelings, attitudes, value judgments or assessments" (Biber et al. 1999: 966) towards a proposition. It is particularly common and important in disciplinary or professional writing where the status of propositions may reflect the unique nature of a given discipline. As with all stance expressions, indicating status is not only subjective and individual but it also reveals the epistemological beliefs and values of a given professional or disciplinary community.

One of the typical resources used to modify status include head nouns (e.g. *assumption*, *belief*, *notion*, etc.) that take a nominal complement in the form of *that*-clause. Hunston (2011: 27) asserts that "evaluation of status essentially reifies propositions into the objects of which the discipline is comprised: hypotheses, results, conclusions, assumptions, implications and so on". Such status-indicting nouns are also commonly found in judicial discourse (Goźdź-Roszkowski and Pontrandolfo 2013). A recent study (Goźdź-Roszkowski (forthcoming 2017) demonstrates how US Supreme Court opinions use a range of status-indicating nouns[2] in the N *that* pattern to perform five major functions: evaluation, cause, result, confirmation and existence. Yet, it turns out that evaluation plays a central role in judicial argumentation and most status-indicating nouns are used to signal sites of contentions, i.e. challenged propositions are likely to be labelled as *arguments*, *assumptions*, *notions* or *suggestions*.

In Example 1 below, taken from a dissenting opinion in the case *City of Chicago, Petitioner v. Jesus Morales et al.*, the proposition 'state courts must apply the restrictive Salerno test' is averred by the writer as *assumption*.

(1) Justice Scalia's assumption *that state courts must apply the restrictive Salerno test* is incorrect as a matter of law.

Labelling the proposition as assumption amounts to evaluation because it aligns the proposition (underlined) with a construed world in which it cannot be subjected to immediate verification. In addition, there is another layer of evaluation marked overtly and negatively by using a value-laden adjective *incorrect*.

When writers use the phrase *the fact that*, one of the problems involved in its interpretation is the distinction between *fact* as a representation of reality or *fact* as an assessment of certainty or other type of evaluation. For example, Examples 2 and 3 provided below show that *the fact that* can be used to indicate very different stances:

(2) Thus, despite the **fact** that the legislature had passed a law mandating nonpartisan judicial elections, despite the **fact** that the new law expressly repealed the old law, despite the **fact** that the Governor had signed the law, and despite the **fact** that the State had submitted the new law to the United States Attorney General for preclearance under §5, this new law was not operative for one reason.
(3) The Court's repeated references to the partners' "opportunity," is potentially misleading because it **ignores the fact** that a plan is binding upon all parties once it is confirmed.

In Example 2, the author presents a clear assertion of what she believes has actually happened, a representation of reality that can be easily verified. On the other hand, in Example 3, the writer provides an overt evaluation of the court's conduct by contrasting the court's description ("opportunity") and "a plan is binding upon all parties once it is confirmed", suggesting that *the fact that* is an expression of evaluation. One of the aims of this chapter is therefore to throw more light on the ways in which *the fact that* is used in legal opinions.

Materials and method

Materials

The study relies on two collections of data. The first one consists of 113 different opinions of the Supreme Court of the United States totaling 1,333,320 words and randomly sampled from the period between 1999 and 2015 via FindLaw.com, a well-known legal information web portal providing free access to cases heard by the US Supreme Court. The Polish data comprises 95 different judgments handed down by the Constitutional Tribunal between 2001 and 2015. The texts, which contain 1,303,141 words, were collected from the on-line database *Internetowy Portal Orzeczeń*, available at http://ipo.trybunal.gov.pl. Despite the differences between the Common Law and the Continental Civil Law, the Supreme Court in the United States and the Constitutional Tribunal in Poland share some similarities with respect to their roles and functions. The US Supreme Court is the highest court in the United States. It consists of the Chief Justice and the eight Associate Justices. Its primary task is to exercise appellate jurisdiction and to serve as the final arbiter in the construction of the Constitution of the United States by providing a uniform interpretation of the law. The Constitutional Tribunal (Pol. *Trybunał Konstytucyjny*) resolves disputes related to the constitutionality of actions undertaken by public institutions and its main task is to ensure the compliance of statutory law with the Constitution of the Republic of Poland. One feature that is shared by both the US Supreme Court opinions and the judgments given by the Constitutional Tribunal is the focus on justifications used in the judicial decision-making. Courts make decisions through legal reasoning. Most of the contexts in which *the fact that* has been examined concern legal reasoning.

Method: phraseology and semantic sequences

This study adopts a somewhat different perspective on phraseology than the other chapters in this volume. It looks at phraseology as the co-occurrence of not only wordforms or lemmas but also of grammatical forms and "broadly-defined elements of meaning" (Hunston 2011: 7). One way of describing textual recurrence involves analyzing a series of meaning elements spread across words and phrases which are usually very diverse in form but which reflect the consistency of function. For example, a recent study of semantic sequences in US Supreme Court opinions documents that the co-texts of the phrase *the argument that* include a wide range of very different lexical items such as *the dissent resorts to the last-ditch argument that*, *This Court finds unpersuasive the argument that*, *The United States' argument that . . . is an astounding assertion*, *The Government of the United States has a valid legal argument that*, etc. Although the wording in each case may be different (there are as many as 65 different expressions evaluating the phrase *argument that*), all these examples share the semantic regularity of signalling evaluative meaning (Goźdź-Roszkowski forthcoming 2017).This suggests that certain types of discourse functions are expressed in varied and idiosyncratic language which avoids repetitive and recurrent sequences of words so typical of certain legal genres, such as contracts and legislation (see for example Biel or Trklja, this volume).

In contrast to other types of phraseological constructs such as lexical bundles (Biber et al. 1999), skipgrams (Guthrie et al. 2006), phrase frames (Fletcher 2002–2007) or concgrams (Cheng et al. 2006), semantic sequences admit of a much greater lexical and structural variation. They are not concerned with the co-occurrence of two or more words. Instead, they are found at a higher level of language organization by displaying regularities of occurrence that go *beyond* the word, the phrase or even the clause. A semantic sequence consists of a core item, which may be a lexical phrase (e.g. *to make sure*), a grammar pattern (e.g. a noun followed by a *that*-clause as in this study) or grammar words (e.g. prepositions). The core item serves as a starting point and a search query in a corpus analysis which then proceeds to identify a co-occurring complementation pattern or patterns and a range of different types of phrases associated with that item. A semantic sequence is identified if the co-occurring elements show a consistency in terms of their meaning and discursive function.

This study aims to identify and analyze semantic sequences which take as their starting point the phrase *fact that* and its Polish counterpart *fakt, że*. The method consisted of carrying out a targeted search (using the WordSmith Tools 5.0) for all instances of *fact that* and *fakt, że/iż*[3] in the two text corpora. The retrieved instances were then manually checked to ensure that the nouns are indeed followed by an appositive *that*-clause and not by the relative pronoun *that* (see Hunston and Francis 2000: 98–99). Once two lists had been compiled, the next stage involved scrutinizing concordance lines centred around *fact that* and *fakt, że/iż* in order to establishing their phraseology. This stage of the analysis focused on examining in detail the preceding prepositions and verbs, and the predicates of *the fact that* depending on their syntactic position (i.e. whether the phrase is in Rheme or Theme, to use the terminology of Systemic-Functional Grammar). The obtained co-occurrence patterns were interpreted in functional terms. As a starting point, I relied on the framework used in Goźdź-Roszkowski and Pontrandolfo (2014) and originally proposed in Hunston (2011). In brief, the phrases with *fact that* and its Italian counterpart *il fatto che* in the former were classified into seven major categories: FACT IS THE BASIS FOR PRACTICAL OUTCOME OR REASONING, FACT EXPLAINS SOMETHING, FACT IS THE CAUSE OF A PROBLEM OR ITS SOLUTION, SOMETHING USES OR ASSUMES A FACT (OR NOT), BE AWARE OR UNAWARE OF A FACT, PEOPLE TALK ABOUT A FACT and AFFECTIVE REACTION TO A FACT.

The study reported in Goźdź-Roszkowski and Pontrandolfo (2014) corroborates the basic usability of this taxonomy as applied to judicial discourse even though it was proposed for the use of facts in popular science writing (Hunston 2011). The study shows that the phrase *the fact that* serves certain basic functions in argumentation, irrespective of a discipline or indeed a language (but see Salkie, this volume). For example, it turns out that the phrase *the fact that* is first and foremost used to support an argument by indicating that it is based on some factual proposition. In a similar vein, Mazzi (this volume) points to the co-occurrence between *the fact that*, which he analyzes as a lexical bundle, and its use as the basis for judges of the Supreme Court of Ireland to express their stance and determine the outcome of their reasoning.

For the purpose of this analysis, this original framework used in Goźdź-Roszkowski and Pontrandolfo (2014) was revisited and configured to paint a more accurate picture of the most prominent and distinct phraseological patterns associated with *the fact that* and identified in both American and Polish texts. As a result, only two of the original discourse functions, namely *fact is the basis for practical outcome or reasoning* and *fact explains something*, have been retained. The former was then modified as facts are the basis for legal reasoning or judicial disposition. A new functional category of *facts are evaluated* has been proposed to reflect the presence of a substantial proportion of instances when the surrounding contexts are overtly or covertly evaluative. In addition, it covers those uses of *fact that* which are associated with a problem and which were included originally in the category of *fact is the cause of a problem or its solution*. Since in this study very few instances of *affective reaction to fact* (e.g. *The Court is troubled by the fact that*) had been found in both corpora, this category was removed. Similarly, the category of *be aware or unaware of a fact* turned out to be virtually non-existent. On closer examination two other functional categories proved to be too general or vague: *something uses or assumes a fact (or not)* and *people talk about a fact*. Instead, the *facts are ignored* category is offered to reflect those cases when a point is made to signal that facts have not been taken into account in specific instances of argumentation. Similarly, when judges 'talk about a fact', they usually do so in order to draw attention to an important descriptive fact (e.g. *We therefore must take into account the fact that*). Thus, the category *people talk about a fact* has been replaced with *facts are emphasized*. Finally, the Goźdź-Roszkowski and Pontrandolfo (2014) study does not propose a specific functional category for those cases when *the fact that* is found in clause-initial position. In this analysis, I argue that *the fact that* and its Polish counterpart are used in that position to communicate that facts do not lead to consequences. In brief, the study reported here relies on a descriptive framework that consists of six new or modified categories described in detail in the next section.

As can be seen from the methodological considerations provided in this section, the present study combines corpus-based, quantitative methods with qualitative analysis that pays attention to detail and context in order to investigate the form and function of judicial language as communicative discourse. In particular, the following specific research questions will be addressed in this chapter:

1. What are the characteristic patterns in which the phrase *the fact that* and *fakt, że/iż* are found and what functions do they perform in the discourse of judicial opinions?
2. What does the analysis of phraseology reveal about how 'fact' is used in judicial writing and how it contributes to the use of argumentative strategies in judicial argumentation?
3. What are the implications of their similarities and differences in terms of epistemology and argumentative strategies?
4. What are the advantages and disadvantages of adopting a corpus methodology to study status and stance in judicial discourse?

Discourse functions of semantic sequences with *fact that* and *fakt, że*

Overview of functional categories in the two corpora

To address the first research question, the frequencies of the different categories of *fact that* and *fakt, że/iż* were compared across the two corpora. The frequencies provided in Figure 8.1 refer to a percentage of instances when the phrase *fact that* or *fakt, że* co-occurs with different lexical items to express a given function. For example, in 26% of all the instances when *fact that* is identified in the corpus of US Supreme Court opinions, it is used to indicate grounds for reasoning and/or judicial decision. As can be seen in Figure 8.1, there are considerable similarities as well as some differences in the way facts are used in the two corpora.

First, the data bring to light a marked preference in both datasets for using facts as the basis for legal reasoning and/or judicial disposition. This is not surprising since legal actors draw upon facts to support their argumentation and to increase the neutrality and reliability of their reasons for reaching particular decisions. In both datasets (with the Polish data showing a slightly higher frequency), facts are also used for their explanatory value. As Solan (1993: 1) observes, "judges usually care deeply about making the best decision they can, and about conveying their decision in a manner that makes the decision appear as fair as possible to the parties, and often to the public". Explaining the reasons behind their decisions by referring to facts is certainly one way of achieving this goal. The first two categories both demonstrate that facts are the cause of things. One of the surprising results of this analysis is the extent to which facts tend to be evaluated in judicial discourse in both US and Polish courts. The present analysis shows there is a much greater presence of evaluative language than previously thought (Goźdź-Roszkowski and Pontrandolfo 2014) and that this occurs equally commonly in Polish and American data. The final point of similarity is relatively infrequent but it signals how things can be oriented around facts by ignoring them or taking them into account. It also indicates that judges are likely to focus on the reasons for

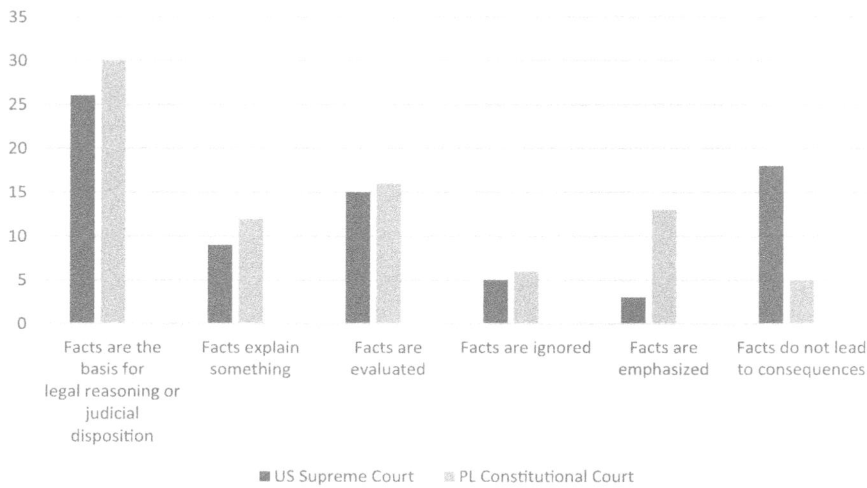

Figure 8.1 Functional categories of *fact that* and *fakt, że/iż* in the two corpora (frequencies expressed in terms of percentages)

Table 8.1 Examples of different linguistic realizations of the *facts are the basis for legal reasoning or judicial disposition* category. Lexical items in square brackets show co-occurring nouns

[presumption] *arise from the fact that*
[plurality] *base its holding on the fact that*
comes from the fact that
confirmed by the fact that
[present case] *consists of the fact that*
[reading] *consistent with the fact that*
derived from the fact that
[conclusion, holding] *does not depend on the fact that*
[Court's conclusion] *did not hinge on the fact that*
due to the fact that
[courts, judge, we] *relied on the fact that*
[report] *reflected the fact that*
[decision, inference] *rested on the fact that*
stems from the fact that
[inference] *strengthened by the fact*
we find additional support for this conclusion in the fact that

a given decision and brush aside the arguments to the contrary (Solan 1993: 2). Facts are emphasized considerably more frequently in Polish data. As will be shown in the next section, this can be attributed to the common strategy in Polish opinions whereby writers use impersonal constructions with obligation/necessity modals to direct the reader's attention to a specific fact (e.g. *one should take into account the fact that . . .*). This use is marginal in the American data. Finally, the two corpora differ in the extent to which *fact that* and *fakt, że/iż* are used in clause-initial position to indicate that an allegedly factual proposition does not lead to an undesirable consequence.

This initial quantitative overview seems to suggest that American and Polish judicial writing is underpinned by essentially the same epistemological assumptions. In the next sections, we will examine each category in much greater detail.

Facts are the basis for legal reasoning or judicial disposition

As shown in Figure 8.1, it turns out that *fact that* in judicial writing, in both types of courts, is most often used to indicate grounds for legal argumentation. In the case of US Supreme Court opinions, this usually leads to reaching specific conclusions and making decisions by announcing dispositions in particular cases. Table 8.1 provides examples of many different ways in which this function is expressed in American opinions.

Despite the seemingly many different expressions, some general observations can be made. Almost all of the phrases listed include a preposition. The preposition *on* is the most frequently used along with several verbs such as *rely*, *rest*, *depend*, *hinge* and *base*, to signal *reliance* on some fact mentioned in the context of a particular opinion. The perception of *fact that* as constituting grounds for propositions made in the opinions is further strengthened by the presence of the preposition *from* and the corresponding verbs such as *arise from*, *come from* or *stem from*.

Sentence Examples 4–7 provide more extended contexts, which enables one to identify other co-occurring items. Facts are relied upon by judges who are defined according to the type of opinion to which they subscribe, i.e. majority, plurality or dissenting:

(4) Second, the Court's decision in Baker v. Carr, supra, **rested** in large part **on the fact that** courts were already involved in overseeing apportionment cases.
(5) The plurality also seems to **base** its sub silentio holding of implied repeal **on the fact that** "[e]ighty percent" of §2a(c) is "dead letter."
(6) Contrary to the dissent's assertion, this conclusion **does not depend on the fact that** interest "was created by the beneficence of a state regulatory program."
(7) Courts that have reached the contrary conclusion have principally **relied on the fact that** 28 U. S. C. §2244(b)(2)(A) contains an explicit requirement that a new rule be "made retroactive . . . by the Supreme Court."

Worth noting is the presence of certain co-occurring epistemic objects, such as *assertion*, *conclusion* or *inference* found in the close vicinity of *fact that*. For example, there are as many as 19 instances of *fact that* co-occurring with *conclusion*. This shows that conclusions can be contested and, as a result, they may need to be strengthened by reference to facts. The use of *fact that* seems to be closely associated with legal argumentation in which different, often conflicting, stances are averred or attributed. This argumentative feature is particularly conspicuous in Examples 6 and 7. In both examples, conclusions contradict arguments put forward by other legal interactants. In Example 6 the conclusion averred in a Court's (majority) opinion is shown to rely on different grounds (even though formulated through negation) than the argumentation (encapsulated here as *assertion*) proposed by the dissent. But there may also be an errant expression which does not strictly follow the formulaic pattern signalled above:

(8) we find additional support for this conclusion in **the fact that** . . .

Still, even though the wording of each example in Table 8.1 is very different, they all share the same function of indicating the grounds for a proposition. In Supreme Court opinions, this function is associated with a clear phraseological pattern, a semantic sequence which can be generalized and formulated as follows:

> LEGAL INTERACTANT [*the Court*, *plurality*, *dissent*, *we (the Court)*, etc.] + RELIANCE VERBS [*rely/rest/depend/hinge/base*] + LEGAL INSTRUMENTS or EPISTEMIC OBJECTS [e.g. *conclusion*, *decision*, *holding*]

This sequence, which does not need to have a fixed order, consists of a legal interactant, typically a judge or a group of judges signalling their decision or argument in a given type of legal opinion (i.e. plurality, majority or dissent opinion), followed by a range of verbs signalling reliance such as *rely*, *rest*, *depend*, *hinge*, *base*, etc. These are followed by the preposition *on* and the phrase *the fact that*. This pattern may also include the element that relies on a given fact: *conclusion*, *decision*, *holding*, etc.

In Polish judgments, facts are also indicated as foundations of propositions but with a view to justifying views, premises, opinions rather than presenting facts as something that writers rely upon. This function is carried out mainly by means of the verb *uzasadnić* (*justify*), which focuses on specific arguments, views, a particular course of action or a legislative intent of a statutory instrument. As can be seen in Table 8.2, Polish judges employ a relatively limited but a more diverse range of different linguistic expressions within this category, the verb *uzasadnić* being by far the most frequent. Thus, one semantic sequence that emerges from Polish data could be summarized as:

LEGAL INTERACTANT + JUSTIFICATION + EPISTEMIC or COGNITIVE OBJECT

Examples 9 and 10 show typical contexts in which facts are invoked to justify a view attributed to a legal interactant, a party to a dispute heard before the Constitutional Tribunal, which in this example is the highest administrative court in Poland (Example 9), and to provide the grounds for a legislative instrument regulating passengers' rights (Example 10).[4]

(9) **Pogląd** ten NSA **uzasadnił faktem, iż** w stanie prawnym właściwym dla rozpoznawanej przez NSA sprawy procedura otrzymywania zasiłku pielęgnacyjnego w sytuacji, kiedy miał on być otrzymywany przez dalszy okres. [The NSA (Supreme Administrative Court) **justified its view by the fact that** given the legal implications of the case . . .]

(10) Jego głównym założeniem jest wzmocnienie praw pasażerów nie tylko w ruchu kolejowym międzynarodowym, lecz także krajowym, **uzasadnione** przede **wszystkim faktem, że** pasażer jest słabszą stroną umowy transportu kolejowego. [Its (the regulation) major premise is to strengthen passengers' rights not only in international but also domestic traffic, **justified by the fact that** passengers are the weaker party to any rail transport contract.]

In a small number of instances, *fact that* is also used to indicate why (on what basis) certain propositions have been deemed problematic. Examples 11–13 illustrate this point. In these examples, facts are related to undesirable situations, i.e. *doubts*, *unconstitutionality* or *constitutional problems*:

(11) Powyższe **wątpliwości** co do siły przedstawionych argumentów **wzmacnia** w opinii Trybunału Konstytucyjnego **fakt, że** [In the opinion of the Constitutional Tribunal, the above-mentioned **doubts** about the strength of the arguments are **exacerbated by the fact that** . . .]

In Example 12, the Tribunal points to a specific fact which lies at the basis of considering a legislative provision as unconstitutional.

(12) W sprawie o sygn. P 28/07 Trybunał uznał, że **podstawą niekonstytucyjności** art. 24 ust. 2 był **fakt, że** [In the case number P 28/07, the Constitutional Tribunal ruled that **the fact that** . . . was the **basis for unconstitutionality** of Art. 24 Section 2.]

Table 8.2 Examples of different linguistic realizations of the *facts are the basis for legal reasoning or judicial disposition* category in the Polish corpus

[*pogląd* [view] *jest uzasadniony faktem, że* [is justified by the fact that . . .]
przemawia za tym fakt, że [this is supported by the fact that]
O czym świadczy fakt, że [as evidenced by the fact that . . .]
wątpliwości . . . wzmacnia fakt, że [doubts are exacerbated by the fact that . . .]
podstawą . . . był fakt, że [the fact that . . . was the basis for . . .]

(13) **Problemem** konstytucyjnym jest **fakt, że** funkcjonowanie mechanizmu, którego część tworzy rozpatrywana norma, nieuchronnie prowadzi do niekonstytucyjnych skutków. [The constitutional **problem lies in the fact that** . . .]

In these cases, the use of *fact that* shows that two different discourse functions can overlap as in Example 13, where the fact is the basis for what is negatively evaluated as problem. Such instances were classified in the *fact as basis* category since this function seems to be primary and it seems to take precedence over the evaluative function.

This correlation between facts and problematic situations is also found in American opinions as Example 14 shows:

(14) The Confrontation Clause **problem lies in the fact that** Lambatos did not have personal knowledge that the male DNA profile that Cellmark said was derived from the crime victim's vaginal swab sample was in fact correctly derived from that sample.

Facts explain something

A distinct albeit related category is proposed to group those expressions centred around *fact that* which provide explanation for propositions included in judicial opinions. In Polish data, this function is expressed by means of a set of fixed phrases such as: *wynika to z faktu, że* [This results from the fact that . . .], *z uwagi na fakt, że*, [given the fact that . . .], *ze względu na fakt, że* [in view of the fact that . . . / due to the fact that], *biorąc pod uwagę fakt, że* [taking into account the fact that], *wziąwszy pod uwagę fakt, że* [having taken into account the fact that], *zważywszy fakt, że* [given the fact that].

In Polish judgments propositions are accounted for by indicating their connection with what the writer considers to be an objectively verifiable fact. In Example 15, the author of the opinion explains the reasons for regarding certain legislative procedures as belonging to the sole competence of the government as the executive power.

(15) Samo przedłożenie projektu ustawy budżetowej jest zarówno uprawnieniem Rady Ministrów, jak i jej obowiązkiem, a wyłączność tej kompetencji Rady Ministrów **wynika z faktu, że** to ona prowadzi gospodarkę finansową państwa i kieruje wykonaniem ustawy budżetowej, za co ponosi odpowiedzialność przed Sejmem. [Submitting a Budget Bill is both a prerogative and a duty vested in the government and the exclusivity of this competence **results from the fact that** it is the government that manages the state finances and implements the budget law and it is held accountable before the parliament.]

Similarly, in Example 16, the judge explains that the town council, a defendant in that case, challenged a certain portion of the Education Act by referring to a specific, descriptive fact, i.e. the way education subsidies are managed. At the same time, the writer of the opinion signals the opposite stance adopted by the Speaker of the *Sejm* [lower house of the Polish parliament], who put forward his counterarguments to exactly the same fact thus leaving it open to interpretation:

(16) Wobec tego, że **niezgodność** art. 90 ust. 2c ustawy o systemie oświaty Rada Gminy Nieporęt **wywiodła z faktu, iż** wysokość subwencji oświatowej nie jest powiązana z kosztami dotacji przekazywanych innym gminom, Marszałek Sejmu sformułował

następujące kontrargumenty: . . . [Since the **non-compliance** of Article 90 Section 2c of the Education Act had been **inferred** by the Town Council of Nieporęt **from the fact that** the amount of the education subsidy is not related to the cost of the subsidies provided to other municipalities, the Speaker put forward the following counterarguments: . . .]

In many cases, the connection between two propositions where one contains the explanatory factor tends to be foregrounded by placing it in sentence-initial position as in Example 16 and 17:

(17) **Z uwagi na fakt, że** pozwany nie miał obowiązku wskazania przyczyny wypowiedzenia, roszczenie o uznanie rozwiązania umowy za bezskuteczne należy uznać za nieuzasadnione (art. 30 § 4 k.p.). [**Given the fact that** the defendant was not under the obligation to indicate the reason for giving the notice, the claim for regarding the termination of a contract as ineffective must be deemed unjustified.]

This use of *fact that* is mirrored in Supreme Court opinions which also rely on a set of fixed expressions to provide explanations as the examples below demonstrate:

(18) There is undeniably a lack of parallelism here, but it seems to us adequately **explained by the fact that** §251 specifically requires the Commission to promulgate regulations implementing that provision, whereas subsection (d) of §252 does not.
(19) After the voir dire, Deck's counsel once again objected, moving to strike the jury panel "**because of the fact that** Mr. Deck is shackled in front of the jury and makes them think that he is . . . violent today."

Other examples of co-occurring phrases include: *due to the fact that*, *be attributable to the fact that*, *despite the fact that*, *given the fact that*.

Facts are evaluated

One of the most surprising findings is the extent to which facts are evaluated in judicial opinions in both US and Polish courts. The way evaluation is expressed can be often difficult to capture. Evaluation can be expressed both explicitly and implicitly. The findings presented in this analysis are confined solely to overt linguistic markers such as value-laden adjectives or nouns and shown in the examples below. The proportion of evaluated facts is similar in both US and Polish data. In both datasets, facts are assessed in terms of their relative importance as shown in Examples 20–23:

(20) In concurrence, Justice Sotomayor **highlighted the importance of the fact that** the forensic report had been admitted into evidence for the purpose of proving the truth of the matter it asserted.
(21) Surely there is no **legal significance to the fact that** immediately after the confirmation of the plan "the partners were in the same position that they would have enjoyed had they exercised an exclusive option under the plan to buy the equity in the reorganized entity, or contracted to purchase it from a seller who had first agreed to deal with no one else."

There are strikingly similar examples in Polish opinions:

(22) Należy więc zaakcentować **znaczenie faktu, iż** wpis ostateczny sąd określa dopiero w wyroku [One should **stress the importance of the fact that** . . .]
(23) **Nie bez znaczenia pozostaje fakt, że** w okresach podejmowania przez ubezpieczonych decyzji o tym, czy całość ich składek ma trafiać do ZUS-u, czy też ich część ma być odprowadzana do OFE, ZUS może prowadzić niczym nieograniczoną kampanię informacyjną. [**The fact that** . . . **remains important**.]

In addition, in American opinions facts are often assessed in negative terms. The most frequent evaluative adjectives are *unremarkable*, *irrelevant* and *unreasonable* but other evaluative words and expressions include *insufficient*, *frivolous*, *have no logical bearing*, *a rational ground*, *says little about*, *is strong evidence*, *is a reliable indicator*, *serves as persuasive evidence*, *is cause enough*, *sufficient reason for*, etc.

In Polish opinions, facts tend to be evaluated using a more restricted lexis. The evaluation is typically expressed using a single lexeme: *znaczenie* (importance). Thus, facts are of *high*, *enormous* or *fundamental* importance. In addition, facts may be with or without a *legal* importance. Most instances of negative evaluation are found when facts are associated with things perceived as negative. The phrase *fakt, że* serves as a link between two propositions one of which refers to something negative.

(24) Trybunał Konstytucyjny dostrzega też pewną **niekonsekwencję** tej tezy związaną z **faktem, że** [The Constitutional Court finds some **inconsistency** in this argument **connected with the fact that** . . .]
(25) **Wątpliwości** wnioskodawców **wiążą się z faktem, że** . . . [The petitioners' **doubts are connected with the fact that** . . .]

Not surprisingly, there are very few instances of what could be called affective reaction to facts in both US and Polish opinions. Below are two of the very few examples:

(26) The Court is **troubled by the fact that** this computation method has enabled Boeing "to deduct some $1.75 billion of expenditures from its domestic taxable earnings under 26 U. S. C. §174 and never deduct a penny of those expenditures from its 'combined taxable earnings' under the DISC statute."
(27) **Razi mnie** też przywoływanie wśród argumentów moralnych za dopuszczeniem uboju rytualnego faktu, że zabijanie zwierząt (bez względu na metodę) zawsze może w praktyce odbywać się w sposób „wadliwy" i „immanentnie" wiąże się z „cierpieniem, bólem i niepokojem", a także zwykły ubój może przebiegać w sposób nieprawidłowy [**I find it offensive** that moral arguments for allowing ritual slaughter include the fact that . . .]

Facts are ignored

Indicating that certain facts have not been taken into account is another way of dealing with arguments in judicial opinions. In US data there are several instances of expressions which assess arguments negatively by asserting that some fact has been missing from the interpretation or discussion as in the examples below:

(28) But this way of reading the statute **simply pays no attention to the fact that** the statute does not speak of liability (and consequent entitlement to recovery) in a free-standing, unqualified way, but in a limited way, by reference to enumerated damages.
(29) This discussion is flawed. **It overlooks the fact that** there was no jury in this case, and as we have explained, the trier of fact did not have to rely on any testimonial hearsay in order to find that Lambatos' testimony about the DNA match was supported by adequate foundational evidence and was thus probative.

There is quite a range of diverse expressions signalling failure to take facts into account. The following semantic sequence can be proposed:

ARGUMENTATION + OMISSION VERBS (e.g. *avoid*, *brush aside*, *ignore*, *leave aside*, *overlook*) + FACT THAT

This use of *fact that* is closely mirrored in Polish where, characteristically, the Constitutional Tribunal tends to be the object of criticism for failing to include some factual circumstances or consequences. It should be pointed out that this use of fact is also evaluative.

(30) Trybunał **nie zwrócił** w uzasadnieniu **należytej uwagi na fakt, że** w trakcie rozprawy wnioskodawca [the Constitutional Tribunal in its opinion **failed to pay sufficient attention to the fact that** . . .]
(31) W konsekwencji Trybunał **nie dostrzega faktu, że** przyjmując zaskarżone przepisy [In consequence, the [Constitutional] Tribunal **does not notice the fact that** . . .]

Facts are emphasized

The other side of the coin is that facts are made often more prominent by signalling how legal actors orient themselves around facts. Example 32 merits some attention because it shows two different uses of *fact that*. The first use seems to be largely rhetorical. The writer attempts to draw attention to what the court did by emphasizing that the action took place more than once and that it did really happen. The use of the phrase *fact that* could be interpreted as adding credibility to the court's inquiry. The other *fact that* refers to a verifiable event, a *material* fact.

(32) In that case, the Court **made repeated reference to the fact that** its inquiry into whether the military tribunal had jurisdiction to try and punish Milligan **turned** in large part **on the fact that** Milligan was not a prisoner of war, but a resident of Indiana arrested while at home there.
(33) Respondents **emphasize the fact that** §252(c)(1), which requires state commissions to assure compliance with the provisions of §251 . . .
(34) We therefore must **take into account the fact that** Martinez was hospitalized and in severe pain during the interview.

As Figure 8.1 shows, Polish judges take into account facts much more frequently. They usually draw attention to facts by using an impersonal construction as in Example 35 and 36.

(35) **Warto też zwrócić uwagę na fakt, że** niewyrażenie zgody na udostępnienie akt przez prokuratora na podstawie art. 156 § 5 k.p.k. wiąże sąd. [**It is worth drawing attention to the fact that** . . .]

(36) Poszukując znaczenia zasady bezstronności władz publicznych **należy zwrócić uwagę na fakt, że** termin „bezstronność" [When seeking the meaning of the impartiality rule, **one should take into account the fact that** . . .]

In other instances, a specific legal actor is mentioned and reported to have focused on a particular fact in his or her argumentation:

(37) Prokurator Generalny **zwrócił uwagę na fakt, że** celem ustawodawcy było . . . [The Attorney General **drew attention to the fact that** . . .]

Facts do not lead to consequences

So far we looked at examples where the construction *fact that* and *fakt, że* are in object position. In fact, the syntactic position has been ignored in order to focus on the semantic and functional components. The findings documented in Goźdź-Roszkowski and Pontrandolfo (2014) show that there is a strong correlation between *fact that* identified in clause-initial position and negative particles and negativity in general. In addition, this observation has been found to hold true for both *fact that* and its Italian counterpart. In the present study, the analysis of Polish opinions leads to similar results. Examples 38 and 39 show that there are structural as well as functional similarities between English and Polish co-texts:

(38) **The fact that** distributors of allegedly obscene materials may be subjected to varying community standards in the various federal judicial districts into which they transmit the materials **does not render** a federal statute unconstitutional.

(39) Sam **fakt, że** dochody jednostek samorządu terytorialnego nie są wystarczające, aby optymalnie realizować wszystkie zadania publiczne, **nie przesądza** o naruszeniu art. 167 ust. 1 Konstytucji. [The very **fact that** the revenue of local government units is not sufficient to carry out its public tasks effectively **does not constitute** a breach of Article 167 Section 1 of the Constitution.]

(40) **Fakt, iż** po tej dacie obowiązywać zaczęła nowa, lepsza z punktu widzenia zasad Konstytucji, procedura, gdyż lepiej realizująca zasadę prawa do sądu, **nie stanowił** pogwałcenia zasady równości, w tym w odniesieniu do praw majątkowych. [The **fact that** . . . **did not constitute** a violation of the equality principle.]

Structurally, the *that*-clause in this construction serves as complement to the noun *fact* (Biber et al. 1999: 676). As far as their function is concerned, the noun phrases beginning with *fact that* and *fakt, że* are meant to indicate that the proposition in the *that*-clause is factual or it contains generally accepted information (cf. Biber et al. 1999: 676). The noun phrases function as theme so they represent departure points for the entire message. In Polish examples, the intended factuality of the proposition is further stressed by modifying the noun *fakt* using the word *sam* which translates as *itself* or *alone*. See Example 39. As can be seen in Figure 8.1, the frequency of the Polish noun phrase *fakt, że* in this functional category is considerably lower than that of the English *fact that*. Further investigation suggests that in Polish opinions, clauses with *fakt, że* in clause-initial position display a consistent pattern. They are found with only two verbs, *przesądzić* (determine) and *stanowić* (constitute), which are used in reference to negative consequences such as *breach*, *unconstitutionality*, *violation*, etc. The overall evaluative prosody is positive because the verbs collocate with the negator *nie* (not). The message communicated in these statements is that the circumstances perceived as factual *do not* lead to undesirable consequences. The corresponding semantic sequence could be formulated as follows:

> FACT THAT in clause-initial position + NEGATION + *przesądzić/stanowić* + NEGATIVE CONSEQUENCE (e.g. *naruszenie*, *pogwałcenie*).

In US opinions, instances of *fact that* in clause-initial position co-occur with a wide range of verbs. Firstly, *the fact that* co-occurs with communication verbs (*suggest* and *imply*) and the mental verb *mean*. See Examples 41 and 42.

(41) Of course, **the fact that** the proponents of a plan offer to pay a fair price for the interest they seek to acquire or retain **does not necessarily mean that** that the bankruptcy judge should approve their plan.

(42) Rather, in these domains, **the fact that** Congress has provided the President with broad authorities **does not imply** – and the Judicial Branch should not infer – that Congress intended to deprive him of particular powers not specifically enumerated.

The co-occurring negation means that the 'facts' are of no consequence and as such should not be taken into account when considering a specific action or proceeding, as in Example 41, or arriving at conclusion, as in Example 42. This lack of consequence seems to be the defining feature shared by many other different lexical items in American opinions as well as in the Polish Examples 39 and 40 provided above. In Polish data, the consequences are confined to a potential violation of a legal norm. In contrast, the scope of consequences in US opinions seems to be much broader:

(43) As we have repeatedly explained, "'**the fact that** the officer does not have the state of mind which is hypothecated by the reasons which provide the legal justification for the officer's action **does not invalidate the action** taken as long as the circumstances, viewed objectively, justify that action.'"

(44) And **the fact that** a state cause of action attempts to authorize remedies beyond those that ERISA §502(a) authorizes **does not put it outside the scope of** ERISA's civil enforcement mechanism.

(45) And **the fact that** the Agency previously reached its interpretation through means less formal than "notice and comment" rulemaking, see 5 U. S. C. §553, **does not automatically deprive** that interpretation of the judicial deference otherwise its due.

Looking at more co-text in Examples 43–45 also shows that the use of *fact that* in clause-initial position may construe dispute and an argumentative stance. This is particularly well illustrated in Example 43 taken from the opinion of the Court delivered by Justice Scalia in *Gerald Devenpeck, et al., Petitioners v. Jerome Anthony Alford*. The propositions contained in *the fact that*-clause invoke arguments which are then rebutted. This use of *fact that* should be thus viewed as another major strategy commonly deployed in legal argumentation.

Summary and conclusions

The findings presented in the previous section point to the centrality of 'fact' in judicial argumentation. This is not surprising given that facts are the essence of narrative in judicial opinions. As is the case with any kind of narration, facts tend to be presented in such a way as to achieve the rhetorical effect of making the reader believe the story. Narrations are thus seldom neutral. In fact, they may be part of an argument. As Klinck (1992: 296) notes, "a judicial recounting of the facts will be determined by the point to which the judge wishes the fact to conduce". In other words, judges will select and focus on those facts that will lead to the desired legal conclusion. Corpus studies of factual status in judicial texts are inevitably impoverished because they are limited to those instances of language use which contain the word *fact*. It is easy to imagine that many factual propositions are not marked explicitly as such in judicial argumentation. This limitation of a corpus-based account of *fact* is offset by its ability to reveal recurrences that are not visible when examining single individual texts or even many texts but in isolation. The analysis reported in this chapter considered *the fact that* and its Polish counterpart as a useful 'point of entry' into the study of the complex argumentative style that characterizes much of judicial writing. It shows that, far from being accidental or idiosyncratic, the use of 'fact' in judicial discourse is strongly patterned. This study arrived at such patterns by examining the most salient semantic sequences with *fact that* and *fakt, że*. Using this methodology, I demonstrated the way that multiple instances of a given sequence occur in broadly similar contexts, even though each instance has been produced in very different circumstances. Those 'broadly similar contexts' have been described in terms of semantic sequences. Semantic sequences reflect the consistency of function manifested through diverse language forms, raising the question of frequency. Semantic sequences are very frequent cumulatively, that is, if we consider all the occurrences of individual linguistic realizations of a particular function. Each individual realization in the form of a particular phrase may be relatively infrequent. For example, some of the different phrases used to indicate that facts are the basis for legal reasoning or judicial disposition (shown in Table 8.1) appear only once or twice. This means that traditional collocational analysis with high minimum frequency thresholds might not capture such regularities of use.

Let us now summarize what the corpus study of *fact* (in the two corpora) has told us.

- Facts are causes. Facts lead to conclusions and outcomes, but also to problems;
- Facts are used to make epistemic and evaluative judgment regarding legal entities and processes;
- Facts provide explanation and justification;
- Facts are ignored or taken into account;
- Facts are at the heart of legal argumentation. Facts provide material evidence which is the primary mode of knowledge and argument construction.

The function-based classification of 'fact' in American and Polish data helps to reveal the general similarity suggesting that American and Polish judicial writing is underpinned by essentially the same epistemological assumptions. Irrespective of the different legal systems and institutions, *the fact that* and *fakt, że* are exploited in judicial rhetoric for basically the same reasons. The comparable analysis also shows that some of the ways in which 'fact' is used in judicial discourse could be both genre- and disciplinary-specific. For example, the frequent co-occurrence of *fact that* with evaluation in both corpora underscores the inherently axiomatic nature of judicial reasoning. It is hoped that the findings presented in this chapter contribute towards building up a picture of common epistemological practices in judicial discourse.

Notes

1 I refer here to data presented in Hunston (2011: 109).
2 Even though *fact* is the most frequent noun identified in the N *that* pattern, it was not considered in this study.
3 The complementizer *that* in English corresponds to two variants in Polish: *że* and *iż*.
4 Polish examples have been glossed in English. The translation is literal and it only covers those relevant parts in which a particular phrase is found.

References

Biber, D., Johansson, S., Leech, G., Conrad, S., and Finegan, D., 1999. *The Longman Grammar of Spoken and Written English*. London: Longman.
Cheng, W., Greaves, C., and Warren, M., 2006. From n-gram to skipgram to concgram. *International Journal of Corpus Linguistics*, (11)2: 411–433.
Fletcher, W., 2002–2007. *KfNgram*. Annapolis, MD: USNA.
Goźdź-Roszkowski, S., forthcoming 2017. Between corpus-based and corpus-driven approaches to textual recurrence. Exploring semantic sequences in judicial discourse. In W. Kopaczyk and J. Tyrkkö (eds.), *Patterns in Text: Corpus Driven Methods and Applications*. Amsterdam: John Benjamins.
Goźdź-Roszkowski, S. and Pontrandolfo, G., 2013. Evaluative patterns in judicial discourse: A corpus-based phraseological perspective on American and Italian criminal judgments. *International Journal of Law, Language and Discourse*, 13(2): 9–69.
Goźdź-Roszkowski, S. and Pontrandolfo, G., 2014. Facing the facts: Evaluative patterns in English and Italian judicial language. In V.K. Bhatia, G. Garzone, R. Salvi, G. Tessuto, and C. Williams (eds.), *Language and Law in Professional Discourse: Issues and Perspectives*. Newcastle upon Tyne: Cambridge Scholars Publishing, 10–28.
Greenberg, M., 2004. How facts make law. *Legal Theory*, 10(3): 157–198.
Guthrie, D., Allison, B., Liu, W., Guthrie, L., and Wilks, Y., 2006. A closer look at skip-gram modelling. In *Proceedings of Fifth International Conference on Language Resources and Evaluation (LREC)*. Genoa, Italy, 1222–1225. <www.cs.brandeis.edu/~marc/misc/proceedings/lrec-2006/pdf/357_pdf.pdf>
Hunston, S., 2011. *Corpus Approaches to Evaluation: Phraseology and Evaluative Language*. London/New York: Routledge.
Hunston, S. and Francis, G., 2000. *Pattern Grammar: A Corpus-driven Approach to the Lexical Grammar of English*. Amsterdam: John Benjamins.
Klinck, D.R., 1992. *The Word of the Law*. Ottawa, Canada: Carleton University Press.
Solan, L., 1993. *The Language of Judges*. Chicago: The University of Chicago Press.

9 *Terms and conditions*

A comparative study of noun binomials in UK and Scottish legislation

Joanna Kopaczyk

Introduction

In the British Isles there are two parliaments steeped in a common linguistic repertoire but belonging to different legal traditions: the UK Parliament at Westminster and the Scottish Parliament in Edinburgh. Following a positive outcome of the referendum in 1997, the Scottish Parliament was reinstated in 1999, after an almost 300-year period of parliamentary union with England. This historic move has equipped the Scots with new legislative powers and an opportunity to mark their separate and independent status within the UK. This was a chance for the Scots to employ their own, equally adequate linguistic tools for making laws. The three centuries of legislating by a Union parliament notwithstanding, Scots law is a product of a continuous indigenous tradition, with major influences from civil law (Walker 2001; Smith 1955; MacQueen 1986), which – to generalize somewhat – can be juxtaposed with common law in the south of the island. This separate legal tradition results in specific linguistic patterns and choices in Scottish legal language (Beaton 1982; Stewart 1995; Styles and Whitty 2003). Even though both the English and Scottish acts of parliament are written in standard English today,[1] lexical and phraseological choices may differ not only because the two parliaments legislate on different matters but also because of different histories and backgrounds of English and Scots law. A document issued by the Office of the Scottish Parliamentary Counsel maintains that "[t]he establishment of the Scottish Parliament has presented an opportunity for divergence in the style of Scottish legislation" (2006: Chapter 2). How much of this style is shared with the UK parliament is one of the issues taken up in the present study.

The purpose of this chapter is to investigate binomials, an area of phraseology which is often singled out as a typical feature of legal language (see p. 161). These are coordinated pairs of the same word-class (Malkiel 1959: 113, Bhatia 1993: 108; Kopaczyk and Sauer 2017), for example *bread and butter*, *man and wife*, *grant and give*, *quick and easy*, etc. Using comprehensive corpora of acts passed in the first decade of the new millennium (2001–2010), I investigate binomials in legislation produced by the UK and the Scottish Parliaments. I first gauge the popularity of nominal binomials (consisting of singular and plural nouns) and then concentrate on what proportion of binomials is shared by texts produced by both parliaments. It should also be possible to assess which one is more conservative or traditional in its style in this respect. Next the most frequent binomials are classified into semantic fields, which will illuminate the question which area of meaning is most conducive to binomials in both corpora. Within the shared binomials I then look at the motivations for creating a lexical pair, paying special attention to binomials unmotivated semantically. The unshared binomials can reveal topics on which the two parliaments concentrated in the naughts but they may also lead us to understand the stylistic preferences in legal drafting which go back to the separate historical roots of the law in Scotland and England. In addition, it is intriguing to see the application of the Plain English campaign directives to legal drafting in both legislative bodies in view of the motivations for binomial pairs.

Binomials as a feature of style in legislation

Justified by the need to establish authority and stability of reference, the language of the law carries its historical residue and typical stylistic and phraseological preferences. This results in a formulaic and conservative nature of the language of the law, which has been recognized by several generations of scholars working at these interdisciplinary crossroads. In his seminal monograph on the history of English as the language of the law, David Mellinkoff complains about wordiness and repetition and characterizes this ancient linguistic residue in legal texts as "unnecessary, confusing and wasteful" (1963: 399). In the same vein, he stigmatizes binomials as a superfluous feature of style, calling them "a worthless doubling" of synonyms (1963: 349). Since then, studies of legal phraseology have been sensitive to the frequency and role of binomials, especially in the context of repetition and formulaicity (Danet 1980; Hiltunen 1990; Danet and Bogoch 1994; Gibbons 1994; Tiersma 1999, 2006; Galdia 2009). The proposed motivations for coining binomials included the translation hypothesis, whereby a post-Conquest borrowing was 'translated' by an older native term, as in *to grant and to give*, as well as the need to ensure precision and all-inclusiveness, as in *fair, just and reasonable* (for a discussion of the interpretative layers for each element of this multinomial, see Phillips 2003: 159–168). The first type of binomials has been discouraged in legal drafting by the proponents of the Plain Language campaign (see the next section), and so have binomials which are purely aesthetic in nature or, in essence, unmotivated semantically.

Outside the British context, recent corpus studies of legal language in the United States show that legal genres are highly formulaic and repetitive in nature, especially "the operative genres, such as legislation" (Goźdź-Roszkowski 2011: 110). Legislative texts contain exceptionally large numbers of recurrent and stable lexico-syntactic patterns. "To date, no other genre or text type has been found to contain such a large proportion of formulaic expressions" (Goźdź-Roszkowski 2011: 142). There is every reason to suspect that this situation holds for legislation in the British Isles, too. Historical inquiries into lexico-syntactic stability in Older Scots legal texts, including legislation, revealed a staggering amount of repetitive phrasal and non-phrasal patterns, with binomials and multinomials featuring prominently in the corpus (Kopaczyk 2013: 188–207). Similar studies for the English historical legal discourse are still to be conducted.

The Plain English campaign

Before moving on to assess the size and overlap of binomial inventories in the present-day Scottish and UK legislation, it is useful to contextualize modern legal drafting in terms of stylistic trends as well as linguistic and social awareness. In his *Lectures*, Foucault drew attention to the fact that "[t]hose who have command of discursive practices have social power" (Phillips 2003: 26). The field of the law offers a very good illustration of this relationship. The law itself, according to modern Western interpretations, should be applicable to everybody in equal measure. As Lord Simon of Glaisdale puts it, "[p]eople who live under the Rule of Law are entitled to claim that that law shall be intelligible. A society whose regulations are incomprehensible lives with the Rule of Lottery, not of Law" (1985: 133). It is then a paradox that the language of the law has long been perceived as complex, impermeable to the outsider and therefore capable of creating and sustaining social inequalities and distance. Critical comments about the complexity and illegibility of legal texts, dating back to the 1960s and especially Mellinkoff's work, inspired scholars and practitioners to look for simpler and more effective ways of communicating in the field of law.

The beginnings of the Plain Language campaign[2] in Britain can be traced back to 1975 when the Renton Committee prepared a Report on the Preparation of Legislation in the UK.[3] The significance of the report and its recommendations have generally been applauded in legal circles (Simon of Glaisdale 1985: 133), however the Report itself warned that "little can be done to improve the quality of legislation unless those concerned in the process are willing to modify some of their most cherished habits" (1975: §1.10). Indeed, while to some legal practitioners the need for simpler language is clear, others find the language of the law "precise, hortatory, impressive and durable" (O.C. Lewis, in Phillips 2003: 27) and therefore efficient in its formal application. While the proponents of the Plain Language campaign blame "professional inertia and conservative attitudes" for this reluctance to change, there is also "a strong apprehension that the use of simple vocabulary may lead to added ambiguity" (Cacciaguidi-Fahy and Wagner 2006: 20).

To address these concerns, "[t]he construction of a good Plain English 'translation' requires input from legal professionals who are highly literate in both legal and lay language" (Mooney 2014: 39; cf. Tiersma 2006). One of the ways advocated for making legal drafting simpler is to avoid wordiness. Of course, binomials are often perceived as unnecessarily wordy and Plain Language publications and guidelines call for replacing them with a single word or avoiding altogether. Since the remit of this chapter is to compare the use of binomials in the UK and Scottish legislation, the data analysis carried out below will also allow us to assess whether both parliamentary bodies comply with the Plain English recommendations by avoiding unnecessary verbosity and whether they do it to the same extent.

Data and methodology

Corpora and counts

All UK and Scottish legislation is available online (legislation.gov.uk). For the present analysis, the years 2001–2010 were selected as this was the first decade when the Scottish parliament was conducting fully-fledged operations. The files were arranged by year, converted to text format from pdfs and POS-tagged with TagAnt (Anthony 2015).[4] Since binomials occurred in all the most important grammatical categories, rendering a comprehensive analysis unwieldy, I decided to focus on nouns, which previous studies identified as the most common group, especially in formal registers (Biber et al. 1999: 1031, 1033; Kopaczyk 2009: 91, 2013: 190; Mollin 2014: 29). Noun binomials were extracted by way of searching for a conjunction preceded and followed by a noun.[5] This procedure rendered over 3,600 types of noun binomials in the UK material and over 1,000 types in the Scottish corpus, which is six times smaller (see Table 9.1). The first general look at the data, supplied

Table 9.1 Binomial counts in the UK and Scottish legislation (2001–2010)

	Overall word-count	*Singular nouns*			*Plural nouns*		
		All tokens	*All types*	*% of overall word-count*	*All tokens*	*All types*	*% of overall word-count*
UK data	12,025,792	17,361	3,627	0.43	13,943	1,987	0.35
Scottish data	2,316,478	9,474	1,039	1.23	3,188	525	0.41

Table 9.2 Counts of shared and unshared binomials in the UK and Scottish corpora

	Shared	*UK (including shared)*	*Scottish (including shared)*
NN_and_NN[1]	33	319	112
NNS_and_NNS	24	203	68
TOTAL	57	522	180

1 NN is a part-of-speech tag denoting singular nouns while NNS denotes plural nouns in the TagAnt tagset. The numbers in the table are slightly different from the strict 10% of the overall number of binomial types (cf. Table 9.1) simply because there may have been more types at the cut-off point with the same number of tokens. For instance, there were 1,987 NNS_and_NNS types in the UK corpus, so this would mean taking 199 types under closer scrutiny. However, in place 199 of the frequency ranking we find the binomial *regulations and rules* with 8 tokens, but *workers and employees* has the same number of tokens but it is lower on the alphabetically arranged list. In all such cases, the types with the same number of tokens as the cut-off-point example had to be included in the analysis.

with a statistical analysis of proportion difference, confirmed that the number of singular binomial types in the UK corpus is significantly lower than in the Scottish corpus. This effect was confirmed for plural nouns.[6] The findings mean that there are relatively more noun binomials in the Scottish legislation than in the UK legislation.

For a comparative qualitative discussion, the data has been narrowed down to the top 10% of types with most tokens in each corpus.[7] The same procedure was followed for singular and plural nouns. Out of the most frequently used binomials, I was interested to check which ones were shared by both legislative bodies and which were typical of one assembly only. For this purpose, I used Meld (version 3.12.3), which is a visual developer tool allowing for two- and three-way comparisons across different files and directories.

The discussion of semantic fields and motivations concentrates on types of binomials that were most frequent (the top 10% of all binomials in the respective corpora) and divides them into three groups: (a) binomials shared by both corpora, (b) those present only in the UK corpus, and (c) those present only in the Scottish corpus (the numbers of tokens would vary in each type). A general look at the shared and unshared proportion of binomial inventories is quite striking (see Table 9.2).

Because the UK corpus is six times as large as the Scottish one, many more binomial types had a chance to make it to the top 10% of the most frequent types. Still, only roughly one-tenth of these are repeated also in the Scottish texts, both in the singular and in the plural.

In other words, more binomials in the Scottish legislation come from the pool of common expressions for both legislative bodies than the other way around.

Semantic fields in legislature

In the years 2001–2010, both parliaments legislated on a number of topics of general and local importance. UK acts concerned, among other themes, criminal defense service (2001), human reproductive cloning (2001), national insurance contributions and statutory payments (2004), horse-race betting and Olympic lottery (2004), finance (2007), serious crime (2007), video recordings (2010) and children, schools and families (2010). Scottish legislation tackled the issues of salmon conservation (2001), Scottish local authorities (2001), protection of children (2003), Gaelic language (2005), smoking, health and social care (2005), prostitution (2007), crofting reform (2010) and budget (yearly). Binomial expressions emerged in each of these contexts. As explained above, the data discussed here has been narrowed down to the most frequent noun binomials from both corpora. Therefore we can assume that the binomial types which made it to the top 10% reflect the degree of phrasal fixedness in a given theme or, in other words, in a given semantic field.

Semantic analysis of binomials is fraught with difficulties; individual lexical items can be polysemous, meaning interpretations can be subjective, and both items in a pair can point in different semantic directions. Still, a good benchmark for semantic evaluations is provided by the USAS tagset for automatic semantic tagging (Archer et al. 2002), which sets forth 21 'major discourse fields', with detailed subdivisions, based on the *Longman Lexicon of Contemporary English* (McArthur 1981). This system has been successfully applied to individual lexemes and multi-word units, to automatic semantic tagging in various genres and periods, and it has served as a backbone for semantic tagsets in other languages (see UCREL Semantic Analysis System webpage). Table 9.3 presents the main semantic categories which will be employed to analyze binomials below. The categories are illustrated with examples – both singular and plural nouns, subject to availability of relevant pairings in the top 10% binomials – from the UK and Scottish legislation corpora.

In order to assign binomials to particular categories, I first subjected them to an automatic semantic analysis using the USAS tool online. Since the tool most often assigned multiple tags to individual items, the results were then assessed one by one and a single main category was decided upon, depending on the context in the parliamentary acts in which a given binomial appeared. I discuss the preferences for specific groups across the two corpora further in the chapter. As far as negative evidence is concerned, the most frequent binomials never belonged, quite understandably, to the categories of 'arts and crafts' (C), 'emotions' (E) and to the more general meta-category containing proper names and grammatical terms (Z). In addition, in the Scottish acts the most frequent binomials never belonged to the categories of 'food and farming' (F), 'numbers and measurements' (N) as well as to 'objects and substances' (O). These general dispreferences may be seen to correlate with the formal character of the genre of legislative writing. Nevertheless, as pointed out above, in the years under investigation the parliaments legislated on a wide range of different themes so, in all fairness, a whole array of topics and semantic fields had a chance to surface in the texts. The results presented in this chapter draw attention to the most frequent, most pervasive uses of formulaic phraseology. We are thus able to discover which semantic areas are most prone to generating frequent binomials and how the two parliaments compare in this respect.

Table 9.3 USAS categories illustrated

Semantic category	*Illustrative noun binomials*	
	UK legislation	*Scottish legislation*
A. General and abstract terms	*nature and extent, times and places*	*art and part, features and characteristics*
B. The body and the individual	*foot and mouth, births and deaths*	*abuse and treatment, drops and tablets*
C. Arts and crafts	–	–
E. Emotion	–	–
F. Food and farming	*alcohol and tobacco*	–
G. Government and public	*imprisonment and detention, duties and powers*	*prohibition and control, witnesses and documents*
H. Architecture, housing and the home	*heritage and architecture, conversions and reconstructions*	*buildings and monuments*
I. Money, commerce, industry[1]	*comptroller and auditor, earnings and pensions*	*land and property, fees and allowances*
K. Entertainment, sports and games	*film and video, museums and galleries*	*tourism and culture*
L. Life and living things[2]	*crabs and lobsters*	*salmon and freshwater (fish)*
M. Movement, location, travel and transport	*catering and accommodation, cars and vans*	*access and egress, piers and harbours*
N. Numbers and measurement	*rate and fraction, reductions and deductions*	–
O. Substances, materials, objects and equipment	*storage and distribution*	–
P. Education	*learning and development, arts and humanities*	*training and experience, conferences and courses*
Q. Language and communication	*information and publicity, censuses and surveys*	*review and release, letters and numbers*
S. Social actions, states and processes	*humanity and war, initiatives and programmes*	*assistance and support, partners and children*
T. Time	*duration and renewal, periods and amounts*	*commencement and completion*
W. World and environment	*oil and gas*	*water and soil*
X. Psychological actions, states and processes	*knowledge and understanding, facts and considerations*	*amenity and convenience, objectives and priorities*
Y. Science and technology	*machinery and plant*	*research and promotion*
Z. Names and grammar	–	–

[1] The original denotation of this category is 'money and commerce in industry' but I find it too restrictive.
[2] In quantitative analyses below the Category L 'life and living things' has been merged with F 'food and farming'.

Semantic motivations for binomials

Another platform of semantic comparison across the corpora is the motivation behind coining the binomial pair. Earlier surveys list various types of synonymy, antonymy and contiguity as the most prevalent semantic relationships within the binomial pair (Leisi 1947; Koskenniemi 1968; Gustafsson 1975; cf. Mollin 2014; Kopaczyk and Sauer 2017). It is perhaps logical to assume that the actual type of semantic motivation may be correlated with genre requirements, so going down this path, one should not expect differences in parliamentary acts from the UK and from Scotland in terms of the number of types. However, the individual inventories turn out to differ, as does the proportion of binomial types motivated in the same way shared by both corpora (see the discussion below).

It is a highly demanding task to assign a binomial to a particular motivation group. When this categorization is done single-handedly, it is best to return to the results after an interval of time and double-check the applied principles for consistency. In this study, the following decisions were taken when deciding upon a semantic motivation behind a given pair of nouns:

Complementation

The primary meanings of both words should contribute in equal measure to the overall meaning of the pair, so that a new whole meaning A + B is created, but the individual meanings are still visible, e.g.:

(1) *time and place*, *powers and duties* (shared), *television and radio*, *places and vehicles* (UK), *noise and vibration*, *proprietors and occupiers* (Scottish)

Contiguity

Here one meaning is an extension of the other; in other words, the meanings overlap partially, as in *knowledge and experience* (shared), but one cannot say that all 'knowledge' is 'experience' and all 'experience' is 'knowledge'. Examples include:

(2) *management and control*, *regulations and orders* (shared), *oil and fuel*, *powers and privileges* (UK), *control and reduction*, *maps and plans* (Scottish)

Thus, *powers and duties* are different in motivation than *powers and privileges* because 'powers' complements 'duties' in creating a new unit of meaning, roughly designating the prerogatives of an individual or institution. The relation between the two elements can be perceived as complementation. On the other hand, because 'powers' in some way place people in a privileged position, and vice versa, having 'privileges' may be seen as a reflection of power. So the relationship between 'powers' and 'privileges' is contiguity.

Cause and effect

It could be argued that the last case is, in fact, a binomial motivated by cause and effect. 'Powers' are the cause and 'privileges' are the effect. However, the rationale applied in this study required that only the very clear-cut cases of cause and effect, often containing a temporal dimension, be classified as such, e.g.:

(3) *search and seizure*, *proposals and policies* (shared), *investigation and report*, *offences and proceedings* (UK), *scrutiny and improvement*, *results and publications* (Scottish)

Hyponymy

When one meaning is clearly subsumed within the meaning of the other word in the pair, the motivation is identified as hyponymy. The difference from contiguity lies in the overarching meaning of one of the elements of the pair, e.g. all types of 'training' are some kind of 'education', so the motivation between *education and training* (shared) is hyponymy. Other examples include:

(4) *care and support*, *fees and expenses* (shared), *information and publicity*, *marriages and relationships* (UK), *money and compensation*, *words and expressions* (Scottish)

Antonymy

Opposite meanings can also give rise to a binomial. These cases are relatively easy to spot due to their contrastive nature but one could argue that they create a new unit of meaning and should therefore be treated as instances of complementation. The distinction lies in the fact that in order to be antonymous, two words need to share a common semantic ground, e.g. both a 'husband' and a 'wife' are effectively spouses of contrastive gender, at least in the traditional understanding of the terms. What is more, there is no third option, unlike in *television and radio*, where the two are, indeed, mass media, but one could extend this inventory further, adding newspapers or the internet. Admittedly, the distinction between antonymy and complementation is not always so straightforward but care should be taken to classify items as consistently as possible. Examples of antonymy include:

(5) *landlord and tenant*, *rights and obligations* (shared), *appointment and removal*, *births and deaths* (UK), *giving and withdrawal*, *fees and allowances* (Scottish)

Binomials proper

Finally, there is a group of binomials which do not seem to be motivated semantically in a transparent manner. Their constituents either display semantic repetition (Wang 2005: 510), which means that a single concept is conveyed twice, as in *terms and conditions*, or the relationship in meaning is obscure altogether and an indivisible unit of meaning is produced, as in *art and part* (SND *airt* n: Phrases: *Art and part*, *airt and pairt* [. . .] 'a Sc[ots] law term'). Such pairs have tentatively been called *binomials proper* (Kopaczyk 2009: 91, 2013: 197–202) because they seem to stand at the core of the binomial inventory (for core and peripheral binomials, see Kopaczyk and Sauer 2017: 15–17), with motivations for their existence to be sought in phonology, etymology style and tradition. Arguably, these are the binomials that typically get stigmatized for their wordiness and incomprehensibility in present-day legal texts because the other types, since they are semantically motivated, can be justified in terms of semantic precision and all-inclusiveness. Examples of binomials proper from the two corpora include:

(6) *practice and procedure*, *regulations and rules* (shared), *peace and reconciliation*, *profits and gains* (UK), *art and part*, *ports and harbours* (Scottish)

Binomials in UK and Scottish legislation

Semantic fields: data overview

When it comes to semantic fields, the top-frequency binomials in both corpora are most often associated with four categories (marked in grey in Table 9.4): G 'government and public', I 'money, commerce, industry', Q 'language and communication' and S 'social actions, states and processes', regardless of whether they are shared by the two corpora or appear in one corpus only. This was to be expected in legal discourse, given its preoccupation with governance, finances and, essentially, the citizens. The prominent position of binomials to do with language stems from the fact that this category includes all expressions which make reference to the legal acts themselves, e.g. *form and content*, as well as to the general communicative behaviour, both in the legal context, e.g. *oath and pledge*, and outside it, e.g. *advice and information*. The remainder of the semantic field ranking differs for the shared, UK and Scottish binomials. It also turns out that there are no shared binomials in several semantic fields: B, F, H, K, L, N and O, even though both corpora make use of these fields in their respective texts, e.g. *abuse and treatment* (B) is used in Scottish legislation but not in the UK legislation, while *prevention and treatment* (B) is found in the UK texts but not in the Scottish texts.

There are also very prominent individual types which render many tokens in semantic fields outside the top type ranks, e.g. more general expressions such as *name and address*

Table 9.4 Semantic fields for the most frequent binomial types (raw counts)

Shared	*NN + NNS*	*UK*	*NN + NNS (including shared)*	*Scottish*	*NN + NNS (including shared)*
G	16	I	145	I	39
I	14	G	96	G	36
Q	8	S	88	S	22
S	5	Q	68	Q	17
A	4	A	24	Y	14
M	3	P	16	A	12
X	2	Y	12	W	9
Y	2	M	11	X	8
P	1	K	10	B	6
T	1	B	9	M	6
W	1	W	9	P	4
B	0	N	7	H	2
F	0	X	8	L	2
H	0	H	6	T	2
K	0	T	6	K	1
L	0	O	4	F	0
N	0	F	2	N	0
O	0	L	1	O	0
TOTAL	57		522		180

(A, see Table 9.6) or more specific ones such as *space and access* in the Scottish data (M, see Table 9.10). The discussion in the analytic sections starts therefore with the shared inventory of binomial types and looks at different UK and Scottish preferences for token frequency within this inventory. The final two sections are devoted to the most frequent binomials which appeared only in the UK or in the Scottish material.

Semantic motivations: data overview

As pointed out above, the two corpora exhibit similar preferences in terms of semantic fields in general, while they differ in terms of individual binomial types with high frequency and with high token counts. With semantic motivations, the situation is very much alike. It is also interesting that the ranking of motivations is basically kept, regardless of the corpus (see Table 9.5).

All in all, complementation comes across as the most powerful motivation behind binomial pairs in both corpora, accounting for 28.8% of the most frequent types in the UK and 26.1% in Scotland. It is interesting to note that the difference between the corpora in scores for all types of motivation behind the binomials (complementation, contiguity, cause and effect, hyponymy, antonymy and binomials proper) is not statistically significant ($p = 0.95$), which means that both the UK and the Scottish assembly produce binomials because of the same reasons to the same degree. Notwithstanding this, there is an inventory of shared types with the same motivation, as well as groups of binomials which crop up in only one corpus. The examples, their contexts and frequencies form the core of the remaining discussion in this chapter. In each section, I first concentrate on binomial types, discussing the preferences for semantic fields and motivations in the shared group, in the UK corpus and in the Scottish corpus. In the second part of each respective section I turn to token and frequency counts, highlighting the semantic background of the types with the highest numbers of tokens.

Shared binomials

It is not surprising that both corpora share the highest number of top binomial types, both singular and plural, in Category G 'government and public' (7 singular and 9 plural types; see Table 9.4), e.g. *management and control*, *search and seizure*, *powers and duties*, *rights*

Table 9.5 Semantic motivations behind the most frequent binomial types (raw counts)

NN + NNS	*Shared types*	*UK types (including shared)*	*Scottish types (including shared)*
Complementation	15	150	47
Contiguity	13	103	43
Cause and effect	9	117	34
Hyponymy	8	62	24
Antonymy	6	48	15
Binomials proper	6	42	17
TOTAL	57	522	180

and obligations. Some shared items appear in boilerplate information attached to all legislation, e.g. *authority and superintendence*:

(7) Printed in the UK by The Stationery Office Limited under the *authority and superintendence* of Carol Tullo, Controller of Her Majesty's Stationery Office and Queen's Printer of Acts of Parliament.

(8) Printed in the UK by The Stationery Office Limited under the *authority and superintendence* of Carol Tullo, the Queen's Printer for Scotland.

Other shared categories include 'general and abstract terms' (A), 'money, commerce and work' (I), 'language and communication' (Q), and 'social actions, states and processes' (S). In singular nouns, Category Q comes second with 5 shared binomial types, e.g. *form and content*, *preparation and publication*, *title and commencement*. Again, some of these were found in boilerplate text. Another 5 types belong to Category I, e.g. *efficiency and effectiveness*, *income and capital*, *sale and purchase*. The contexts for these binomials are very similar in the respective corpora, e.g.:

(9) [T]he Treasury shall have regard to the desirability of (a) identifying protecting and facilitating the return of client assets (b) protecting creditors rights (c) ensuring certainty for investment banks creditors clients liquidators and administrators (d) minimising the disruption of business and markets and (e) maximising the *efficiency and effectiveness* of the financial services industry in the United Kingdom.
(uk_20090001)

(10) The inspectors of constabulary must, from time to time, carry out an inspection of the police support services provided by the Authority for the purpose of ascertaining the *efficiency and effectiveness* of those services.
(asp_20060010)

When it comes to plural nouns, the category of 'money, commerce and work' (I) delivered as many shared top types as Category G, mentioned earlier. It turns out that there are more contexts for coordination here than in the singular (9 types), e.g. *costs and fees*, *goods and services*, *grants and loans*. Again, these binomials are employed in a similar fashion in both the UK and Scottish legislation:

(11) Expenditure by the HM Procurator General and Treasury Solicitor's Department comprising the Treasury Solicitor's Department Agency, the Attorney General's Office and HM Crown Prosecution Service Inspectorate on administration, *costs and fees* for legal and related services, residual matters following the closure of the Government Property Lawyers Agency and associated non-cash items.
(uk_20070010)

(12) . . . community justice services including probation and supervised attendance orders; grants to voluntary organisations; court services, including judicial pensions; the Accountant in Bankruptcy; certain legal services; *costs and fees* in connection with legal proceedings, prison land, buildings, staff quarters, vehicles, equipment and property NUM.[8]
(asp_20040002)

Turning now to semantic motivations behind the 57 types in the shared group, complementation and contiguity are most productive. Quite a few types from these two motivation categories are, in fact, among the most frequent shared binomials: *name and address*, *form and manner*, *time and place*, *form and content*, *advice and information*, *title and commencement*, *owners and occupiers* (complementation) and *research and development* and *orders and regulations* (contiguity) (see Table 9.6 below for individual counts). For singular nouns, cause and effect is also an important motivation, rendering such shared binomials as *search and seizure*, *establishment and administration* or *fire and rescue*. Hyponymy and antonymy have motivated 8 and 6 shared binomials respectively, e.g. *education and training*, *wishes and feelings* (hyponymy) and *sale and purchase*, *rights and obligations* (antonymy). Shared binomials proper, unmotivated semantically, present an interesting inventory where the phonological factors, such as alliteration, come forward very strongly:

(13) singular: *practice and procedure*, *efficiency and effectiveness*
(14) plural: *duties and liabilities*, *regulations and rules*, *repeals and revocations*, *terms and conditions*

It seems that both assemblies keep these word pairings not because they expand the intended meaning, present alternatives or signal other types of semantic relationships. Here the appeal is stylistic in nature, based largely on sound but also on the frequency with which these binomials appear in the texts, e.g. *terms and conditions* is the most frequent shared binomial in the Scottish texts (see Table 9.7).

Talking about token frequencies, in the shared group of binomials several types stand out (see Table 9.6 for singular and Table 9.7 for plural nouns). The items have been arranged

Table 9.6 Most frequent shared singular binomials: semantic fields and motivations

Singular shared noun binomials	*Semantic field*	*Motivation*	*UK legislation*		*Scottish legislation*	
			Raw tokens	*/100,000 words*	*Raw tokens*	*/100,000 words*
research and development	Y	Contiguity	522	13.0	19	2.5
fire and rescue	W	Cause and effect	311	7.8	52	6.7
authority and superintendence	G	Hyponymy	291	7.3	130	6.8
name and address	A	Complementation	265	6.6	155	20.1
form and manner	A	Complementation	164	4.1	77	10.0
time and place	A	Complementation	134	3.3	36	4.7
form and content	Q	Complementation	86	2.1	47	6.1
advice and assistance	S	Hyponymy	69	1.7	69	8.9
husband and wife	S	Antonymy	62	1.5	37	4.8
landlord and tenant	I	Antonymy	51	1.3	41	5.3
advice and information	Q	Complementation	30	0.7	47	6.1
title and commencement	Q	Complementation	15	0.4	124	16.1

Table 9.7 Most frequent shared plural binomials: semantic fields and motivations

Plural shared noun binomials	*Semantic field*	*Motivation*	*UK legislation*		*Scottish legislation*	
			Raw tokens	*/100,000 words*	*Raw tokens*	*/100,000 words*
rights and liabilities	G	Antonymy	512	12.8	27	3.5
terms and conditions	Q	Proper	461	11.5	264	34.2
orders and regulations	G	Contiguity	270	6.7	85	11.0
repeals and revocations	G	Proper	263	6.6	12	1.6
allowances and gratuities	I	Contiguity	32	0.8	61	7.9
owners and occupiers	I	Complementation	19	0.5	59	7.6

according to the normalized proportion of the word-count involved in creating a given type in the UK legislation (per 100,000 words).[9] The Scottish counterparts (top scores marked in grey) display a slightly different frequency ordering and scores within the shared group. For instance *research and development* (Y) features prominently in the UK acts while the more general binomials *name and address*, *form and manner* (A) and *title and commencement* (Q) are more typical of Scottish legislation. Complementation comes across as a motivation behind the most frequent Scottish binomials in a more pronounced manner than it does for the UK material. Other important motivations behind the most numerous binomial types include hyponymy and antonymy.

Among the most frequent shared plural binomials, the numeric preferences are slightly different again. It is especially striking how often Scottish acts make reference to *terms and conditions*, a binomial proper (Table 9.7).

Both tables show that Scottish legislation uses the shared binomials relatively more frequently than UK legislation – the scores per 100,000 words are overall higher for Scotland. Nevertheless, each legislating body has its own favourite binomials within the shared group.

UK binomials

Turning now to the inventories of top noun binomials which were not shared between the two corpora, it seems that in the UK texts the relative frequencies are generally higher than those for the shared group. Simply speaking, when the UK texts share some binomials with Scottish texts, these binomials are less frequent than the ones appearing only in the UK legislation. This finding may indicate that legal drafters in Westminster have their own stylistic preferences and, conversely, that legal drafters in Edinburgh do not employ these stylistic choices in their legislation (compare the discussion on typically Scottish binomials, in the next section). Table 9.8 presents token scores for the most frequent singular binomials in the UK corpus, their semantic fields and proposed motivations.

Singular binomials preferred by the UK drafters come from several semantic fields, with a slight emphasis on financial and administrative contexts (I, G, Q, S). The financial slant is much more visible in plural binomials, where practically all of the most frequent constructions refer to money (I, Table 9.9).

It is also clear that antonymy gives rise to quite numerous binomials, especially in the plural, while other motivations are represented to a similar degree. Interestingly, *amounts*

Table 9.8 Most frequent singular binomials typical of UK legislation

Singular noun binomials	*UK legislation*			
	Semantic field	*Motivation*	*Raw tokens*	*/100,000 words*
title and chapter	Q	Complementation	632	15.8
tax and capital	I	Contiguity	610	15.2
advice and consent	X	Cause and effect	351	8.8
plant and machinery	Y	Complementation	302	7.5
crime and disorder	G	Hyponymy	243	6.1
overview and scrutiny	Q	Antonymy	193	4.8
employment and support	S	Hyponymy	191	4.8

Table 9.9 Most frequent plural binomials typical of UK legislation

Plural noun binomials	*UK legislation*			
	Semantic field	*Motivation*	*Raw tokens*	*/100,000 words*
amounts and sums	I	Proper	971	24.2
earnings and pensions	I	Contiguity	812	20.3
gains and losses	I	Antonymy	283	7.1
contributions and benefits	S	Cause and effect	238	5.9
credits and debits	I	Antonymy	171	4.3
profits and losses	I	Antonymy	162	4.0

and sums, classified as a binomial proper, ranks top among the plural binomials found in the UK texts only.

Scottish binomials

In Scotland, binomials connected with money are not as prominent. Among singular pairs, one can sense a preference for binomials in more socially oriented contexts (Table 9.10). Again, the scores for individual Scottish binomials are higher than those for shared binomials discussed above, which confirms the observation made earlier: when legal drafters in Edinburgh compose their texts, they employ their own inventory of binomials more frequently than the binomials which stand a chance of appearing in the UK legislation too. It is doubtful that this practice results from a conscious effort to avoid UK binomials and leave a mark of own identity on Scottish legislation but nevertheless such a tendency is corroborated in corpus data by automatic, and thus objective, retrieval methods.

Two Scottish plural binomials showed high enough frequency to enter the discussion (see endnote 9) and both of them are linked to issues of governance and property (Table 9.11).

In terms of motivations, the most frequent Scottish binomials rely on complementation and contiguity, and, to a lesser extent, cause and effect. This provides an interesting contrast

Table 9.10 Most frequent singular binomials typical of Scottish legislation

Singular noun binomials	*Scottish legislation*			
	Semantic field	*Motivation*	*Raw tokens*	*/100,000 words*
space and access	M	Contiguity	122	15.8
water and sewerage	W	Contiguity	68	8.8
scrutiny and improvement	Y	Cause and effect	54	7.0
custody and community	S	Complementation	51	6.6
owner and occupier	I	Complementation	34	4.4
removal and use	A	Cause and effect	33	4.3

Table 9.11 Most frequent plural binomials typical of Scottish legislation

Plural noun binomials	*Scottish legislation*			
	Semantic field	*Motivation*	*Raw tokens*	*/100,000 words*
commissions and commissioners	G	Complementation	56	7.3
lands and heritages	I	Contiguity	35	4.5

with the most frequent UK binomials, where antonymy stood out while the general inventory of motivations was more diverse (Tables 9.8 and 9.9).

Conclusions: binomials in the UK and Scottish legislation

The main observation stemming from the data overview presented in this chapter is that the number of noun binomials in present-day legislation in English is small, regardless of the legal tradition. This may be to do with the Plain Language guidelines, which may have inspired both assemblies to reduce wordiness in a conscious effort. It may well be the sign of the changing phraseology and style of legal English in general. Still, the number of singular noun binomials in the Scottish texts was significantly higher. This runs counter to Williams's observation that the Scottish Parliament is leading the way in Plain Language drafting (2011: 141–142). It is possible that some Scottish stylistic choices are still continuing some tendencies from the past. Even though there are no historical corpus studies of binomials in legal English, the historical corpus data for Scots clearly show that noun binomials used to be more frequent than today but altogether not much more frequent that present-day singular Scottish binomials (1.23% today vs 1.66% of total word-count in a historical corpus of Scottish legal and administrative texts; Kopaczyk 2013: 144, 190). There has been a change in the formation of binomials, however. In historical Scots texts, binomials proper featured prominently (Kopaczyk 2009) while today this motivation does not seem to play much of a role. The only conspicuous binomials unmotivated semantically were *terms and conditions* in the Scottish texts and *amounts and sums* in the UK texts. It seems that the wordiness of legal texts, often sought in the employment of semantically opaque binomials, is now being reduced, possibly due to the Plain Language campaign.

It is interesting that the number of shared binomials in the same genre, dealing with the same type of topics, is rather small, compared to the exclusive inventories for both corpora. It is striking, for instance, that the UK texts talk about *crime and disorder* while the Scottish texts do not, and that the Scottish texts refer to *scrutiny and improvement* while the UK texts do not. Still, among the most frequent binomial types, Scottish texts share more binomials with the UK texts than the other way around.

There is conspicuous phrasal fixedness in the semantic fields G, I, Q and S. Within these fields, the UK texts seem to prefer repetition in government- and money-related contexts while Scotland displays more fixedness in socially oriented contexts. One might suspect that this distinction is due to the nature of topics dealt with by the respective parliamentary acts but, as explained earlier, both corpora contain a wide coverage of diverse topics and their multi-million word-count also alleviates semantic bias. The conspicuous nature of particular semantic fields is then due to the (subconscious) preference of the drafters to create more stability, more fixedness, more complete semantic coverage in the fields that stand out.

When it comes to the motivation behind the pairs, the ranking of options is the same in both corpora with complementation on top. Most frequent binomials in the UK texts are often motivated by antonymy while in Scotland it is complementation and contiguity. It seems that in Scotland the drafters are keen on covering multiple readings and contexts which would not be covered by a single noun, hence the drive to add another noun and create a binomial. Possibly this is also the reason why, on the whole, there are relatively more noun binomials in the Scottish legislation than in the UK texts.

This study has been limited to nouns but in order to gain a complete picture of binomial constructions across parliamentary discourse in the British Isles today one should also consider modifiers – adjectives and adverbs – and especially verbs, as they carry important pragmatic and discoursal functions in legal contexts. A quick glance at the data for verbs suggests that many of them are motivated by cause and effect, as was also the case in historical texts, at least in Scotland. This is one of the strands for further investigations.

Notes

1 The earliest acts of the Scottish parliament were written on and off in Scots. A continuous record of legislation in Scots can be dated back to James II's act of 1466, when it was ordered for "þe kingis rollis and regesteris be put in bukkis" (Reeves 1893: 6).

2 In fact, the trend towards simplification is also visible in other formal, information-oriented and utilitarian texts, e.g. in business communication, designing manuals or offers (see for instance Bailey 1996).

3 The first suggestions that the language of the UK statutes should be made more comprehensible date back to 1946 (Simon of Glaisdale 1985: 133). Since the 1980s, the Plain Language movement has spread to the United States and other English-language legal contexts all over the world (Asprey 1991: 32–38).

4 I thank Dariusz Stróżyński, Tom Booth, Alistair Tullo and Jukka Tyrkkö for their technical help in data preparation.

5 Since capitalization needs to be retained for POS-tagging, I had to merge capitalized and non-capitalized binomials post hoc, as well as perform some additional pruning of tokens which did not comply with the definition of a binomial.

6 A Z-test for two population proportions showed a score of −11.3543 for singular binomials and −6.4674 for plural binomials in the UK corpus against the Scottish corpus. The amount of overall word-count involved in the creation of noun binomials (the number of tokens times

three, for the three elements of the binomial) is also much smaller in the UK corpus than in the Scottish corpus (Z-Score –148.089). See also the counts in Table 9.1.

7 Interestingly, the top 10% most numerous types in the UK legislation start at 6 tokens for singular and 8 tokens for plural binomials, and in Scottish legislation above 5 tokens in the singular and 7 in the plural, which seems to be a reasonable cut-off point.

8 All numbers in the corpora were replaced with a NUM label.

9 For instance, *research and development* appears 522 times in the UK corpus, so this number is multiplied by 3 (since three lexical items are involved in making up a binomial) and set against the whole corpus word-count, relative to 100,000 words. To be included in Tables 9.6 to 9.11, a binomial needed a relative word-count frequency above 4. A score below 4 essentially means that a binomial appeared once in 100,000 words, which I regarded as too infrequent to discuss in more detail.

References

Anthony, L., 2015. *TagAnt* (Version 1.2.0) [Computer Software]. Tokyo, Japan: Waseda University. <www.laurenceanthony.net/>

Archer, D., Wilson, A., and Rayson, P., 2002. Introduction to the USAS Category System. *Benedict Project Report.* <http://ucrel.lancs.ac.uk/usas/usas%20guide.pdf>

Asprey, M.M., 1991. *Plain Language for Lawyers.* Sydney: The Federation Press.

Bailey, E.P., 1996. *Plain English at Work.* Oxford: Oxford University Press.

Beaton, J.A., 1982. *Scots Law Terms and Expressions.* Edinburgh: W. Green & Sons.

Bhatia, V.K., 1993. *Analysing Genre: Language Use in Professional Settings.* London: Longman.

Biber, D., Johansson, S., Leech, G., Conrad, S., and Finegan, E., 1999. *Longman Grammar of Spoken and Written English.* London: Longman.

Cacciaguidi-Fahy, S. and Wagner, A., 2006. Searching for clarity. In A. Wagner and S. Cacciaguidi-Fahy (eds.), *Legal Language and the Search for Clarity: Practice and Tools.* Bern: Peter Lang, 19–32.

Danet, B., 1980. Language in the legal process. *Law and Society Review*, 14(3): 445–564.

Danet, B. and Bogoch, B., 1994. Orality, literacy, and performativity in Anglo-Saxon wills. In J. Gibbons (ed.), *Language and the Law.* London: Longmans, 100–135.

Galdia, M., 2009. *Legal Linguistics.* Frankfurt a/Main: Peter Lang.

Gibbons, J. (ed.), 1994. *Language and the Law.* London: Longmans.

Goźdź-Roszkowski, S., 2011. *Patterns of Linguistic Variation in American Legal English: A Corpus-based Study.* Frankfurt a/Main: Peter Lang.

Gustafsson, M., 1975. *Binomial Expressions in Present-Day English: A Syntactic and Semantic Study.* Turku: Turun Yliopisto.

Hiltunen, R., 1990. *Chapters on Legal English: Aspects Past and Present of the Language of the Law.* Helsinki: Suomalainen Tiedakademia.

Kopaczyk, J., 2009. Multi-word units of meaning in 16th-century legal Scots. In R.W. McConchie, A. Honkapohja, and J. Tyrkkö (eds.), *Selected Proceedings of the 2008 Symposium on New Approaches in English Historical Lexis (HEL-LEX2).* Somerville, MA: Cascadilla Proceedings Press, 88–95.

Kopaczyk, J., 2013. *The Legal Language of Scottish Burghs: Standardization and Lexical Bundles 1380–1560.* Oxford: Oxford University Press.

Kopaczyk, J. and Sauer, H., 2017. Defining and exploring binomials. In J. Kopaczyk and H. Sauer (eds.), *Binomials in the History of English: Fixed and Flexible.* Cambridge: Cambridge University Press, 1–23.

Koskenniemi, I., 1968. *Repetitive Word Pairs in Old and Early Middle English Prose.* Turku: Turun Yliopisto.

Legislation.gov.uk. <legislation.gov.uk> [Accessed: June 2012].

Leisi, E., 1947. *Die tautologischen Wortpaare in Caxton's* Eneydos*: Zur synchronischen Bedeutungs- und Ursachenforschung*. Cambridge, MA: Murray.
MacQueen, H., 1986. Pleadable brieves, pleading and the development of Scots Law. *Law and History Review*, 4(2): 403–422.
Malkiel, Y., 1959. Studies in irreversible binomials. *Lingua*, 8: 113–160.
McArthur, T., 1981. *Longman Lexicon of Contemporary English*. London: Longman.
Mellinkoff, D., 1963. *The Language of the Law*. Boston: Little Brown.
Mollin, S., 2014. *The (Ir)reversibility of English Binomials: Corpus, Constraints, Developments*. Amsterdam: John Benjamins.
Mooney, A., 2014. *Language and Law*. Basingstoke: Palgrave Macmillan.
Office of the Scottish Parliamentary Counsel, 2006. *Plain Language and Legislation Booklet*. <www.gov.scot/Publications/2006/02/17093804/0> [Accessed: February 2015].
Phillips, A., 2003. *Lawyers' Language: How and Why Legal Language Is Different*. London/New York: Routledge.
Reeves, W.P., 1893. *A Study in the Language of Scottish Prose Before 1600*. Johns Hopkins University dissertation. Baltimore: John Murphy & Co.
Report of the Renton Committee on the Preparation of Legislation (Command Paper No. 6053). 1975. London: H.M.S.O.
Simon of Glaisdale, Lord, 1985. The Renton Report – Ten years on. *Statute Law Review*, 6(1): 133–138.
Smith, T.B., 1955. *The United Kingdom: The Development of Its Laws and Constitutions. Vol. 1. Scotland. The Channel Islands*. London: Stevens & Sons.
Stewart, W., 1995. *Scottish Contemporary Judicial Dictionary of Words and Phrases*. Edinburgh: W. Green/Sweet & Maxwell.
Styles, S. and N.R. Whitty (eds.), 2003. *Glossary: Scottish and European Union Legal Terms and Latin Phrases*, 2nd ed. Edinburgh: Law Society of Scotland, LexisNexis UK.
Tiersma, P., 1999. *Legal Language*. Chicago: University of Chicago Press.
Tiersma, P., 2006. Some myths about legal language. *Law, Culture and the Humanities*, 2: 29–50.
UCREL Semantic Analysis System. <http://ucrel.lancs.ac.uk/usas/> [Accessed: January 2015].
Walker, D.M., 2001. *The Scottish Legal System: An Introduction to the Study of Scots Law*, 8th ed. Edinburgh: W. Green/Sweet & Maxwell.
Wang, S., 2005. Corpus-based approaches and discourse analysis in relation to reduplication and repetition. *Journal of Pragmatics*, 37: 505–540.
Williams, C., 2011. Legal English and plain language: An update. *ESP Across Cultures*, 8: 139–151.

Appendix

Shared singular noun binomials

administration and operation
advice and assistance
advice and information
authority and superintendence
care and support
date and time
development and delivery
education and training
efficiency and effectiveness
entry and inspection
establishment and administration
fire and rescue
form and content
form and manner
husband and wife
income and capital
information and assistance
knowledge and belief
knowledge and experience
landlord and tenant
maintenance and publication
management and control
marketing and processing
name and address
practice and procedure
preparation and publication
research and development
sale and purchase
search and seizure
site and access
time and place
title and commencement
town and country

Scottish-only singular noun binomials

abuse and treatment
access and egress
acquisition and use
act and warrant
age and maturity
alteration and reconstruction
amalgamation and dissolution
amenity and convenience
application and commencement
art and part
assistance and support
care and preservation
clearance and repair
commencement and completion
conduct and practice
construction and maintenance
construction and operation
control and reduction
conveyancing and executry
conviction and acquittal
custody and community
deposit and return
dismissal and withdrawal
efficiency and safety
election and holding
equipment and property
exclusion and restriction
execution and action

expenditure and grant
extension and variation
force and effect
giving and withdrawal
improvement and demolition
information and awareness
inspection and seizure
installation and maintenance
land and equipment
land and property
landscape and habitat
layer and subsoil
lighting and road
maintenance and operation
management and maintenance
mitigation and protection
money and compensation
monitoring and surveillance
noise and vibration
order and restriction
owner and occupier
prohibition and control
propriety and regularity
protection and enhancement
provision and maintenance
publicity and consultation
quarantine and hospital
reduction and recycling
removal and use
removal and detention
research and promotion
research and publicity
retention and use
review and release
rod and line
salmon and freshwater (fish)
scrutiny and improvement
secretary and chairman
seizure and removal
signature and designation
space and access
staff and property
supervision and care
teaching and conference
tenure and removal
tourism and culture
training and experience
use and operation
value and accountability
water and soil

UK-only singular noun binomials

ability and fitness
access and recreation
accommodation and family
accommodation and maintenance
accommodation and subsistence
acquisition and disposal
act and section
action and capacity
address and date
advice and guidance
advice and support
advice and training
affirmation and declaration
aircraft and boat
aircraft and hovercraft
alcohol and tobacco
appeal and quash
application and interpretation
appointment and constitution
appointment and removal
appointment and tenure
approval and signing
assessment and advice
assistance and advice
assistance and supervision
attendance and examination
catering and accommodation
certification and registration
charge and rate
childcare and transport
coal and shipbuilding
collection and enforcement
collection and management
collection and recovery
commencement and duration
commencement and extent
community and business
compensation and pension
comptroller and auditor
conciliation and mediation

construction and maintenance
construction and use
consultation and publicity
consultation and representation
content and publication
contract and conveyance
control and independence
control and management
countryside and wildlife
creation and acquisition
crime and disorder
date and place
debtor and creditor
deprivation and disadvantage
detention and training
development and production
development and regeneration
direction and control
disapplication and modification
disposal and acquisition
disposal and reacquisition
dissolution and restoration
driver and licensing
driver and vehicle
duration and renewal
duty and stamp
election and referendum
electricity and gas
employment and support
employment and training
entry and search
equipment and weapon
establishment and maintenance
establishment and operation
evidence and procedure
excise and registration
exclusion and poverty
expenditure and disposal
exploration and access
father and mother
film and video
financing and money
food and drink
foot and mouth
form and amount
fuel and power
gas and electricity
gender and faith
governance and audit
grant and revocation
guidance and welfare
harm and neglect
health and safety
health and welfare
hearing and determination
heritage and architecture
hospital and community
humanity and war
identification and recovery
immigration and asylum
immigration and nationality
importation and exportation
importation and storage
imposition and modification
imprisonment and detention
income and adjustment
income and exemptions
income and expense
income and material
income and property
infanticide and suicide
information and evidence
information and explanation
information and guidance
information and inspection
information and publicity
inspection and audit
inspection and search
installation and use
interest and royalty
interest and share
investigation and determination
investigation and report
involvement and consultation
involvement and scrutiny
judge and jury
jurisdiction and procedure
jurisdiction and recognition
knowledge and understanding
land and burial
land and infrastructure
law and practice
leader and cabinet
leadership and management
learning and development
lease and finance

lease and rent
leave and pay
liability and exemption
library and archive
life and liberty
litigation and enforcement
machinery and plant
management and collection
management and development
management and discharge
management and disposal
management and relief
management and use
manner and form
mayor and cabinet
mayor and council
mining and oil
misconduct and performance
misdeclaration and neglect
modification and revocation
music and ballet
music and dance
name and contact
name and surname
nature and amount
nature and extent
nomination and selection
oath and pledge
oil and gas
oil and fuel
opening and closing
order and conduct
order and statement
overview and scrutiny
ownership and control
parish and community
participation and representation
payment and enforcement
peace and reconciliation
peacemaking and peacebuilding
pension and superannuation
place and time
plan and description
plant and machinery
policing and crime
policy and legislation
possession and use
preparation and adoption
preparation and dissemination
prevention and detection
prevention and treatment
procedure and practice
production and acquisition
production and publication
profit and loss
promotion and advice
promotion and protection
promotion and provision
promotion and regulation
property and staff
prosecution and punishment
provision and renewal
provision and savings
purchase and entry
purchase and resale
purchase and sale
quality and delivery
quality and effectiveness
rate and dividend
rate and fraction
rating and valuation
realisation and reinvestment
rebate and rate
reconstruction and acquisition
recovery and interest
recovery and postponement
recovery and taxation
reduction and prevention
refurbishment and acquisition
register and information
registration and inspection
regulation and advice
regulation and inspection
relief and reconstruction
relief and vaccine
remediation and support
removal and disposal
removal and reinterment
rent and leasehold
repayment and interest
report and summary
resignation and removal
revenue and capital
revocation and amendment
safety and hygiene
safety and mobility

sale and finance
sale and leaseback
sale and reacquisition
sale and repurchase
sale and supply
schedule and section
seal and proof
section and schedule
security and independence
security and intelligence
security and pension
seizure and detention
seizure and forfeiture
service and labour
signature and date
skill and diligence
staff and equipment
state and management
statement and report
stock and work
stop and search
storage and distribution
storage and maintenance
storage and use
strategy and guidance
student and trainee
study and training
supervision and punishment
supervision and surveillance
support and assistance
suspension and revocation
taking and sale
tax and capital
tax and stamp
teaching and research
television and radio
terrorism and intelligence
title and reference
training and education
training and enterprise
training and recreation
transferor and transferee
travel and subsistence
treatment and testing
trial and punishment
use and disclosure
use and maintenance
use and possession
validity and revision
vehicle and traffic
violence and disorder
warhead and fissile

Shared plural noun binomials

allowances and gratuities
allowances and expenses
amendments and repeals
costs and fees
duties and liabilities
facts and circumstances
fees and expenses
goods and services
grants and loans
orders and directions
orders and regulations
owners and occupiers
persons and bodies
powers and duties
proposals and policies
provisions and savings
regulations and orders
regulations and rules
repeals and revocations
representations and objections
rights and liabilities
rights and obligations
terms and conditions
wishes and feelings

Scottish-only plural noun binomials

baits and lures
bodies and organisations
buildings and monuments
burdens and servitudes
commissions and commissioners
conferences and courses
contractors and practitioners
contributions and grants

drops and tablets
features and characteristics
fees and allowances
fees and charges
functions and activities
inhibitions and adjudications
inspectors and constables
interests and liabilities
lands and heritages
letters and numbers
liabilities and obligations
maills and duties
maps and plans
objections and representations
objectives and priorities
orders and undertakings
partners and children
piers and harbours
plans and programmes
plans and sections
ports and harbours
practitioners and ophthalmologists
premises and facilities
proprietors and occupiers
publications and statistics
rents and wayleaves
reports and accounts
results and publications
sales and grants
schemes and directions
services and inspections
sewers and passages
standards and outcomes
views and representations
witnesses and documents
words and expressions

UK-only plural noun binomials

accounts and reports
acts and defaults
acts and omissions
acts and proceedings
acts and threats
adaptations and modifications
affairs and transactions
agencies and individuals
allowances and charges
allowances and reliefs
amounts and sums
appeals and applications
applications and notices
arrangements and reconstructions
arts and humanities
arts and sports
assessments and adjustments
assessments and appeals
assets and liabilities
bands and percentages
benefits and expenses
births and deaths
bodies and offices
bodies and projects
buildings and structures
cars and vans
cases and circumstances
censuses and surveys
charges and payments
children and dependants
claims and proceedings
companies and trusts
conditions and exceptions
contracts and policies
contributions and benefits
conversions and reconstructions
corporations and shareholdings
costs and expenses
costs and loans
crabs and lobsters
credits and debits
data and services
debits and credits
decisions and appeals
deductions and reliefs
departments and authorities
directors and employees
disposals and acquisitions
disposals and changes
disputes and appeals
drugs and medicines
duties and levies
duties and powers
duties and responsibilities

earnings and benefits
earnings and pensions
elections and referendums
enactments and instruments
establishments and agencies
establishments and facilities
exemptions and exceptions
exemptions and reliefs
expenses and allowances
expenses and receipts
facilities and services
facts and considerations
families and communities
fingerprints and samples
firms and people
forces and personnel
functions and duties
futures and options
gains and losses
grants and payments
honours and dignities
individuals and businesses
individuals and firms
individuals and members
initiatives and programmes
institutions and services
institutions and teachers
interests and rights
investigations and reports
investments and loans
judgments and orders
landlords and tenants
laws and regulations
leases and licences
leases and loans
liabilities and rebates
loans and advances
loans and grants
loans and investments
losses and liabilities
losses and profits
losses and releases
lotteries and amusements
marriages and relationships
measurements and photographs
meetings and proceedings
men and women
mergers and divisions
methods and principles
monuments and sites
museums and galleries
names and addresses
networks and services
obligations and liabilities
offences and proceedings
officers and employees
officers and men
orders and rules
parties and elections
payments and benefits
payments and grants
payments and loans
payments and subscriptions
pensions and allowances
pensions and gratuities
people and adults
periods and amounts
perpetuities and accumulations
places and vehicles
plans and specifications
policies and contracts
powers and privileges
principles and procedures
proceedings and proceeds
proceedings and remedies
professions and vocations
profits and deficits
profits and gains
profits and losses
programmes and measures
prohibitions and restrictions
provisions and limitations
qualifications and examinations
rates and fractions
rates and rebates
receipts and assets
receipts and deductions
receipts and expenses
reductions and deductions
regulations and directions
reliefs and exemptions
rents and profits
repayments and credits
reports and measures
reports and recommendations
resolutions and meetings

restrictions and conditions
reviews and commissions
reviews and investigations
rights and duties
rights and opportunities
rights and powers
rules and directions
rules and practices
rules and regulations
salaries and allowances
salaries and pensions
schemes and arrangements
services and activities
services and facilities
services and initiatives
services and purposes
services and schemes
shareholdings and holdings
shares and securities
subscriptions and contributions
sums and assets
systems and services
taxes and duties
times and places
transitionals and savings
tribunals and inquiries
undertakings and orders
weights and measures
workers and employees

Part III

Phraseology and English legal discourse

10 "By partially renouncing their sovereignty . . ."

On the discourse function(s) of lexical bundles in EU-related Irish judicial discourse

Davide Mazzi

Introduction: the Republic of Ireland and/in the European Union

The creation and expansion of the European Union has generated wide interest and increasing recognition across disciplinary perspectives. This has been so for a number of reasons, the first and most intuitive one being that the EU legal framework has brought not only speakers but also different and at times heterogeneous legal systems closer together (Maley 1994; Tomkin 2004). Consequently, as the impetus towards the integration of the Member States within the EU gathered momentum, the Union itself progressively increased the range of its activities, so that "friction between the laws of the individual Member States is likely to increase" (Collins and O'Reilly 1990: 322).

In the case of the Irish Republic, a wide array of studies has thoroughly and critically discussed the relationship between the country and the EU, along with any peaks and troughs in the application of EU law within domestic legislation. Going back 25 years, Collins and O'Reilly (1990) pointed out that the incorporation of certain provisions in isolated matters such as intellectual property or product liability may not have been as swift as was desired, but this was very much the exception to the rule.

Roughly ten years on, however, the majority of the Irish electorate (54%) voted No in a referendum to ratify the 2001 Nice Treaty, thereby giving a profound shock to the Government, its partners in the Union and the candidate states eagerly awaiting Membership (Laffan and Tonra 2005). Although the Treaty was eventually approved by a majority of Irish voters in 2002, a sense of tension between ever closer EU integration and the attempt to preserve sovereignty and control over the national legal system has been documented in more than one scholarly work.

First of all, Fahey (2008) deals with the serious repercussions of the implementation of the EU Framework Decision on the European Arrest Warrant (EAW) into Irish domestic law. The EAW was an important provision of EU law designed to replace traditional extradition systems and surrender procedures across Member States. While ensuring that the EAW surrender procedures may satisfactorily protect fundamental rights norms through Section 37 of the European Arrest Warrant Act of 2003, Fahey explains, the Irish State decided not to accept the jurisdiction of the Court of Justice of the European Union in respect of Third Pillar issues, as of Article 35 of the EU Treaty. The so-called Third Pillar concerns judicial review aspects and most importantly, judicial co-operation in criminal matters: the refusal to abide by its rules, Fahey contends, may be symptomatic of the consequences of a somewhat antagonistic stance adopted by the Irish State at a European level.

In the second place, Phelan (2008) points to elements of constitutional disobedience inherent in Irish law with respect to EU legislation. At the outset, the author shows that Article 29.6 of the Irish Constitution underlies the dualist approach taken by the Irish legal order to international treaty obligations such as those deriving from the EU framework. More specifically, Phelan observes that international law has only been effective in the Republic's law as a result of domestic legislation. Accordingly, although EU judges have kept stressing that EU law is in principle directly applicable and therefore binding on national judges, their Irish counterparts have repeatedly disagreed with such views. As Phelan surmises, in fact, Irish judges have constantly tended to conceive of the supremacy and direct effect of EU law as a derivative of successive amendments to the European Communities Act and the norms of the Irish Constitution that introduce EU law into the Irish legal order.

The spate of interest generated by the discussion of the competing pressures on Ireland as an instance of small yet open polity (Laffan and Tonra 2005: 459) – i.e. benefiting from EU integration while at once preserving its sovereignty – is a motivation for this research, too. Expatiating on the growing body of research documented earlier on, the aim of this paper is to bring a corpus and discourse perspective (Hunston 2002; Baker 2006; Römer and Wulff 2010) to bear on the study of the judicial discourse of the Supreme Court of the Republic of Ireland within EU-related disputes. The analysis combined and implemented computer-assisted quantitative methods of language study and qualitative analysis, in the attempt to discern recurrent phraseological patterns and their function(s) in the Court's discourse. In particular, the research questions fielded by the investigation are the following: To what extent can phraseology, as instantiated by lexical bundles, bring insights into the Court's judicial practice and/or stance about EU matters? What, if anything, can it reveal in terms of the judges' own line of argument? How accurate is the reading of judicial texts provided by a corpus study of phraseology, compared to the viewpoint of legal experts?

The relevance of the use of corpora to discourse analysis and the role of phraseology in the study of specialised discourse may be seen as well established traditions of current applied linguistics research. Serving as they do as a background to the present investigation as well, they will briefly be discussed in the following section.

The study of judicial discourse: corpora and phraseology

As a prime example of specialised language in use, judgments are a prominent genre of legal discourse, and they have attracted scholarly attention from a variety of perspectives. From a legal-theoretical point of view, judgments have been studied as the site where the judges' adjudicating power takes concrete form. Emphasis has therefore been laid on the role of justification in judicial decision-making (Alexy 1989), and a large number of works have focused on the methods through which judges weigh and balance the sources of law they rely upon, e.g. statutes, *travaux préparatoires* and prior court decisions (Peczenik 1989; Barcelò 1997; Doyle 2008; Byrne et al. 2014).

From a discursive point of view, research has turned to the relationship between the structure of judicial texts and their distinctive rhetorical properties (Mazzi 2007). Within such a context, specialised corpora (McEnery and Hardie 2011; Gabrielatos et al. 2012) as sources of authentic data can be acknowledged to lend remarkable insights into the process of socialising law students and practitioners into the distinctive communicative practices of the judicial discourse community.

This aspect seems central when it comes to the prolific output of corpus investigation to show the recurrence of co-occurring items in text. In that regard, the adoption of corpus approaches to the study of naturally occurring language has shed light on a large number of discourse regularities. Among these, phraseology as the tendency of words to go together and make meaning by virtue of their combination has been a favourite subject of investigation over the last two decades.

Co-occurring items have been variously termed. For instance, Sinclair (1996) talks about 'units of meaning' as longer sequences to be described in terms of collocation, colligation and semantic preference. These respectively denote firstly the regular co-occurrence of words; secondly, the co-occurrence of grammatical choices; and thirdly, "the restriction of regular co-occurrence to items which share a semantic feature" (Sinclair 2004: 142) as in the case, for instance, of an adjective co-occurring with nouns from the lexical field of sports.

Likewise, in their project aimed at a corpus-driven pedagogic grammar, Hunston and Francis (1998) look at the close association between 'verb patterns' and meaning in the 250-million-word Bank of English. Furthermore, Biber et al. (1999: 990) conduct a cross-register investigation of 'lexical bundles', i.e. "sequences of word forms that commonly go together in natural discourse" regardless of their idiomaticity, while Wray (2002) discusses 'formulaic expressions or sequences' as linguistic units composed of multiple words, which she analyses in the light of different frames of interpretation, e.g. individual motivations for achieving novelty and pragmatic notions of shared knowledge between speaker/writer and listener/reader.

Co-occurring patterns have been variously ascribed to such widespread phenomena as Sinclair's (2004) idiom principle, Hoey's (2005) lexical priming and Goldberg's (2009) construction grammar, and they represent the primary focus of Hunston's recent analysis of 'semantic sequences'. These are defined by Hunston (2008: 271) as "recurring sequences of words or phrases [. . .] more usefully characterized as sequences of meaning elements rather than as formal sequences", and they have been analysed as a clue to the main aspects related to the presentation and discussion of research findings in specialised academic journals (cf. Groom 2010; Mazzi 2015).

The centrality of phraseology to specialised language analysis may well go beyond the realm of academic discourse. Thus, for instance, Pontrandolfo (2013) adopts a contrastive approach focusing on prepositional phrases across English, Spanish and Italian judicial texts. His comprehensive qualitative and quantitative analysis shows that phraseological mechanisms are instrumental to expressing crucial conceptual relations in the drafting practices of criminal judgments by courts of last resort in Spain (*Tribunal Supremo*), Italy (*Corte Suprema di Cassazione*) and England/Wales (Supreme Court of the United Kingdom/House of Lords).

In the attempt to sharpen our knowledge of phraseology as a leading principle of discourse organisation, the analysis proposed here delves into lexical bundles as a suitable candidate for the description of regularity in judicial text. The rest of the paper is organised as follows. In the next section, the criteria of corpus design are discussed, and the methodological tools are introduced: this will allow for a presentation of the dataset as well as a preliminary review of the procedure through which the corpus was interrogated. The findings of the study are then presented and eventually discussed in the light of the relevant literature in the last section.

Materials and methods

The study was undertaken on a small synchronic corpus of 82 judicial opinions by the Supreme Court of Ireland (henceforward, 'the SCI'). The text of the opinions was retrieved from the

Court's official website at www.supremecourt.ie/Judgments.nsf/SCSearch?OpenForm&l=en as of 15 October 2014, when corpus design was completed. On that page, the advanced search function allows one to insert any string in the quest for judgments, in addition to any judge's name one or more cases may be accessed with. For the purpose of this paper, the item *European Union* was used as the search term. The 82 texts displayed as search results cover a time span between 2001 and 2014, and they altogether amount to 742,194 words.

From a methodological point of view, the study was carried out as follows. In order to examine key instances of phraseology in context, emphasis was laid on 'lexical bundles' (Biber et al. 1999; Biber et al. 2004; Pecorari 2009). Lexical bundles are aptly defined by Breeze (2013: 230) as "multi-word sequences that occurred most frequently in particular genres, regardless of whether or not they constituted idioms or structurally complete units". Bundles were taken as a case in point in light of recent scholarly research (Goźdź-Roszkowski 2011), whereby the adoption of corpus-driven methods and multi-dimensional analysis pointed to their frequency as evidence of their operative function in communicating key procedural aspects of judicial decisions.

In order to identify bundles, the linguistic software package *AntConc* (Anthony 2006) was used. More specifically, the on-screen function *Clusters* was launched in the attempt to generate an *n-gram* list. This is a list of the most frequent clusters, i.e. multi-word sequences, in the corpus, and it was used to extract the items of interest to the current work. By virtue of its preliminary nature, the analysis was circumscribed to the top-ten most recurrent lexical bundles. These were identified on the basis of the following criteria: first of all, a minimum size of three and a maximum size of six words per bundle; secondly, a minimum frequency of ten tokens per bundle; finally, a distribution of each bundle across a minimum of five different texts, in order to ensure an adequate degree of generality to the analysis.

Once the bundles were detected, they were classified by combining the criteria in Biber et al. (2004), Pecorari (2009) and Breeze (2013). As will be clarified in the upcoming section, this essentially amounted to integrating semantic (Breeze 2013) and syntactic (Biber et al. 2004) criteria for a preliminary exploration of the *prima facie* characteristics of the bundles. In addition, *Concordance* – a software function displaying the whole of the occurrences of a search word or phrase on the same page – was operated, with the aim of uncovering and quantifying the main discourse function of each bundle in context (Stubbs 2001).

Lexical bundles: forms and functions in context

By applying the criteria laid down in the prior section to the *n-gram* list of the corpus, the most frequent bundles were identified. These are displayed in Table 10.1 below with their respective raw and per 1,000-word frequency.[1]

Moving beyond mere frequency counts, the items in the table could be classified by following the guidelines provided in the literature. To begin with, Pecorari's (2009) subdivision of bundles into 'content' and 'non-content' forms appears to apply well to a preliminary categorisation. All bundles in Table 10.1 are 'content' in that they "contain one or more words from the specialist register within which [texts] were written" (Pecorari 2009: 96), the only exceptions being *seems to me*, *the fact that*, *in respect of* and *in relation to*.

On the one hand, the latter fall within the scope of Biber et al.'s (2004: 381) chiefly syntactic framework: thus, *the fact that* can be ascribed to Type 2 bundles – namely those that "incorporate dependent clause fragments"; and *in respect of* as well as *in relation to* are definitely to be attributed to Type 3 bundles, which, among others, incorporate prepositional phrase fragments.

Table 10.1 Most frequent lexical bundles and related frequency

Bundle	*Frequency (raw)*	*Frequency (per 1,000 words)*
of the Act	753	1.014
in respect of	560	0.754
European Arrest Warrant	437	0.588
in relation to	435	0.586
the fact that	394	0.530
the purposes of	260	0.350
the European Union	233	0.313
the basis of	227	0.305
seems to me	213	0.286
the principle of	207	0.278

On the other hand, 'content' bundles can be read in the light of Breeze's (2013: 238) semantic categorisation of lexical bundles in case law texts. Accordingly, they may denote 'agents' (*the European Union*), 'documents' (*of the Act* and *European Arrest Warrant*) or 'abstract concepts' (*the purposes of*, *the basis of* and *the principle of*).

Leaving aside such formal properties of lexical bundles, it is by looking at them in context that one manages to know more about the textual functions they fulfil at a broader corpus level. In this respect, the analysis provided substantial evidence that bundles perform three main functions: first of all, defining the relationship between State and EU law; secondly, indicating peculiarities of the Court's argumentation; thirdly, identifying the core element of the dispute, from the Court's own perspective. These functions are reviewed in the remainder of this section.

The first function, i.e. a definition of the relationship and ever shifting boundaries between Irish and EU law, is served by bundles in four main ways. One of these is the expression of the Court's critical stance towards the EU and the implementation of its norms or policies. This takes the form of two phraseological patterns schematised as follows: (a) [Evaluative marker + *purpose(s)* + *of the Act*]; (b) [Evaluative marker + 'objective' + *the European Union*].[2]

The former may also be read as an example of two lexical bundles merging together – chiefly *the purposes of* and *of the Act* – to form a longer phraseological unit. More generally, it concerns 13.1% of the co-occurrences between *of the Act* and the lemma *purpose*, preceded by a marker of the Court's critical attitude, e.g. *it is difficult to decipher* or as in (1) below, *there is great difficulty in attributing any effective meaning to*. As of (b), *the European Union* typically collocates with words sharing a semantic preference of 'objective' – either the word *objective* itself or a lexicalisation of the specific objective discussed in the text, e.g. the enlargement of the Union. In turn, this is again preceded by formulations reflecting SCI Justices' negative perceptions about the putative mismatch between proposed legislation and the goals to be pursued at an EU level – cf. *represents a disproportionate implementation of*, *does not seem to be relevant to* or *problems that would arise from the enlargement of*, as in (2):[3]

(1) That particular part of the section is worth repeating, "a person shall not be surrendered to an issuing state under this Act in respect of an offence unless the offence is

an offence that consists of conduct specified in [paragraph 2 of Article 2]". There is great difficulty in attributing any effective meaning for the purposes **of the Act** to that particular provision.

(Minister for Justice v. Ferenca)

(2) Accordingly, there continued to be a surplus of milk in the community. Various methods were adopted by the EEC of dealing with the resultant problems. Eventually, what was called "Agenda 2000" was adopted by the EEC Commission with a view to preparing the dairy sector for the further problems which would arise from the enlargement of **the European Union** and the liberalisation of trade within the World Trade Organisation. The latter developments would mean, not merely a new threat of surpluses in milk production, but also an undermining of the effectiveness of the quota regime in maintaining milk prices.

(Maher et al. v. Minister for Agriculture et al.)

In (1), Murray C.J. notes that the obscurity of the reported provision of EU law on the surrender of subjects to another State is indeed what makes its implementation in the domestic legal order so problematic. In (2), similarly, Keane C.J. points to the purported discrepancy between the scope of the Commission's *Agenda 2000* and the scale of the problems related to the milk quota regime within the enlarged Union envisaged at the beginning of the new century.

Another aspect relevant to the first function of lexical bundles in context was the Court's reflection upon and appreciation of the impact of EU law on the domestic legal framework. In this regard, it is noteworthy that in 5.6% of its 233 entries, *the European Union* collocates with items sharing a semantic preference of 'consequence' in that they deal with the nature or scope of legislative tools the State had to incorporate into its own legal order by virtue of EU membership, e.g. *was necessitated by the obligations of the membership of* (echoing the exact wording of Article 29.4.6 of the Irish Constitution), *a historic transfer of legislative, executive and judicial sovereignty to*, and *as a consequence of Ireland's membership of* – as in (3).[4]

A similar pattern applies to the bundle *European Arrest Warrant*: the innovative nature of this document is often discussed in the case law sampled through the corpus, as per the collocation of the bundle with items such as *is a novel instrument* or *constitutes a complete change of direction* in (4):

(3) The democratic system in Ireland functions through three branches of government. However, in addition, the State is subject to European institutions and provisions made therein. These regulations are directly applicable. These regulations are part of Irish laws as a consequence of Ireland's membership of **the European Union**.

(Browne v. Attorney General et al.)

(4) The move from extradition to the **European arrest warrant** constitutes a complete change of direction. It is clear that both concepts serve the same purpose of surrendering an individual who has been accused or convicted of an offence to the authorities of another State so that he may be prosecuted or serve his sentence there. However, that is where the similarities end.

(Minister for Justice v. Ostrowski)

In (3), Denham J. addresses the notion of the direct applicability of regulations, which is argued to be due to the country's full EU membership, while in (4) McKechnie J. delves into the aspects that differentiate prior legislation on extradition from the current regime set up under the EAW.

A context acting as an actual counterpart to the Court's critical stance – as of (1) and (2) above – is represented by those passages where SCI Justices emphasise the value of domestic legislation as a benchmark against which to evaluate EU norms. Interestingly, the bundle *of the Act* recurrently collocates with a specification of the year the legislation at issue was enacted, and an evaluative marker through which the Court expresses its satisfaction with the overall quality of the Act mentioned. In 6.5% of its occurrences, [*of the Act* + year] is followed by such markers as *is stated clearly*, *I find no ambiguity* and *terms are very specific and unambiguous*. In (5), therefore, Denham C.J. does more than simply introduce the content of Section 21A of the European Arrest Warrant Act of 2003: she also stresses that that piece of domestic legislation displays a desirably high degree of quality and explicitness:

(5) Under Irish law, s. 21A **of the Act** of 2003, as amended, ensures persons are not surrendered for the purposes of investigation. [. . .] <u>The national law is clear on the requirements it lays down</u>.

(Minister for Justice v. Bailey)

The finding that the Court attaches fundamental importance to the framework of domestic legislation also appears to be corroborated by the bundle *of the Constitution*. Being mainly confined to judgment Pringle v. Government of Ireland et al., this bundle failed to meet the eligibility criterion of distribution across a minimum of five different texts. Although it was not formally included in the analysis, it is interesting that its main collocates are *Article* (139 entries), *provision* (43) and *breach* (7). As the careful scrutiny of the co-occurrence with *breach* revealed, *of the Constitution* can be found in contexts where Justices assess the effects of adhesion to EU-driven initiatives in terms of their compatibility with the Irish Constitution – cf. *to ratify a treaty that is in breach of the Constitution* (Pringle v. Government of Ireland et al.).

Moreover, *of the Constitution* displays a similar usage pattern when it keeps the company of its two other top collocates. As a matter of fact, 14.4% of [*Article(s)* + *of the Constitution*] are preceded by such items as *inconsistent with*, *contrary to*, *breach*, *infringe*, *confuse the interpretation of* or *in clear disregard to* – e.g. *Such a transfer would be contrary to Articles 5, 6 and 17 of the Constitution* (Pringle v. Government of Ireland et al.). Furthermore, the collocation of [*provision(s)* + *of the Constitution*] with the nouns *contravention*, *breach* or *violation* as well as the verb *contravene* amounts to a significant 25.6% of its 43 tokens. In the cases documented here, the passages where the bundle is embedded confirm the emphasis placed on constitutional architecture as the framework for evaluating the viability of prospective EU norms.

As a way of expatiating into the relationship between State and EU law, one more aspect worth mentioning is the tendency of SCI Justices to stress the need to make sure that domestic legislation is harmonised with and construed in light of EU objectives and/or principles. This is primarily true of the co-occurrence patterns of the prepositional bundle *in respect of*, which indicate that harmonisation may be invoked about both procedural matters – e.g. *reliefs*, *charges*, *appeals* and *grounds of appeal* – and, even more so, factual aspects of cases. This is apparent in 85.7% of the 21 occurrences of the pattern [*in respect of* + *a person* + relative clause denoting a fact in the dispute] – e.g. *in respect of a person, who falls within one of the prescribed categories, subject to* [. . .] *the Council Framework Decision* (Minister for Justice v. Ciarán) – as well as in 45.4% of the co-occurrence pattern between *in respect of* and the noun *offence*. Similar usage patterns were also documented for a limited amount of the collocation entries of *in relation to* with either *a criminal trial* or *framework decisions*. In (6) and (7), the Irish Justice delivering the opinion begins by identifying a specific matter around which the dispute revolves, before suggesting an interpretation of the facts of the case consistent with the overarching EU framework, most often in the field of the highly controversial EAW:

(6) By section 44 of the Act of 2003, Ireland adapted into Irish law Article 4.7.b. of the Framework Decision [. . .]. I construe s. 44 as enabling Ireland to surrender a person **in respect of** an offence alleged to have been committed outside the territory of the issuing State in circumstances where the Irish State would exercise extra-territorial jurisdiction in reciprocal circumstances.

(Minister for Justice v. Bailey)

(7) The sole matter which I wish to make clear here is that the mere fact that a trial or sentence may take place in a requesting State according to procedures or principles which differ from those which apply, even if constitutionally guaranteed, **in relation to** a criminal trial in this country does not of itself mean that an application for surrender should be refused pursuant to s. 37(2) of the Act.

(Minister for Justice v. Stapleton)

What the examples show so far is that in critically assessing the impact of EU law on the Irish legal order at various levels, the discourse of SCI Justices is indicative of the tension between the growing pressure to incorporate EU law into State legislation as swiftly as possible, and the willingness to emphasise and preserve the prerogatives of the country's domestic law. This aspect has been singled out by legal scholars (see the introductory section), but it is interesting that it can be documented with corpus analytic tools as well.

The second main function performed by the phraseological patterns of lexical bundles is their capability of bringing insights into the Court's argumentation. In this respect, bundles appear to reflect a pattern of legal text through which they act as signposting or navigating words pointing to specific elements in the reasoning of judges, most notably abstract ideas or principles. To mention but two examples, the bundle *the principle of* mainly collocates with a precise denotation of the specific principle considered by SCI Justices, e.g. *conforming interpretation*, *mutual recognition*, *effectiveness* and *proportionality*. In the vast majority of these contexts, what the collocation shows is the Justice's recourse to 'argument from substantive reasons'. This argument form is observed by Summers (1991: 418) to be common in Supreme Court opinions, where the mode of the argument derives "from an authoritative source of law, such as a statute, or case or legal principle". As far as our opinions are concerned, the most widely mentioned principle appears to be *equivalence*: its use as the basis of the Court's reasoning follows a clear two-part sequence attested for 70.6% of the tokens of the pattern. First of all, a definition of the scope of the principle, testified to by the collocation between [*the principle of* + *equivalence*] and the verbs *meet* and *comply with*, or the nouns *observance* and *breach*. Secondly, an outline of the criteria for the Court to bear in mind while determining whether the principle itself has been complied with (cf. (8) below):

(8) Observance of **the principle of** equivalence implies, for its part, *that* the procedural rule at issue applies without distinction to actions alleging infringements of Community law and to those alleging infringements of national law, with respect to the same kind of charges or dues. [. . .] In order to determine whether **the principle of** equivalence has been complied with in the present case, the national court – which alone has direct

knowledge of the procedural rules governing actions in the field of employment law – must consider both the purpose and the essential characteristics of allegedly similar domestic actions.

(TD et al. v. Minister for Justice et al.)

In addition, the bundle *(for) the purposes of* includes the verb *assume* among its top collocates. In the greater majority of these occurrences, the discourse of the SCI Justice in question makes use of the larger pattern *even assuming for the purposes of . . . that*, in order to respond to and criticise someone else's – e.g. one of the parties' – causal argumentation. In causal argumentation, "the argument is presented as if what is stated in the argumentation is a means to, a way to, an instrument for or some other kind of causative factor for the standpoint or vice versa"(Van Eemeren and Grootendorst 1992: 97).

In (9) below, O'Donnell J. expresses his own disagreement with the appellant's argument requesting an interlocutory injunction. In order to strengthen his argument, he stretches the potential validity of the plaintiff's case to the extreme (*and even assuming for the purposes of this stage of the argument that*), only to argue that there is no causal connection between the claim that the European law argument can also be framed in domestic constitutional terms, and the standpoint that the Court should issue the requested injunction:

(9) In analysing the issues in this way, I do not lose sight of the argument made on behalf of the plaintiff that a breach of the Treaties is ipso facto a breach of the Irish Constitution. [. . .] It is apparent however that this constitutional point is an entirely consequential one. It is completely dependent on, and follows ineluctably from, the European law argument. The alleged breach of the Constitution occurs because there is an alleged breach of the Treaties. [. . .] In my view therefore, and even assuming for **the purposes of** this stage of the argument *that* there is or may be merit in the contention that a breach of the Treaties is a breach of the Constitution (on which I express no view), it adds nothing to the calculation the court must carry out on an application for interlocutory injunction to say that the European law argument can also be framed in domestic constitutional terms.

(Pringle v. Government of Ireland et al.)

As regards the third function fulfilled by the phraseology of bundles, notably the identification of the core element of the dispute from the Court's own perspective, this is primarily shown by *seems to me*. As an indicator of "stance expression" (Breeze 2013: 245), the bundle tends to collocate with evaluative markers such as *it is important to keep in mind that* or *significant weight needs to be attached to*. In 4.7% of these cases, characterised by the deployment of meaning elements intensifying the Court's attitude in reading the case, what underlies the pattern is the Justices' emphasis on what they single out as the key issue in the dispute. In (10) below, it is significant that in pronouncing judgment in a sensitive case on asylum applications, Hardiman J. points out that public interest is a parameter of paramount importance in securing a rational and effective immigration system (*seems to me to constitute a grave and substantial matter of high importance*):

(10) All these considerations emphasise the social and legal need for a proper discretion in these cases to be exercised with due regard to the individual circumstances of applicants (including applicant families) and the common good of the Irish community. This includes the public interest in a fair rational and effective asylum and immigration

system. This interest **seems to me** to constitute a grave and substantial matter of high importance.

(Minister for Justice v. Osayande et al.)

In a further 10.4% of attested occurrences, the Court's reasoning takes on an inherently axiomatic character. More specifically, the form taken by the related pattern was identified as being [*seems to me* + *to be* + *beyond argument/clear/elementary/obvious* + *that*], typically within contexts where the SCI sets about to settle the dispute through the "overly literal interpretation" of an Act of Parliament or EU norm, based on the principle that "plain words must be given their plain meaning save where this would lead to an absurdity, whether in the light of common sense or of the policy of the instrument" (Morgan 2001: 93). In (11), therefore, Fennelly J.'s stance is that the prohibition against the High Court issuing an arrest warrant requested by Germany pursuant to the Extradition Act 1965 stems from the wording of Article 32 of the new EU Framework Decision prevailing upon prior legislation on the matter:

(11) It **seems to me** to be clear beyond argument that the High Court cannot issue a warrant pursuant to Part II for the arrest of a person for extradition to a country to which that part does not any longer apply, even if the request has been received at a time when it did. What then is the effect of Article 32 of the Framework Decision? It reads:

"Extradition requests received before 1 January 2004 will continue to be governed by existing instruments relating to extradition. Requests received after that date will be governed by the rules adopted by Member States pursuant to this Framework Decision."

(Attorney General v. Abimbola)

An idea of consistency between the judge's stance and the wording as well as the enactment itself of relevant legislation also emerges from the use of *the fact that*. Interestingly, there is a correlation between the function of the bundle in the present corpus and the findings in Goźdź-Roszkowski and Pontrandolfo's (2014) analysis of *fact that* along with its Italian equivalent *fatto che* across US Supreme Court opinions and judgments from the criminal division of the Italian *Corte di Cassazione*. In those two corpora, the *fact that* is often established to be the ground on which judicial reasoning rests, mainly in a collocational environment where *fact that* is preceded by a preposition. In SCI opinions, 12.4% of the occurrences of *the fact that* keep the same kind of collocational company, as it were – cf. *the order was invalid by reason of the fact that* (Dublin City Council v. Williams); *the interim legal protection which Community law ensures for individuals before national courts must remain the same* [. . .] *in view of the fact that* (Dowling et al. v. Minister for Finance); *the grant of planning permission is invalid by virtue of the fact that* (Arklow Holidays Ltd. v. An Bord Pleanála).

Such entries suggest that their surrounding contexts may be covertly evaluative, in so far as the fact ascertained by the Court serves as the basis for judges to express their stance and thereby determine the outcome of their reasoning. This is illustrated by (12), where both the words and the very approval of a draft proposal by the *Oireachtas* [the Irish Parliament] allow Murray C.J. to conclude that the contested passages of the European Arrest Warrant Act of 2003 did in fact enjoy full constitutionality:

(12) The Act of 2003 benefits, in any event, from the normal presumption of constitutionality. The resolutions of the Houses passed on 12th December 2001 benefit from the

> same presumption. [. . .] It follows from **the fact that** the resolutions of 12th December approved a draft proposal for a Framework Decision that the Houses approved any reasonable and usual drafting changes, amendments to improve and clarify the document.
>
> (Iqbal et al. v. Minister for Justice et al.)

Discussion and conclusions

The findings presented over the whole of the last section may be read at various levels. First of all, they provide evidence that corpus tools can be a rich source of insights about the texts under investigation, as far as the study of lexical bundles is concerned. In spite of their lack of inherent idiomaticity, these were observed to act as significant "lexical units that cut across grammatical structures" and "have identifiable discourse functions, suggesting that they are important for the production and comprehension of texts" (Biber 2006: 155). Although Biber's research mainly focuses on university classroom teaching and textbooks, its value can fruitfully be extended to judicial texts, too, where bundles form an integral part of the 'legal grammar' postulated by Goźdź-Roszkowski and Pontrandolfo (2014) to consist of a wide array of stylistic conventions at the heart of the judges' discourse strategies.

More specifically, bundles were described earlier on as keys to judicial discourse as a practice and system of statements that systematically construct the object of which it speaks (Baker 2006). In the case of the study undertaken here, that 'object' was the EU, or even more precisely the underlying tension between State and EU law, a critique of the Union or the implementation of its policies and a genuine appreciation of domestic legislation, coupled with an assessment of the impact of EU law and the inevitable need to harmonise the Republic's legal order with EU objectives and/or principles. The findings may be indicative of the oft taken for granted yet at times problematic relationship between the EU and its Member States, especially when it comes to traditionally pro-EU countries such as Ireland: hence the potential interest of replicating an analysis such as that proposed here to other comparable national contexts.

Predictably, some legal commentators might suggest that the centrality of cases such as those instantiated by the corpus could be easily grasped even without recourse to corpus tools. On the one hand, for instance, Cahill (2014) thoroughly discusses case Pringle v. Government of Ireland et al. as a landmark decision that documents the revival of the doctrine of implied amendment in the Irish system. In addition, Noonan and Linehan (2014: 129) propose that "the judgment reveals much that is of interest about the nature of legal reasoning, in particular the blend of text, background purpose, and teleology that constitutes the very essence of legal discourse". In this vein, they delve into what they see as the major procedural aspects of the case, e.g. the tight timescale for the Irish courts to examine the issues raised, and the composition of the EU's Court of Justice as it sat for a preliminary ruling on the case.

On the other hand, it should first of all be pointed out that the study of the procedural matters and technicalities of jurisprudence is neither offset nor questioned but rather profitably integrated by the application of quantitative and qualitative methods to the investigation of phraseology in judicial texts. In fact, corpus linguistics needs not only and not necessarily be seen as a primary source of insights – as it has been in this paper – but also as a handy tool and a flexible instrument to check and support the trained analyst's first-hand intuition. Secondly, the fact that corpus findings may either integrate or indeed overlap with the legal scholars' research skills should neither surprise nor disappoint anyone. In keeping with Stubbs's (2001: 143) views, although "the method seems to add little to what an intelligent reader knows already", the fact remains that "we would be rightly suspicious of a technique which was completely at odds with the interpretations of trained readers".

By using corpus methods, we may indeed "have the beginnings of an explanation of the human reader's interpretation, because we can make explicit some of the textual features which a human reader (perhaps unconsciously) attends to" (Stubbs 2001: 143). If that is the case – as it was with lexical bundles like *in respect of* or *in relation to* providing the 'frame' that encloses the key 'slot' of the legislative item to be harmonised with EU law (Biber 2006: 172), as well as *the principle of* providing the frame whose slot is the Court's substantive argumentation – then legal scholars' expertise is likely to benefit from a sound textual basis enriching or consolidating their specialised profile.

Notes

1 As can be noted straight away, the table only includes three-word bundles. In this respect, the implementation of the methodological criteria laid down in the prior section led to homogeneity rather than variety. However, the fact that the bundles eventually investigated in the paper were chosen as the most frequent was considered a benefit, because that secured proper generality to the findings.
2 By 'patterns', reference is made here to the larger sequences in which bundles were observed to be embedded upon the achievement of the distinctive communicative purposes illustrated throughout the section.
3 In all numbered examples, the realisation of the patterns is signalled by the use of bold typeface for the lexical bundle involved, and an underline for the rest of the pattern. In addition, the case passages are taken from is reported in parentheses at the end of each example.
4 Here as well as elsewhere, co-occurrence percentages are not as high as one might expect. This is not simply correlated with the overall small size of the corpus. In fact, it should be borne in mind that the interest was less in collocation per se than in the occurrence of extended patterns. While these may be quantitatively less significant, their role as sequences instrumental to the achievement of specific goals in the Court's discourse was considered qualitatively worth pointing out as occurring across the bundles in Table 10.1.

References

Alexy, R., 1989. *A Theory of Legal Argumentation: The Theory of Rational Discourse as Theory of Legal Justification*. Oxford: Clarendon.

Anthony, L., 2006. *AntConc 3.2.1*. <www.laurenceanthony.net/>

Baker, P., 2006. *Using Corpora in Discourse Analysis*. London: Continuum.

Barceló, J., 1997. Precedent in European community law. In N. MacCormick and R. Summers (eds.), *Interpreting Precedents: A Comparative Study*. Aldershot: Dartmouth, 407–436.

Biber, D., 2006. *University Language: A Corpus-Based Study of Spoken and Written Registers*. Amsterdam: Benjamins.

Biber, D., Conrad, S., and Cortes, V., 2004. *If you look at . . .*: Lexical bundles in university teaching and textbooks. *Applied Linguistics*, 25(3): 371–405.

Biber, D., Johansson, S., Leech, G., Conrad, S., and Finegan, E., 1999. *Longman Grammar of Spoken and Written English*. London: Longman.

Breeze, R., 2013. Lexical bundles across four legal genres. *International Journal of Corpus Linguistics*, 18(2): 229–253.

Byrne, R., McCutcheon, P., Bruton, C., and Coffey, G., 2014. *The Irish Legal System*. Dublin: Bloomsbury.

Cahill, M., 2014. *Crotty* after *Pringle*: The revival of the doctrine of implied amendment. *Irish Journal of European Law*, 17(1): 1–25.

Collins, A.M. and O'Reilly, J., 1990. The application of Community Law in Ireland. *Common Market Law Review*, 27: 315–339.
Doyle, O., 2008. *Constitutional Law: Text, Cases and Materials*. Dublin: Clarus Press.
Fahey, E., 2008. How to be a third pillar guardian of fundamental rights? The Irish Supreme Court and the European Arrest Warrant. *European Law Review*, 33(4): 563–576.
Gabrielatos, C., McEnery, T., Diggle, P.J. and Baker, P., 2012. The peaks and troughs of corpus-based contextual analysis. *International Journal of Corpus Linguistics*, 17(2): 151–175.
Goldberg, A., 2009. The nature of generalization in language. *Cognitive Linguistics*, 20(1): 93–127.
Goźdź-Roszkowski, S., 2011. *Patterns of Linguistic Variation in American Legal English: A Corpus-based Study*. Bern: Peter Lang.
Goźdź-Roszkowski, S. and Pontrandolfo, G., 2014. Facing the facts: Evaluative patterns in English and Italian judicial language. In V.K. Bhatia, G. Garzone, R. Salvi, G. Tessuto, and C. Williams (eds.), *Language and Law in Professional Discourse: Issues and Perspectives*. Newcastle upon Tyne: Cambridge Scholars Publishing, 10–28.
Groom, N., 2010. Closed-class keywords and corpus-driven discourse analysis. In M. Bondi and M. Scott (eds.), *Keyness in Texts*. Amsterdam: Benjamins, 59–78.
Hoey, M., 2005. *Lexical Priming: A New Theory of Words and Language*. London: Routledge.
Hunston, S., 2002. *Corpora in Applied Linguistics*. Cambridge: Cambridge University Press.
Hunston, S., 2008. Starting with the small words. Patterns, lexis and semantic sequences. *International Journal of Corpus Linguistics*, 13(3): 271–295.
Hunston, S. and Francis, G., 1998. Verbs observed: A corpus-driven pedagogic grammar. *Applied Linguistics*, 19(1): 45–72.
Laffan, B. and Tonra, B., 2005. Europe and the International dimension. In J. Coakley and M. Gallagher (eds.), *Politics in the Republic of Ireland*. London: Routledge, 430–461.
Maley, Y., 1994. The language of the law. In J. Gibbons (ed.), *Language and the Law*. London: Longman, 11–50.
Mazzi, D., 2007. *The Linguistic Study of Judicial Argumentation: Theoretical Perspectives, Analytical Insights*. Modena: Il Fiorino.
Mazzi, D., 2015. Semantic sequences and the pragmatics of medical research-article writing. In M. Gotti, S. Maci, and M. Sala (eds.), *Insights into Medical Communication*. Bern: Peter Lang, 353–368.
McEnery, T. and Hardie, A., 2011. *Corpus Linguistics*. Cambridge: Cambridge University Press.
Morgan, D.G., 2001. *A Judgment Too Far? Judicial Activism & the Constitution*. Cork: Cork University Press.
Noonan, J. and Linehan, M., 2014. Thomas Pringle v. The Government of Ireland, Ireland and the Attorney General. *Irish Journal of European Law*, 17(1): 129–137.
Pecorari, D., 2009. Formulaic language in biology: A topic-specific investigation. In M. Charles, D. Pecorari, and S. Hunston (eds.), *Academic Writing: At the Interface of Corpus and Discourse*. London: Continuum, 91–105.
Peczenik, A., 1989. *On Law and Reason*. Dordrecht: Kluwer.
Phelan, W., 2008. Can Ireland legislate contrary to EC Law? *European Law Review*, 33(4): 530–549.
Pontrandolfo, G., 2013. La fraseología como estilema del lenguaje judicial: El caso de las locuciones prepositivas desde una perspectiva contrastiva. In L. Chierichetti and G. Garofalo (eds.), *Discurso profesional y lingüística de corpus. Perspectivas de investigación*. Bergamo: CELSB, 187–215.
Römer, U. and Wulff, S., 2010. Applying corpus methods to written academic texts: Explorations of MICUSP. *Journal of Writing Research*,2(2): 99–127.
Sinclair, J., 1996. The search for units of meaning. *Textus*, 9(1): 75–106.
Sinclair, J., 2004. *Trust the Text: Language, Corpus and Discourse*. London: Routledge.
Stubbs, M., 2001. *Words and Phrases: Corpus Studies on Lexical Semantics*. Oxford: Blackwell.

Summers, R., 1991. Statutory interpretation in the United States. In N. MacCormick and R. Summers (eds.), *Interpreting Statutes.* Aldershot: Dartmouth, 407–459.

Tomkin, J., 2004. Implementing Community legislation into national law: The demands of a new legal order. *Judicial Studies Institute Journal*, 4(2): 130–153.

Van Eemeren, F.H. and Grootendorst, R., 1992. *Argumentation, Communication, and Fallacies.* Hillsdale, NJ: Lawrence Erlbaum Associates.

Wray, A., 2002. *Formulaic Language and the Lexicon.* Cambridge: Cambridge University Press.

11 Extended binomial expressions in the language of contracts

Katja Dobrić Basaneže

Introduction

Legal English has long been criticized for its tendency to use redundant expressions, long sentences and archaic and synonymous words. Members of the legal profession, on the other hand, have advocated this complex style of drafting legislation and other documents, stating precision and all-inclusiveness as arguments. To a non-specialist, however, such language "is a mere ploy to promote solidarity between members of the specialist community, and to keep non-specialists at a respectable distance" (Bhatia 1993: 102). Regardless of this long debate between 'Legalese' and 'Plain English', legal documents continue to be perceived as complicated and confusing to ordinary people. The same is, of course, true of contracts. This chapter will, thus, focus on one of such style markers of legal language. It will investigate binomial expressions in a corpus of English-language contracts. Since these expressions have been mostly dealt with in isolation, the aim of the chapter is to study the wider context of these expressions, i.e. to see which lexical items extend them in order to allow for their "distinctive meaning" (Sinclair 2004: 30) to emerge. It will be shown in this chapter that the co-texts of these expressions may reveal interesting findings on both the function of binomial expressions and the genre in which they are used.

Binomial expressions

Terminology and definitions

The term *binomial* was first adopted by Yakov Malkiel in 1959 and he defined it as "a sequence of two words pertaining to the same form-class, placed on an identical level of syntactic hierarchy, and ordinarily connected by some kind of lexical link" (Malkiel 1959 cited in Gustafsson 1984). The term was, of course, not new since it had already been used in philology and rhetoric. Subsequently, many authors have proposed definitions of 'binomials', 'binominals', 'doublets', 'binominal expressions', 'binomial phrases', 'nominal stereotypes', 'binomial pairs', 'paired forms', 'couplets', 'conjoined phrases', all these being "synonyms or near-synonyms on the semantic level, and . . . hyponyms or co-hyponyms on the terminological level" (Bukovčan 2009: 62) for the same syntactic units. Following the analogy, numerous definitions of binomials can be found in several studies devoted to these expressions. Gustafsson, for instance, defines a binomial expression as "a sequence of two words which belong to the same form-class, and which are syntactically coordinated and semantically related" (1984: 123), whereas Bhatia defines it as "a sequence of two or more words or phrases belonging to the same grammatical category having some semantic relationship and joined by some syntactic device such as 'and' or 'or'" (1993: 108), the latter scholar thereby 'extending' lexical units which form binomial expressions to more than one word. According to Bhatia, these expressions are "an extremely effective linguistic device to make the legal document precise as well as all-inclusive" (ibid.: 108). Danet claims that these expressions had originally been used to facilitate communication, since some of them consist of a word of Anglo-Saxon origin and of a word of French or Latin origin (e.g. *will and testament*, *break and enter*) (1980: 469). Gustafsson (1984: 134) points out that, although the two words forming a binomial expression might seem synonymous to a layperson, specialists make a clear distinction between them (e.g. *discrimination or segregation*). In addition, she suggests that another reason for the emergence of these doublets might lie in the vagueness of the first term, which needs to be precisely defined by the second one (e.g. *full and equal*). Mellinkoff also indicates that "there would be more loss than gain in dropping a synonym for the sake of brevity, or even to tailor law language to a more logical pattern of word usage" (1963: 349). Some of these expressions, however, as suggested by Mellinkoff, have outlived their function and can be considered as "worthless doubling". Nevertheless, they "insinuate themselves into the lawyer's subconscious" (ibid.: 363) and, as a result, legal documents abound in such expressions.

Typology of binomial expressions

Typologies of binomial expressions have been proposed by different scholars. Gustafsson (1984), for instance, dedicated her research to analyzing binomial expressions in terms of thematic structure, i.e. to how old and new information is distributed in the sentence; clausal structure, i.e. to the distribution of binomials between independent and dependent clauses; sentence elements, i.e. to the function of binomials in sentences; and parts of speech, i.e. to the word classes of binomial expressions. As far as thematic structure is concerned, Gustafsson (1984) finds that binomials in legal English are mostly used for conveying new and additional information and are, therefore, placed towards the end of the sentence. As far as clausal analysis is concerned, it seems that the distribution of binomials between dependent and independent clauses in legal English is similar to that in English prose. The analysis of sentence elements, however, is more revealing, since Gustafsson finds that "the proportion of adverbials in binomials is extremely high in relation to the other major sentence elements" (ibid.: 130). In other words, legal texts show a tendency towards the end-weight principle, since binomial expressions used as predicate verbs, subjects and objects seem to be underrepresented. In terms of parts of speech or word classes, Gustafsson finds only a few adjectival binomials and a total absence of adverbs, but also a high frequency of binomials consisting of nominalized verb forms and prepositional binomials. Typically, however, a binomial consists of a pair of nouns. Based on her analysis one can classify binomial expressions according to the word classes of their members as well as according to their function in the sentence. Gustafsson, however, touches only briefly upon the semantic relations between the constituents of binomial expressions, while Bukovčan (2009: 64) takes this semantic relation one step further and classifies binomial expressions as:

a) Sequences of two or more synonymous or near-synonymous terms (e.g. *aider and abettor*)
b) Semantically related terms with interpretative or explanatory function (e.g. *breaking and entering*)

c) Two or more terms representing a chronological sequence of events (e.g. *arrest, charge and trial*)
d) Expressions where the second member is a varied repetition of the first (e.g. *arrest and apprehension*)
e) Expressions where the second member is the consequence of the first (e.g. *shoot and kill*)
f) Sequences of antonymous terms (e.g. *guilt or innocence*)
g) Sequences of complementary terms (e.g. *bribery and corruption*)
h) Sequences of two terms representing contradictory notions (e.g. *drink and drive*).

Bukovčan also analyzes binomial expressions taking into account their reversibility (e.g. *danger and risk* vs *risk and danger*), modifications (e.g. *law and order* vs *law and justice*) and morphological oppositions (e.g. *Ordnung und Unordnung* vs *Ordnung und Chaos*).

Gačić (2009), alternatively, takes into account synonymity and all-inclusiveness and distinguishes between doublets and triplets, which are considered to be sequences of synonymous units (e.g. *agreed and declared*; *force and effect*; *give, devise, and bequeath*), and binomial and multinomial expressions, the constituents of which belong to the same grammatical category, but represent sequences of antonymous units or sequences which contribute to all-inclusiveness of legal language (e.g. *advice and consent*; *by or on behalf of*; *executed and signed*; *freehold conveyed or long lease granted*; *jointly and severally*).

This chapter, however, will classify binomial expressions taking into consideration the word classes of their constituent parts (Gustafsson 1984). It will also investigate corpus data in order to reveal whether they can be reversed or modified and whether other equivalent legal binomials occur in the corpus.

Analyzing extended binomial expressions by means of genre analysis

Since this chapter deals with extended binomial expressions in contracts, the key issues that must be taken into account before any study of legal phraseology are the legal genre involved in the analysis and the legal system that strongly affects its features. Given the fact that the corpus analyzed for the purpose of this chapter consists of common-law contracts, it is clear that the interpretation of phraseological units found in these legal documents is strongly influenced both by the genre of contracts and the legal system in which these documents are used.

According to Swales, genre refers to "a class of communicative events, the members of which share some set of communicative purposes" (1990: 58). Based on Swales' definition of genre, Bhatia defines it as

> a recognizable communicative event characterized by a set of communicative purpose(s) identified and mutually understood by members of the professional or academic community in which it regularly occurs. Most often it is highly structured and conventionalized with constraints on allowable contributions in terms of their intent, positioning, form and functional value. These constraints, however, are often exploited by the expert members of the discourse community to achieve private intentions within the framework of socially recognized purposes(s).
>
> (1993: 13)

He further suggests that there are several aspects of this long definition that need to be taken into consideration. Firstly, the fact that each genre has communicative purpose shared by its members shapes the genre. If communicative purpose changes significantly, this results in a new genre. If, however, there is a minor change in communicative purpose, a sub-genre is created (e.g. the genre of contract within the legal genre). Secondly, the fact that the genre is highly structured and conventionalized is the result of the long experience within the specialist community, which in turn gives the genre its internal structure. Thirdly, the fact that the genre establishes constraints on allowable contributions strongly affects the language of the genre. In other words, although one has an abundance of linguistic resources at one's disposal, one must conform to the standards of a particular genre. This enables one, for instance, to clearly distinguish between a contract and an academic research article. Fourthly, the fact that the constraints are exploited by the members of the discourse community suggests that members of this professional community have greater knowledge about the purpose, structure and the use of genre than the non-specialists. The third aspect of Bhatia's definition is of special interest to this study, since sometimes one needs to take both the statute and case law into consideration in order to explain the meaning of extended binomial expressions. As Bukovčan suggests, "in the field of law they not only have their roots in national legal systems but also in specific legal cultures" (2009: 62). This chapter is therefore an attempt to suggest that the analysis of extended binomial expressions can, apart from revealing the typical phraseological patterns thereof, also reveal the reasons for such patterns, by taking into account the above factor of constraint imposed by the genre and the respective legal system.

Data and methodology

Data

Although the initial intention was to create a corpus consisting of authentic contracts, this proved to be impracticable due to the confidentiality of information included in private legal documents. For this reason, it was decided that the corpus will be based on the online edition of *Encyclopaedia of Forms and Precedents* (Millet and Walker 2014), "the UK's most comprehensive source of precedents for (non-litigating) solicitors, covering the whole of law of England and Wales at a transactional level".[1] The authority of the *Encyclopaedia* may also be supported by the fact that lawyers never draft contracts from scratch; they rely instead on standard forms, "which are used for all contracts of the same kind, and are only varied so far as the circumstances of each contract require" (Treitel 1995: 196). This trend towards the form-production process may be explained by three dynamics (Hill 2001): status quo bias, which favors the existing form-production process; anchoring effect, which favors one's initial point (again the form); and conformity bias, which favors the attitude of one's peers (if they use the form, one conforms to them). Therefore, although many lawyers would agree that the forms they use are far from perfect in terms of their unnecessary length and complexity, they would not deviate from them. Adding a new clause to the existing form, on the other hand, is less frowned upon than deleting an existing one.

The corpus may be divided into several groups of contractual undertakings: contracts for purchase and sale (8 documents), lease agreements (11 documents), lien agreements (5 documents), easement agreements (5 documents), service agreements (6 documents), insurance policy agreements (4 documents), banking law agreements (6 documents), gift agreements (7 documents), pre-nuptial agreements (3 documents), employment agreements (4 documents). The corpus contains 59 documents only, but its size amounts to 372,150 tokens, the latter being a sufficient size for special-purpose corpora, given the fact that "corpora intended for LSP can be smaller than those used for LGP studies" (Bowker and Pearson 2002: 48).

It follows from the above-listed types of contracts included in the corpus that most contractual undertakings are actually titled agreements, despite the fact that some authors (see, for instance, Alcaraz Varó and Hughes 2002) propose elements which distinguish contracts from legal agreements. Rossini, however, suggests that "agreement is an acceptable title for any contract" (1998: 11). Furthermore, if one looks at the list of titles for different types of contracts that Rossini (ibid.: 11–14) defines, it is clear that the term *agreement* is preferred in terms of phraseology (only six types of contractual undertakings actually use the term *contract* out of a total of 33 listed by Rossini). This was noticed in the context of European contract law as well, where "in a large number of texts the word 'agreement' is used to refer to a type of 'contract'" (Fauvarque-Cosson and Mazeaud 2008: 17). Thus, for the purpose of this chapter, the term *contract* has a wider meaning, encompassing both contracts and legal agreements. The discrepancy between a small number of texts and a substantial corpus size, however, may on one hand be attributed to the above-mentioned trend towards the form-production and on the other to the complete freedom to contract given to parties in a common-law system. The fact that the parties in a common-law system enjoy complete autonomy with regard to the content and the value of the contract strongly affects the language of these legal documents. Since the parties want to predict everything that may go wrong, they also offer all possible solutions in the body of the contracts. In other words, the parties are afraid of opportunism and they therefore "prefer a solution specified *ex ante* notwithstanding that they can predict that the optimal solution *ex post* might be quite different" (Hill and King 2004: 901). The judge in a common-law system, apart from not being asked to determine the adequacy of consideration, does not take the conduct of the parties during negotiations into consideration either. This is in contract law referred to as the *parol evidence* rule and it "prevents the parties from producing any evidence to add to, vary or contradict the wording of a contract, and imposes to read the contract exclusively on the basis of the provisions that are written therein" (Moss 2007: 5). This in turn affects the length of common-law contracts, which tend to be significantly longer than, for example, their civil-law counterparts, the latter being to a large extent regulated by statute.

Method

The corpus was searched by means of WordSmith Tools 6.0 (Scott 2012) and its tools ConcGram and Concordance. Scott has adopted the definition of concgrams from Cheng et al. who define them as "instances of co-occurring words irrespective of whether or not they are contiguous, and irrespective of whether or not they are in the same sequential order" (2008: 237). The search for concgrams is fully automated and can find "the associated words even if they occur in different positions relative to one another (i.e. positional variation) and even when one or more words occur in between the associated words (i.e. constituency variation)" (Cheng et al. 2006: 413). Parameters in the settings were therefore modified to display binomial expressions which occur at least twice, but stop at sentence breaks.

The procedure had first involved creating a wordlist and adding the wordlist to an index. This index was chosen for the procedure, and all items which occur together at least twice (Sinclair 2004: 28) were saved as potential constituents of each concgram. A tree view of concgrams was then produced, where "each branch of the tree shows how many sub-items and how many items of its own it has".[2] The resulting concgrams were analyzed and compared in their concordances.

Since all these binomial expressions share common conjunctions 'and' and 'or', the search for concgrams started from these conjunctions. Due to the fact that these conjunctions occur in numerous combinations (e.g. joining two clauses), it was expected that not all concgrams would represent binomial expressions. As a result, it was also necessary to analyze concordances of the listed concgrams, which means that the analysis was a semi-automatic one.

Extended binomial expressions

Extended units of meaning

A model that has had considerable influence on corpus semantics is John Sinclair's model of extended lexical units (2004: 24), which proposes that focus should be put on large phraseological units, rather than on individual words. Sinclair suggests that phrases "have to be taken as wholes in their contexts for their distinctive meaning to emerge" (ibid.: 30). If one looks at the wider context of lexical phrases, one discovers that they are prone to variation. Therefore, Sinclair takes the binary unit *naked eye* as the starting point and, by extending it, he detects that the unit is dominated by the prepositions *to* and *with*, that it co-occurs with verbs of 'visibility' and that it involves the semantic prosody of difficulty (e.g. *too faint to be seen with the naked eye*).

It has already been pointed out above that the chapter is concerned with extended units of meaning. Since "phraseologists must carefully define the linguistic level(s) at which they observe a potential phraseologism" (Gries 2008: 8), the extended unit of meaning will at this point be precisely defined, taking into account six parameters established by Gries (2008). With respect to the nature of the elements involved in a phraseologism, the extended unit of meaning will encompass a lexical item extended by other lexical items (e.g. *to place contracts, orders and engagements*). In terms of the number of the elements involved in a phraseologism, the extended unit of meaning will include at least three elements (a binomial expression extended by at least one lexical or grammatical item). As regards the frequency parameter, the extended unit of meaning "has to occur a minimum of twice" (Sinclair 2004: 28) in the corpus. Since it has been pointed out above that phraseologisms in legal language are frequently discontinuous, the extended unit of meaning will, thus, include units consisting of both adjacent and non-adjacent elements. As to the fifth criterion, the extended unit will include flexible patterns, but sometimes only part of the unit might be flexible. The latter claim holds especially true for irreversible and non-modifiable binomials and multinomials. Finally, regarding the sixth criterion, the extended unit of meaning has to represent a semantic unity but does not have to be non-compositional.

Extended binomial expressions

Binomial expressions may be extended into larger units of meaning, the latter thereby forming extended binomial expressions. Bukovčan points out that "doublets can be extended to trinomial and multinomial expressions representing a special type of phraseological units which call for in-depth linguistic and extralinguistic study" (2009: 63). For instance, the binomial *law and order* can be extended to *law, order and peace.* She claims, however, that "the third member constituting the new trinomial unit defines a particular notion as system-embedded" (ibid.: 73). The trinomial expression *Freiheit, Ordnung und Recht* thus suggests that in German culture the concept of law and order is closely related to the concept of freedom.

Enumeration is another style marker of legal language and encompasses "listing more than two syntactically and semantically interrelated elements" (ibid.: 74), and, hence, these larger chunks of enumerated elements may sometimes represent extended binomial expressions. For instance, the binomial *fees and charges* may become part of the enumeration *to pay all costs, fees, charges, disbursements and expenses*, the latter listing all types of amounts that are to be paid.

The main objective of this chapter, however, is to study the lexical and grammatical items that extend the extracted binomial or trinomial expressions. For instance, if one extends the binomial expression *repair and condition*, one discovers that the phrase tends to co-occur with the modifier *good* and the preposition *in*. If one further extends it, one discovers that the expression favors verbs of 'preservation' (e.g. *to keep/maintain in good repair and condition*). Sometimes the wider context can even reveal another binomial expression that serves as a modifier or a collocate (e.g. *to become* ***wholly or partly*** *void or voidable*; ***to assign and transfer*** *all rights and obligations*).

Results

Since binomial expressions are either joined by 'and' or 'or', the analysis was based on concgrams of both 'and' and 'or'. The search in the corpus was quite extensive, since the conjunction 'and' displays 31,114 concgrams, whereas the conjunction 'or' displays 36.036 concgrams. The results were, therefore, categorized according to the connective element of a binomial or trinomial expression ('and' or 'or'). The second criterion that was taken into account upon classification of extracted binomial expressions was the word class of the binomial expression. There is a group of these expressions that is extended by another binomial expression (e.g. *to hold and enjoy the Premises peaceably and quietly*). The deciding factor within this group was the sequence of binomial expressions. If, for instance, a binomial expression consisting of two verbs preceded the one consisting of two nouns, then this extended binomial was grouped as V + V + N + N. The last group consists of extended trinomial expressions, i.e. trinomials extended by an additional lexical item(s).

It has to be pointed out that there is a group of binomials/trinomials with which no stable extension can be detected, i.e. they do occur in numerous co-texts, but their extensions do not occur frequently enough to be able to draw conclusions concerning their phraseological status. In regards to their respective semantic field, however, similarities can be detected. For instance, unit 1.1 listed in Table 11.1 is used in the context of executing and delivering a legal document (e.g. *to execute and deliver a deed*; *to execute and deliver a duplicate of the document*; *to execute and deliver a counterpart of the document*). Unit 1.3, on the other hand, refers to establishing and maintaining funds for the benefit on an individual or organization (e.g. *to establish and maintain a trust*; *to establish and maintain funds*; *to establish and maintain scholarship*).

Although Table 11.1 suggests that there is a group of units with which one cannot detect stable phraseological extensions, there is a significant number of those with which one can detect a stable extension as well as the relative stability of each member of these binomials/trinomials (see Tables 11.2–11.10). Some extensions act as phrases in their own right, which holds especially true for the group of binomial expressions extending other binomial expressions. The same also applies to extensions consisting of a binary collocation typically represented in dictionaries (e.g. *to incur expenses* in the unit *properly and necessarily incurred expenses*).

Table 11.2 illustrates that the most frequent base is the one consisting of a pair of nouns. It also makes it evident that adjectival and verbal bases are equally represented in the corpus,

Table 11.1 List of binomials/trinomials with no stable phraseological extension in the corpus

List of binomials/trinomials with no stable extension
1.1. *to execute and deliver* (13)
1.2. *to acknowledge and agree* (11)
1.3. *to establish and maintain:* a) *trust* (1); b) *funds* (1); c) *scholarship* (2)
1.4. *to represent and warrant* (4)
1.5. *fair and reasonable* (4)
1.6. *to represent, warrant and undertake* (3)
1.7. *right or remedy* (43)
1.8. *to keep or store* (8)
1.9. *right, title or interest* (3)

Table 11.2 Extended binomial expressions with 'and'

Base V + V	*Base N + N*	*Base Adj + Adj*	*Base Adv + Adv*
1.1. *to carry out and complete the outstanding obligations* (2)	2.1. *to incur costs and expenses* (13)	3.1. *to constitute a valid and binding agreement* (2)	4.1. *set (out) below and overleaf* (7)
1.2. *to carry out and complete the works* (5)	2.2. *to keep in good condition and repair* (7)	3.2. *substantial and reputable insurer/ insurance office* (25)	4.2. *properly and necessarily incurred expenses* (2)
1.3. *to obtain and produce a permission* (7)	2.3. *to purchase sth. with full knowledge of the actual state and condition* (5)	3.3. *to be final and binding on/upon the parties* (9)	
1.4. *to sign and return a copy of the document* (7)	2.4. *to remain in full force and effect* (4)	3.4. *to be conclusive and binding on/upon the parties* (5)	
1.5. *to undertake and complete the works* (8)	2.5. *other than fair wear and tear* (3); *beyond normal wear and tear* (2)	3.5. *to maintain good and accurate records* (2)	

whereas there are only a few examples of adverbial bases (see Figure 11.1 below for frequency counts).

Similarly, Table 11.3 indicates that the only base within the group of extended trinomials connected with 'and' is the one consisting of three nouns, which in turn suggests that Gustafsson's claim on the most frequent binomial type may be extended to trinomial types as well.

Table 11.4 again proposes that nominal binomials constitute the most frequent base type; they are typically accompanied by a pair of verbs, but there are only a few examples in which they are extended by either adjectival or nominal binomials. Unlike Gustafsson's (1984) research, which suggests that adverbial binomials are non-existent in legal English, this study reveals two types of adverbial binomials accompanied by verbal binomials.

Table 11.3 Extended trinomial expressions connected with 'and'

Base N + N+ N
1.1. *rights, easements and privileges reserved to sb.* (2)
1.2. *to carry out additions, alterations and improvements to the Building/Premises* (7)
1.3. *to place contracts, orders and engagements* (2)
1.4. *validity, legality and enforceability of the remaining terms/provisions* (2)

Table 11.4 Binomial expressions extended by other binomial expressions

(V + V) + (N + N)	*(N + N) + (N + N)*	*(Adj + Adj) + (N + N)*	*(V + V) + (Adv + Adv)*
1.1. *to observe and perform the covenants and conditions* (6)	2.1. *non-observance or non-performance of covenants and conditions* (5)	3.1. *joint and several obligations and liabilities* (8)	4.1. *to hold and enjoy the Premises peaceably and quietly* (8)
1.2. *to vary and modify terms and conditions* (2)		3.2. *valid and effective terms and provisions* (6)	4.2. *to observe and perform duly and punctually* (3)
1.3. *to observe and comply with the provisions and requirements* (9)			
1.4. *to assign and transfer all rights and obligations* (3)			
1.5. *to supersede and replace any prior written or oral agreements* (5)			

As far as enumerations connected with 'and' are concerned, it seems that, as put forward by Table 11.5, the most frequent type is the one consisting of enumerated nouns and that they are typically extended by a verbal element.

The group of extended binomials joined by 'or' again supports Gustafsson's (1984) claim on the high frequency of nominal binomials in legal English, although verbal binomials also occur frequently in the corpus. In addition, as suggested by Table 11.6, there are five instances of prepositional bases (see Figure 11.2 below for frequency counts).

Within the group of extended trinomial expressions connected with 'or', however, there are no instances of prepositional binomials; hence, the most frequent base type is again the one consisting of nouns, although there is also one instance of an adjectival binomial.

Table 11.8 lists only two types of binomial expressions extended by other binomial expressions, whereby one consists of a nominal and the other of an adjectival base.

As far as the group of trinomial expressions extended by binomial expressions is concerned, however, nominal trinomials prevail and they are either preceded or followed by adverbial or nominal binomials, as shown in Table 11.9.

Table 11.5 Enumerations connected with 'and'

Nominal enumerations with 'and'
1.1. *to keep indemnified against all actions, costs, claims, demands and liabilities* (3)
1.2. *to pay all costs, fees, charges, disbursements and expenses* (7)

Table 11.6 Extended binomial expressions connected with 'or'

Base V + V	*Base N + N*	*Base Adj + Adj*	*Base Prep + Prep*
1.1. *to be inconsistent with or in breach of the provisions* (6)	2.1. *to make any objection or representation* (9)	3.1. *equal to or greater than* (3)	4.1. *in or on the Premises* (8)
1.2. *to affect or impair the continuation in force of the remainder of the Agreement/remaining provisions* (8)	2.2. *transferred at nil or nominal consideration* (2)	3.2. *to sell with full or limited title guarantee* (5)	4.2. *initialed by or on behalf of* (8)
1.3. *to unreasonably withhold or delay consent/approval* (46)	2.3. *transferred for no or nominal consideration* (2)		4.3. *during or after the end of the term* (9)
1.4. *to omit or delete all the alternative statements* (20)	2.4. *imposed by law or bylaw* (9)		4.4. *before or after the date of this Agreement* (9)
1.5. *varied or extended by this deed* (2)	2.5. *to make good the loss or damage* (7)		4.5. *by or pursuant to this deed* (2)
1.6. *sent or supplied in electronic form* (2)	2.6. *to vary terms or provisions* (6)		
1.7. *to grant or reserve easements* (9)	2.7. *prior written consent or approval* (8)		
	2.8. *to enjoy the Premises/Property without any interruption or disturbance/interference* (9)		

Table 11.7 Extended trinomial expressions connected with 'or'

Base N + N + N	*Base Adj + Adj*	*Base Adv + Adv + Adv*
1.1. *period of holding-over or extension or continuance of the Contractual Term* (8)	2.1. *written, oral or implied representation* (8)	3.1. *in contract, tort or otherwise* (8)
1.2. *to require approval, consent or permission* (5)		

Table 11.8 Binomial expressions extended by other binomial expressions ('or')

(N + N) + (Prep + Prep)	*(Adv + Adv) + (Adj + Adj)*
1.1. without any interruption or disturbance from or by sb. (9)	*2.1. to be/become wholly or partly void or voidable* (8)

Table 11.9 Trinomial expressions extended by other binomial expressions ('or')

(N + N + N) + (Adv + Adv)	*(Adv + Adv) + (N + N + N)*	*(N + N + N) + (N + N)*
1.1. *to render any debts, obligations or liabilities void or otherwise unenforceable* (2)	2.1. *to arise directly or indirectly out of any act, omission or negligence* (9)	3.1. *conviction, judgment or finding of any court or tribunal* (15)
		3.2. *invalidity, illegality or unenforceability of any term or provision of this Agreement* (6)

Table 11.10 Enumerations with 'or'

Nominal enumerations with 'or'
1.1. *notice, direction, order or proposal* (16)
1.2. *to be or become or cause a nuisance or annoyance, disturbance, inconvenience, injury or damage to sb.* (8)

Finally, Table 11.10 reveals two examples of nominal enumerations. It needs to be pointed out, however, that a stable extension consisting of a verbal trinomial tends to cluster around enumeration 1.2 listed in Table 11.10.

Analysis and discussion

Regarding the typology of binomial expressions, the most frequent ones in the corpus are the ones in which the base consists of N + N (see Tables 11.2 and 11.6). The same applies to extended trinomials, in which the most frequent type is again the one consisting of the base N + N + N (see Tables 11.3 and 11.7), as well as to binomial expressions extended by other binomial expressions, where the most frequent type is (V + V) + (N + N). Among the group of trinomial expressions extended by other binomial expressions the most frequent type is (N + N + N) + (N + N) (see Tables 11.4 and 11.8). Finally, with enumerations joined by either 'and' or 'or' the only word classes that are enumerated are nouns (see Tables 11.5 and 11.10). This, as suggested above, supports Gustafsson's (1984) claim that in legal language a binomial expression typically consists of a pair of nouns (see Figures 11.1 and 11.2).

It also seems that there is greater variation within the group of binomial expressions extended by other binomial expressions and joined by 'and', whereas in the same group joined by 'or' the only two types extracted from the corpus are (N + N) + (Prep + Prep) and (Adv + Adv) + (Adj + Adj). In the group joined by 'or', on the other hand, there is one group of trinomial expressions extended by other binomial expressions which is not present in the group joined by 'and'.

By extending the prototypical binary units, one discovers their possible variations and relative stability of their constituents. For instance, units 2.2 (*transferred at nil or nominal consideration*) and 2.3 (*transferred for no or nominal consideration*) from Table 11.6 suggest that the constituent *nominal* is rather stable. The other constituent, however, displays a certain degree of variation (*nil* or *no*). The same applies to phrase 2.8 listed in Table 11.6

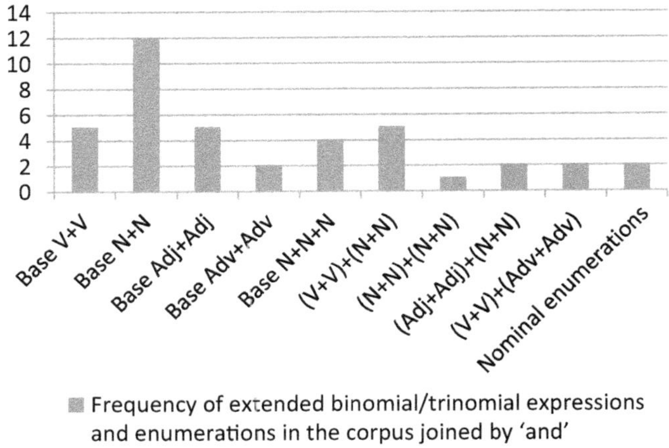

Figure 11.1 Frequency of extended binomials/trinomials/enumerations joined by 'and'

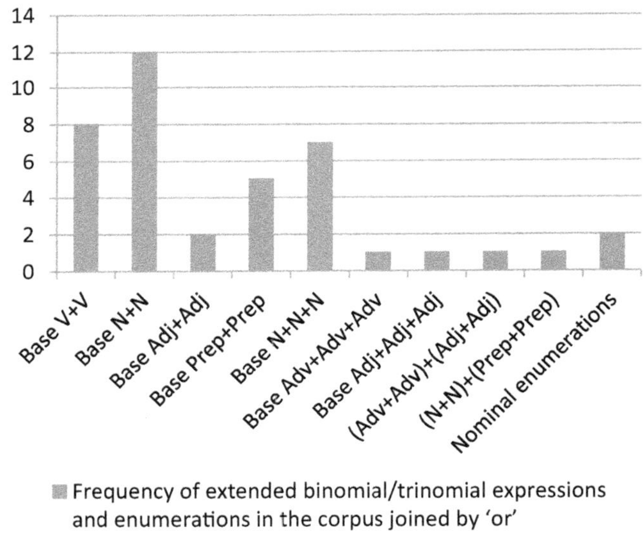

Figure 11.2 Frequency of extended binomials/trinomials/enumerations joined by 'or'

(*to enjoy the Premises/Property without any interruption or disturbance*). Corpus data, however, reveal that the second member of the binomial expression is modifiable (e.g. *to enjoy the Premises/Property without any interruption or interference*). This is also true of units 3.3 and 3.4 from Table 11.2, where the first member is modifiable (e.g. *to be final and binding upon the parties* and *to be conclusive and binding upon the parties*).

By extending binomial and trinomial expressions it is possible to detect which member of the expression determines the extension (e.g. *to* **place** *contracts,* ***orders*** *and engagements*). The extension can also provide information on the naturally sounding language of the original. This is best illustrated by item 2.5 listed in Table 11.6 (*to make good the loss or* *damage*), where it is suggested that the collocate used in this context is *to make good* and not *to repair*, which might be one of the options a translator would consider.[3] Similarly, if one extends the binomial *terms and conditions*, it is revealed that the unit is extended by the verb *to vary*, thereby suggesting that something that needs to be changed in a contract is subject to variation and not amendment thereof, the latter also referring to the act of changing and modifying legislations and legal documents. The usefulness of the Sinclairian wider-context-perspective may also be illustrated by the binomial expression *repair and condition*, where one discovers that the pattern is dominated by the modifier *good* and the preposition *in*. If one further extends it, it is revealed that the expression favors verbs of 'preservation' (e.g. *to keep/maintain in good repair and condition*).

Sometimes the wider context can reveal quite significant facts not only about the language of documents but also about the legal background. This is the case with phrase 2.5 in Table 11.2. The extension *other than/beyond* extending the binomial *fair/normal wear and tear* suggests that this binomial is something that constitutes an exception. If one further extends the binomial, one discovers that verbs of 'repair' determine it, i.e. that the party is responsible for making good any damage except for the normal/fair wear and tear. Similarly, if one studies the wider context of the trinomial *validity, legality, enforceability*, it becomes clear that the unit frequently refers to the *remaining provision* or *remaining part of the agreement*. And, indeed, by further extension, it is revealed that the prerequisite for this extended trinomial is that a term or provision of the agreement be held invalid, illegal or unenforceable first, which does not in turn affect the validity, legality and enforceability of the remaining part of the agreement.

A similar interpretation may also be applied to the meaning of the unit *to supersede and replace any prior written or oral agreements* since the binomial indicates the existence of something or someone in order to supersede and replace prior written or oral agreement. The co-text of this binomial suggests that the agreement needs to represent the entire agreement between the parties in order to supersede and replace any prior or written agreements. In other words, one of the typical boilerplate clauses of common-law contracts is called the entire agreement clause (Cao 2007) and its purpose is

> to make clear that the agreement between the parties is solely what is stated in the written contract, and to prevent the parties to the contract from subsequently raising claims that statements or representations made during contractual negotiations, and prior to the signing of the written contract, constitute additional terms of the agreement or some form of side agreement. That is, the parties include an entire agreement clause in the contract to prevent those pre-contract statements and representations from having any contractual force.[4]

It therefore seems that the more extended the binomial expression becomes, the more legal knowledge needs to be applied to the interpretation thereof. In a similar vein, although many units in the corpus are extended by vague or "flexible" (Mellinkoff 1963: 301) modifiers (e.g. to ***unreasonably*** *withhold or delay a consent/approval)*, such words, when used in law, are never used as isolates; they are always attached to other units and "it is assumed that attachment can work a reformation, and that a word wild and amorphous can suddenly become tame and purposeful" (ibid.: 302). This also becomes obvious when one takes into account the non-linguistic context of extended units of meaning, which, as pointed out above, imposes constraints on allowable combinations a word can enter into. Additionally, the meaning of these combinations is strongly influenced by the respective legal system.

For instance, in the case of the unit to ***unreasonably** withhold or delay consent/approval*, one discovers that there have been a significant number of cases in which courts had to decide when it is reasonable to withhold consent, thereby resulting in the establishment of four principles for the determination thereof:

> it is for the party that requested consent to show that the other party's refusal to give consent was unreasonable; what is reasonable in each case will depend on the facts; a legitimate refusal does not have to be right or justified. However, it must be based on reasonable commercial grounds; and the party required to give consent is not obliged to have regard to the other party's interests when making its decision. However, if the party requesting consent would suffer disproportionate detriment as a result of a refusal, that refusal may nonetheless be deemed unreasonable.[5]

These principles are to be kept in mind when one determines the meaning of the modifier *unreasonably* extending the binomial expressions *to withhold or delay*. Thus, it follows that the non-linguistic context sometimes contributes to on-its-face an ordinary word with no specific meaning being recognized as a modifier that carries considerable weight as part of an extended binomial expression. Furthermore, the non-linguistic context might also remove the veil of vagueness created by the legalese style of writing. For instance, the unit *to unreasonably withhold consent or approval* always uses the double negative (*such consent or approval not to be unreasonably withheld*), which suggests that it can be construed as either *not withhold unreasonably* or *not unreasonably withhold*, depending on whether the drafter wanted to negate the modifier or the verb. The above-stated principles, however, make it clear that in this particular context, the intention is to negate the verb. Similarly, the phrase *joint and several obligations and liabilities* refers to the obligations and liabilities made "together and separately" (Triebel 2009). In other words, if two parties "A and B each separately promise to pay C £10 this does not amount to one promise by several to one, but to two independent promises" (Treitel 1995: 523). The item does not make it clear, however, whether this principle of plurality of debtors also applies to the plurality of creditors. By examining the co-text of this expression, it is revealed that the expression applies to both parties to the contract, as witnessed by the following example from the corpus:

> Where any party comprises more than one person the obligations and liabilities of that party under this Agreement shall be *joint and several obligations and liabilities of those persons*.

Another example in which the extension represents vague modifiers is *to hold end enjoy the Premises peaceably and quietly*. The unit *quiet enjoyment*, however, refers to "the right to exclude others from the premises, the right to peace and quiet, the right to clean premises, and the right to basic services such as heat and hot water and, for high-rise-buildings, elevator service."[6] It therefore adds a new dimension to the extension *peaceably and quietly*, since the unit, apart from referring to the right to peace and quiet, also includes other rights (e.g. the right to heat and hot water). If, on the other hand, some of the rights included in the definition of *quiet enjoyment* would be denied, the possession would be interrupted. Advocates of plain English contract drafting style therefore propose that *peaceably and quietly* should be replaced with *uninterrupted possession* (Triebel 2009) in order to add precision to the phrase *to hold and enjoy the Premises*. This is also supported by unit 1.1 listed in Table 11.8 (*without any interruption or disturbance from or by sb.*), which represents yet another extension of the unit *to hold and enjoy the Premises peaceably and quietly.* In some respect this covenant of quiet and peaceful enjoyment is similar to an Implied Warranty of habitability, "which warrants that the landlord will keep the premises in good repair".[7] The English-language corpus of contracts, however, includes the extended variant of this warranty (e.g. *to keep in good condition and repair*), which in effect represents two separate covenants, hence, "a covenant to keep the property in good and substantial repair and a covenant to keep the property in good and substantial condition".[8] Not surprisingly, the meaning of this phrase has been subject to judicial discretion in many cases. For instance, in *Lurcott v Wakely and Wheeler* [1911] 1 KB 905 the court decided that the covenants to keep in good condition and to keep in good repair refer to the obligation of keeping the premises in a certain state, whereas the covenant to keep in good repair also imposes the obligation to repair the premises.[9]

It therefore follows that extensions clustering around binomial expressions in legal English, apart from revealing their typical phraseological behavior, also reveal their deep rootedness in the English legal culture, characterized by the intertwinement of the principles of English contract law and the opinion of the judge in a certain case.

Concluding remarks

The aim of this chapter was to show that extended units of meaning can reveal many interesting and useful findings for the study of binomial and trinomial expressions in contracts. Although a considerable amount of research has thus far been conducted to describe the formulaic nature of these expressions, it has been shown in this chapter that by focusing on extended binomials and trinomials, it is possible to detect both their variations in a wider context and the communicative role they play in the genre of contracts.

The wider context helps one to reveal which member of the binomial/trinomial is the strongest one and therefore determines the collocate (e.g. *to place contracts, orders and engagements*). It also makes it possible to determine typical collocational patterns of binomial expressions. For instance, the binomial expression *loss or damage* is in the corpus extended by the collocate *to make good* and not *to repair*, the latter probably being the verb most translators unfamiliar with the context of contracts would resort to.

Very often, however, there is a need to focus on the generic conventions of contracts in order to successfully interpret the meaning of the extended binomial expression (e.g. in the case of the entire agreement clause and the unit *to supersede and replace any prior written or oral agreements*) and other non-linguistic contexts which impose constraints on the meaning of these units (e.g. judicial interpretation of the unit *to unreasonably withhold consent*). Furthermore, by drawing attention to the non-linguistic context of these expressions, lawyers may be reminded of the fact that "law must in some degree be comprehensible not merely to those who work at it but to those who are expected to be governed by it" (Mellinkoff 1963: 395). This claim especially applies to contracts, since they represent private legal documents and are as such usually concluded between persons unacquainted with the non-linguistic context affecting the interpretation of words in contracts. The chapter, however, has tried to point out the fact that lawyers still tend to use "flexibles" (Mellinkoff 1963), which, as suggested above, either tend to raise confusion (e.g. the double negative in the unit *not to unreasonably withhold consent or approval*) or constitute mere repetitions (e.g. *to hold and enjoy the Premises peaceably and quietly without any interruption or disturbance from or by sb.*). Lawyers should thus be made aware of the communicative function of these expressions since "case law only rarely makes the pretension of being a dictionary of precise definition" (ibid.: 375). Even if precedents account for the definition of extended binomial expressions, it seems that their meaning is rarely conclusively defined and that it depends upon the circumstances of a given case. Instead of cluttering contracts with extended binomials that serve the mere purpose of "precaution of legal actors against variation in the wording of legal documents" (Kjaer 2007: 510), it would be advisable to refrain from the form-production process and resort to omission. It seems, however, that this objective may be achieved only by means of careful study of extended units of meaning which signal the need for studying legal phraseological units in the context of a certain genre embedded in its respective legal system. This way one can both create "the appropriate LSP environment" (Picht 1987: 154) and preserve certainty of legal effect.

Notes

1 Encyclopaedia of Forms and Precedents, www.lexisnexis.co.uk/en-uk/products/encyclopaedia-of-forms-and-precedents.page (Accessed November 27, 2016)
2 www.lexically.net/downloads/version5/HTML/?viewing_concgrams.htm (Accessed January 20, 2015)
3 This assumption may be supported through the fact that nowadays there is a general lack of university programs on legal translation and interpretation (Bajčić 2015) in most EU Member States, which results in the development of various (or sometimes no) certification schemes by EU Member States, whereby it needs to be pointed out that in some states hiring bilinguals with no legal competence whatsoever has been a common practice (Bajčić and Dobrić Basaneže 2016).
4 www.lexology.com/library/detail.aspx?g=ab1e0ed6-f91d-485a-a69d-87f68beec265 (Accessed November 5, 2016)
5 Norton Rose Fullbright, www.nortonrosefulbright.com/knowledge/publications/114754/when-is-it-unreasonable-to-withhold-consent (Accessed May 26, 2015)
6 Legal Dictionary, http://legal-dictionary.thefreedictionary.com/quiet+enjoyment (Accessed October 29, 2016)
7 Ibid. (Accessed October 29, 2016)
8 New Law Journal, www.newlawjournal.co.uk/content/read-small-print (Accessed October 29, 2016)
9 Ibid. (Accessed October 29, 2016)

References

Alcaraz Varó, E. and Hughes, B., 2002. *Legal Translation Explained*. Manchester: St. Jerome Publishing.

Bajčić, M., 2015. The way forward for court interpreting in Europe. In S. Šarčević (ed.), *Language and Culture in EU Law: Multidisciplinary Perspectives*. Farnham, UK: Ashgate, 219–239.

Bajčić, M. and Dobrić Basaneže, K., 2016. Towards the professionalization of legal translators and court interpreters in the EU: Introduction and overview. In M. Bajčić and K. Dobrić Basaneže (eds.), *Towards the Professionalization of Legal Translators and Court Interpreters in the EU*. Newcastle upon Tyne: Cambridge Scholars Publishing, 1–11.

Bhatia, V.K., 1993. *Analysing Genre*. Harlow: Longman.

Bowker, L. and Pearson, J., 2002. *Working With Specialized Language. A Practical Guide to Using Corpora*. London/New York: Routledge.

Bukovčan, D., 2009. Binominal expressions in the German and English language of criminal law. In L. Sočanac, Ch. Goddard, and L. Kremer (eds.), *Curriculum, Multilingualism and the Law*. Zagreb: Nakladni zavod Globus, 61–78.

Cao, D., 2007. *Translating Law*. Clevedon/Buffalo/Toronto: Multilingual Matters.

Carvalho, L., 2007. Translating contracts and agreements from a corpus linguistics perspective. In Kredens, K., and Goźdź-Roszkowski, S. (eds.). *Language and the Law: International Outlooks*. Frankfurt am Main: Peter Lang, 109–121.

Cheng, W., Greaves, C., Sinclair, J., and Warren, M., 2008. Uncovering the extent of phraseological tendency: Towards a systematic analysis of concgrams. In K. Hyland and J. Hellerman (eds.), *Applied Linguistics*, 30/2. Oxford: Oxford University Press, 236–252.

Cheng, W., Greaves, C., and Warren, M., 2006. From n-gram to skipgram to concgram. *International Journal of Corpus Linguistics*, 11(2): 411–433.

Danet, B., 1980. Language in the legal process. *Law & Society Review. Contemporary Issues in Law and Social Science*, 14(3): 445–564.

Encyclopaedia of Forms and Precedents. <www.lexisnexis.co.uk/en-uk/products/encyclopaedia-of-forms-and-precedents.page> [Accessed: 27/11/2016].

Fauvarque-Cosson, B. and Mazeaud, D., 2008. *European Contract Law: Materials for a Common Frame of Reference: Terminology, Guiding Principles, Model Rules*. Munich: Walter de Gruyter.

Gačić, M., 2009. *Riječ do riječi: lingvistička istraživanja odnosa engleskoga i hrvatskog jezika na području prava i srodnih disciplina*. Zagreb: Profil International.

Gries, S., 2008. Phraseology and linguistic theory: A brief survey. In S. Granger and F. Meunier (eds.), *Phraseology: An Interdisciplinary Perspective*. Amsterdam: John Benjamins, 3–25.

Gustafsson, M., 1984. The syntactic features of binomial expressions in legal English. *Interdisciplinary Journal for the Study of Discourse*, 4(1–3): 123–142. [Online]. <www.degruyter.com/dg/viewarticle/j$002ftext.1.1984.4.issue-1-3$002ftext.1.1984.4.1-3.123$002ftext.1.1984.4.1-3.123.xml> [Accessed 10/06/2015].

Hill, C.A., 2001. Why contracts are written in legalese. *77 Chicago Kent Law Review*: 59–85. [Online]. <http://scholarship.kentlaw.iit.edu/cklawreview/vol77/iss1/5> [Accessed 11/10/2015].

Hill, C.A. and King, Ch., 2004. How do German contracts do as much with fewer words? In *79 Chicago Kent Law Review*: 889–926. [Online]. <http://scholarship.kentlaw.iit.edu/cklawreview/vol79/iss3/23> [Accessed 11/10/2015].

Kjær, A.L., 2007. Phrasemes in legal texts. In H. Burger, D. Dobrovol'skij, P. Kühn, and N.R. Noerrick (eds.), *Phraseologie/Phraseology. Ein internationales Handbuch zeitgenössischer Forschung/An International Handbook of Contemporary Research*. Berlin/New York: de Gruyter, 506–515.

Legal Dictionary. <http://legal-dictionary.thefreedictionary.com/quiet+enjoyment> [Accessed 29/10/2016].

Malkiel, Y., 1959. Studies in irreversible binomials. *Lingua*, 8: 113–160.

Mellinkoff, D., 1963. *The Language of the Law*. Oregon: Wipf and Stock Publishers.

Millett, P. and Walker, R. (eds.), 2014. *Encylopaedia of Forms and Precedents*. London: LexisNexis Butterworths.

Moss, G.C., 2007. International contracts between common law and civil law: Is non-state law to be preferred? The difficulty of interpreting legal standards such as good faith. *Global Jurist*, 7/1. [Online]. <www.bepress.com/gj/vol7/iss1/art3> [Accessed 11/10/2015].

New Law Journal. <www.newlawjournal.co.uk/content/read-small-print> [Accessed 29/10/2016].

Norton Rose Fullbright. *When Is It Unreasonable to Withhold Consent?* [Online]. <www.nortonrosefulbright.com/knowledge/publications/114754/when-is-it-unreasonable-to-withhold-consent> [Accessed 26/05/2015].

Picht, H., 1987. Terms and their LSP environment – LSP phraseology. *Meta* 32/2. [Online]. <http://id.erudit.org/iderudit/003836ar> [Accessed 11/10/2015].

Rossini, C., 1998. *English as a Legal Language.* London: Kluwer Law International.

Scott, M., 2012. *WordSmith Tools* (Version 6). Liverpool: Lexical Analysis Software.

Sinclair, J., 2004. *Trust the Text: Language, Corpus and Discourse.* London/New York: Routledge.

Swales, J., 1990. *Genre Analysis: English in Academic and Research Settings.* New York: Cambridge University Press.

Treitel, G.H., 1995. *The Law of Contract.* London: Sweet and Maxwell.

Triebel, V., 2009. Pitfalls of English as a contract language. In F. Olsen, A. Lotz, and D. Stein (eds.), *Translation Issues in Language and Law.* Hampshire/New York: Palgrave Macmillan, 147–182.

ZAKON.HR. *Pročišćeni tekstovi zakona.* [Online]. <www.zakon.hr/z/75/Zakon-o-obveznim-odnosima> [Accessed 27/06/2015].

12 Giving voice to the law

Speech act verbs in legal academic writing

Ruth Breeze

Introduction

Academic publications clearly have a dialogic purpose. Of course, they convey the writer's view of the subject, but in doing so, they also project, mediate and respond to the positions of other writers, as well as those of potential readers. A considerable number of publications has focused on various ways in which writers convey their own points of view, represent the views of others, and construct a relationship with previous writers and potential readers. One particular thread in this discussion relates to the importance of the verbs used to represent arguments or ideas: texts are polyphonic (Bakhtin 1981), and one of the ways the writer orchestrates the different voices is through the careful use of reporting verbs (Ducrot 1986). The writer's own assertions using the appropriate professional tone ("we assume", "the present writer considers"), his/her presentation of others' words ("Smith maintains", "Brown suggests"), and his/her representation of anonymous voices ("many authors discuss", "it has been suggested") all contribute to the overall argumentation in the text. Moreover, within specific disciplinary areas such as law, these combinations, though not completely fixed, tend to fall into regular patterns, and thus represent an instance of what might be termed "phraseological patterning". They are conventional combinations of lexical elements which are used to project disciplinary voices. Analysis of such patterns can provide insights not only into the writer's personal stance and position within the discourse community, but also into the epistemological underpinnings of the discipline itself (Hyland 2000).

Although there has been some research into textual voices in other legal contexts (Mazzi 2007a, 2007b; Yovel 2014; Breeze 2014), so far relatively little attention has been paid to their role in legal academic writing. This chapter considers the nature of the reporting verbs used to introduce different voices in a corpus of legal academic articles, and the typical combinations and patterns in which they occur. This study thus takes a broad view of phraseology, aiming to reveal how the patterning in legal language weaves "an intricate web of semantic meanings" (Goźdź-Roszkowski and Pontrandolfo 2015, p. 134). In order to provide a contrastive perspective on legal academic writing, I also explore to what extent their characteristic style of polyphony overlaps with what is found in other legal genres (law reports), or academic genres from other disciplines (business management).

Theoretical background

The area of reported speech and attribution has attracted considerable interest over the last 20 years, particularly because acts of attribution involve a shift in responsibility away from the writer, and afford the writer a means of subtly evaluating what is being said (Hunston 2000). In the context of academic publications in English, the question of reporting verbs has been investigated mainly in the specific case of first person constructions. According to Biber (2006), since the most overt expressions of a writer's own position are those structures with a first person subject, the writer's use of lexical verbs with an "I" or "we" subject is important because it explicitly voices his/her attitude towards the matter at hand. Reporting verbs have a role in modulating the degree of certainty attached to particular propositions, and are therefore important in argumentative texts. Biber identifies three principal types of reporting verbs in this context: verbs with primarily epistemic meaning, verbs that convey attitude and verbs that represent a speech act. Epistemic verbs fall into two basic categories, namely those conveying certainty as to the truth of the proposition being voiced (such as "show" or "know") and those which indicate likelihood (such as "assume" or "believe"). Attitude verbs express the writer's feelings or agreement (in Biber's view, this includes verbs such as "hope" or "agree"), while speech act verbs articulate the way in which the statement is being made ("argue", "assert", "explain").

This taxonomy has subsequently been modified and developed in a number of ways, some of which may seem contradictory. To analyse the types of verb used with writer subjects, Hyland (2000) divides them into three categories: discourse verbs (corresponding to Biber's speech act verbs); verbs of cognition (which appears to cover Biber's epistemic and attitude verbs); and a third type, which he terms "research verbs", which denote actions carried out as part of the research process. These categories provide a convenient framework for determining whether the writer is taking on a writer, thinker or researcher role at any given point (see also Breeze 2010). If a comparison is made between Hyland's framework and that of Biber (2006), Hyland's discourse verbs can be seen to correspond to Biber's speech act verbs, while the category of verbs of cognition appears to include many of Biber's epistemic and attitude verbs. However, Hyland's category of research actions includes some of the verbs of certainty included in Biber's epistemic category: those relating to findings and proofs ("demonstrate", "observe", "discover"), i.e. the outcome of the research process; and those which represent the process itself ("analyse", "measure", "calculate"). In a similar context, Fløttum et al. (2006) develop Hyland's framework somewhat differently, preferring to distinguish between a researcher role, a writer role, an arguer role, and an evaluator role. In their categories, the role of writer is restricted to non-evaluative statements ("state", "describe") and discourse-organising verbs ("begin"), while the role of arguer is represented in the use of verbs such as "argue", "claim", "reject" and so on. Their evaluator role seems to correspond roughly to Biber's category of attitude verbs, since it comprises verbs such as "feel". It is not clear where verbs such as "agree" and "disagree" would fit in this framework, but it seems likely that these would be classed as verbs of argument, rather than attitude.

Although all these taxonomies are interesting and lay some of the foundations for the present analysis, if our main concern is polyphony, there is an obvious flaw in these frameworks: they focus almost entirely on the writer's own explicit presence in the text, complemented (at best) by an analysis of reader involvement manifested through the use of the inclusive "we", and perhaps occasionally "you". To design an analysis that takes account of the polyphonic nature of academic texts, we have to examine the "other" voices in the text, and the co-occurring reporting verbs used to present or represent them. This has previously been considered mainly in the area of citation analysis, often in isolation from the question of actual writer voice (Thompson 2001; Harwood 2009). One example of a study that does try to bring together these perspectives is that of Malmström (2008), who proposes a scalar concept of discourse voice. In this model, discourse voices can be staged as "Self" or "Other". Writers can make both "Self" and "Other" known to the addressee to varying degrees (scalar vocal presence), by using various metadiscursive features, and importantly by the choice of reporting verb (Hyland 2001, 2005). In Malmström's analysis, the type of reporting verb used not only provides insights into the relationships developed in the text, but also sheds light on the epistemological assumptions that underpin different disciplines. Potentially, the choice of different knowledge-stating verbs, the combination of those verbs with Self or Other subjects in typical patterns, or their use in semi-conventionalised impersonal constructions, should shed light onto the way knowledge is understood in a particular discipline, and on the nature of accountability – that is, how writers take responsibility for what they write. Unfortunately, Malmström's own study comparing academic papers in linguistics and literary studies failed to bring to light any major differences that could be interpreted in this way. However, his findings do not mean that other disciplines might not yield more interesting results in this respect. In fact, the rather high degree of formulaicity and conventionalisation which permeates legal language across genres (Breeze 2013; Ruusila and Lindroos 2016) makes legal academic writing a good candidate for investigating regularities and contrasts across disciplines.

The present chapter starts from an exploration of reporting verbs found in a corpus of legal academic articles, compared and contrasted with a corpus of academic articles from the field of business management and with the British law report corpus as a representative sample of judicial language. After providing an overview of the lexical frequencies and phraseological patterning appearing in association with the use of reporting verbs in the three corpora, I conduct an in-depth analysis of the dramatic differences observed in the frequency of speech act verbs used, examining the patterns that emerge in their co-text, and draw conclusions concerning the epistemology of legal academic writing.

This chapter will therefore address the following research questions:

1 What are the characteristic patterns in which reporting verbs are found in the legal academic corpus?
2 What are the implications of these differences in terms of epistemology and disciplinary values?

Framework and method

Framework

Since the aim of this study was to investigate polyphony in texts through the patterns associated with the most frequent verbs associated with writer (Self or Other) actions, it was first necessary to identify and quantify verbs that would fit into this category. A taxonomy of research and report verbs was therefore developed, based on Biber (2006), Hyland (2000), Fløttum et al. (2006) and Malmström (2008), with certain adaptations to the legal context based on Trosborg (1997) and Conte (2002):

1 Verbs of cognition indicating thought processes (such as "assume", "think", "understand", "consider" or "believe"; see Hyland 2000).
2 Research act verbs conveying physical or intellectual actions that form part of the process of inquiry (such as "explore", "investigate", "develop", "examine" "show", "demonstrate", "find", "uncover", "reveal", "discover" or "know"; see Hyland 2000).

3 Speech act verbs:

- 3a reporting verbs properly speaking, that is, verbs used to introduce something that is said (in other words, non-thetic rhetic performative verbs, like "say", "state", "indicate", "argue", "claim", "suggest", "agree", "promise" or "assert"; see Conte 2002).
- 3b discourse-organising verbs, a particular kind of non-thetic rhetic verb used to establish order or importance within the text ("conclude", "add"; see Hyland 2000).
- 3c speech act verbs of the type classified as thetic performative speech act verbs ("consent", "dismiss", "authorise", "convict", "abdicate"; see Conte 2002), often associated in legal documents with "hereby", which have been analysed at length by philosophers and legal linguists interested their "world-changing" function (Searle 1989; Trosborg 1997).

4 Attitude verbs which convey feelings ("hope", "regret", "feel"; see Biber 2006).

Several points need to be made with regard to this taxonomy. First, category 1 (verbs of cognition) reflects Hyland's category of the same name, and Biber's category of epistemic likelihood. This choice was made mainly for practical reasons, since the interest of the present paper centres on polyphony as represented by writer voices (Self and Other), rather than on epistemological issues. Similarly, category 2 (research act verbs) incorporates Hyland's research act verbs, which overlap with Biber's "epistemic certainty" verbs. Here, too, the nature of the agency voiced in the text is prioritised over the epistemological dimension. Thirdly, category 3 with its threefold division based partly on Conte (2002) is designed to account better for the complexity of the speech acts encountered in these texts. It was thus devised with specifically academic, and within that, legal and business academic, texts in mind. The fourth category, attitude verbs, was included to complete the taxonomy of polyphonic options, even though such verbs are relatively rare in academic writing.

Two verbs merit particular attention here. One is "agree", classed by Biber (2006) as an attitude verb. In this corpus, "agree" with a writer subject is more easily understood as a speech act verb, since it is usually used to convey contributions to an argument or debate. An added complication is that in legal contexts, "agree" can be thetic, since in legal contexts it sometimes functions as a commissive (Trosborg 1997: 69 and 84), but outside the context of legal documents and ceremonies it is mainly non-thetic, used simply to indicate acceptance of a particular argument, for example. The second is "provide", which is common in both the legal and the business corpus, but with slightly different uses. While the polysemy of "provide" in legal contexts ("the law provides that . . .") clearly accounts for its much higher frequency in the legal corpus, "provide" appears fairly often in both corpora with a meaning approximating "make available for the reader", which seems to lie closer to the ambit of research actions than to speech acts. Given the polysemy on the one hand, and questionable status on the other, it was decided to omit this verb from the calculations.

Finally, regarding the nature of polyphony and "voice", in order not to overcomplicate the present study, and at the risk of oversimplification, Malmström's notion of accountability and Fløttum's scheme of writer roles were used to operationalise "voice" in three simple categories: "authoritative voice", when a subject is framed as speaking as an authority with the endorsement of the writer (and to endorse the writer); "polemical voice", when the writer adopts some distance to the voice; and "neutral voice", where the writer simply reports what the source says, without apparently committing him/herself to what is said.

Method

The legal academic corpus (LAC) and business academic corpus (BAC) were constructed by the present author. Each consisted of half a million words from open-access academic journals published in the area of business and corporate law, on the one hand, and business management, on the other. All the articles were research papers, and had been published between 2008 and 2015. Both corpora were uploaded to SketchEngine. The British Law Reports Corpus (BLRC), which was used as the third point of comparison, is publicly available in SketchEngine. It is an 8.85-million-word legal corpus of 1,228 judicial decisions issued between 2008 and 2010 by British courts and tribunals (Marín Pérez and Rea Rizzo 2012).

The reporting verbs identified from the bibliography were compared with the list of the most frequent verbs found in the three corpora. This made it possible to generate a list of verbs that were salient in at least one corpus that might belong to one of the categories on the taxonomy explained above. By taking a cut-off point of 60 occurrences per million words in at least one corpus, it was possible to narrow down the field of enquiry to the most frequent research and reporting verbs. Once a definitive list of verbs had been obtained in this way, and classified using the taxonomy, the frequencies of these verbs were calculated in all three corpora. The patterns associated with each verb were then analysed both in concordance lines, and in sample texts.

Results and discussion

Overview of reporting verbs in the three corpora

To address the first research question, namely how do the reporting verbs in LAC differ from or resemble those in the other two corpora, the frequencies of the different categories of verb were compared across the three corpora. Figures 12.1–12.5 show the most frequent verbs (f > 60/M in at least one of the corpora) found in the different categories.

Figures 12.1–12.5 present considerable differences between the three corpora, and particularly between BAC and the two legal corpora, above all in the area of research

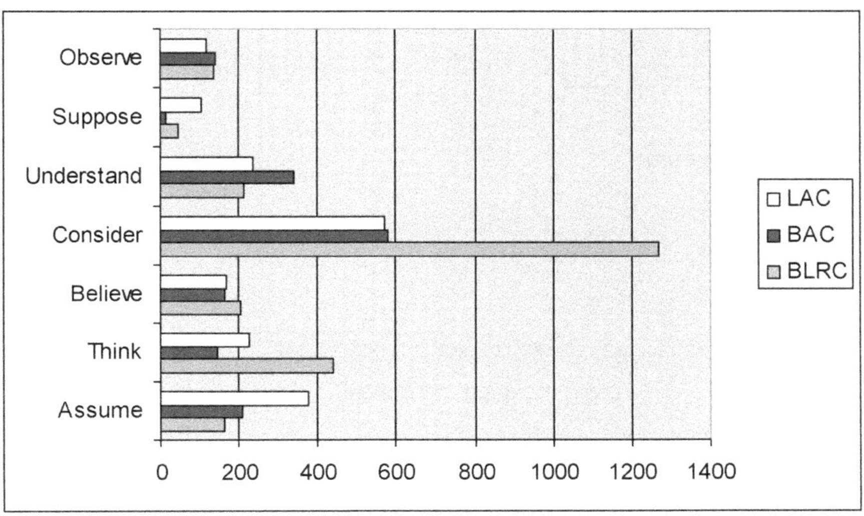

Figure 12.1 Verbs of cognition in the three corpora (frequency per million words)

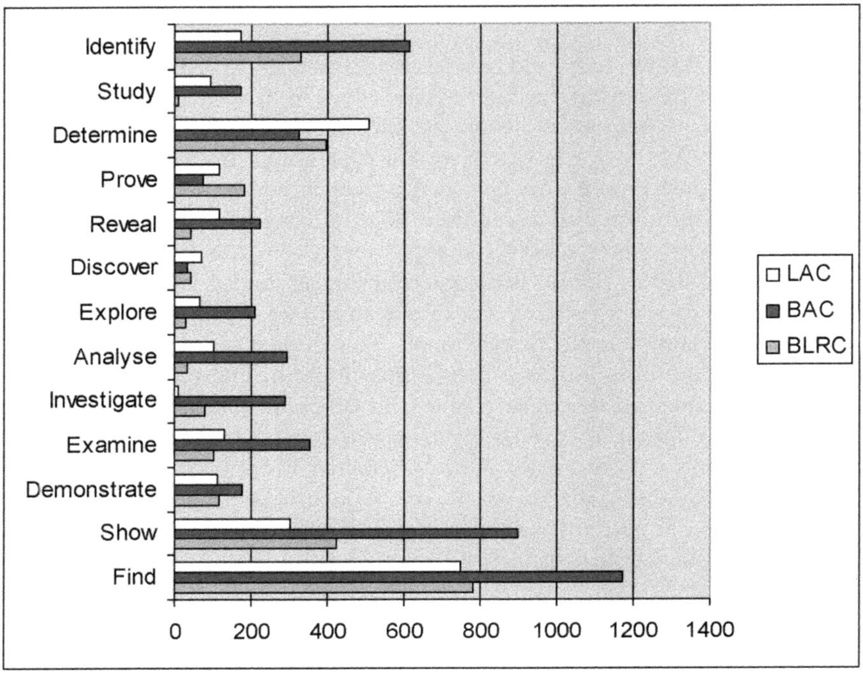

Figure 12.2 Research act verbs in the three corpora (frequency per million words)

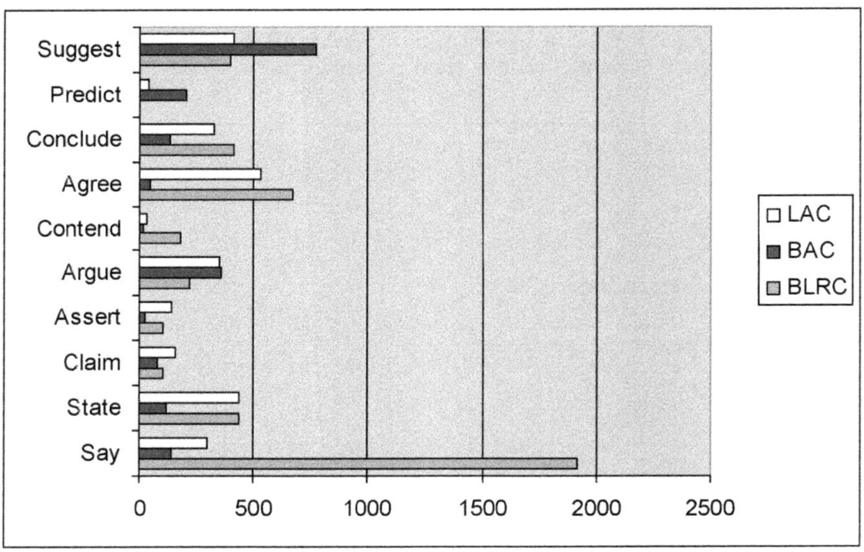

Figure 12.3 Non-thetic speech act verbs in the three corpora (frequency per million words)

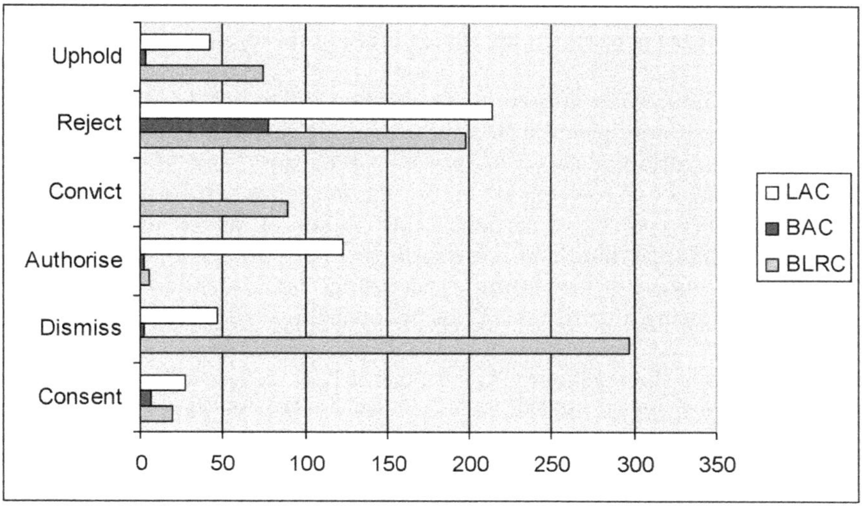

Figure 12.4 Thetic speech act verbs in the three corpora (frequency per million words)

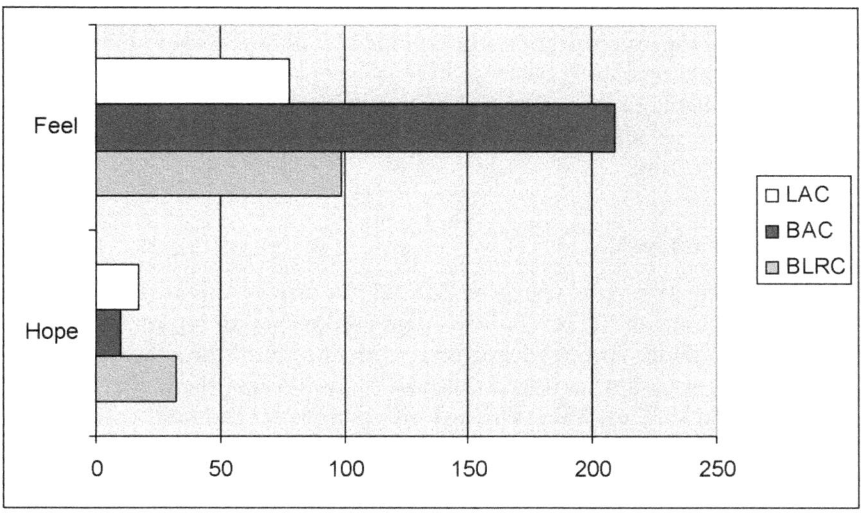

Figure 12.5 Attitude verbs in the three corpora (frequency per million words)

actions and speech act verbs. Before focusing on these, however, it may be useful to provide a brief explanation for three differences that do not warrant in-depth discussion. First, the data for verbs of cognition in Figure 12.1 bring to light a marked preference in the BLRC for using "consider" and "think", which is a consequence of the oral nature of law reports, and the need to provide accounts of the different parties' positions. Second, Figure 12.4 shows, unsurprisingly, that thetic verbs are also much more common in the BLRC except in the case of "reject", which is more frequent in LAC. Third, Figure 12.5

indicates that "feel" is more important in BAC than in the legal corpora, which can be explained in terms of two features common in business management research which are unusual in legal academic research: the frequent use of survey data, and the concern with psychology.

Regarding the underlying epistemology, the first difference relevant to our present purpose is the importance given in BAC to presenting research actions. As Figure 12.2 shows, with the exception of the verbs "prove", "determine" and "discover", BAC has a much higher frequency of research act verbs than the other two corpora. The choice of these verbs appears to point to a particular epistemological stance, in which knowledge is understood to be something that is attained through a process of empirical investigation. Through a process of "exploring", "analysing" and "identifying", the writers in this area aspire to being able to "show" or "demonstrate" that their hypothesis is valid (Hyland 2000).

By contrast, while the legal corpora fall behind BAC in research actions, they easily overtake it in speech act verbs. Not only do they predictably have more thetic speech act verbs, they also have a higher frequency of non-thetic rhetic speech act verbs, the only exceptions being "suggest" and "predict". These two verbs, arguably, match better with the rhetoric of empirical science detected in BAC, and less with the legal corpora, where forward predictions are rare and assertions are characteristically less tentative. The verb "conclude" was the only potential discourse-ordering verb that was frequent in these corpora ("add" was initially investigated, but most instances were accounted for by "value added" and "emphasis added"). This initial quantitative overview seems to suggest that legal academic writing is underpinned by different epistemological assumptions from those that operate in business and management, where an empirical paradigm seems to be dominant. In what follows, these non-thetic speech act verbs will be analysed in more depth, in order to shed further light on the epistemological underpinnings of legal academic writing.

Non-thetic speech act verbs

Since thetic performative verbs (category 3c) did not prove particularly revealing here in terms of the polyphony of the text, as they were used mainly to report what happened in cases, they were set aside, although I shall return briefly to this issue in my conclusions. The scope of the study was thus narrowed down to centre on non-thetic rhetic performative verbs (categories 3a and 3b), which are used with both writer and non-writer subjects, and play an essential role in configuring the polyphony of these texts.

The most frequent non-thetic performative speech act verbs are displayed in Figure 12.3. Although BAC has a much higher frequency of the two speculative verbs "predict" and "suggest", LAC and BLRC have a higher frequency of almost all the other speech act verbs than BAC. The only verb for which similar values were obtained across all three corpora was "argue". Since "predict", "suggest" and "argue" appeared not to be of particular salience in LAC, this study will focus on the remaining speech act verbs, all of which were more frequent in LAC (and BLRC) than in BAC.

In what follows, these verbs are analysed separately, in terms of their subjects in LAC, the type of voice with which they appear to function in the polyphonic structure of the text, and the patterns within which they characteristically occur. Where appropriate, comparisons are drawn with their behaviour in BAC and BLRC.

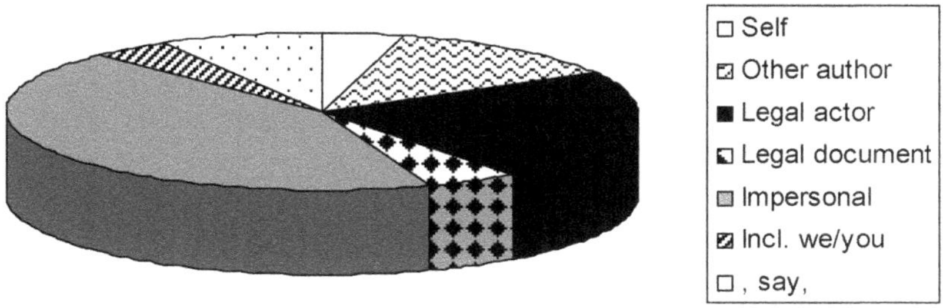

Figure 12.6 Subjects of "say" in LAC

Say

The frequency of the verb "say" is one of the most striking findings that emerges from this comparison. LAC has twice as many instances of the lemma "say" as BAC, while the BLRC has almost five times as many again. The nature of case law as a site of struggle between conflicting accounts and theories is fully borne out by the figures in this case.

As Figure 12.6 shows, the most salient use of "say" in LAC was in impersonal constructions, often of a rather elaborate kind, mainly expressing a degree of difficulty: "it is often difficult to say", "it is not easy to say", "it is an exaggeration to say", "it is incongruous to say", "it is circular to say". Although none of these constructions appears to be a stable phraseological unit, together they share a type of family resemblance, so that they could be described as a loose phraseological pattern fitting into the category of the "habitual routine phrases" identified by Kjaer (2007: 512), which are not subject to constraint and whose variation implies few or no consequences.

Similarly, passives of "say" also fall into conventionalised patterns, but these are loosely repetitive rather than highly formulaic. Such passive forms can be divided into three categories here, representing three different types of "voice" in the textual polyphony. First, some of the constructions belong to the class of "determine", mentioned above. Thus writers state, "If the dispute cannot be said to arise under the previous . . .". In this case, "be said" means something akin to "be found" or "be determined". Similarly, when the writer states, "An agreement is said to be self-enforcing when . . .", he/she means that it is generally defined in this way. Secondly, many instances of passive "say", such as the frequent "it has been said that", appear to refer to legal arguments or principles mentioned by other writers who have been cited previously in the text, or who are subsequently credited with these ideas. We should note that these do not simply fall into the "hearsay" category associated with passives of "say" (Bednarek 2006). The following example illustrates this characteristic way of referring to previous case law:

(1) For example, it has been said that contract rights can be impaired under the Constitution, but property rights cannot (Kuehner v. Irving Trust Co., 299 U.S. 445, 451–52, 1937).

Thirdly, a moderate proportion of the impersonal uses also fall into a particular category which might be termed the rhetoric of self-restraint, such as repetitions of the frequent phrase "much more could be said":

(2) Again, much more could be said on this and there is a substantial body of case law especially in the U.S., but further elaboration is not necessary to make this basic point.

The second most frequent type of subject classified here is "legal actors", namely people or groups of people defined by their legal roles, such as "the plaintiff", "judges", "applicants" or "arbitrators", or collective entities such as "the court". In fact, the most frequent grammatical subject of "say" in LAC was "court" or "courts", followed by "the judge" or "judges", "the contract" and "lawyers". Many of these examples are presented neutrally, suggesting that the writer does not take full accountability for what is said:

(3) To illustrate the foregoing concepts, the court says: The final measure is to test the fairness of this result.

"Say" also appeared occasionally after documents or part-documents such as "the contract" or "the clause" (see also Breeze 2013: 237–241, Trosborg 1997: 114–122):

(4) The first term on the right-hand side of the equation, x, represents the first stage in determining the meaning of the contract, the stage at which the parties decide what the contract shall say.

Finally, only a few of the instances of "say" represent the voice of other academic writers or their work:

(5) Guido Calabresi and Douglas Melamed's famous 1972 article said that a legal entitlement is protected by a "property rule" when "someone who wishes to remove the entitlement from its holder must buy it from him in a voluntary transaction."

As far as comparisons are concerned, it is hardly surprising that the BLRC also has a high frequency of "say". This can be put down to the nature of legal hearings, in which the proceedings are enacted as a war of words, a conflict between opposing or contradictory accounts by diverse actors. Open and flexible patterns along the lines of "it is/was (also/sometimes) said that" or "more could/might/can be said" are frequent here, as in LAC, and seem to form part of the routine phraseology accompanying legal activity. In BLRC, as in LAC, legal roles, institutions and entities have a considerable voice ("the applicants", "the defendant", "the court", "the ECJ", "the statute", "the contract"), as do named individuals. By contrast, "say" in BAC is relatively infrequent, and is generally used either impersonally ("it is safe to say that consumers' attitude towards online shopping is affected by different product types"), to preface interview data or, on two occasions only, to report what other authors have written.

State

The verb "state" is twice as frequent in LAC as in BAC, and almost twice as common again in BLRC (see Figure 12.7).

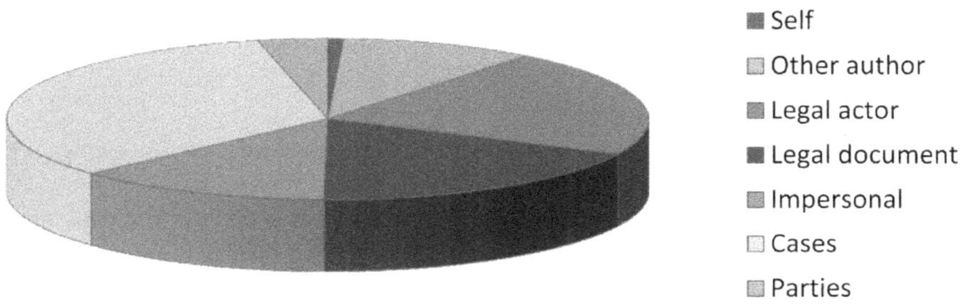

Figure 12.7 Subjects of "state" in LAC

When the subjects are analysed in LAC, it becomes apparent that "state" is mainly used to denote what is set forth in a written text (51%), either case law, legislation or some other form of legal document, which is framed as one of the non-negotiable pillars of the writer's argument:

(6) Section 761(8) of the Bankruptcy Code states that "commodity" has the meaning assigned to the term by the CEA. "Commodity" is defined under section 1a(4) of the CEA as "wheat, cotton, rice . . .".
(7) The contract stated that it was a forward contract.

When these authors are citing case law, "state" is frequently used to introduce a literal quotation, presumably from the relevant law report, which is presented to support the writer's own line of argument. The following example is typical of a large number of instances in this corpus, which provide the citation reference, and then include the main precedent in parentheses, introduced by "stating that":

(8) United States v. One Parcel of Land, 965 F.2d 311, 316 (7th Cir. 1992) (stating that "as a legal fiction, a corporation cannot 'know' like an individual 'knows'. We treat corporations as separate legal entities and enable them to own property and enter contracts by relying on agency precepts. . . . A corporation acts through its agents").

As would be expected, "state" is also used to represent what named people actually say, preceding either a direct quotation or a paraphrase or summary. Again, most instances seem to imply endorsement rather than distancing:

(9) Justice O'Connor has stated that "over the past decade, the Court has abandoned all pretense of ascertaining congressional intent with respect to the Federal Arbitration Act, building instead, case by case, an edifice of its own creation."

By extension, legal institutions often also appear as the speaking subject here. In fact, "court" is the single most frequent subject of "state", occurring 22 times:

(10) The Court stated in note 158: Despite the real obligations of courts to apply international law and foster comity, domestic courts do not sit as internationally constituted tribunals.

Even more strikingly, it is evidently also possible for abstract notions such as "case law" or "principles" to "state" something: in this way, the contribution of these abstract entities is also brought on stage, given voice in the discourse and used as authority to support the writer's own argument:

(11) Case law expresses this by stating that the "cash forward" exception applies if there is a legitimate expectation of physical delivery under the contract.
(12) The harm principle states that it is illegitimate for the state to interfere with an individual's liberty unless that individual has harmed (or is about to harm) another individual.

In short, with all of these subjects, "state" appears to stage an authoritative voice: when a law, case law or "the court" states something, this not only has weight in the present discourse: there is a kind of mutual endorsement, by which the (usually prestigious) subject of "state" endorses what is stated, and the writer, by citing in this authoritative tone, imbues the "stater" with validity. In Malmström's (2008) terms, the writer is fully accountable for this voice. Moreover, a high degree of conventionalisation characterises these uses: the pattern (legal actor/legal document/case + states + that) seems to constitute the standard way of reporting the authoritative voice of the law within the polyphonic texture of the discourse.

If we turn to the comparison with the BLRC, where "state" is a highly frequent verb, we find that institutional collective legal actors and non-human speaking subjects are there also among the most salient subjects of the verb. Implications here seem to be less clear: the voice associated with "state" ranges from neutral reporting to authoritative endorsement. The most frequent subject of "state" in the BLRC is "the court", followed by "the letter", "the report", etc.:

(13) Then following a lengthy citation from Connors the court stated first that the reasoning in Connors was not confined to gypsies . . .
(14) The affidavit stated that the receivers had discovered the telex by chance because it had been misfiled.

The main human actors forming the subject of "state" are named judges, and figures such as "the claimant", "the respondent", "the coroner" and "the solicitor":

(15) Mummery LJ had earlier stated in his judgment that the setting aside of the order of Harman J was of practical significance in this case.

In short, the behaviour of "state" in BLRC and LAC is clearly very similar, which suggests that such patterns are transversal to legal discourse in general rather than genre-specific.

The behaviour of "state" in BAC contrasts sharply with the patterns found in the legal corpora. Here, the verb "state" is relatively infrequent, and is almost always used to introduce a citation from the bibliography of the field, or to report on a statement by a speaking subject:

(16) Raheman and Nasr [2] state that delaying payment of accounts payable to suppliers allows firms to access the quality of bought products and can be inexpensive and flexible source of financing.
(17) The Indian minister of commerce has stated on several occasions that foreign direct investments in India are safe [7].

The only non-human subjects characteristically used with "state" in BAC are "hypothesis" and "model" and "equation":

(18) Kwiatkowski et al [25] present a test where the null hypothesis states that the series is stationary.
(19) Hauschildt and Kirchmann's (2001) promoter model, which states that in innovation processes, different persons with different powers are needed to overcome the barriers of unwillingness and of ignorance.

In only one instance in this corpus does a document figure as the subject of "state", curiously echoing the common practice identified in LAC and BLRC:

(20) In addition, the committee must have a written charter that states the purposes and responsibilities of the committee.

Agree

In LAC, the most frequent subject of "agree" is "party/ies" (found in 15% of instances), but many other named individuals and individual legal roles also figure ("consumer", "creditor", "respondent", "plaintiff", "member of the Bar", "buyer", "seller"):

(21) A party who agrees to dispute resolution in a certain forum should not later be able to renege on his promise.

Collective non-human subjects ("the court", "the organisation", "Peat Marwick") are also frequently represented as "agreeing":

(22) The court agreed with the shareholders, stating that even though the LBO transaction was an extraordinary one and was not an ordinary securities "trade," payments in the LBO qualified as settlement payments.

Writer subjects ("we", "I", "the present writer") are rare in LAC. It thus seems that the staging of agreement in these texts is part of the matter being discussed, rather than part of the action of the writer with regard to other actors in the text.

In the BLRC, the word "parties" also has one of the strongest associations with the verb "agree" (co-occurring in 7% of cases), as well as members (1%) (found in combinations such as "members of the court", or "members of the committee"), and identifiers associated with individual judges, such as "Lord" (7%), and "LJ" (3%). "Agree" is also strongly associated with "court" (2%), although here the concordance lines are fairly equally divided between those which position "court" as the grammatical subject, those which refer more accurately to the different members of the court and those indicating a first person subject who is in agreement with the court. One of the striking differences between uses of "agree" in BLRC is its use in the first person, a phenomenon which can be explained by the nature of the law report genre. Among the principal collocates of "agree" in BLRC, and their percentages of co-occurrence, are: "I" (28%) and "we" (6%). Interestingly, these are often found in the following formulaic combinations: "we also agree", "we entirely agree", "we respectfully agree", and "we therefore agree". Given the special authoritative nature of judicial rulings, the judges' explicit agreement forms an integral part of the way that power is negotiated through the text: by accepting a point of view, they are not merely debating, they are actually validating an interpretation of the law, or finding in favour of one of the parties. The following example shows how in the BLRC the judges' "agreement" assumes complete accountability for what is said, and builds up to the authoritative declaration permitting the appeal, expressed through the thetic speech act verb "allow" (no such evidence was found in LAC):

(23) The jury duly retired at eight minutes past 3 after this direction and returned with guilty verdicts within the hour. We agree with counsel that the speed with which they returned suggested there was a danger that the answer they had just received had been decisive. We agree that there was a very real risk here that the jury were thoroughly confused and approached the statutory defence wrongly. For all these reasons we think this conviction is unsafe. This application is allowed. We allow the appeal against conviction on counts 2 to 8.

In BAC, "agree" is almost exclusively used to report questionnaire data, particularly the kind based on Likert-type items. Only very occasionally is "agree" used here to indicate consensus among experts:

(24) Measurement theorists agree that content validity is a necessary prerequisite for establishing the construct validity of a measure.

Assert

As Figure 12.8 shows, parties (either represented as "parties" or identified by their more specific legal role as "claimant", "respondent" and so on) are the most frequent subjects of "assert", although it should be noted that in both cases, the most frequent use of the verb "assert" is in the context of asserting claims, which are reported factually by the writer.

Another characteristic use of "assert" appears to be similar to the use of "state" in the representation of precedents from case law. The difference is that here there almost always seems to be an implication that the writer is adopting some distance to the reported proposition, shrugging off accountability or even advancing it as a polemical statement. In the following example, the writer is citing case law that backs up the view he opposes:

(25) See also Green Tree, 531 U.S. at 96 (Ginsburg, J., dissenting) (asserting that businesses, as "repeat players" in arbitration, have more knowledge about the process and its costs).

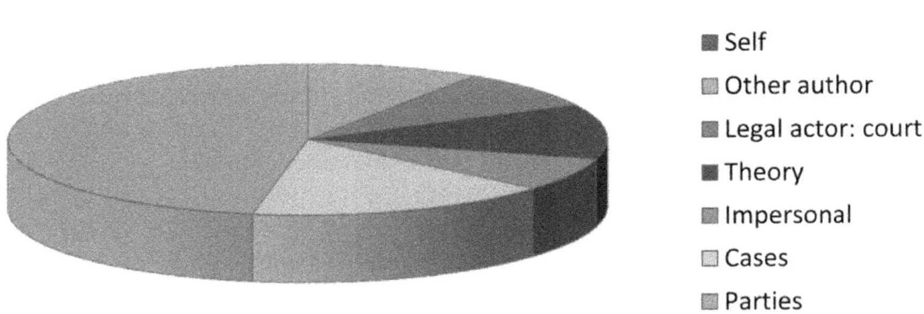

Figure 12.8 Subjects of "assert" in LAC

Aside from this, LAC is notable in the role it accords to theoretical entities as the subjects of "assert":

(26) Death of contract theory asserts the lack of integrity of contract law and contract's identity with other areas of law.

"Assert" in BLRC is also used mainly to dissociate the writer from the statements being reported. It is associated with parties in the case ("claimant", "respondent") and with adverbs ("falsely", "merely") that shed doubt on the content or importance of the assertion:

(27) I am of this view notwithstanding that I do not consider that Mr O'Donoghue was correct to assert . . . that the extent of the State's obligation to investigate the circumstances of the death of a deceased will only arise in circumstances where the State is implicated in the taking of that person's life.

Claim

In LAC, "claim" is used principally to report neutrally what parties ask for or argue in legal cases. In this case, it is clearly used in the sense of "the parties say/ask for this", without any commitment to the truth or fairness of what is stated. "Claim" thus has a role similar to that identified by Mazzi (2007a) for verbs such as "submit" or "contend", associated with non-factive stance in legal judgments. Interestingly, however, it is also used for staging arguments. In this case, various semi-fixed expressions appear: the verb is preceded by "one might claim", "some would claim", "no one would claim", "it would be an exaggeration to claim", "we do not claim", all of which seem to indicate the writer's intention to evade accountability:

(28) Second, one might claim that firms that maximize profits sometimes do bad things – pollute the environment, for example – that the law should attempt to deter.

Occasionally the various positions in an argument are embodied in more descriptive textual roles, such as "the contextualist", "arbitration advocates":

(29) The textualist, in contrast, claims that variance does not shrink materially with a broader evidentiary base because contracts often have plain meanings.

The following example illustrates how this verb is used to advance ideas that are to be refuted:

(30) For our second example, return to the relation-specific investment model set out above. There, we claimed that permitting the seller to sue for the price would deter the buyer's threat to renegotiate after the seller had invested. This claim is too strong because sellers in some cases could not make a credible threat to sue.

In short, although the first use of "claim" is to report actions, another very frequent use is to advance an argument which is going to be refuted or at least modified by the writer. The use of this verb, particularly in phraseological patterns such as "one might claim" or "some would claim", alerts the reader to exercise suspicion when processing the content of the "claim" and plays a special role in the dialogical structure of the text.

Contend

"Contend" is principally used in LAC to preface positions in argument that are disputed or disputable, for which the writer takes no personal responsibility. The following example positions the speaker cataphorically as an "arbitration critic", preparing the reader for her contentious statement by using loaded lexis ("misuse", "one-sidedly"):

(31) Arbitration critics argue that corporations misuse this power by including provisions in arbitration clauses that one-sidedly favor the corporation. Professor Jean Sternlight contends: Drafters of arbitration clauses will inevitably be tempted to use arbitration clauses to provide themselves with various unfair advantages.

Although not all the evidence in this corpus is conclusive in this respect, it seems that "contend" is mainly associated with the advancement of arguments that the writer does not support. In the following example, the writer places this account of what the court "contended" before launching a highly critical attack on the court's ruling in this case:

(32) The court contended that because she received Social Security and other benefits and owned the trailer home in which she lived, Foster might have had "other sources of income or owned other assets besides her trailer home".

However, in a few cases, "contend" seems to be used neutrally, to present statements which are disputed in the circumstances, but to which the writer holds a neutral stance. In general, there is a strong resemblance between "contend" and "claim", but the former is less frequent and seems (in this corpus) to be used more freely, without discernible phraseological patterns.

Conclude

The overwhelming majority of instances of "conclude" (84%) in LAC have a meaning close to "reach the conclusion that", and this idea is supported by the fact that the collocation "conclude that" occurs in 69% of the instances. The other 16% of instances simply indicate the termination of legal proceedings, or the position of something in the text. The most frequent subject of "conclude" in LAC is "the court" (21%):

(33) The United States Court of Appeals for the Third Circuit, for example, concluded that the confidentiality provisions incorporated in an employment agreement were not unconscionable.

"Conclude" is often used, like "state" and "assert" above, to report precedents. In such cases, "conclude" connotes the weight of judicial authority:

(34) See Helvey v. Wabash County REMC, 278 N.E.2d 608, 610 (Ind. App. 1972) (concluding electricity is goods under the U.C.C.).

In short, evidence from LAC suggests that "conclude" is mainly used to preface the final outcome of arguments, presented as authoritative backing for the writer's present line of argumentation, rather than simply to indicate that something comes at the end of the text. In BAC, only 67% of instances of "conclude" meant "reach the conclusion that", while 33%

were used simply to order the discourse. In BLRC, however, 84% of occurrences of "conclude" were followed by "that", indicating the presentation of conclusions (see also Mazzi 2007b). The use of "conclude" to project an authoritative voice was thus equally prevalent in the two legal corpora, but much less frequent in BAC.

Summing up

In the polyphony of these legal texts, each speech act verb is characteristically associated with a particular type of voice and certain categories of subject in the LAC. An overview of the main voices and subjects found with each verb in LAC is provided in Table 12.1, using the three categories of "voice".

The first group of verbs ("state", "conclude") is typically used to state what the writer regards as true, sound and authoritative. "State" is frequently used with laws, precedents and documents, or with citations which the present writer incorporates into his/her own line of argument. "Conclude" is used to report decisions, precedents or arguments by other writers which have the present writer's full endorsement. Indeed, with these verbs a kind of mutual endorsement occurs: the writer boosts his/her arguments by citing authoritative sources, and by according this important to those sources, he/she thereby endorses the source. The second group of verbs ("claim", "assert", "contend") is used to distance the writer from what is said, warning the reader that such views, though perhaps worthy of consideration, are ultimately going to be refuted. The third group of verbs ("say", "agree") is generally used neutrally in the LAC to represent what parties or other writers say: the writer does not exercise distance, but neither does he/she take full responsibility for what is said. From the perspective of phraseological patterning, it is particularly noticeable that "say" is very frequently used in combinations such as "difficult/incongruous/unreasonable to say that", that is, impersonal constructions used to map out the limits of what is "sayable" within the legal academic community, and in passive constructions such as "it has been said that" to report others' views. These characteristic patterns draw attention to the primordial importance of "saying" as the outward representation of legal reasoning, perhaps reflecting pervasive genre conventions from courtroom practice.

In this context, we have also seen that the patterns associated with these verbs in LAC strongly resemble those of the judicial decisions in the BLRC, rather than those found in BAC. The only exception to this is "agree", which exerts a further authority-building function in BLRC. This general resemblance constitutes further evidence of the specificity of legal academic writing in comparison to other academic genres: there seems to be evidence

Table 12.1 Main voices and subject categories associated with non-thetic speech act verbs in LAC

Voice	*Subject*	*Speech act verb*
Authoritative voice (writer endorsed)	Legal actor, legislation, document, case law, impersonal, other writers, present writer	State, conclude
Polemical voice (writer distanced)	Legal actor, case law, staged argumentative positions, other writers	Claim, assert, contend
Neutral voice (writer neutral)	Legal actor, other writers	Say, agree

of considerable discursive flow between legal academia and other legal genres (Breeze 2011). Moreover, the high frequency of these authoritative speech act verbs in LAC brings out an essential aspect of what academic enquiry means in the legal world. Unlike the epistemological underpinning of business management articles, which is fundamentally empirical, based on cycles of explore-test-show to advance in disciplinary knowledge, the underlying paradigm of legal academic enquiry could be described as a search for authority and coherence. Writers proceed by scrutinising accepted sources for relevant principles or interpretations, on the one hand, and discerning between different arguments to identify the one which is most coherent and most compatible with previous authority, on the other. Like the judges analysed by Mazzi (2007b), these writers orchestrate the different voices in such a way as to lead the audience towards the desired outcome. Although an academic writer *de facto* lacks the authority of the judge, his/her ethos is built up through the text through a similarly asymmetrical deployment of discursive resources. Polyphonic resources, particularly as encapsulated in the choice of speech act verb, are of crucial importance in assigning roles to the different sources cited, and in signalling how much accountability the writer wishes to assume for what is being said.

On a different note, the high frequency of these particular speech act verbs also points to one of the hallmark features of legal argumentation (present in academic writing, as well as in judgments or opinions), in which arguments are, so to speak, brought forward discursively, or staged, as though a practised barrister were delivering them to a packed courtroom. In this process, the type of "voice" used for each argument plays a special role in modulating the discourse, and in guiding the reader towards the desired conclusion. The conventional phraseological patterns within which each of these verbs occur are important in configuring these "voices" and setting the appropriate tone and pitch for each stage in the argument. Future research should consider further aspects of legal "voices", exploring how they are operationalised and deployed in different legal genres.

References

Bakhtin, M., 1981. *The Dialogic Imagination: Four Essays.* Austin/London: University of Texas Press.

Bednarek, M., 2006. Epistemological positioning and evidentiality in English news discourse: A text-driven approach. *Text & Talk*, 26(6): 635–660.

Biber, D., 2006. *University Language: A Corpus-based Study of Spoken and Written Registers.* Amsterdam: John Benjamins.

Breeze, R. 2010. They say, we do: Writers' strategic positioning in the discourses of political communication research. In R. Lorés and P. Mur (eds.), *Constructing Interpersonality: Multiple Perspectives and Applications to Written Academic Discourse.* Newcastle upon Tyne: Cambridge Scholar's Publishing,163–180.

Breeze, R., 2011. Disciplinary values in legal discourse: A corpus study. *Ibérica*, 21: 93–116.

Breeze, R., 2013. Lexical bundles across four legal genres. *International Journal of Corpus Linguistics*, 18(2): 229–253.

Breeze, R., 2014. Constructing authority in international investment arbitration. Insights from separate opinions at ICSID. In V.K. Bhatia, G. Garzone, R. Salvi, G. Tessuto, and C. Williams (eds.), *Language and Law in Professional Discourse: Issues and Perspectives.* Newcastle upon Tyne: Cambridge Scholars Publishing, 93–108.

Conte, A., 2002. Atto performativo: il concetto di performatività nella filosofia dell'atto giuridico. In G. Lorini (ed.), *Atto Giuridico.* Bari: Adriatica, 29–108.

Ducrot, O., 1986. *El decir y lo dicho. Polifonía de la enunciación.* Barcelona: Paidós.

Fløttum, K., Kinn, T., and Dahl, T., 2006. 'We now report on . . .' versus 'let us now see how . . .': Author roles and interaction with readers in research articles. In K. Hyland and M. Bondi (eds.), *Academic Discourse Across Disciplines*. Bern: Peter Lang, 203–224.

Goźdź-Roszkowski, S. and Pontrandolfo, G., 2015. Legal phraseology today: Corpus-based applications across legal languages and genres. *Fachsprache*, 3–4: 130–138.

Harwood, N., 2009. An interview-based study of the functions of citations in academic writing across two disciplines. *Journal of Pragmatics*, 41: 497–518.

Hunston, S., 2000. Evaluation and the planes of discourse: Status and value in persuasive texts. In S. Hunston and G. Thompson (eds.), *Evaluation in Text: Authorial Stance and the Construction of Discourse*. Oxford: Oxford University Press, 176–207.

Hyland, K., 2000. *Disciplinary Discourses: Social Interactions in Academic Writing*. London: Longman/Pearson.

Hyland, K., 2001. Bringing in the reader: Addressee features in academic writing. *Written Communication*, 18: 549–574.

Hyland, K., 2005. Stance and engagement: A model of interaction in academic discourse. *Discourse Studies*, 7(2): 173–191.

Kjaer, A.L., 2007. Phrasemes in legal texts. In H. Burger, D. Dobrovol'skij, P. Kühn, and N.R. Norrick (eds.), *Phraseology: An International Handbook of Contemporary Research*. Berlin: de Gruyter, 506–515.

Malmström, H., 2008. Knowledge-stating verbs and contexts of accountability in linguistic and literary academic discourse. *Nordic Journal of English Studies*, 7(3): 35–60.

Marín Pérez, M.J. and Rea Rizzo, C., 2012. Structure and design of the British Law Report Corpus (BLRC): A legal corpus of judicial decisions from the UK. *Journal of English Studies*, 10: 131–145.

Mazzi, D., 2007a. Reporting verbs: A tool for a polyphonic reading of judgments. In D. Heller and K. Ehlich (eds.), *Studien zur Rechtskommunikation*. Bern: Peter Lang, 183–206.

Mazzi, D., 2007b. The rhetoric of judicial texts: The interplay of reported argumentation and the judge's argumentative voice. In G. Garzone and S. Sarangi (eds.), *Discourse, Ideology and Specialized Communication*. Bern: Peter Lang, 379–399.

Ruusila, A. and Lindroos, E., 2016. Conditio sine qua non: On phraseology in legal language and its translation. *Language and Law*, 3(1): 120–140.

Searle, J., 1989. How performatives work. *Linguistics and Philosophy*, 12: 535–558.

Swales, J., Ahmad, U., Chang, Y., Chavez, D., Dressen, D., and Seymour, R., 1998. Consider this: The role of imperatives in scholarly writing. *Applied Linguistics*, 19(1): 97–121.

Thompson, G., 2001. Interaction in academic writing: Learning to argue with the reader. *Applied Linguistics*, 22(1): 58–78.

Trosborg, A., 1997. *Rhetorical Strategies in Legal Language*. Tübingen: Narr.

Yovel, J., 2014. Language and power in a place of contingencies: Law and the polyphony of self representation. *New York University Public Law and Legal Theory Working Papers*. Paper 456. <http://lsr.nellco.org/nyu_plltwp/456>

13 *Verba dicendi* in courtroom interaction

Patterns with the progressive

Magdalena Szczyrbak

Introduction

That law is constructed through the use of language cannot be disputed. Nor can it be denied that the two are virtually inseparable. On the one hand, written statutes and contracts would not exist were they not coded in language and mediated through language. On the other hand, lawyers' routine expressions and prefabricated formulae uttered during trials frame witnesses' testimony and thus affect judges' and juries' assessments. Clearly, the courtroom becomes a place where "talk about the talk," or "saying what is being said," constructs legal stories and so few would negate the importance of *verba dicendi* in reporting and perspectivising information. Naturally, since talking is central to the process of evidence construction, the choice of verbs of speaking is anything but random. Rather, it can be argued, their selection and patterning are pragmatically motivated. And yet, unlike more obvious lexical indicators of evaluative meaning (see, e.g., Heffer 2007), the role of grammar patterns in conveying attitude in court proceedings has not been sufficiently explored. To fill this gap, this study centres on recurrent patterns with the progressive form of four common verbs of speaking, namely: *say*, *talk*, *tell* and *speak*. Seeking to demonstrate their role in the discursive construction of evidence, it examines the speakers' mutual positioning strategies, including the ways in which they negotiate authority and claim epistemic priority.

Key theoretical concepts

Before selected patterns with the verbs are discussed, it is essential that the key theoretical concepts informing the analysis be clarified. It may be useful to define *verba dicendi* first. This term denotes verbs referring to speech events and speakers use them to talk about their own or other speakers' utterances. In the literature, *verba dicendi* appear under several labels – including *speech act verbs* (see, e.g., Wierzbicka 1987; Allan and Brown 2009), *saying verbs* (see, e.g., Hwang 2000), *reporting verbs* (see, e.g., Thompson and Ye 1991; Caldas-Coulthard 1994) and *communication verbs* (see, e.g., Biber et al. 1999)[1] – and they are described from various perspectives. From the semantic point of view, *verba dicendi* belong to the broader category of "verbs of cognition" and they involve an act of conveying information by the speaker, who mentally "possesses" it, to the addressee, who is transferred from the state of "not knowing" the information to the state of "possessing" it (Hirschová 2009: 1072). Taking a frequency-based perspective, Biber et al. (1999: 365) observe that speakers of English "commonly report what someone has said or written using verbs such as *ask*, *call*, *say*, *speak*, *talk*, *tell*, *write*." At the same time, they observe that *say* is the most common of all communication verbs, and of all verbs in general (Biber et al. 1999: 373). Here, it should be noted that even though communication verbs are a diverse class of verbs, "there is no single verb which would contain and convey all aspects of a speech act, and there are few verbs which are employed to describe only speech acts" (Kleszczowa 1989 quoted in Gawlik 2010: 52).

That said, equally relevant to the present investigation is the clarification regarding the notion of *phraseological units* or *phrasemes*. Departing from the well-trodden path of traditional phraseology concerned mainly with non-compositional items such as idioms or proverbs, this study applies a wider perspective and draws on more recent, frequency-based methodologies abandoning the notion of the fixedness of word combinations. The distributional approach, as this view is described, clearly favours lexicogrammar and it equates phraseological units with word combinations which do not necessarily correspond to predefined linguistic categories, but which are identified on the basis of their frequencies (Granger and Paquot 2008: 29). Also applicable to the patterns examined in this study is the notion of *collostructional analysis*, as proposed by Stefanowitsch and Gries (2003), which looks at dependences between particular words and specific constructions. Supporting the view that syntactic structures are signs, Stefanowitsch and Gries (2003: 236) aptly note that if they "served as meaningless templates waiting for the insertion of lexical material, no significant associations between these templates and specific verbs would be expected." With regard to the progressive aspect, Stefanowitsch and Gries (2003: 230) observe that communication verbs are reasonably frequent among the most strongly attracted collexemes of the progressive construction. At the same time, they note that these verbs are not found among the most strongly repelled verbs.

Moving on to the legal domain, a point which needs to be raised is that the term *legal phraseology* is differentiated from *phraseology in legal language*, with the latter concept extending its scope well beyond legal phrasemes with a specific judicial meaning (Ruusila and Lindroos 2016: 129) and thus forming part of the phraseological system as a whole (Ruusila and Lindroos 2016: 130). Since much of the focus of legal phraseology scholarship falls on formulaicity and terminology, one notable area, it can be argued, that such studies do not fully explore is the way in which grammar patterns index attitude in spoken legal genres, although elsewhere it has been recognised that "collocational and colligational patterning (lexical and grammatical choices respectively) are intertwined to build up a multi-word unit with a specific semantic preference [. . .] performing an attitudinal and pragmatic function in discourse" (Tognini-Bonelli 2002: 79). The present analysis can then be seen as one complementing studies focused on "fixed word patterns, routine expressions and prefabricated formulas that are reproduced in certain oral communicative situations" such as police interviews or court proceedings (Ruusila and Lindroos 2016: 121). It can also be situated alongside corpus-based investigations "that focus on the way legal patterns weave an intricate web of semantic meanings by resorting to a wider notion of phraseology" (Goźdź-Roszkowski and Pontrandolfo 2015: 134; see also Goźdź-Roszkowski and Pontrandolfo 2013; Pontrandolfo and Goźdź-Roszkowski 2014).

As mentioned earlier, recurrent grammar patterns can index the speaker's attitudes, assessments and judgments and, therefore, they can be rightly thought of as markers of *stance*. It should also be explained that unlike more "static" views on the expression of attitude (e.g. Biber et al. 1999: 966), the concept adopted here is that of *stancetaking*, understood as an intersubjective (collaborative) effort,[2] involving the mutual positioning of subjects and the evaluation of objects (du Bois 2007), which is realised through varied conversational practices (Englebretson 2007).[3] This ties in with the belief that in interaction, meanings are dynamically co-constructed by multiple participants, who simultaneously produce sound, gesture, lexicogrammar and recurrent structures of collaborative action (Ford 2004: 31). In line with this approach, recurrent grammar patterns with speech verbs can be regarded as signals of speakers' epistemological positioning, betraying their orientation vis-à-vis other speakers as well as their own and others' utterances. In this way, *verba dicendi* are also positioned as interactional evidentials with which speakers claim *epistemic priority* against other speakers and which, importantly, need to be interpreted in the sequential (interactional) frames in which they appear (Clift 2006: 586).

With this in mind, in what follows I argue that patterns with the progressive form of some verbs of speaking can reveal the speaker's stance in courtroom talk, which is marked by visible social and interactional power asymmetries.

Data and method

The study reported here is based on 32 transcripts (totalling 1,484,574 words, including metadata) from the *David Irving v. Penguin Books Ltd and Deborah Lipstadt* trial.[4] Since it was a bench trial, there was no jury and so the participants included the judge, the defendants' counsel, the claimant (who represented himself) and expert witnesses. Another thing to note is that the trial followed the adversarial procedure and as such contained competing narrative representations, with the participants aiming to "display evidence" (Holt and Johnson 2010: 22), rather than seeking to exchange information. It should also be acknowledged that since the data come from one trial, this piece of research is in fact a case study and so the findings may not accurately reflect trends or practices found in other proceedings. Yet, since examinations of other trials (e.g. Taylor 2009; Partington et al. 2013) corroborate some of the results obtained in this study, this seems to suggest that the deployment of progressives is not uncommon, but rather that similar interactional mechanisms underpin other legal-lay encounters, too.

To be precise, trying to reconcile interactional linguistics with a corpus-assisted discourse studies (CADS) approach, the analysis examines the use of four common verbs of speaking, i.e. *say*, *talk*, *tell* and *speak*, believed to be most representative of the category of *verba dicendi* (cf. Biber et al. 1999; Gawlik 2010). In order to identify recurrent patterns with these verbs, I used the Concord function of *WordSmith Tools* 6.0 (Scott 2012). First, I queried the corpus to check the frequencies of the *–ing* forms of the verbs selected for analysis. Since not all the occurrences of *saying*, *talking*, *telling* and *speaking* were progressives, all instances which did not meet the adopted criterion were removed manually. Next, the most frequent collocates within a 2L, 2R span of the progressives *saying*, *talking*, *telling* and *speaking* were examined. These results were then used as a starting point for a more detailed analysis of the various configurations including three- and four-word clusters. The final stage of the analysis involved a qualitative examination of selected patterns as well as of longer chunks of the co-text in which they appeared (i.e. preceding and subsequent turns at talk). At this point, it needs to be explained that a bottom-up approach was adopted, since it was believed that in this way a range of patterns with selected progressives would be generated, some of which would be more salient than others. This is in line with the view that, given the "serendipitous nature of CADS research" and the fact that "unforeseen subquestions can arise" during the process of data investigation, "induction and hypothesis testing combine and interact," which may require that the original dataset be re-configured and re-examined (Partington 2009: 282).

Finally, it should also be stressed that since the analysis focuses only on recurrent grammar patterns, it excludes paralinguistic elements which, it is admitted, can be equally revealing in interpreting (inter)subjective meanings in spoken interaction.

Verba dicendi in courtroom interaction

Verba dicendi are particularly potent interactional tools in asymmetrical legal-lay encounters and their evaluative potential has been discussed in several studies. For instance, Johnson (2002) and Holt and Johnson (2010) demonstrate what is accomplished in court trials and police interviews through the use of *so-* and *and-*prefaced questions, some of which contain verbs of speaking such as *say* and *tell*. In police interviews with children, as they observe, *so*-prefacing has an empowering effect, as it aids children's narratives, whereas in the questioning of adults, the same strategy serves to label and evaluate the interviewees' responses (Holt and Johnson 2010: 25–26). Elsewhere, Johnson (2014) discusses various uses of *say* in legal questioning, focusing on the role of *say* in reporting and quoting witnesses' words, that is on the processes of "making evidence" and authority construction. Drawing on the notion of "collocational frameworks" (Renouf and Sinclair 1991: 128),[5] she looks at patterns with *say* such as: *what XX saying*, *you say* + quotation, *you say this*: + quotation, *you say* + direct quotation + probing question and *what X said was*, observing that professional questioners have "institutionally-derived conversational dominance" as well as "power derived from formal and informal naming of the interviewee in the course of questioning" (Johnson 2014: 531). Along the same lines, the role of patterns with *when you say* in paraphrases and reformulations found in trial and police interview data is addressed in Szczyrbak (in preparation), where three schemata emerge: *when-you-say-A,-(do)-you-mean-B?*, *are-you-saying-A,-when-you-say-B?* and *when-you-say-A,-are-you-saying-B-or-C?* These structures, it is argued, underlie disagreement-seeking questions which aim to challenge the respondent's credibility. Partington et al. (2013: 252–254), similarly, focus on the *you are + ing* phraseologies marking shifts from transactional to interactional modes in hostile examination. Taylor (2009: 218), on the other hand, analyses the strategies of attribution deployed by the questioner, which, as she validly observes, limit "both the quantity and quality of the response turn." At the same time, she notes that *tell us* is more frequent in friendly examination, while *told us*, used to threaten negative face, is preferred in hostile examination (Taylor 2009: 219), where an increased frequency of progressive forms is also observed (Taylor 2009: 220).[6]

Building on the above research, this study casts light on the pragmatics of the progressive forms of *say*, *talk*, *tell* and *speak* in courtroom interaction and focuses on selected patterns which emerged during the analysis. As predicted, in the dataset analysed, *saying* proved to be the most frequent of all the progressives and it was represented by 755 tokens.[7] With 652 instances, *talking* turned out to be the second most preferred form, while *telling* and *speaking* were decidedly less common, with 95 and 72 occurrences, respectively. It was observed that while *speaking* and *talking* referred to the speaking activity itself, *saying* and *telling* tended to focus on the message instead (cf. Dirven et al. 1982; Gawlik 2010). Equally relevant, *I*-orientedness vs *you*-orientedness, that is the confrontational dimension involving the shifting of standpoints, was perceptible as well, especially in the case of the verbs *say* and *tell*. Finally, it was also evident that the progressives introduced "a shift to focus on the present time and place" as well as involved "a repositioning of the beneficiary," with the participants interacting personally instead of following conventions typical

Table 13.1 Collocates of the progressive *saying* in the corpus

L2	*L1*	*NODE*	*R1*	*R2*
you 165	**are 164**		**that 166**	**is 66**
I 132	is 139		is 50	the 47
he 93	am 131	**SAYING** (755)	it 37	that 42
am 89	not 86		you 30	a 37
are 70	you 52		this 27	you 30

of discourse enacted for a non-participatory audience (Partington et al. 2013: 252). These patterns will be examined in the ensuing sections of this chapter.

Patterns with "saying"

As already noted, the corpus query yielded as many as 755 occurrences of the progressive *saying*, which proved to be the most productive of the four analysed verbs. Rather predictably, *that* turned out to be its most frequent R1 collocate, *you* was the most common L2 collocate, while *are* was the most frequent L1 collocate and *is* the most frequent R2 collocate (Table 13.1). The most noticeable three- and four-word clusters containing the progressive *saying* are discussed below.

You are saying (that)

With as many as 137 occurrences, *you are saying* was the most frequent of all the analysed patterns and it subsumed 32 tokens of *you are saying that*. The most immediate observation was that these patterns were found in confrontational contexts and that their use created a sense of tension between the speakers, as is plain in (1) and (2), where the declarative form *you are saying* is used in leading questions. In the first excerpt, *and*-prefaced *you are saying* serves to challenge the relevance of the claimant's statement regarding the pits in Riga (whose relevance is questioned during the ongoing interaction). In the second interaction, *so*-prefaced *you are saying that* is found in the judge's clarification-seeking question about the purpose of the "special room." In both instances, the claimant relies on hedging and distancing devices (*this is, well, as you can tell . . . this is probably; I do not want to try and establish a complete link . . . I was only asked to support my "bizarre hypothesis". . .*) to avoid giving a straightforward answer. Importantly, it may be speculated that a great share of the attitudinal meaning in (1) and (2) is carried by the speakers' tone of voice and intonation. This, however, may not be verified, given the absence of prosodic marking.

(1) *[Claimant]* My Lord, that is a very hazardous operation if you are standing at the bottom of the pit and you dig it without any kind of shoring. I would now draw your Lordship's attention to one such pit which is photographed in the little bundle I gave you. It is the last item in the bundle. It provides a useful check point for the depth that these pits go when they are only three metres wide.

[Expert witness 2] *And **you are saying**, are you, Mr Irving, that this is one of the pits in Riga? This is an authenticated photograph of one of them?*[8]

[Claimant] *This is, well, as you can tell by the British soldier standing around with machine guns, this is probably Bergen-Belsen or Buchenwald,* where the victims of Nazi atrocities are being buried by some of the perpetrators.

[Expert witness 2] *And what does that tell us about the pits in Riga, Mr Irving?*

[Day 22, P-36]

(2) [Claimant] *That is precisely what my contention is,* what this room was being used as. They had installed this room Liechenkeller 1, as a disinfestation room, as a sonderkeller for treating the infested bodies which were delivered to the crematorium during the appalling plague which hit Auschwitz in 1942 and 1943.

[Judge] *So* ***you are saying that*** *this invoice, or whatever it is, can be tied in to the chamber from which the zinc covers came?*

[Claimant] *I do not want to try and establish a complete link* in that linkage in that manner, my Lord. *I was only asked to support my "bizarre hypothesis", as Mr Rampton calls it,* that an alternative use of this room was not just a mortuary but also as a disinfestation chamber.

[Day 8, P-106–107]

Are you saying (that)

Though far less common than *you are saying*, *are you saying* (50 tokens, including 28 tokens of *are you saying that*), similarly, served to challenge the respondent's views. In (3), for instance, the counsel tries to undermine the claimant's truthfulness by demanding that he should admit to not having read the passage in Fleming's book. The claimant resists the implied claim by producing a circuitous answer, before eventually admitting to not having read the passage. In (4), in turn, the claimant re-focuses the object of contention and defiantly asks the question about the authorities cited in his book, expecting that the counsel will confirm the claim embedded in the question. The claim is, however, resisted. Here, too, it should be expected that, like in (1) and (2), the evaluative meaning of the questions derives not only from the interactional frame in which they appear, but also from the speakers' modality coded in the prosodic features, which, however, are not accessible in the written data.

(3) [Counsel] *Do you remember that I put it to you in cross-examination that, contrary to what you said in court, you were indeed familiar with* the Muller order of 1st August?

[Claimant] *You put to me, yes.*

[Counsel] ***Are you saying*** *you did not read* this passage in Fleming's book?

[Claimant] *I have to say that you are asking me about something 18 years later but I can say with great confidence that, as there are no kind of markings on those pages, then, with the high degree of probability, I did not read them.*

[Day 29, P-85]

(4) [Counsel] *No, no, Mr Irving. You mistake me completely. I am not trying to prove* a case about the number of deaths at Dresden one way or another. *This is a mistake you habitually make. You make the same mistake* in relation to

Auschwitz and elsewhere. No, Mr Irving. *I am wondering why it is that an honest, upright, careful, meticulous, open minded historian does not mention two alternative sources, the one of which claims to be a direct witness of what happened.*

[Claimant] ***Are you saying that*** *nowhere in my Dresden book do I state that there are authorities which hold that lower figures are more accurate? Is that what are you are suggesting?*

[Counsel] *No, I am not.*

[Claimant] *And that this person is not included among those authorities?*

[Counsel] *I am very puzzled why an open minded historian desiring to give a balanced account of what the figures might be would not include this man who, on the face of it, appears to be a very powerful witness for the opposition.*

[Day 13, P-135]

What you are saying

In addition to the patterns presented above, various configurations of *what you are saying* (57 tokens) were also prominent and they were linked, again, to leading questions which suggested the preferred answer, as in *Is this/that what you are saying? What you are saying . . . is.*[9] This phenomenon is neatly exemplified by the excerpts shown in (5) and (7), in which the implied claim is resisted: (*That is not quite what I am saying*; *No, I am not going to say yes or no . . .* ; *I am not saying that at all. I am saying it is . . .*).

(5) *[Claimant]* ***What you are saying****, this is your expert evidence, is that "Judentransport" could under no circumstances be translated as "transportation of Jews from Berlin"?*

[Expert witness 2] *That is not quite what I am saying.*

[Claimant] *Will you accept that it can?*

[Expert witness 2] Just let me answer.

[Claimant] *Just say yes or no. Will you accept that it can?*

[Expert witness 2] *No, I am not going to say yes or no, I am going to give you a full answer.*

[Day 22, P-58]

I am (not) saying

Moving on to the patterns with the first person singular, *I am saying* (122 tokens) and *I am not saying* (56 tokens), too, proved to be useful for the mutual positioning of the speakers and the negotiation of their respective viewpoints (as already indicated above). For instance, in (6), by repeating *I am not saying*, the claimant tries to dissociate his viewpoint from the one being attributed to him by the judge. A similar pattern is visible in (7), where the witness resists the interpretation suggested by the claimant.[10] *I am saying*, in turn, allows the speaker to signal insistence and argument continuity, as illustrated by the following examples, where this pattern appears in the *I-am-not-saying-A,-I-am-saying-B* schema.

(6) *[Judge]* There are two points. One is that it is not authentic because it is not stamped "Geheim" and the other is that it is janitorial.

[Claimant] ***I am not saying*** *– no, my Lord.* ***I am not saying*** *it is not authentic, my Lord.* ***I am saying*** *the fact that* it is given no security classification, even by an SS officer, *indicates that it is as harmless as it appears to be.*

[Day 8, P-138]

(7) [Claimant] *You would like to see it censored, would you? You would like to have automatic filters installed? Is that* ***what you are saying****?*

[Expert witness 2] ***I am not saying*** *that at all.* ***I am saying*** *it is your responsibility for what you do.*

[Day 20, P-141]

What I am saying

Similarly, *what I am saying* (50 tokens) marked emphasis and insistence, as shown in (8). It is also interesting to note that while *not* was found among the most frequent collocates of *I*-oriented patterns (suggesting some form of resistance), it was not found in the environment of *you*-oriented patterns.

(8) [Claimant] *Excuse me, I did not say* "reluctantly got to".

[Counsel] *– you do not accept that is the sense of it?*

[Claimant] *Not at all.* ***What I am saying*** *quite clearly here is that* that let us get one thing quite plain, *we have to accept* there were these mass murders on the Eastern Front.

[Day 4, P-112]

He is saying

As became evident, it was not only the *I* vs *you* opposition that played a role in the analysed patterns, since *he is saying* proved to be relatively frequent, too (78 tokens). The referents of *he*, as transpired, included either the co-present participants (witnesses), as in (9), or non-present speakers whose statements or beliefs were being referred to (and thus supported) during the ongoing interaction, as illustrated by (10). Relevant in this context are the switches between the simple and progressive forms, as illustrated, for instance, by *he talks* vs *he is (basically) saying*, shown in (9) or *it says/it does not say* vs *it is saying*, shown in (10). More precisely, in (9), the expert witness interprets the meaning of the document in question and shifts to interactional mode using the words: *he is basically saying*; *he is saying, yes, we* . . . ; or *he is saying, well, actually* . . . In (10), similarly, the same witness utters the words: *it is saying, you know*, . . . to introduce his metalinguistic comment, rather than stress duration or temporality (cf. Mair 2012: 806).

(9) [Expert witness 4] As far as I can see from the document, *he is basically saying* two things. ***He is saying****, yes, we carried out the Holocaust*, the Final Solution, we killed, we tried and we were able to, we killed millions of Jews. *He talks about* Millionen Morden on page 5, and on the other hand ***he is saying****, well, actually Himmler did it on his own initiative* because he thought that he could fulfil Hitler's ideas. So I do not know, I mean I do not know how you put your case, you know, how you want to deal with the document. ***Are you saying*** *this is a kind of confirmation that* millions of Jews were actually

killed in extermination camps? I mean what is the way you want to deal with the document? *Are you only relying on parts of it* and you would then refuse other parts of the documents?

[Day 25, P-208–209]

(10) *[Expert witness 4]* Well, I cannot, you know, I cannot read so fast but under "Clothing" it is stated here: "I decide that during the winter, as far as far as available, prisoners should wear coats, pullover, socks", so that should give you an idea about the standards which actually existed in the concentration camps before this letter arrived, *and it says, it says* "as far as available", *so it does not actually say*, "Give the men, you know, proper clothing". ***It is saying***, *you know*, "You can give them socks if they are available and nothing more". So I think this gives you a kind of an idea of this.

[Day 25, P-23]

At this point, it needs to be explained that the progressives used in all of the above instances represent the so-called "interpretive" or "explanatory" progressive (Huddleston and Pullum 2002: 165). This kind of progressive, also described as "experiential," focuses on the speaker's consciousness, rather than duration or temporality, and involves his or her "interpretation or evaluation of some state of affairs" (Wright 1995: 156). In other words, it "interprets the speaker's attitude and perspective of the situation" and conveys his or her "epistemic stance at a particular moment in the context of utterance" (Wright 1995: 157). In the dataset analysed, subjective uses of the progressive were noted not only in patterns with *saying* (such as, e.g., *you are saying (that)*, *what you are saying*, *I am saying*, *it is saying*, *he is saying*), but also in patterns with *talking* (such as *he is talking*), as shown in (16), and *telling* (such as *he is telling the truth*), as illustrated by (18).

Patterns with "talking"

The progressive *talking* proved to be the second most frequent among the analysed verbs (652 tokens). Unlike the patterns with *saying*, however, in the case of which the *I* vs *you* opposition was quite clear, *talking* tended to co-occur with *we*. To be more specific, *we* was its most frequent L2 collocate, *are* its most frequent L1 collocate, while *about* turned out to be its most frequent R1 collocate and *the* proved to be the most frequent R2 collocate (Table 13.2). The two most noticeable patterns, i.e. *we are talking (about)* and *you are talking (about)*, are discussed below.

Table 13.2 Collocates of the progressive *talking* in the corpus

L2	*L1*	*NODE*	*R1*	*R2*
we 169	**are 238**		**about 473**	**the 123**
are 85	is 102	**TALKING (652)**	here 25	about 32
he 75	a 57		to 17	a 25
you 70	not 35		of 9	what 12
I 64	we 27		in 9	this 12

We are talking (about)

It was noted that *we are talking* appeared 147 times, while *we are talking about* had 110 occurrences. In the case of the latter pattern, two practices were identified. Firstly, *we are talking about* was used in declarative questions seeking confirmation or disambiguation, as in (11). Secondly, the pattern was found in assertions, with which, it can be speculated, the speaker tried to stress obviousness and convey authority, as in (12), as well as appeal to shared knowledge in order to provide a broader background for his claim, as in (13). In these instances, by using the inclusive *we*, the speaker draws the whole audience into the discourse, suggesting a common epistemological perspective. Another element to note is the use of the historic present (*There are large numbers of Jews . . . are being gassed*), which introduces "the dramatic immediacy of an eye-witness account" (Quirk et al. 1985: 181).

(11) *[Judge]* ***We are talking about*** *1944?*

[Day 10, P-123]

[Expert witness 1] ***We are talking about*** *Stark now, the Stark testimony?*

[Day 10, P-92]

(12) *[Expert witness 1]* – must be kept steady with constant ventilation, especially in the summer.

[Claimant] *We are not concerned with summer here.* ***We are talking about*** *Poland, which gets notoriously cold in the winter.*

[Expert witness 1] The point which is here is that the next sentence says there should be at a certain moment in this case some heating and cooling installation in this building, yes.

[Claimant] Yes.

[Expert witness 1] I will leave it to you. You will spring another trap on me right now and then I will try to answer it.

[Claimant] *No. This is not a trap. We are trying to educate the court. I have to admit that I have learned a lot* out of Neufert as I went along as well.

[Day 10, P-169–170]

(13) *[Claimant]* I was going to ask the witness, *Professor Evans, what interpretation would you place on that, that* "The Fuhrer has given me the job, placed on my shoulders a job of rendering the occupied Eastern territories free of the Jews"?

[Expert witness 2] *Yes, well,* ***we are talking about*** *July 1942, as I have said*, when the death camps were already in full swing. *There are large numbers of Jews* from the occupied territories *are being gassed* in Belzec, Sobibor and Auschwitz, Treblinka, and so on. *So I think, given that context, it clearly means that* the Fuhrer has told Himmler to kill the Jews in the occupied Eastern territories.

[Claimant] *That is how you would read between the lines of that document?*

[Expert witness 2] *It does not require too much reading between the lines.*

[Day 22, P-190]

You are talking (about)

As regards *you are talking*, this pattern had 57 occurrences, out of which *you are talking about* was identified 43 times. Similarly to *we are talking about*, *you are talking about* was found in declarative questions seeking confirmation or disambiguation, as in (14). Unlike patterns with *saying*, patterns with *talking* were not manifestly evaluative. However, they were useful for shifting perspectives, as is the case in (15), where *we are talking about* is contrasted with *you are talking about*. Clearly, the claimant's switch from *we* to *you* is a distancing mechanism, whose effect is additionally strengthened by the use of *well*. On the other hand, the counsel's response (*Yes, surely, but . . .*) articulates defiance and resistance.[11]

(14) *[Judge]* ***You are talking about*** *photograph 3 on 3B?*

[Day 11, P-32]

[Claimant] *Any of your suspects, like Remer or Kussel or any of these names* ***you are talking about****? Are they in that photograph or the next one?*

[Day 28, P-19]

(15) *[Claimant]* I am not sure what that question means, but if I say that one of his staff, Walter Havel, whose diary I had, said that if you want to understand Hitler's attitude to humanity was the way that a man might look on an ant heap, and that is how he regarded the Eastern peoples whether they were Jewish or not, *but he very definitely intervened to stop the killing of German Jews at the time that I specified. So there was clearly a distinction in his own mind at that time.*

[Counsel] ***We are talking about*** *two events a year apart.*

[Claimant] *Well,* ***you are talking*** *about two events a year apart. Also* ***you are talking about*** *the giving of the order and the receiving of melding.*

[Counsel] *Yes, surely, but that is in a completely different context, Mr Irving, as you very well know. You use what you say* as Hitler's opposition to the Riga killings as having some kind of relevance to this document. *Tell me what the relevance is.*

[Day 2, P-276–277]

He is talking (about)

Finally, the pattern *he is talking* (65 tokens) also deserves a brief discussion. In the dataset analysed, by analogy to *he is saying*, *he is talking (about)* served explanatory purposes, and revealed the speaker's assessment of the situation, as illustrated by (16). Here, again, the progressive should not be analysed in terms of truth-conditional meaning (by contrast to the factual *he says*), but rather as the witness's own interpretation of Dr Frank's speech (additionally signalled by *I think*).

(16) *[Claimant]* *You say that is exaggerated, but, of course, Dr Frank* in his famous December 16th 1941 speech *talks of* 3.5 million Jews?

[Expert witness 4] *No, he says* at 2.5 and they are [German] – the families, their relatives, or everybody, ***he is talking about****, I think* ***he is talking***

about the so-called mixed Mischlinger or mixed Jews. He gives two figures. *I think* one is 2.5 *and then he says*, "Well, and their dependents and people that are related to them" and then he comes to 3.5. The figure 3.5 is too high.

[Day 25, P-190]

Patterns with "telling"

Unlike the patterns with *saying* and *talking* described above, phraseologies with the progressive *telling* (95 tokens) were decidedly less frequent. As Table 13.3 demonstrates, the most frequent collocates of *telling* included *you* (L2 collocate), *are* (L1 collocate), *the* (R1 collocate) and *that* (R2 collocate). Also, three patterns emerged, namely: *you are telling*, *telling the truth* and *I am telling you.*

You are telling (us/me)

The pattern *you are telling* occurred 14 times and, similarly to *(is this/that what) you are saying*, it was used in leading questions restricting the respondent's answer, as in (17). It needs to be observed that, unlike the patterns with *saying*, *you are telling* always indicated the audience, that is *us*, *me* or *this audience.* This enabled the speaker to side with the court and to create the *us/you* divide, as seen in (17), where the counsel positions himself in opposition to the claimant and his words.

(17) *[Counsel]* Then the fourth line is "Keine Liquidierung", so this could mean that none of those three groups, categories, is to be liquidated. *Is that what* ***you are telling*** *us?*

[Claimant] *I do not think I said that. I am saying that* all four lines can be taken separately because the first three lines are quite clearly separate topics from each other.

[Day 3, P-122]

Telling the truth

As for *telling the truth*, in all the 14 instances found, *telling* was used in the progressive construction. In the excerpt shown in (18), the counsel says *he is always telling the truth* to indicate his evaluation of the claimant's words, rather than to stress duration or temporality.

Table 13.3 Collocates of the progressive *telling* in the corpus

L2	*L1*	*NODE*	*R1*	*R2*
you 22	**are 20**		**the 29**	**that 16**
he 11	is 18		me 17	truth 13
I 10	was 10	**TELLING (95)**	us 15	what 5
one 10	am 10		you 12	about 5
is 4	you 5		what 2	reader 3

Again, the interpretive progressive of *tell* is contrasted with the purely descriptive *he says* (cf. patterns with *saying* and *talking*).

(18) *[Claimant]* Goebbels, remember, is an arch liar. He is a minister of propaganda. The diaries show this again and again – an extremely dangerous weapon to use.

[Counsel] *He is always* ***telling the truth*** *when he says something which in your mind is favourable to him, but whenever he says anything which is unfavourable to Hitler, he in your mind is a liar* and, therefore, you feel justified in obliterating that from the text of your books, do you not?

[Day 5, P-33]

I am telling you

Finally, although rather infrequent, *I am telling you* (8 tokens) was used to convey an air of authority and as such it demonstrated the speaker's claim to epistemic priority, as shown in (19). Here, the witness stresses his conviction and authority as well as undermines the claimant's credibility (*and I am telling you that you have no right to say that*; *You do not read. . . . You have no idea.*). Noteworthy in this context is not only the use of the verbs *say* and *tell*, but also the use of turn-initial *well.*

(19) [Expert witness 2] *Well, how can you say that if you do not read other historians' work, Mr Irving?*

[Claimant] *Well, I am asking you as the expert on historiography.*

[Expert witness 2] *And you are just telling me, and* ***I am telling you*** *that you have no right to say that. You do not read* what other historians have written on the subject. *You have no idea.*

[Day 21, P-99]

Patterns with "speaking"

Turning now to the last of the analysed verbs, i.e. *speak*, it was noted that the words co-selected with *speaking* (72 tokens) proved to be even less frequent than those including the progressive *telling*. The most frequent collocates of *speaking* included *I* (L2 collocate), *am* (L1 collocate), *to* (R1 collocate) and the indefinite article *a* (R2 collocate), as shown in Table 13.4.

Table 13.4 Collocates of the progressive *speaking* in the corpus

L2	*L1*	*NODE*	*R1*	*R2*
I 19	**am 14**		**to 16**	**a 13**
you 12	is 12		from 6	the 7
he 7	was 11	**SPEAKING (72)**	at 5	on 4
was 6	are 11		out 4	this 3
who 3	not 7		in 4	and 3

As it emerged, in the case of the progressive *speaking*, none of the patterns seemed to be linked to stancetaking. By contrast to the argumentatively-oriented *are you saying* and the clarification-seeking *are you talking about*, the pattern *are you speaking* was not identified in the data at all. On the other hand, *you are speaking* was attested seven times. This pattern, as illustrated by (20), was used with reference to the very activity of speaking and not to the witness's words.

(20) *[Claimant]* So when you talk about millions, it is not a deliberate manipulation or a perverse distortion of figures. It is just a loose approximation because ***you are speaking*** *without a script?*

[Expert witness 1] No. First of all, ***I am speaking*** *without a script.* I mean, you know exactly how Errol Morris interviews people because you were interviewed in the same way and also appear in the same movie.

[Day 9, P-49]

By analogy, *I am speaking*, which was a bit more frequent (13 tokens), referred to the utterance itself. For instance, it was found in patterns such as: *I am speaking without a script/from a prepared script/from memory/at various meetings/here on oath* and it did not seem to show any evaluative leanings.

Conclusions

As represented by the data discussed in this study, in courtroom talk speakers rely on phraseologies with verbs of speaking to convey evaluative meanings and to negotiate the validity of their respective standpoints. Thus, the findings seem to indicate that such patterns play an important role in the discursive construction of evidence during courtroom examinations and, further, that they contribute to the role projection that trial participants can attain. Moving on to the specifics, in terms of frequency, it was found that combinations with *saying* unquestionably took centre stage. It was also observed that patterns with *talking* were relatively frequent, whereas patterns with *telling* and *speaking* were decidedly less common. As regards the pragmatics of the analysed progressives, their stancetaking potential was realised thanks to their interaction with other discourse elements. For instance, patterns with *saying* displayed a negative discourse prosody resulting from the cumulative interplay of the co-occurring lexical items as well as the wider interactional context. These patterns (e.g. *you are saying (that)*, *are you saying (that)*, *what you are saying*) were found predominantly in contexts where the opposing party's views were being questioned or challenged. In addition, *(what) I am saying* was deployed to bolster the speaker's stance, while *I am not saying* signalled resistance and was used to deflect actual or anticipated criticism. The my-account-against-yours schema, on the other hand, was visible in patterns with *telling* which signalled an asymmetrical relation between the interactants (as in, e.g., *you are telling (me/us)*, *I am telling you*) and which, it may be argued, allowed them to be "consciously aggressive in an acceptable way" (Locher 2004: 90). In the case of *talking*, conversely, the relation between the speakers was symmetrical and so *we are talking* resurfaced as the most visible pattern, used to draw all participants into the discourse and to signal a collaborative effort. Further still, unlike patterns with *saying* and *telling*, patterns with *talking* and *speaking* seemed to focus on the speaking activity itself, rather than betrayed the speaker's attitude. It is also worthy of note that the pronoun *we*, suggesting a shared epistemological perspective, was not found among the most strongly attracted collocates of the progressive forms of *say*, *tell* and *speak*, in the case of which the relation between the speakers was always asymmetrical.

In light of the foregoing, it may be convincingly argued that some phraseologies with the present progressive of *verba dicendi* are an important stancetaking resource, whose evaluative potential in courtroom talk should not be ignored. Not only do they introduce the here-and-now perspective and focus on "saying what is being said," but they also convey the speaker's stance and mark intersubjectivity, which becomes apparent after the contributions of the co-present speakers are considered. It, too, needs to be reiterated that, as the data bear out, not all the *I*- and *you*-oriented progressives signal the same degree of subjectivity. To be precise, while the analysis showed that patterns with *saying* clearly betrayed the speaker's stance, the attitudinal uses of patterns with *talking* and *telling* were less frequent (although they were palpable as well). In the case of the progressive *speaking*, in turn, no evaluative meanings were evident at all. It may then be argued that patterns with the progressive *saying*, which were most visible in the data, not only belong to spoken grammar and the phraseological system as a whole, but also form part of *courtroom idiom*, that is the "preferred ways of saying things" in courtroom interaction, where *say* seems to be found chiefly in negative contexts. It should also be added that although they do not have any specific judicial meaning, patterns with the progressive *saying* can be viewed as phraseological units typical of courtroom discourse – that is *phraseology in legal discourse* rather than *legal phraseology* – given that they appear to be routine expressions which are reproduced in the courtroom setting. What follows, the current study shows, is that not only fixed word combinations, but also specific grammar constructions "can and do play a role in the phraseological universe" (Goźdź-Roszkowski and Pontrandolfo 2013: 20), even more so when the less overt expression of positive and negative assessments is concerned. These, in turn, can be identified based on the distribution of lexical and grammatical resources as well as their co-occurrence patterns, that is if a broad understanding of evaluative phraseology is adopted. Last but not least, since the deployment of interactional patterns, such as the ones discussed above, is correlated with the distribution of institutional and interactional power, it may, as is believed, affect the outcome of a trial. Therefore, analysing the way in which courtroom interactants "construct truth and lies" (Johnson 2014: 645) or, put differently, fix "states of knowledge against legal and moral discourses" (Johnson 2014: 525), may provide more insight into the processes of making evidence and the power dynamics of courtroom discourse.

That being said, several methodological considerations deserve attention as well. Firstly, intersubjective positioning strategies resist automatic detection and, like the evaluation which they subsume, they are dispersed and "parasitic" (Thompson 1997: 65) on various structures. As such, they may be easily overlooked in analyses targeting more obvious lexical indicators of evaluative meaning. Secondly, as is often the case, many discourse phenomena interact with one another and that is why a broader context is needed for the pragmatic meanings of grammatical structures to be recovered in the context of the co-occurring lexical items and interactional patterns. Thirdly, in any investigation of spoken discourse, in which subjective meanings are co-constructed interactionally over larger stretches of talk, plausible interpretations can be achieved only through "reaching back" and "looking forward," i.e. after a detailed analysis of prior and subsequent turns at talk, and not just the immediate collocational co-occurrences of the target items. Further still, while some attitudinal phenomena can indeed be identified in corpus-assisted analyses, some things, admittedly, will not be achieved. If, trying to account for spoken phenomena, the analyst looks only at the material which represents "once-was-discourse" (Partington et al. 2013: 2), in which intonation contours and hesitation phenomena are no longer present, then inferences about the speakers' intentions can never be perfect.[12] Nonetheless, it may be concluded that – despite the fact that stance and evaluation emerge in myriad intangible ways and despite the limitations that less-than-perfect corpus-assisted analyses of spoken data inevitably involve – counting "the countable" can shed more light on how meanings emerge in interaction, provided that this is always complemented by a detailed investigation of the co-text and a careful consideration of the non-linguistic context.

Notes

1 Although not completely synonymous, these terms are used interchangeably in this study.
2 It should also be added that *intersubjective meaning* is understood as the speaker's attribution of "particular attitudes, knowledge, and stance to an addressee or interlocutor" (Fitzmaurice 2004: 429).
3 In the literature, different conceptualisations of *stance* and *evaluation* can be found. For instance, du Bois (2007) sees *evaluation* as part of *stancetaking*, whereas Hunston (2011: 51) distinguishes between *evaluation* and *stance*, which are both covered by the term "evaluative language."
4 The transcripts were downloaded from: www.hdot.org/en/trial/transcripts/index.html (date of access: 31 January 2013).
5 In Renouf and Sinclair's (1991: 128) words, a collocational framework is "a discontinuous sequence of two words, positioned at one word remove from each other."
6 In Taylor's (2009: 220) data, *saying*, *talking*, *suggesting*, *speaking* and *trying* were the most frequent progressive forms in hostile examination.
7 For the sake of clarity, it should be reiterated that the figures refer only to these occurrences of *saying*, *talking*, *telling* and *speaking* in which these forms were progressives.
8 Here and in the following examples the bolding and the italics have been added.
9 It might also be added that the grammatical question *what are you saying?* had only seven occurrences, but even in these instances the questions suggested the preferred response, as illustrated by the counsel's words: *What are you saying if you are not saying that?* or the judge's clarification-seeking question: *What are you saying that the reason was?* Interestingly, three instances of *what are you saying* were used incorrectly in declarative sentences, as, e.g., in: **Is that what are you saying?* or **So what are you saying is that this view* . . . The above seems to suggest that in courtroom talk, the verb *say* is rarely used (if at all) in open questions inviting the respondent's free narrative and that it tends to appear in questions that restrict the response as well as betray the questioner's stance.
10 Cf. Craig and Sanusi's (2000: 434) observation that *I'm not saying* is used to deflect actual or anticipated criticism.
11 As observed by Downing (2009: 85), *surely* involves antagonism and it "is essentially the confidence marker of a speaker who challenges, contradicts or tries to persuade a prior speaker."
12 A similar view is expressed, for instance, by Miller and Johnson (2009: 40), who – drawing on Slembrouk (1992) – observe that "any transcription that fails to account for the prosodic features that only an audio-video recording of the speech event can provide is necessarily an imperfect representation of the modality that speaker intonation construes. It also fails to provide extralinguistic multimodal information."

References

Allan, K. and Brown, E.K., 2009. *Concise Encyclopedia of Semantics.* Boston: Elsevier.

Biber, D., Johansson, S., Leech, G., Conrad, S., and Finegan, E., 1999. *The Longman Grammar of Spoken and Written English.* London: Longman.

Caldas-Coulthard, C.R., 1994. On reporting reporting: The representation of speech in factual and factional narratives. In M. Coulthard (ed.), *Advances in Written Text Analysis.* London: Routledge, 295–308.

Clift, R., 2006. Indexing stance: Reported speech as an interactional evidential. *Journal of Sociolinguistics*, 10(5): 569–595.

Craig, R.T. and Sanusi, A.L., 2000. *I'm just saying . . .* Discourse markers of standpoint continuity. *Argumentation*, 14: 425–445.

Dirven, R., Goossens, L., Putseys, Y., and Vorlat, E., 1982. *The Scene of Linguistic Action and Its Perspectivisation by Speak, Talk, Say and Tell*. Amsterdam/Philadelphia: John Benjamins.

Downing, A., 2009. *Surely* as a marker of dominance and entitlement in the crime fiction of P.D. James. *Brno Studies in English*, 35(2): 79–92.

du Bois, J.W., 2007. The stance triangle. In R. Englebretson (ed.), *Stancetaking in Discourse: Subjectivity, Evaluation, Interaction*. Amsterdam/Philadelphia: John Benjamins, 139–182.

Englebretson, R. (ed.), 2007. *Stancetaking in Discourse: Subjectivity, Evaluation, Interaction*. Amsterdam/Philadelphia: John Benjamins.

Fitzmaurice, S., 2004. Subjectivity, intersubjectivity and the historical construction of interlocutor stance: From stance markers to discourse markers. *Discourse Studies*, 6(4): 427–448.

Ford, C.E., 2004. Contingency and units in interaction. *Discourse Studies*, 6(1): 27–52.

Gawlik, O., 2010. *Basic Verba Dicendi in Academic Spoken English*. PhD dissertation, Uniwersytet Śląski.

Goźdź-Roszkowski, S. and Pontrandolfo, G., 2013. Evaluative patterns in judicial discourse: A corpus-based phraseological perspective on American and Italian criminal judgments. *International Journal of Law, Language and Discourse*, 3: 9–69.

Goźdź-Roszkowski, S. and Pontrandolfo, G., 2015. Legal phraseology today: Corpus-based applications across legal languages and genres. *Fachsprache: International Journal of Specialized Communication*, 3–4: 130–138.

Granger, S. and Paquot, M., 2008. Disentangling the phraseological web. In S. Granger and F. Meunier (eds.), *Phraseology: An Interdisciplinary Perspective*. Amsterdam/Philadelphia: John Benjamins, 27–49.

Heffer, C., 2007. Judgment in court: Evaluating participants in courtroom discourse. In K. Kredens and S. Goźdź-Roszkowski (eds.), *Language and the Law: International Outlooks*. Frankfurt am Mein: Peter Lang, 145–179.

Hirschová, M., 2009. Speech acts in Slavic languages. In T. Berger, K. Gutschmidt, S. Kempgen, and P. Kosta (eds.), *The Slavic Languages: An International Handbook of their History, Their Structure and Their Investigation*, Vol. 1. Berlin: Walter de Gruyter, 1055–1090.

Holt, E. and Johnson, A., 2010. Socio-pragmatic aspects of legal talk: Police interviews and trial discourse. In M. Coulthard and A. Johnson (eds.), *The Routledge Handbook of Forensic Linguistics*. London/New York: Routledge, 21–36.

Huddleston, R.D. and Pullum, G.K., 2002. *The Cambridge Grammar of the English Language*. Cambridge: Cambridge University Press.

Hunston, S., 2011. *Corpus Approaches to Evaluation: Phraseology and Evaluative Language*. London/New York: Routledge.

Hwang, J.L., 2000. Historical development of reported speech in Chinese. *Berkeley Linguistics Society: Proceedings of the Annual Meeting*, 26: 145–156.

Johnson, A., 2002. *So . . . ?* Pragmatic implications of *so*-prefaced questions in formal police interviews. In J. Cotterill (ed.), *Language in the Legal Process*. Hampshire/New York: Palgrave Macmillan, 91–110.

Johnson, A., 2014. Legal discourse: Processes of making evidence in specialised legal corpora. In K.P. Schneider and A. Barron (eds.), *Pragmatics of Discourse, Handbook of Pragmatics*, Vol. 3. Berlin/New York: Mouton de Gruyter, 525–554.

Kleszczowa, K., 1989. *Verba dicendi w historii języka polskiego. Zmiany znaczeń*. Katowice: Uniwersytet Śląski.

Locher, M.A., 2004. *Power and Politeness in Action: Disagreements in Oral Communication*. Berlin: Mouton de Gruyter.

Mair, C., 2012. Progressive and continuous aspect. In R.I. Binnick (ed.), *The Oxford Handbook of Time and Aspect*. Oxford: Oxford University Press, 806–827.

Miller, D.R. and Johnson, J.H., 2009. Strict vs. nurturant parents? A corpus-assisted study of congressional positioning on the war in Iraq. In J. Morley and P. Bayley (eds.), *Corpus-assisted Discourse Studies on the Iraq Conflict: Wording the War*. London/New York: Routledge, 34–73.

Partington, A., 2009. Evaluating evaluation and some concluding thoughts on CADS. In J. Morley and P. Bayley (eds.), *Corpus-assisted Discourse Studies on the Iraq Conflict: Wording the War*. London/New York: Routledge, 261–303.

Partington, A., Duguid, A. and Taylor, C., 2013. *Patterns and Meanings in Discourse: Theory and Practice in Corpus-assisted Discourse Studies (CADS)*. Amsterdam/Philadelphia: John Benjamins.

Pontrandolfo, G. and Goźdź-Roszkowski, S., 2014. Exploring the local grammar of evaluation: The case of adjectival patterns in American and Italian judicial discourse. *Research in Language*, 12(1): 71–91.

Quirk, R., Greenbaum, S., Leech, G.V., and Svartik, J., 1985. *A Comprehensive Grammar of the English Language*. London: Longman.

Renouf, A. and Sinclair, J., 1991. Collocational frameworks in English. In K. Aijmer and B. Altenberg (eds.), *English Corpus Linguistics: Studies in Honour of Jan Svartvik*. London/New York: Longman, 128–143.

Ruusila, A. and Lindroos, E., 2016. *Conditio sine qua non:* On phraseology in legal language and its translation. *Language and Law/Linguagem e Direito*, 3(1): 120–140.

Scott, M., 2012. *WordSmith Tools* (Version 6). Stroud: Lexical Analysis Software.

Slembrouk, S., 1992. The parliamentary Hansard 'verbatim' report: The written construction of spoken discourse. *Language and Literature*, 1(2): 101–119.

Stefanowitsch, A. and Gries, S., 2003. Collostructions: Investigating the interaction between words and constructions. *International Journal of Corpus Linguistics*, 8(2): 209–243.

Szczyrbak, M., in preparation. *When you say over here, you mean . . .* Reformulation strategies in confrontational institutional talk.

Taylor, C., 2009. Interacting with conflicting goals. In J. Morley and P. Bayley (eds.), *Corpus-assisted Discourse Studies on the Iraq Conflict: Wording the War*. London/New York: Routledge, 208–233.

Thompson, G., 1997. *Introducing Functional Grammar*. London: Arnold.

Thompson, G. and Ye, Y.Y., 1991. Evaluation in the reporting verbs used in academic papers. *Applied Linguistics*, 12: 365–382.

Tognini-Bonelli, E., 2002. Functionally complete units of meaning across English and Italian: Towards a corpus-driven approach. In B. Altenberg and S. Granger (eds.), *Lexis in Contrast: Corpus-based Approaches*. Amsterdam/Philadelphia: John Benjamins, 73–95.

Wierzbicka, A., 1987. *English Speech Act Verbs: A Semantic Dictionary*. Sydney: Academic Press.

Wright, S., 1995. Subjectivity and experiential syntax. In D. Stein and S. Wright (eds.), *Subjectivity and Subjectivisation: Linguistic Perspectives*. Cambridge: Cambridge University Press, 151–172.

14 Formulaic word *n*-grams as markers of forensic authorship attribution

Identification of recurrent *n*-grams in adult L1 English writers' short personal narratives

Samuel Larner

Introduction

This chapter diverts somewhat from previous chapters in this collection. Rather than focussing on legal phraseology per se, this chapter explores how phraseology may be useful as evidence in civil and criminal legal contexts; that is, the potential contribution that phraseology – specifically formulaic word *n*-grams – may make to forensic linguistics and authorship attribution. In forensic authorship attribution, the goal of the linguist is to compare documents whose authorship is unknown (such as terrorist threat letters, hate mail or blackmail, for instance) – so called 'Questioned Documents' (QD) – against documents known to have been written by potential authors, with a view to determining the most likely author. For this purpose lexis has been well explored as a marker of style (e.g. Chaski 2001; Kredens 2001; Hoover 2002; Coulthard 2004). The problem is that authors can attempt to change aspects of their authorial style (Shuy 2001). Finding a marker of authorship which operates at a deeper level – and which therefore would be harder to disguise – would be the holy grail of authorship analysis (Tomblin 2013). Phraseology offers one such possibility.

Evidence from psycholinguistics (e.g. Wray 2002; Hoey 2005), sociolinguistics (e.g. Coulmas 1979), corpus linguistics (e.g. Moon 1998) and both L1 and L2 language acquisition (Pawley and Syder 1983; Peters 1983, 2009; Vihman 1982) repeatedly demonstrates that language users exhibit formulaic patterns in language and have "preferred formulations" for expressing ideas (Wray 2006: 591). Wray (2002: 9) found 57 different terms each describing characteristics of language that can be thought of as formulaic including collocations, idioms, fixed expressions, multi-word items, phrasal lexemes and recurrent phrases. In order to unify previous research into formulaic language, Wray (2002) coined the term *formulaic sequence* as an over-arching, inclusive definition to cover all characteristics of formulaic language:

> [A] sequence, continuous or discontinuous, of words or other elements, which is, or appears to be, prefabricated: that is, stored and retrieved whole from memory at the time of use, rather than being subject to generation or analysis by the language grammar.
> (p. 9)

The underlying principle is that formulaic sequences are not created through the analysis of the individual words within a sequence. Indeed, holistic storage and processing is a key aspect of formulaic language research (Pawley and Syder 1983; Sinclair 1991; Erman 2007). Therefore, authors will likely produce sequences of words without necessarily thinking about each individual word. It naturally follows that if authors are unaware that they are using particular sequences of words it will be much harder for them to disguise their writing style. This point is made by Lancashire (1998):

> Word, phrase, and collocation frequencies . . . can be signatures of authorship because of the way the writer's brain stores and creates speech. Even the author cannot imitate these features, simply because they are normally beyond recognition, unless the author has the same tools and expertise as stylometrists undertaking attribution research. Reliable markers arise from the unique, hidden clusters within the author's long-term associative memory.
>
> (p. 299)

Previous research has explored *n*-grams in relation to authorship attribution (e.g. Hoover 2002; Clement and Sharp 2003; Bel et al. 2012; Johnson and Wright 2014). For instance, Coulthard (2004) demonstrated the evidential value of word *n*-grams by entering successively longer strings of words into the *Google* search engine. He found that whilst a word *n*-gram such as *I asked* returned 2,170,000 hits, a longer word *n*-gram such as *I asked her* returned 284,000, whilst *I asked her if I could* returned 7,770 hits and *I asked her if I could carry her bags* returned no hits (p. 441). He argues that whilst the word *n*-gram *I asked her* appears to be idiomatic, co-selection of items in sequence becomes rare, with successively longer word *n*-grams becoming increasingly rare (p. 441). However, whilst word *n*-grams such as these may be indicative of authorship, there is no reason to suspect that they are stored holistically (i.e. as formulaic sequences), meaning authors may be aware of, and therefore able to, disguise their use of them, and furthermore, results into the general reliability of word *n*-grams for authorship purposes have been mixed. Therefore, providing that there is an appropriate way to identify them, formulaic sequences may more reliably mark out the writing style of an individual author than traditional sequences of words. As will become clear below, word *n*-grams can be argued to be formulaic based on the number of occurrences *and* the consistency with which individual word *n*-grams occur across a series of texts. It is this recurrence and consistency which separates the research presented here from other investigations which have explored *n*-grams more generally as a marker of authorship.

Formulaic sequences and authorship

There is very limited empirical evidence which explores the relationship between formulaic sequences (as defined by Wray 2002) and individual style. In a cognitive-overload experiment, Schmitt et al. (2004) presented 34 participants with a selection of 25 recurrent *n*-grams ("recurrent clusters" in their terms) interspersed in dialogue. The participants were required to recite back the dialogue on the basis that with working memory being overloaded, those recurrent clusters that were remembered were likely to be stored holistically, and therefore formulaically, as a way to compensate for the increased cognitive load. They found that some recurrent clusters were always remembered by their participants whilst others were not even attempted by all participants. However, they also found that some participants recited some of the recurrent clusters, whilst others did not, leading them to argue that some of the recurrent clusters were formulaic for some individuals, but not for everyone. In other words, in addition to the mental lexicon containing a majority of formulaic sequences which are shared across the speech community, there is also a "unique inventory of formulaic sequences" (p. 138) based on individual abilities in fluency and powers of expression.

In a study of supermarket checkout operators, Kuiper (2009) found that during the greetings phase of an interaction with a customer, some formulaic sequences (in his terms, "formulae") were used by all operators, whilst others were used more regularly by only one checkout operator, suggesting again that at least some sequences may be formulaic for some but not for others. Indeed, Kuiper argued that the combination of formulaic sequences used by checkout operators was "equivalent to a signature" (p. 114).

Larner (2014) was the first to explore this individual potential of formulaic sequences specifically in the forensic authorship context. To determine whether formulaic sequences distinguished between individual authors' writing styles, he developed a quantitative dictionary-matching approach, in which a list of 13,412 formulaic sequences was constructed from online sources. These formulaic sequences were then matched against a corpus of 100 texts produced by 20 authors. He found that the specific types of formulaic sequences used by authors were not used consistently or distinctively enough to differentiate between authors. However, some authors did appear to use more formulaic sequences than others, so he investigated the normalised count of formulaic sequences (i.e. the number of words making up a formulaic sequence per 100 words) to determine whether authors were more or less formulaic than others. The results showed that inter-author variation was greater than intra-author variation. However, in determining the likely author of a QD, reliability was low, with only 20 *per cent* of attributions being correct. In other words, this study lends support to the findings of Kuiper (2009) and Schmitt et al. (2004) in that individuals appear to use formulaic sequences differently, but with insufficient reliability to be used as a marker of authorship in the forensic context.

The research was followed up in Larner (2016), in which a different approach to the identification of formulaic sequences was adopted. Whereas Larner's (2014) approach identified mostly fixed formulaic sequences, Larner (2016) outlined a method which allowed for far greater variability by identifying semantically related formulaic sequences which occur in different forms. Larner (2016) argued that if a single word which occurs predominantly in formulaic sequences can be identified, then by finding all instances of that core word in a corpus, a reasonable subset of sequences should by virtue also be identified, the majority of which should be formulaic. The word *way* was selected for this purpose since it occurs in numerous formulaic sequences (e.g. *in a way*, *by way of*, *ways and means*), and since it occurred frequently in his corpus. Using the same data as Larner (2014), Larner (2016) identified 103 concordances which contained the nodes *way* or *ways*. The *way*-phrase was then identified from the concordance by including all of the words surrounding *way* which would need to be removed for an alternative formulation to be used (e.g. *all the way*, *in several ways*). This method resulted in 55 separate *way*-phrases being identified. A semantic gloss was then produced for each phrase (e.g. *go out of my way to* = 'do more than necessary/expected') and a series of synonyms for these glosses were then identified so that a range of semantically related phrases could be identified in the corpus. The findings indicated that only one of the 20 authors expressed the same meaning in a consistent form (*in a way*) across all five of her texts.

A limitation of Larner's (2016) method is that whilst it allows for complete variability in form in terms of the formulaic sequences identified, it is still limited in that only a very small subset of formulaic sequences was identified: only those semantically related to one of 55 phrases which contained the word *way*. An alternative approach is therefore presented in the current research which attempts to bridge this gap. By focussing on recurrent word *n*-grams of different lengths it should be possible to identify a much wider range of formulaic sequences, whilst also identifying sequences which are formulaic for one individual rather than a whole speech community. Of course, in order to do this, it is firstly necessary to define in an operational way what will actually be identified in the data.

Defining 'formulaic word *n*-grams'

Wray's (2009) definition of the *formulaic sequence* is intended to be as inclusive as possible so that it can be used as a cover-all term for any part of language that has been considered formulaic by previous definitions (p. 9). However, whilst the definition of the formulaic sequence is intended to be inclusive, it is not intended to be a definition that enables identification of formulaic material in texts: "Although the formulaic sequence can be used for identification at the general level of items that 'appear to be prefabricated', what appears to be prefabricated needs its own clear definition" (Wray 2008: 97).

Some types of word *n*-grams are explicitly linked to genre (notably, lexical bundles, e.g. Biber and Conrad 1999; Biber et al. 2004). Since a forensic approach to authorship requires a method which is universally applicable, a robust method for authorship attribution needs to be independent of genre or context. The term *formulaic word n-gram* has been coined here for this purpose, and is defined as follows:

> Sequences of three words or more which are not necessarily complete meaningful units and which are not overtly related to context. Formulaic word *n*-grams occur in the majority of texts produced by an individual author and can be argued to be idiolectal based on the recurrence of form across separate texts, and to be formulaic in terms of their frequency.

The fact that formulaic word *n*-grams are found in the majority of texts demonstrates that they are a strong and, crucially, recurring part of that author's lexical repertoire (as opposed to word *n*-grams, which might be very frequent in one text but not across a series). Repetition across texts also reduces the likelihood of word *n*-grams being content-specific or chance occurrences. A cline will naturally be generated between word *n*-grams which occur more frequently across fewer texts and those which occur less frequently over more texts. The threshold for determining what 'majority' means will be dependent on the data available. In the next section, the author corpus is described in which each author produced a total of five texts. As a guide, occurrence in three of the available texts is justified as the minimum since this equates to over half of the texts produced by an author (and obviously, formulaic word *n*-grams which occur in four or five of the texts should be more characteristic of an author's style). Other researchers wishing to draw on this definition would be required to justify their own thresholds based on their specific data.

The definition specifies that formulaic word *n*-grams must consist of at least three words. This is on the basis that two-word *n*-grams will typically consist of grammatical items (Biber et al. 2004). Although the diagnostic potential of grammatical items has been claimed in an authorship context (Mosteller and Wallace 1964), it may be less convincing to argue that they will be useful in identifying formulaic sequences related to authorship. After all, grammatical items are in many cases required for the organisation of text whereas lexical items allow for more variability. Although combinations of grammatical items may well be stored formulaically, being a smaller set of words means that there is more limited variation in how authors can use them compared to lexical words, so two-word *n*-grams consisting of only grammatical items provide less opportunity to be used distinctively between authors. Indeed, whilst previous studies have explored grammatical words in relation to authorship (e.g. Holmes and Forsyth 1995), more recent studies tend to focus on the most frequent words in texts, which combine grammatical and lexical words (Wright 2014: 15) rather than the grammatical words in isolation.

Finally, focussing on the recurrence of form means that variability cannot be tolerated; in other words, authors must produce the identical forms over at least three of their texts. The limitation of this approach is that word *n*-grams which naturally allow for some variability (e.g. *it's his choice* and *it's her choice*, where the pronominal choice is content dependent) will not be identified as formulaic word *n*-grams in this research. However, this potential limitation is outweighed by the fact that the method will enable an initial automated analysis, meaning that if inter-authorial differences can be identified, the method will be reliable enough for use in forensic contexts, rather than relying on purely qualitative methods which entail some subjectivity.

The empirical study

Data: the author corpus

The data used in this research is the same as that described in Larner (2014, 2016). Twenty authors, identified through a snowball sampling technique, were recruited to participate in the study. Their ages ranged from 18 to 48 years old, with an average age of 24, comprising nine males and 11 females. Education levels ranged between post-16 further education (n = 6), undergraduate level (n = 10) and postgraduate level (n = 3), and one participant had a doctorate; in other words, all participants at that time had completed compulsory formal education and had engaged with optional further and higher education within the UK. Participants completed a daily structured writing task over a period of five days, resulting in 100 texts overall. The structured writing task involved each participant being sent two essay-style questions daily, from which they answered one. If they could not answer either of the questions, a list of five substitute questions was provided. In the introduction, it was noted that authors are likely to produce formulaic sequences automatically. Therefore, to inform participants that this particular aspect of their authorial style was important to the present study would be to foreground an otherwise automatic behaviour which could affect the reliability of the formulaic sequences elicited as a marker of authorship. For this reason, participants were not told the real aim of the research at the outset, although they were fully debriefed at the end of the task and were provided with the opportunity to withdraw their data (none did). Labov (1970) proposes an additional measure for reducing the experimental effect. Labov proposed that through describing past events – *producing narratives of personal experience* – participants focus less on their writing style. As such, the questions posed to participants as part of the structured writing task were therefore open-ended and designed to engage participants with their personal experiences. All question prompts are provided in the Appendix.

In designing this data collection task, it was necessary to consider how many texts should be created and, indeed, the length of those texts, to ensure validity of the results for a forensic context. No threshold has been established for the optimum quantity and length of texts in forensic linguistics research, although Chaski (2001) used three texts per author for testing markers of authorship, whilst Grant (2007) used an average of 3.5 texts per author. Hänlein (1999) used between 13 and 17 texts per author. Therefore, five texts were collected per author which falls within this range and ensured that the task was not too onerous for participants. In terms of length, participants were advised to write approximately 500 words in response to each question. Acknowledging that authentic forensic texts are often very short, previous empirical research into markers of authorship has been conducted on shorter texts. For instance, Chaski (2001) focussed on texts with an average word length of 260 words, and Nini and Grant (2013) used texts containing 300 words. Winter (1996) analysed texts with words lengths ranging from 481 to 805. Therefore, despite no universal minimum word-limit threshold having been established, encouraging participants to write approximately 500 words generated a sufficient amount of text to explore formulaic sequences, whilst not being too cumbersome for participants to complete. The total corpus consisted of 65,113 words. Each author produced an average of 3,325 words across their five texts. The shortest text contained 485 words whilst the longest contained 822 words. The average text length was 651 words.

Method

Using *Wordsmith Tools* (Scott 2008), a list of word *n*-grams for each author's group of five texts was created. In line with the definition of formulaic word *n*-grams presented earlier, all word *n*-grams of between three and six words which occurred at least twice were extracted from each author sub-corpus. Requiring each word *n*-gram to occur minimally only twice in the five texts was a deliberately low threshold set to generate as many potentially formulaic word *n*-grams as possible. A total of 1,424 word *n*-grams were identified (98 types). Table 14.1 shows the total number of word *n*-grams per author (ranked from highest to

Table 14.1 Number of word *n*-grams per author

Author	*Number of word **n**-grams*
Rose	166
Elaine	101
Rick	93
Jenny	93
Mark	83
Hannah	77
Sue	76
John	75
Alan	72
Nicola	66
Keith	66
Sarah	66
Judy	61
Thomas	60
Carla	59
David	49
Melanie	46
Greg	45
June	41
Michael	29
Total	1,424

Table 14.2 Examples of word *n*-grams found in the author corpus

Length of word n-grams	*Types (tokens)*	*Examples*
3 words	85 (1,294)	A COUPLE OF ALL THE TIME AT THE TIME DOWN THE ROAD IN A WAY THE SAME TIME WHAT HAD HAPPENED
4 words	11 (116)	AND AS A RESULT AT THE SAME TIME FOR THE REST OF I WAS GOING TO IN A WAY I
5 words	2 (14)	ENJOYING EACH OTHER'S COMPANY MOMENT OF MY LIFE WAS
Total	98 (1,424)	

lowest) whilst Table 14.2 shows how many types and tokens of each length of word *n*-gram were identified, along with some representative examples.

As would be expected, there are many more of the shorter three-word *n*-grams, both types and tokens, than the four-word *n*-grams. Likewise, the frequency of types and tokens drops dramatically with an increase in size to five-word *n*-grams, and no *n*-grams of six words or greater being identified at all. The authors vary significantly in their use of word *n*-grams, ranging from 29 to 166.

Although 1,424 word *n*-grams have been identified, there is no reason to believe they are formulaic. To establish this, all word *n*-grams which occurred in at least three texts produced by a single author were selected in line with the definition of formulaic word *n*-grams presented earlier. This created for each author a range of word *n*-grams which could be argued to be formulaic on the basis of recurrence across separate texts. A total of 140 formulaic word *n*-grams (93 types) were identified in the entire corpus. Five of these word *n*-grams were directly primed by the data-eliciting questions: *moment of my life*, *moment of my life was*, *my life was*, *of my life* and *of my life was*, all of which were in response to the three questions: *what has been the best moment of your life*, *what has been the worst moment of your life* and *what has been the most embarrassing moment of your life?* As such, to comply with the context-free nature of formulaic word *n*-grams, these were excluded from further analysis. Representative examples of the remaining formulaic word *n*-grams for eight of the authors are presented as Table 14.3, a redacted version of the entire data set which characterises the most salient points. Column 2, 'Formulaic word *n*-grams (FWN)', lists the formulaic word *n*-grams identified for each author. The third column indicates in how many of each author's five texts each word *n*-gram occurred. This figure merely indicates the number of texts in which a formulaic word *n*-gram occurred so the totals range from a minimum of three to a maximum of five. The actual frequency of occurrence for each author is indicated in column four, 'Total occurrences of FWN across all five texts'. The fifth column, 'Total occurrences in entire corpus', shows how many tokens of the formulaic word *n*-gram type occurred across the entire author corpus, and the final column indicates how many of the

Table 14.3 Formulaic word *n*-grams identified for eight authors and in comparison to all other authors

Author	*Formulaic word n-grams (FWN)*	*In N files*	*Total occurrences of FWN across all five texts*	*Total occurrences in entire corpus*	*Used by N authors*
Carla	AT THE TIME	5	6	34	15
	IT WAS A	5	6	41	17
	THE WHOLE THING	3	3	11	5
Elaine	AND I JUST	3	4	8	5
	AND WE WERE	3	4	12	9
	IT WAS TIME	3	4	9	6
	THAT I WAS	3	3	45	17
	THAT IT WAS	4	5	14	9
	TO GET OUT	3	4	9	6
	TO GO TO	3	3	26	15
Hannah	AT THE TIME	4	5	34	15
	GOING TO BE	3	3	15	8
	HAVE EVER BEEN	3	3	8	6
	I HAVE EVER	3	3	15	11
	I HAVE EVER BEEN	3	3	8	6
	I REMEMBER THINKING	3	3	3	1
	I WAS SO	3	3	23	10
	WAS GOING TO	3	3	24	9
	WAS GOING TO BE	3	3	11	6
Jenny	AND AS A RESULT	3	3	3	1
	AND I WAS	4	4	33	16
	AS A RESULT	3	4	6	3
	AS I WAS	3	4	21	12
	I WAS REALLY	3	3	7	3
	IN THE END	4	4	20	9
	SOME OF THE	3	3	9	7
	THAT I WAS	3	4	45	17
	THOUGHT IT WOULD	3	3	3	1
	WAS WHEN I	3	3	9	6
	WHEN I WAS	3	3	41	18
Mark	AND I WAS	3	3	33	16
	AT THE SAME TIME	3	3	9	5
	FOR THE REST OF	3	3	6	4
	IN THE END	3	4	20	9
	IN THE SAME	3	3	8	6
	ME AND MY	3	3	11	6
	THE REST OF	3	3	25	12
	THE SAME TIME	3	3	11	7
	WENT TO MY	3	3	3	1

(*Continued*)

Table 14.3 (Continued)

Author	*Formulaic word n-grams (FWN)*	*In N files*	*Total occurrences of FWN across all five texts*	*Total occurrences in entire corpus*	*Used by N authors*
Michael Rose	ENJOYING EACH OTHER	3	3	3	3
	A COUPLE OF	3	4	23	11
	A LOT OF	3	3	14	8
	A WAY I	3	3	8	5
	AND I WAS	3	3	33	16
	AS I WAS	3	3	21	12
	BUT I KNEW	3	3	3	1
	BY THE TIME	3	3	19	9
	I KNEW THAT	4	5	18	10
	I REALLY FELT	3	4	4	1
	I THINK THE	3	5	11	5
	I WAS GLAD	3	3	4	2
	I WAS GOING	3	4	16	10
	I WAS SO	3	5	23	10
	IN A WAY	5	10	19	8
	IN A WAY I	3	3	7	4
	IT WAS A	3	4	41	18
	LOOKING FORWARD TO	3	3	7	5
	MADE ME FEEL	3	4	8	5
	ME IN A	3	3	3	1
	THAT I WAS	3	3	45	17
	THE WHOLE THING	3	4	11	5
	WAS GOING TO	3	6	24	9
	WHEN I WAS	3	3	41	18
	WHICH I WAS	4	5	6	2
Sarah	FRIENDS AND FAMILY	3	4	6	3
	HE TOLD ME	3	4	12	6
	THAT I HAD	5	7	42	16
	TOLD ME THAT	3	3	7	5
	THE END OF	3	4	23	11
	THE FACT THAT	3	7	30	15

20 authors used each particular formulaic word *n*-gram. These two columns are discussed further below.

For each of the 20 authors, at least one formulaic word *n*-gram was identified although no single word *n*-gram was used by all 20 authors: the word *n*-grams most shared were *when I was* and *it was a*, which were used by 18 authors. It is also apparent that more formulaic word *n*-grams have been identified for some authors than others. This difference is perhaps most evident between Michael, with only one formulaic word *n*-gram, and Rose, for whom 24 formulaic word *n*-grams were identified.

The majority of the formulaic word *n*-grams (118) occurred in only three of the five texts written by a single author, although there were a few formulaic word *n*-grams which occurred at least once in all five texts: *at the time*, *it was a* (Carla), *in a way* (Rose) and *that I had* (Sarah). Some formulaic word *n*-grams are particularly noteworthy because of their frequency. For example, Carla used both *at the time* and *it was a* a total of six times across all five of her texts. Rose used *in a way* ten times across all her five texts and Sarah used *that I had* a total of seven times across all her texts.

A set of formulaic word *n*-grams has been isolated – that is, word *n*-grams that occur at least once, and often more, across a series of at least three texts for each author. However, what is not known is the significance of the formulaic word *n*-grams for an individual author – whether they are commonplace items for the speech community in general or whether they are potentially diagnostic of authorship. The entire corpus was therefore searched and all the instances of the formulaic word *n*-grams identified in Table 14.3 were counted (indicated in the fifth column). A total of 1,311 tokens were identified for the 93 formulaic word *n*-gram types, of which 22 types were shared with another author. The sixth column shows how many authors across the entire corpus used the formulaic word *n*-gram. By examining these two columns, it is possible to determine how distinctive each formulaic word *n*-gram is for each author, e.g. Rose's use of *I really felt* four times across three texts appears to be more prominent in her written output since she is the only author to use this word *n*-gram, whereas another word *n*-gram such as *to go to* occurs 26 times across the author corpus and is used by 15 authors, so the fact that Elaine uses this three times across three texts is not sufficient to claim this word *n*-gram to be distinctive for her, although it may still be formulaic.

Of particular interest in this regard are word *n*-grams produced by only one author and produced in at least three of their texts. For example, Hannah's use of *I remember thinking*, Jenny's use of *and as a result* and *thought it would*, Mark's use of *went to my* and Rose's use of *but I knew, I really felt* and *me in a*, none of which occur in the rest of the corpus (in other words, each author's uses of these formulaic word *n*-grams accounts for 100 *per cent* of occurrences in the whole corpus). In fact, Rose's use of *I really felt* occurs in three separate texts, a total of four times (so in one text she uses this formulaic word *n*-gram twice) and these four occurrences are the only occurrences in the corpus. This is in contrast to other formulaic word *n*-grams which occur relatively frequently for each author and for other authors in the corpus. Such examples include Carla's use of *at the time*, which occurs in all her five texts and a total of six times but a total of 34 times across the whole corpus, and Sarah's use of *that I had*, which occurs seven times across all five of her texts, against a total of 42 occurrences across the whole corpus. These findings suggest that authors use different patterns of word *n*-grams with some consistency across their texts. It is now possible to determine whether these formulaic word *n*-grams can be used as a marker of authorship.

Results

Establishing variation

Jaccard's coefficient is a statistical test which compares the level of (dis)similarity between sample sets. Specifically, Jaccard's coefficient considers whether particular features (in this case, formulaic word *n*-grams) are present within the samples, rather than the frequency with which they occur, making it particularly suited for short texts, where frequencies would typically be very low. As such, it is gaining in prominence in forensic linguistics research (e.g. Grant 2010; Larner 2014, 2016; Johnson and Wright 2014). Jaccard's coefficient score is calculated between linked pairs (a text by the same author compared to another text by the same author) and unlinked pairs (a text by one author and a text by another author) resulting in a distance measure of between zero and one where zero indicates that two texts are completely different and one indicates that they are identical. Decimals between zero and one indicate variation between these two extremes. The statistical significance of the resulting distance measure is then calculated using an appropriate test (in this case, the non-parametric Mann-Whitney *U*). Each formulaic word *n*-gram constituted a feature, resulting in 93 features. All 100 texts in the corpus were used in the analysis, resulting in 4,950 pairs of texts.

The Jaccard's coefficient for each of the two groups of linked and unlinked pairs was tested to see if the coefficients were normally distributed. Although Jaccard values for linked pairs showed no significant difference from normal (KSZ = 0.768, N = 200, $p = 0.597$), the unlinked pairs were significantly different from normal (KSZ = 7.661, N = 4750, $p < 0.001$). Therefore, the non-parametric Mann-Whitney *U* test was carried out to test whether Jaccard was significantly lower in unlinked pairs. The Mann-Whitney *U* test showed a significant difference in mean ranks between linked and unlinked pairs (Z = 11.3, N = 4950, $p < 0.001$) where unlinked pairs were lower. This means that texts produced by the same author are more similar in their use of specific formulaic word *n*-grams than texts by different authors.

Having established that inter-author variation is greater than intra-author variation, it is now necessary to determine whether a QD can successfully be attributed to its author. However, the point of using Jaccard's coefficient is that it is not an authorship attribution in the traditional sense (e.g. attributing a QD to one of a small sample of candidate authors). Rather, it is a statistical method for describing consistency and distinctiveness, and therefore Jaccard's coefficient is not sufficient to tell whether a feature is unique to an author; only whether it is consistently used across the data. As a result, in order to attribute a QD to its author, it is necessary to use qualitative analysis to describe the consistent and distinctive features between writers. Such an approach is in keeping with Grant (2010), who established inter-author variation between SMS text message authors through the use of Jaccard's coefficient and then attributed QDs through qualitative analysis based on the occurrence of features shared between the texts.

Attributing a QD

Two candidate authors

Two authors were randomly selected for the analysis: Rose and Mark. Of the ten texts produced by these two authors, one text was randomly chosen as the QD: the first text produced by Mark.

Selecting one of the documents as a QD means that there will be a five-text to four-text comparison, and although the majority of word *n*-grams occur in only three texts, this uneven comparison may skew the results. Whilst the argument can be made that in a forensic investigation it is less likely that exactly the same number of texts will be available for analysis, in an exploratory study such as this, limits must be established where possible. Therefore, the first part of the analysis will proceed with the five-text to four-text comparison, before reducing Rose's texts by one to see how the results are affected by a four-text to four-text comparison.

The results of this analysis are presented in Table 14.4. Column 1 shows the formulaic word *n*-grams identified for Rose. The third column lists all of the formulaic word *n*-grams

Table 14.4 Formulaic word *n*-grams used by Rose, Mark and QD in comparison to all other authors

Formulaic word n-grams used by Rose	*Word n-grams occurring in QD*	*Formulaic word n-grams used by Mark*	*Total authors using formulaic word n-gram*
A COUPLE OF			11
A LOT OF			8
A WAY I			5
AND I WAS	AND I WAS		16
AS I WAS			12
		AT THE SAME TIME	5
BUT I KNEW			1
BY THE TIME	BY THE TIME		9
I KNEW THAT			10
I REALLY FELT			1
I THINK THE			5
I WAS GLAD			2
I WAS GOING			10
I WAS SO	I WAS SO		10
IN A WAY			8
IN A WAY I			4
	IN THE END	IN THE END	9
		IN THE SAME	6
IT WAS A	IT WAS A		18
LOOKING FORWARD TO			5
MADE ME FEEL			5
		ME AND MY	6
ME IN A			1
THAT I WAS			17
		THE SAME TIME	7
THE WHOLE THING			5
WAS GOING TO			9
		WENT TO MY	1
WHEN I WAS			18
WHICH I WAS			2

identified in the four texts produced by Mark (i.e. those that occurred in at least three texts). The QD was then searched for each of Rose's and Mark's formulaic word *n*-grams and those which were present are shown in the second column. It is important to point out that those items in the second column are only 'candidate formulaic word *n*-grams', since by definition a formulaic word *n*-gram would need to occur in three texts whereas only one QD is available for analysis. Therefore, this column represents the occurrence of a word *n*-gram which has been claimed to be formulaic for another author (either Rose or Mark), and it is predicted that more word *n*-grams in the QD should be shared with its author (Mark) than with the other candidate author (Rose). The fourth column is discussed further below.

As can be seen from Table 14.4, 24 formulaic word *n*-grams were identified in Rose's texts, whilst only six were identified in Mark's texts, and five word *n*-grams were identified in the QD. The first thing to notice is that Rose and Mark do not share any of the same formulaic word *n*-grams. This adds some weight to the argument that there is inter-author variation in the use of formulaic word *n*-grams. Secondly, far fewer formulaic word *n*-grams were identified for Mark than for Rose. Referring back to Table 14.3, it is evident that nine formulaic word *n*-grams were originally identified for Mark, based on five texts. Here, since one of Mark's texts has been selected as a QD, only four texts were available for analysis, explaining why fewer formulaic word *n*-grams were identified than previously.

Given that only a total of five word *n*-grams were identified in the QD and that four are formulaic for Rose and one is formulaic for Mark, it is unlikely that persuasive evidence can be found for authorship. However, the fact that they are formulaic word *n*-grams for an author only means that they are used frequently (at least once in three texts) for that author, not that they are used exclusively by that author. In other words, in line with Solan and Tiersma (2005: 156), the distinctiveness of a feature needs to be assessed in relation to other authors. This is shown in the fourth column in Table 14.4. With the benefit of 18 other authors with whom to compare the texts, it is possible to show how many of the 20 authors also used the identified formulaic word *n*-grams in their texts. Note, though, that the occurrence could be as low as once across all five texts produced by an individual author, so the claim is not necessarily that the word *n*-gram is also distinctive, or even formulaic, for them; rather, that it is also available in their lexical repertoire. Table 14.4 shows that *and I was* was used by 16 authors, *by the time* by 9 authors, *I was so* by 10 authors, *in the end* by 9 authors and *it was a* by 18 authors. Viewed in this light, it can be seen that whilst Rose shares the majority of the formulaic word *n*-grams identified in the QD (rather than Mark), they do not seem to offer any discriminatory power since all of the formulaic word *n*-grams are used by several other authors – almost 50 *per cent* in each case, with *and I was* and *it was a* being used by 80 and 90 *per cent* of the authors, respectively. Therefore, no attribution is possible, and nor is it possible to exclude either author as a potential author of the QD. It is important to acknowledge though that if an attribution had been based purely on the quantity of 'matched' formulaic word *n*-grams, the wrong attribution would have been made with Rose looking like the more likely author.

At this stage, it is necessary to consider the fact that five texts produced by Rose have been compared against four texts produced by Mark and that the extra text available for analysis in Rose's set of texts may well have skewed the results. The point was made above that using fewer texts reduced the quantity of formulaic word *n*-grams identified for Mark. Therefore, reducing the number of texts written by Rose should also affect the outcome of the qualitative analysis. As such, one of Rose's texts was randomly selected and removed from the analysis, resulting in four texts by Rose, four by Mark and one QD. The formulaic word *n*-gram analysis based on these texts is presented as Table 14.5.

Table 14.5 Formulaic word *n*-grams used by Mark and Rose in comparison to QD (four texts each)

Formulaic word n-grams used by Rose	*Word n-grams occurring in QD*	*Formulaic word n-grams used by Mark*	*Total authors using formulaic word n-grams*
A COUPLE OF			11
AND I WAS	*AND I WAS*		16
		AT THE SAME TIME	5
BY THE TIME	BY THE TIME		9
I REALLY FELT			1
I THINK THE			5
I WAS GLAD			2
I WAS GOING			10
	IN THE END	IN THE END	9
		IN THE SAME	6
LOOKING FORWARD TO			5
		ME AND MY	6
THAT I WAS			17
		THE SAME TIME	7
THE WHOLE THING			5
WAS GOING TO			9
		WENT TO MY	1
WHEN I WAS			18

As predicted, the number of Rose's formulaic word *n*-grams was significantly reduced from 24 to 12 and, as a consequence, two of the word *n*-grams which occurred in the QD are discounted. The result is that there are now only two of Rose's formulaic word *n*-grams to place against the one for Mark. This in no way clarifies or otherwise strengthens/weakens the conclusions reached above but simply reduces the data on which conclusions can be based. This reinforces the position of forensic linguists that more data (i.e. more and longer texts) enable stronger conclusions and, more importantly for this method, it appears that data sets should be similar in size to enable more valid comparisons. Furthermore, no forensic linguist would attribute a QD to an author with any certainty based on the occurrence or absence of just one feature in isolation. A stronger attribution to an author would likely be more possible if other established markers of authorship were also taken into consideration (for example, see Eagleson 1994).

So far, formulaic word *n*-grams which occur in five texts and four texts have been identified and no attribution was possible. It may be the case that formulaic word *n*-grams do still hold potential to be diagnostic of authorship, but that a larger set of candidate authors is required to make differences more apparent. The next investigation tests this assertion.

Five candidate authors

Five authors were randomly selected: Keith, Jenny, Sue, Michael and Judy. Of the 25 texts they produced, the first text produced by Jenny was randomly selected as the QD. Since this left Jenny with only four texts for comparison, and taking into account the findings from the previous section, the first text for all of the other authors was also removed from the analysis so that just four texts were analysed for each author.

The definition of formulaic word *n*-grams offered here states that word *n*-grams need to occur in the majority of texts and that just how many texts this equates to will vary depending on how many are available for analysis. In this investigation, four texts for each author are available for analysis and so the threshold could be lowered to word *n*-grams which occur at least once in two texts, which would certainly generate more formulaic word *n*-grams. However, this would lead to the identification of a range of word *n*-grams which occur at least once in only 50 *per cent* of an already small range of texts, so the decision was made to test the method with a threshold of occurrence set to at least once in three texts. A smaller range of formulaic word *n*-grams will be identified, but stronger evidence of formulaicity based on recurrence can also be argued as a result of this decision. The following 12 formulaic word *n*-grams were identified in the texts: *I had been*, *and I was*, *in the end*, *was when I*, *when I was*, *at the time*, *back into the*, *I could not*, *I did not*, *a couple of*, *I don't know* and *I went to*.

The QD was searched for each of these word *n*-grams, but only one word *n*-gram was found: *in the end* – a formulaic word *n*-gram for Jenny. Whilst it is true that Jenny is the author of the QD, the occurrence of this one formulaic word *n*-gram is certainly less than persuasive as evidence of authorship, although only two other authors in the corpus actually used this word *n*-gram. Therefore, whether or not *in the end* is formulaic, this word *n*-gram does show how rarity may be used as a feature in authorship analysis, particularly since it is used by only three authors.

Discussion

The method reported in this chapter attempts to do something slightly different from previous investigations which explore the relationship between word *n*-grams and authorial style. Rather than simply identifying word *n*-grams, a decision was made to focus only on those word *n*-grams which can be argued to be formulaic for an author because of their recurrence across a minimum threshold of texts, and these formulaic word *n*-grams were assessed for distinctiveness in comparison to other authors. Using the Jaccard's coefficient statistical test demonstrated that inter-author variation was greater than intra-author variation. However, it was not possible to attribute a QD to its correct author through the ensuing descriptive approach; a situation which became further compounded when fewer texts were available for analysis.

As expected, reducing the number of texts available for analysis (from five to four) meant that fewer formulaic word *n*-grams were identified. The significance of this is that the method outlined in this chapter may carry more investigative value if larger data sets are available for analysis and it is perhaps not a suitable approach for those investigations where fewer texts are available. Whilst it may not be possible to speculate about the ideal number of texts that would be required to make the method more robust, it is important to note that few reliable predictions could be made about which particular word *n*-grams might occur in another random text, since the majority of formulaic word *n*-grams were not used sufficiently frequently or regularly. Table 14.3 shows that only Carla's use of *at the time* and *it was a*, Rose's use of *in a way*, and Sarah's use of *that I had* occurred in all five of their texts at least once. There may therefore be grounds to predict that these word *n*-grams would also occur in a sixth, seventh or *n*th text also by that author. However, the fact that the majority of formulaic word *n*-grams were identified based on their recurrence across three texts already suggests that 40 *per cent* of the texts produced by an author will not contain that word *n*-gram. Likewise, it is likely that the length of the texts themselves affected the success of the method. The current trend in forensic linguistics research is to focus on shorter texts so that results have ecological validity against authentic forensic texts which are characteristically short (such as e-mails and SMS text messages). However, it may be the case that a feature such as formulaic word *n*-grams has insufficient opportunity to manifest in shorter texts. This suggests that either the method needs testing on a larger corpus of longer texts, or simply that formulaic word *n*-grams do not occur with enough frequency to be useful as a marker of authorship, despite the fact that inter-author variation is greater than intra-author variation.

It is now possible to consider these findings against previous research in this specialised area. Larner (2014) found that by identifying formulaic sequences using a pre-defined list, formulaic sequences were not used consistently or distinctively enough to differentiate texts by different authors. However, when considering the overall number of formulaic words compared to novel words, inter-author variation was greater than intra-author variation and furthermore, in some instances it was possible to correctly attribute a text to its author. Importantly though, this was not to any reliable forensic standard (i.e. a level of accuracy which would secure a safe conviction, which one would hope might be 100 *per cent* in such a high-stakes context). Support for these results is provided by the present study. The specific types of formulaic word *n*-grams used by authors do not, in this case, allow a text to be attributed to its author. However, statistical testing did again show that inter-author variation was greater than intra-author variation. Larner (2016) adopted a very different approach which allowed for far greater flexibility in the form that formulaic sequences were expressed, focussing instead on the message that the author conveyed. In this case, it was found that only one author expressed the same meaning in a consistent way (through the formulaic sequence *in a way*) across all five texts. Incidentally, this same formulaic sequence was identified for the same author, Rose, through the method reported here (see Table 14.3). It can therefore be argued that this one formulaic sequence, identified in separate research through two disparate approaches, does appear to characterise something about Rose's authorial style. Overall, despite the fact that three different methods have been used to identify formulaic sequences, statistical testing consistently seems to show differences, but this only goes so far as showing that inter-author variation is greater than intra-author variation. The problem is that this variation cannot yet be identified in a forensically reliable or usable way.

In light of this, it is necessary to question the validity of formulaic word *n*-grams as formulaic sequences. The case has been made in this chapter that formulaic word *n*-grams are valid as formulaic sequences since they recur across a series of texts; they therefore hold potential to be pre-fabricated in these particular forms, ready for use when required. Whilst some of the formulaic word *n*-grams may appear to be quite acceptable as evidence of formulaic sequences (e.g. *the whole thing*, *the next day*, *as a result*, *in the end*, *all the time*), others, due to their semantic incompleteness, appear less so (e.g. *it was a*, *and I just*, *to go to*, *out of the*, *me and my*). There are certainly features in common with previous research into formulaic language. Notably, Wray (2002) and those who use the *formulaic sequence* as their definition of choice do not see the lack of meaning (in other words, the fact that the units are incomplete) as a problem. Therefore, the fact that formulaic word *n*-grams such as *it is a*, *and I was* and *I was really* are semantically incomplete does not preclude them from being formulaic. They are, though, certainly less intuitively satisfying. A stronger argument for the classification of these word *n*-grams as formulaic is based on the frequency approach to formulaic language. That is, they occur over a certain threshold for a particular author and can therefore be argued to be formulaic for a particular individual based on their recurrence in texts. In other words, the individual appears to have found a particular formulaic word *n*-gram which enables them to express their meaning, or produce cohesive discourse, in a way which operates best for them. In this way, formulaic word *n*-grams can be argued to be formulaic sequences.

One final issue that is worthy of mention but which falls outside the scope of the present research is the actual number of formulaic word *n*-grams that were identified for each author – should any significance be attached to the fact that 26 formulaic word *n*-grams (based on at least one occurrence in three out of five texts) were identified for Rose, whilst only one was identified for Michael, or 12 for Elaine but only four for Sarah (see Table 14.3)? It is likely that this level of recurrence would create the sense of a repetitive style for Rose and presumably more novel language and less repetition for Michael. This finding suggests that some authors' styles (certainly in terms of formulaic word *n*-grams) may be more amenable to forensic authorship analysis than others, since for some authors there are more formulaic word *n*-grams to analyse. This is not an unusual finding in forensic authorship analysis, and Foster (2001) claims that if you "[g]ive anonymous offenders enough verbal rope and column inches . . . they will hang themselves for you, every time" (p. 12); that is, more data makes the analysis more feasible. The main point, of course, is that a forensic linguist would never seek to attribute a text on the basis of one variable alone, and so whilst an individual author may use a comparatively minor proportion of formulaic word *n*-grams compared to another, they may indeed use comparatively more of another feature (such as misspellings, syntactic features and stylistic features, for example).

Conclusion

From a statistical perspective, results demonstrate that formulaic word *n*-grams were used distinctively between authors. It can therefore be concluded that individual authors use different formulaic sequences. However, in attempting to qualitatively attribute a text to its correct author, the method was unsuccessful. Therefore, whilst differences in formulaic sequence usage between authors can be demonstrated, formulaic word *n*-grams themselves are too few in short personal narratives to be of practical use as a marker of authorship. Whereas this research adopted a word-*n*-gram-based approach in an effort to identify a wider range of formulaic sequences than previous research, the more principled and selective approaches outlined by Larner (2014, 2016), despite identifying only a smaller subset of formulaic sequences, were more successful in characterising authorial differences in formulaic sequence usage. Given the statistical evidence that formulaic sequences are used differently by authors, a better understanding of how formulaic sequences are actually used by authors, coupled with different approaches to identification, is likely to enable a more effective description of individual usage for forensic purposes.

Returning to the main theme of this collection, it is necessary to reflect on phraseology and its relevance to legal contexts. Within the field of forensic linguistics a distinction is often drawn between descriptive forensic linguistics (the analysis of language produced at any stage throughout the legal process with a view to characterising different genres and text types) and investigative forensic linguistics (in which language that in some way constitutes a crime is analysed) (e.g. Coulthard and Johnson 2007; Cotterill 2012). As the chapters in this collection have clearly demonstrated, legal discourse – whether spoken or written – can in many cases be characterised by the patterns of word sequences which occur within. Although the contributors to this collection may not necessarily define themselves as forensic linguists, their work does clearly fall within the domain of descriptive forensic linguistics. This chapter, by contrast, has argued that phraseology offers a further opportunity for academic enquiry; that is, the relevance of phraseology beyond the description of legal texts towards the domain of investigative forensic linguistics. Drawing on the wealth of established literature surrounding phraseology, coupled with the relatively young field of investigative forensic linguistics, there are numerous opportunities for exploring the extent to which linguists may contribute to solving crimes. Indeed, outside of authorship analysis, my own research has started to explore the role that formulaic sequences may play in deception detection (Larner, in preparation). To take an area of study as fundamental to language as phraseology, and to apply it to a domain in which justice and liberty are at stake, highlights the essence of what it means to be an 'applied' linguist.

References

Bel, N., Queralt Estevez, S., Spassova, M.S., and Turell, M.T., 2012. The use of sequences of linguistic categories in forensic written text comparison revisited. In S. Tomblin, N. MacLeod, R. Sousa-Silva, and M. Coulthard (eds.), *Proceedings of the International Association of Forensic Linguists' Tenth Biennial Conference*. Aston University, Birmingham, UK: The Centre for Forensic Linguistics, 192–209. <www.forensiclinguistics.net> [Accessed: April 2012].

Biber, D. and Conrad, S., 1999. Lexical bundles in conversation and academic prose. In H. Hilde and S. Oksefjell (eds.), *Out of Corpora: Studies in Honour of Stig Johansson*. Amsterdam: Rodopi, 181–190.

Biber, D., Conrad, S., and Cortes, V., 2004. *If you look at* . . . : Lexical bundles in university teaching and textbooks. *Applied Linguistics*, 25(3): 371–405.

Chaski, C., 2001. Empirical evaluations of language-based author identification. *Forensic Linguistics: The International Journal of speech, Language and the Law*, 8(1): 1–65.

Clement, R. and Sharp, D., 2003. Ngram and Baysian classification of documents for topic and authorship. *Literary and Linguistic Computing*, 18(4): 423–447.

Cotterill, J., 2012. Corpus analysis in forensic linguistics. In C. Chapelle (ed.), *The Encyclopedia of Applied Linguistics*. London: Wiley-Blackwell.

Coulmas, F., 1979. On the sociolinguistic relevance of routine formulae. *Journal of Pragmatics*, 3: 239–266.

Coulthard, M., 2004. Author identification, idiolect, and linguistic uniqueness. *Applied Linguistics*, 25(4): 431–447.

Coulthard, M. and Johnson, A., 2007. *An Introduction to Forensic Linguistics: Language in Evidence*. Abingdon: Routledge.

Eagleson, R., 1994. Forensic analysis of personal written texts: A case study. In J. Gibbons (ed.), *Language and the Law*. London: Longman, 362–373.

Erman, B., 2007. Cognitive processes as evidence of the idiom principle. *International Journal of Corpus Linguistics*, 12(1): 25–53.

Grant, T., 2007. Quantifying evidence in forensic authorship analysis. *The International Journal of Speech, Language and the Law*, 14(1): 1–25.

Grant, T., 2010. Text messaging forensics: txt 4n6: Idiolect free authorship analysis? In M. Coulthard and A. Johnson (eds.), *The Routledge Handbook of Forensic Linguistics*. Abingdon, Oxford: Routledge, 508–522.

Hänlein, H., 1999. *Studies in Authorship Recognition – A Corpus-based Approach*. Frankfurt: Peter Lang.

Hoey, M., 2005. *Lexical Priming: A New Theory of Words and Language*. Abingdon, Oxon: Routledge.

Holmes, D. and Forsyth, R., 1995. The federalist revisited: New directions in authorship attribution. *Literary and Linguistic Computing*, 10(2): 111–127.

Hoover, D.L., 2002. Frequent word sequences and statistical stylistics. *Literary and Linguistic Computing*, 17(2): 157–180.
Johnson, A. and Wright, D., 2014. Identifying idiolect in forensic authorship attribution: An n-gram textbite approach. *Language and Law/Linguagem e Direito*, 1(1): 37–69.
Kredens, K., 2001. Towards a corpus-based methodology of forensic authorship attribution: A comparative study of two idiolects. In B. Lewandowska-Tomaszxzyk (ed.), *PALC 2001: Practical Applications in Language Corpora*. Frankfurt: Peter Lang, 405–446.
Kuiper, K., 2009. *Formulaic Genres*. Basingstoke: Palgrave MacMillan.
Labov, W., 1970. The study of language in its social context. In J.B. Pride and J. Holmes (eds.), *Sociolinguistics: Selected Readings*. Harmondsworth: Penguin, 180–202.
Lancashire, I., 1998. Paradigms of authorship. *Shakespeare Studies*, 26: 296–301.
Larner, S., 2014. A preliminary investigation into the use of fixed formulaic sequences as a marker of authorship. *The International Journal of Speech, Language and the Law*, 21(1): 1–22.
Larner, S., 2016. Using a core word to identify different forms of semantically related formulaic sequences and their potential as a marker of authorship. *Corpora*, 11(3): 343–369.
Larner, S., in preparation. 'At the end of the day, when all is said and done, honesty is the best policy': An investigation into the potential role of formulaic sequences as a marker of deception.
Moon, R., 1998. *Fixed Expressions and Idioms in English*. Oxford: Clarendon Press.
Mosteller, F. and Wallace, D., 1964. *Inference and Disputed Authorship: The Federalist*. Reading, MA: Addison-Wesley Publishing Company Inc.
Nini, A. and Grant, T., 2013. Bridging the gap between stylistic and cognitive approaches to authorshop analysis using Systemic Functional Linguistics and multidimensional analysis. *The International Journal of Speech, Language and the Law*, 20(2): 173–202.
Pawley, A. and Syder, F., 1983. Two puzzles for linguistic theory: Nativelike selection and nativelike fluency. In J. Richards and R. Schmidt (eds.), *Language and Communication*. New York: Longman, 191–226.
Peters, A., 1983. *The Units of Language Acquisition*. Cambridge: Cambridge University Press.
Peters, A., 2009. Connecting the dots to unpack the language. In R. Corrigan, E. Moravcsik, H. Ouali, and K. Wheatley (eds.), *Formulaic Language: Acquisition, Loss, Psychological Reality, and Functional Explanations*, Vol. 2. Amsterdam: John Benjamins Publishing Co. 387–404.
Schmitt, N., Grandage, S., and Adolphs, S., 2004. Are corpus-derived recurrent clusters psycholinguistically valid? In N. Schmitt (ed.), *Formulaic Sequences: Acquisition, Processing and Use*. Amsterdam: John Benjamins Publishing Company, 127–151.
Scott, M., 2008. *WordSmith Tools* (Version 5). Liverpool: Lexical Analysis Software.
Shuy, R., 2001. DARE's role in linguistic profiling. *DARE Newsletter*, 4(3 (Summer)): 1–5.
Sinclair, J., 1991. *Corpus, Concordance, Collocation*. Oxford: Oxford University Press.
Solan, L. and Tiersma, P., 2005. *Speaking of Crime: The Language of Criminal Justice*. London: The University of Chicago Press.
Vihman, M., 1982. Formulas in first and second language acquisition. In L. Obler and L. Menn (eds.), *Exceptional Language and Linguistics*. London: Academic Press Ltd., 261–284.
Winter, E., 1996. The statistics of analysing very short texts in a criminal context. In H. Kniffka (ed.), *Recent Developments in Forensic Linguistics*. Frankfurt am Main: Peter Lang, 141–179.
Wray, A., 2002. *Formulaic Language and the Lexicon*. Cambridge: Cambridge University Press.
Wray, A., 2006. Formulaic language. In E.K. Brown (ed.), *The Encyclopedia of Language and Linguistics*. Oxford: Elsevier, 590–597.
Wray, A., 2008. *Formulaic Language: Pushing the Boundaries*. Oxford: Oxford University Press.
Wright, D., 2014. *Stylistics Versus Statistics: A Corpus Linguistic Approach to Combining Techniques in Forensic Authorship Analysis Using Enron Emails*. PhD thesis, School of English, University of Leeds.

Appendix

Data-generating question prompts

Participants were sent two questions per day in the following order:

Day 1: i) What has been the best moment of your life? ii) When did you last cry and what made you cry?
Day 2: i) Have you ever told a lie and what were the consequences? ii) What has been the worst moment of your life?
Day 3: i) How did you find out that Santa Claus doesn't exist? ii) What is the biggest decision you have ever made and did you make the right one?
Day 4: i) What is the most life-threatening situation you have ever been in? ii) What is the angriest you have ever been?
Day 5: i) What has been the most embarrassing moment of your life? ii) How close have you ever got to having your heart broken?

If participants were unable to answer either question from each day's set, they were provided with the following list of five substitute questions, from which any one could be selected:

i) If you could change anything in the world, what would it be and why?
ii) Who you do admire and why
iii) If you could be invisible for a day, what would you do?
iv) What would you do if you won £1,000,000?
v) Would you like to be a housemate on *Big Brother* and what are your reasons?

Index

For Product Safety Concerns and Information please contact our EU representative GPSR@taylorandfrancis.com
Taylor & Francis Verlag GmbH, Kaufingerstraße 24, 80331 München, Germany

www.ingramcontent.com/pod-product-compliance
Ingram Content Group UK Ltd.
Pitfield, Milton Keynes, MK11 3LW, UK
UKHW022116190926
475702UK00013B/1479
9780367313050